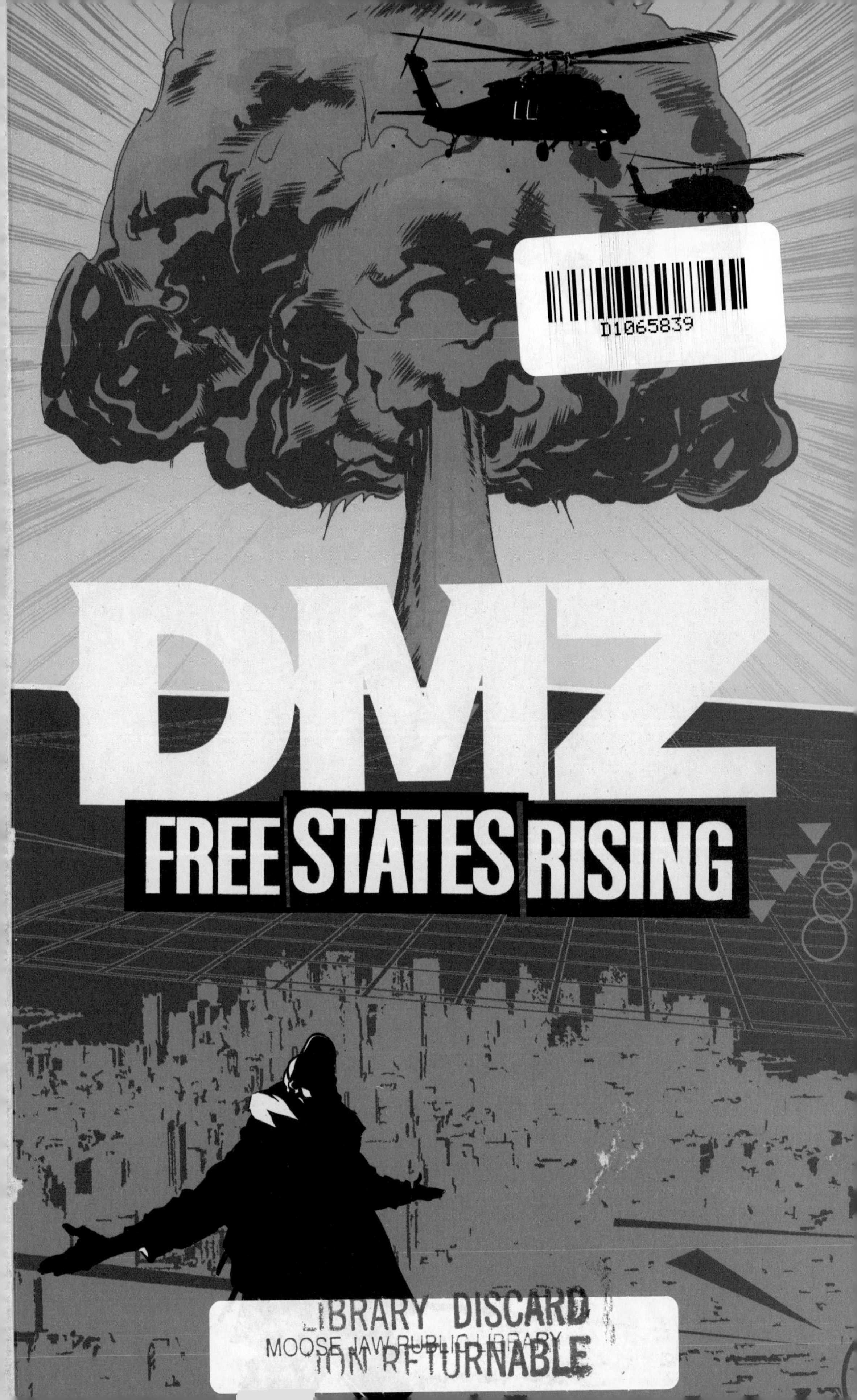
DMZ
FREE STATES RISING

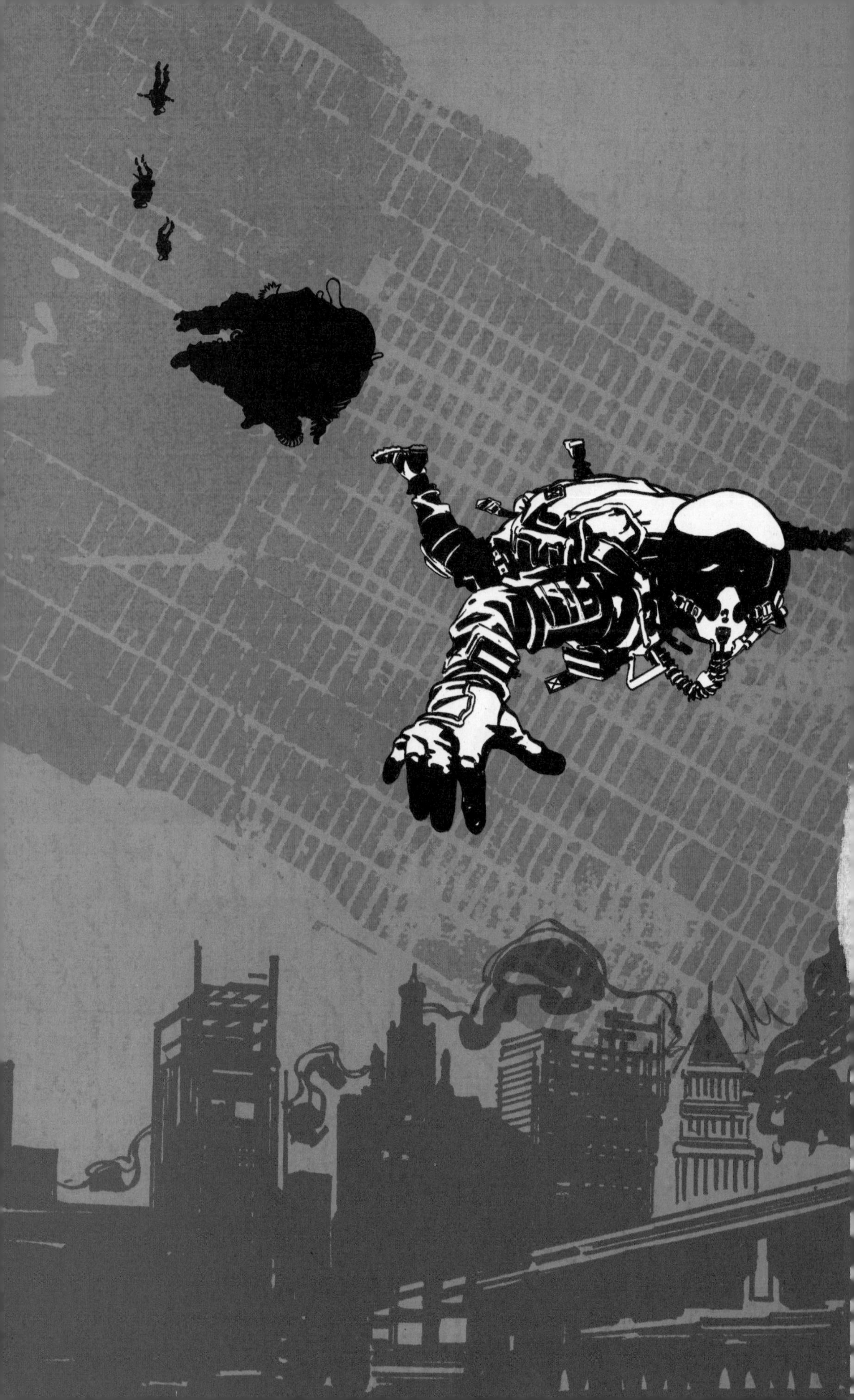

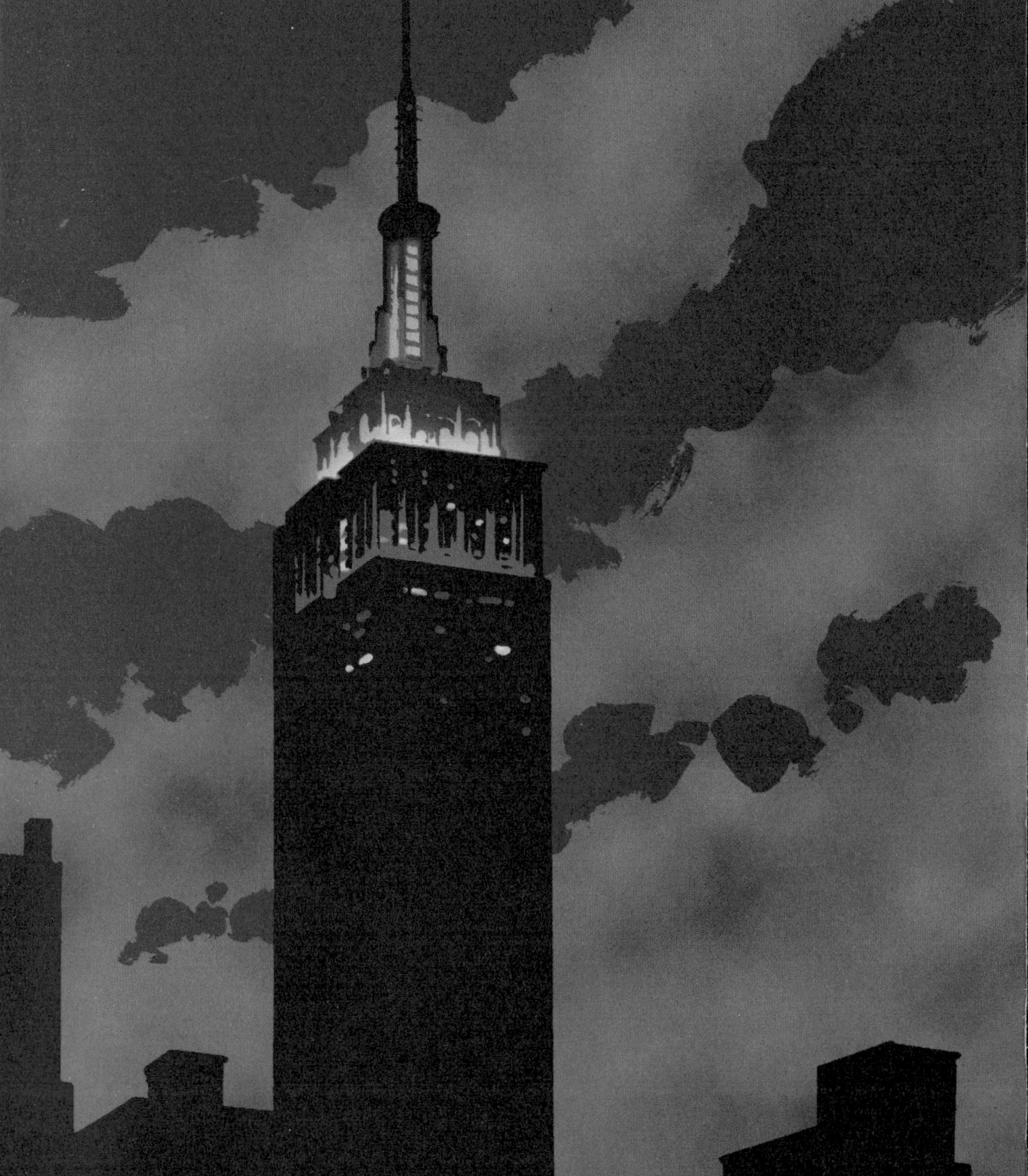

Will Dennis Editor - Original Series **Mark Doyle** Associate Editor - Original Series
Ian Sattler Director - Editorial, Special Projects and Archival Editions
Robin Wildman Editor **Robbin Brosterman** Design Director - Books
Robbie Biederman Publication Design

Karen Berger Senior VP - Executive Editor, Vertigo **Bob Harras** VP - Editor-in-Chief

Diane Nelson President **Dan DiDio** and **Jim Lee** Co-Publishers **Geoff Johns** Chief Creative Officer
John Rood Executive VP - Sales, Marketing and Business Development **Amy Genkins** Senior VP - Business and Legal Affairs **Nairi Gardiner** Senior VP - Finance
Jeff Boison VP - Publishing Operations **Mark Chiarello** VP - Art Direction and Design **John Cunningham** VP - Marketing **Terri Cunningham** VP - Talent Relations and Services
Alison Gill Senior VP - Manufacturing and Operations **David Hyde** VP - Publicity **Hank Kanalz** Senior VP - Digital **Jay Kogan** VP - Business and Legal Affairs, Publishing
Jack Mahan VP - Business Affairs, Talent **Nick Napolitano** VP - Manufacturing Administration **Sue Pohja** VP - Book Sales
Courtney Simmons Senior VP - Publicity **Bob Wayne** Senior VP - Sales

Logo and front cover designed by Brian Wood.

DMZ: FREE STATES RISING

DC Comics, 1700 Broadway, New York, NY 10019. A Warner Bros. Entertainment Company. Printed in the USA. 2/24/12. First Printing. ISBN: 978-1-4012-3389-1

SUSTAINABLE FORESTRY INITIATIVE Certified Sourcing
www.sfiprogram.org
SFI-01042
APPLIES TO TEXT STOCK ONLY

DMZ

FREE STATES RISING

BRIAN WOOD WRITER

RICCARDO BURCHIELLI
SHAWN MARTINBROUGH (PARTS ONE & TWO) ARTISTS

JEROMY COX COLORIST

JARED K. FLETCHER LETTERER

COVER BY **BRIAN WOOD**

ORIGINAL SERIES COVERS BY **JOHN PAUL LEON**
DMZ CREATED BY **BRIAN WOOD** AND **RICCARDO BURCHIELLI**

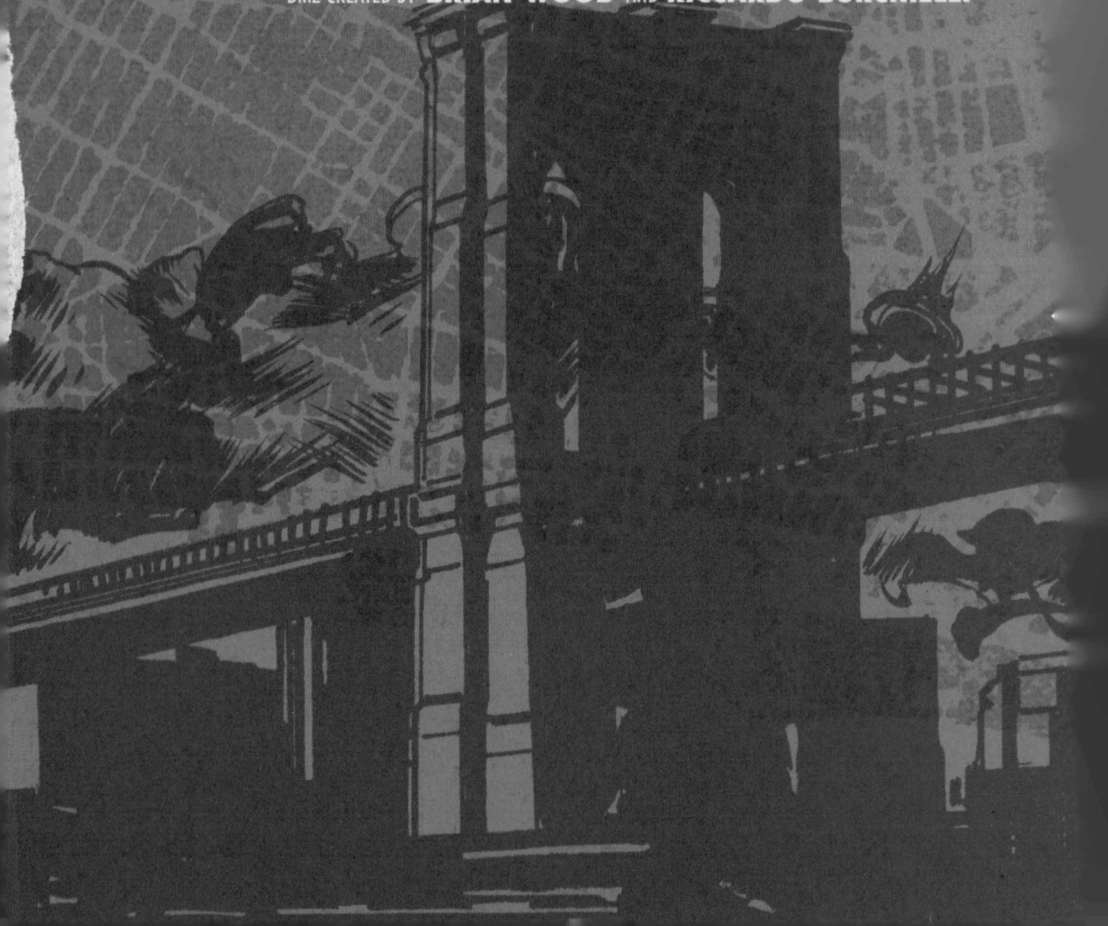

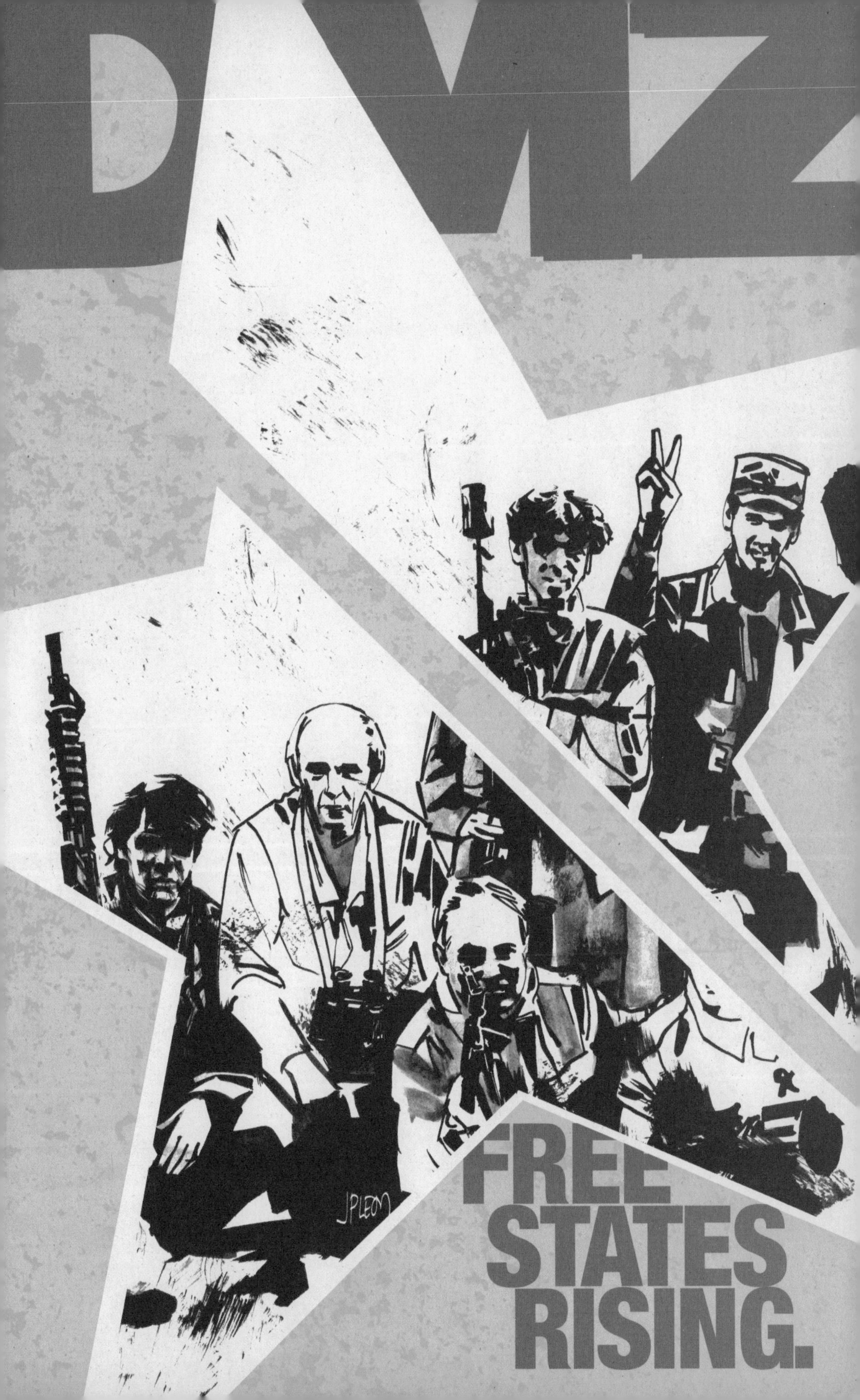
DMZ
JP LEON
FREE
STATES
RISING.

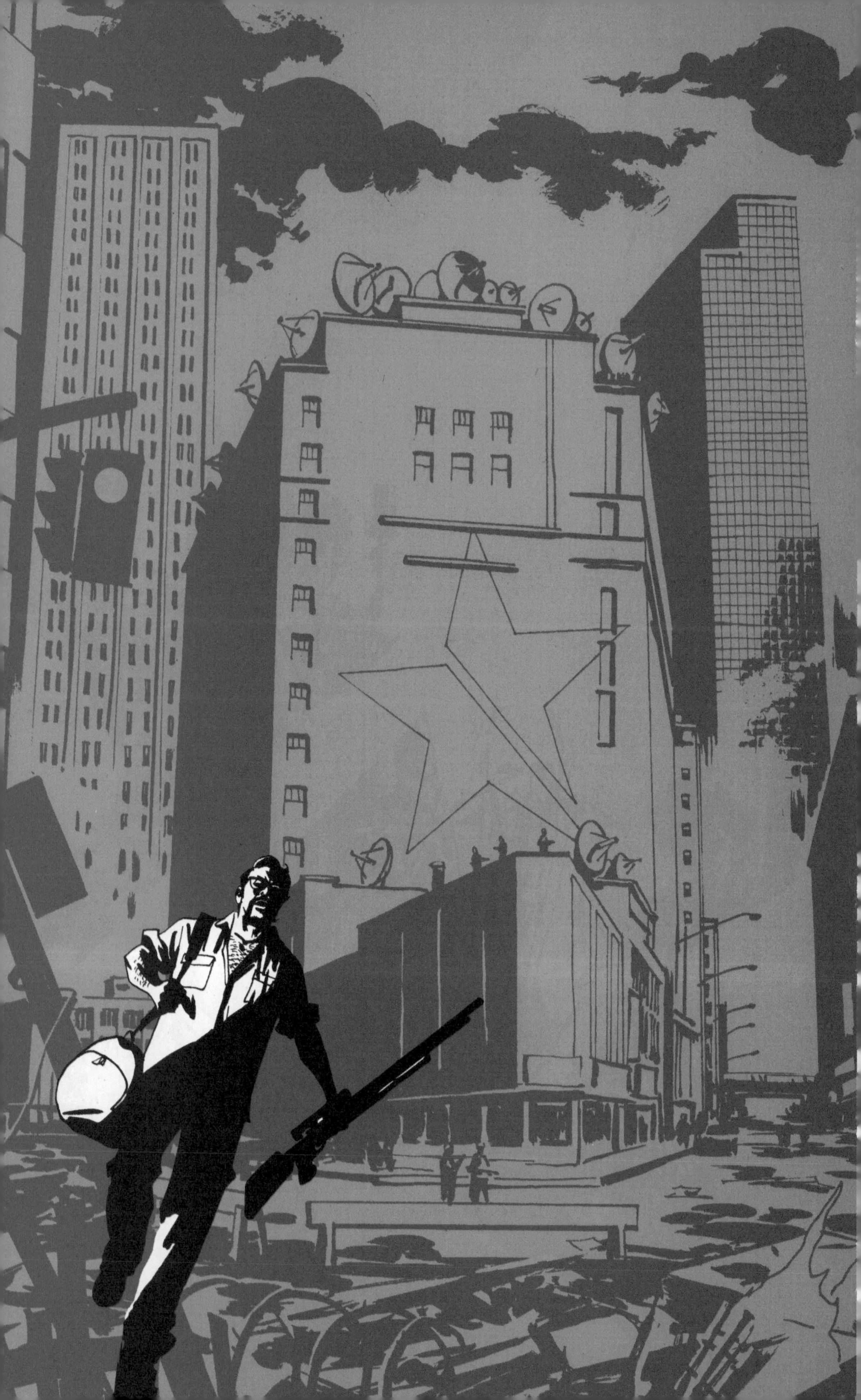

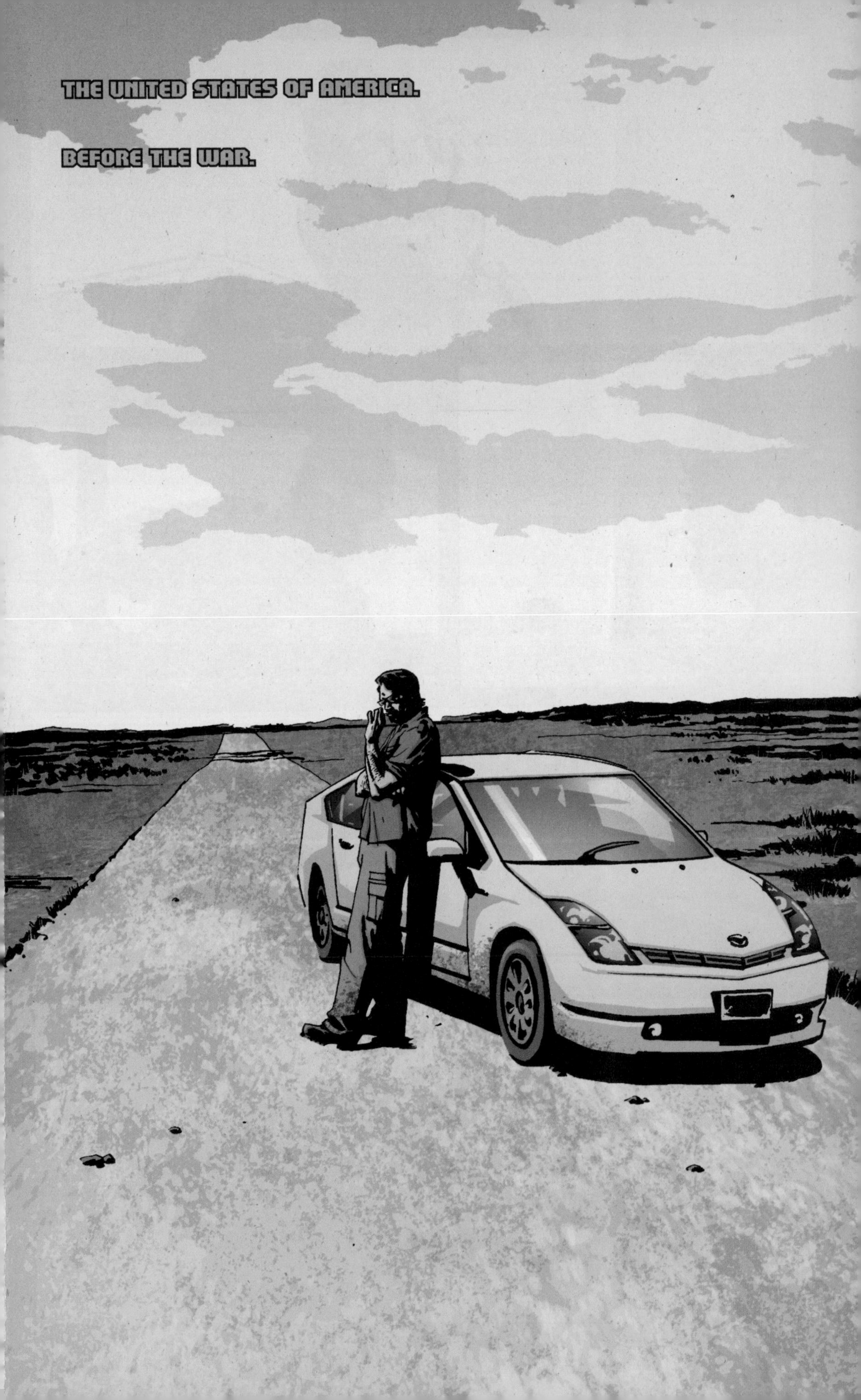
THE UNITED STATES OF AMERICA.
BEFORE THE WAR.

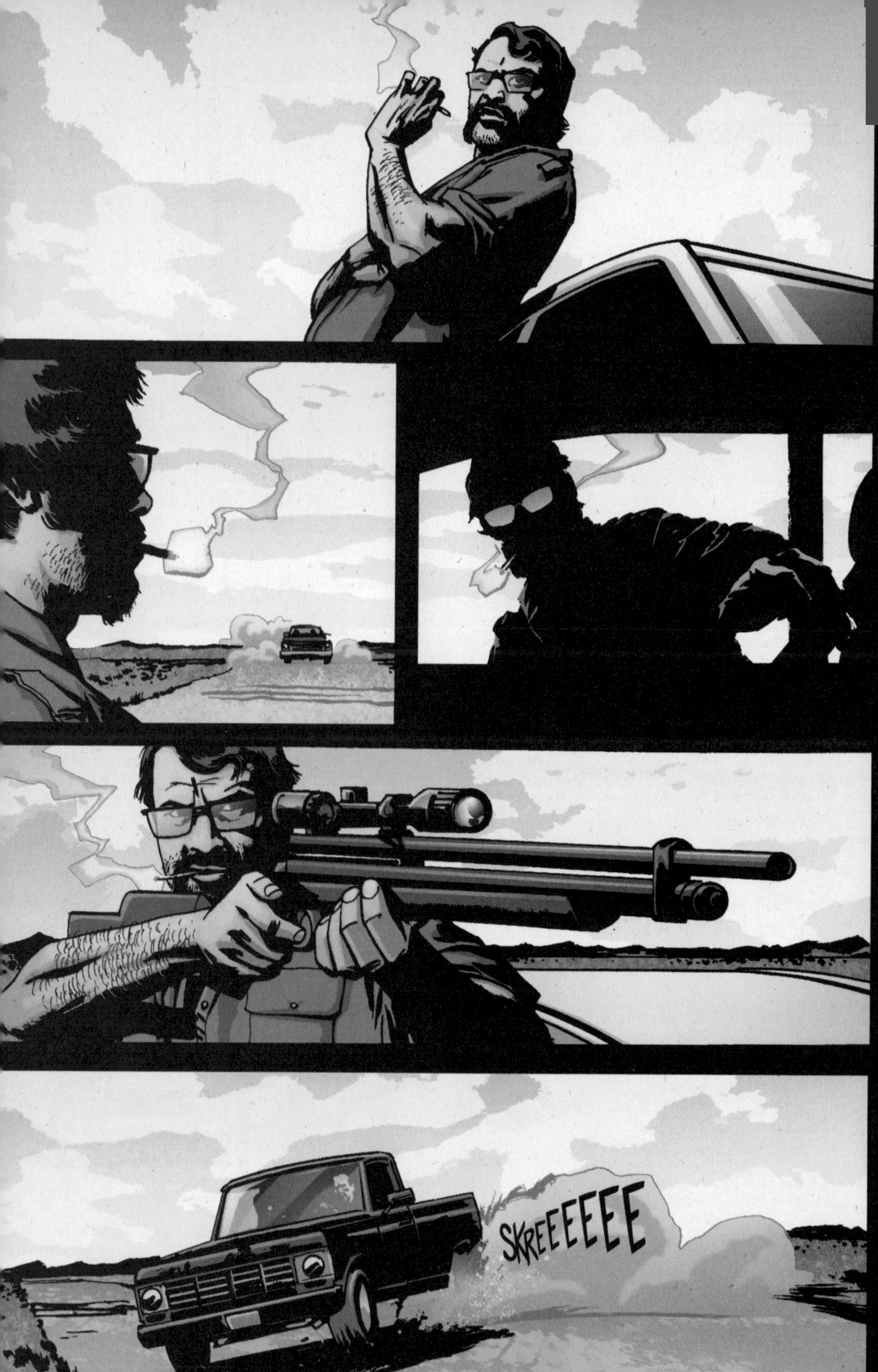
SKREEEEEE

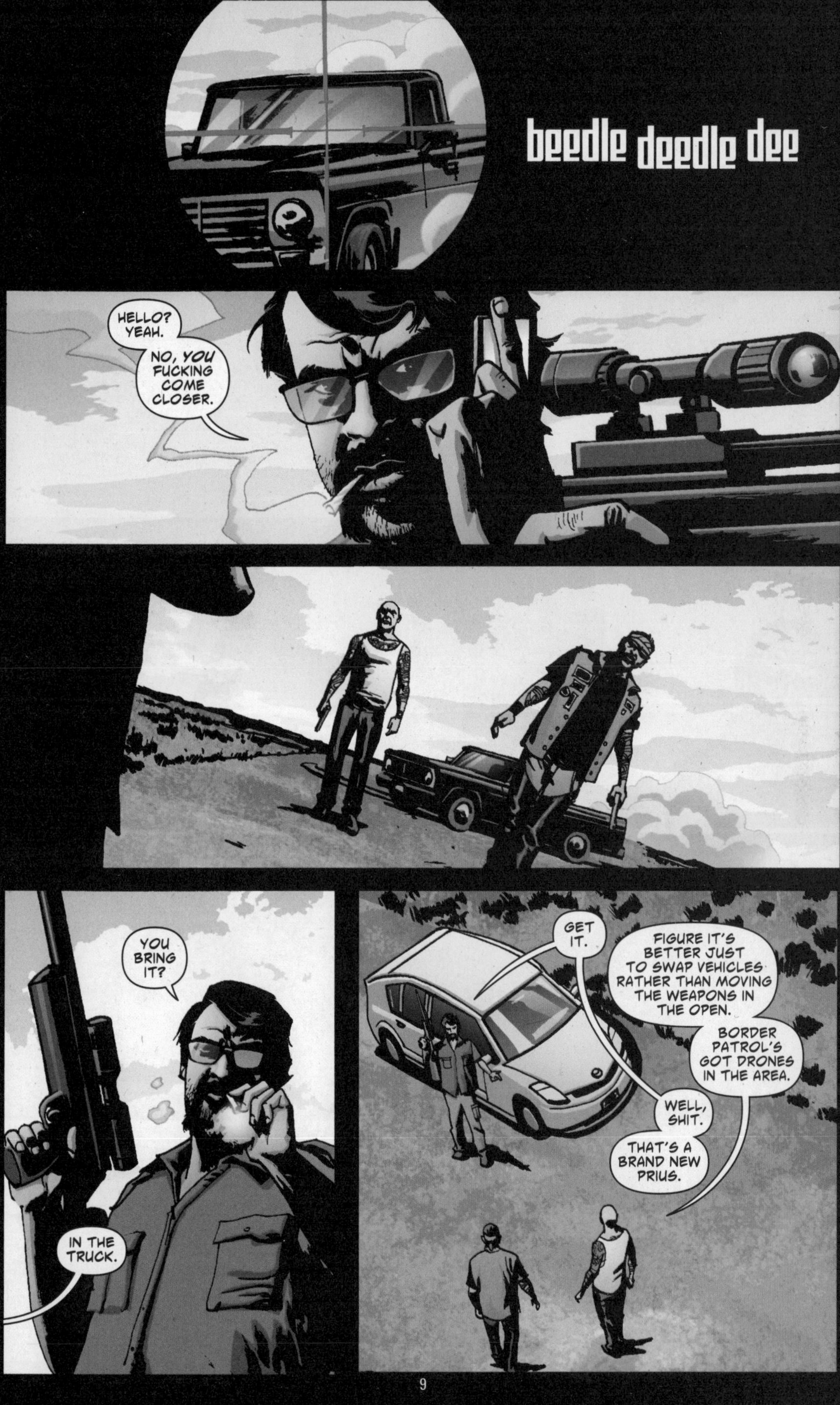
beedle deedle dee
HELLO? YEAH.
NO, YOU FUCKING COME CLOSER.
YOU BRING IT?
IN THE TRUCK.
GET IT.
FIGURE IT'S BETTER JUST TO SWAP VEHICLES RATHER THAN MOVING THE WEAPONS IN THE OPEN.
BORDER PATROL'S GOT DRONES IN THE AREA.
WELL, SHIT.
THAT'S A BRAND NEW PRIUS.

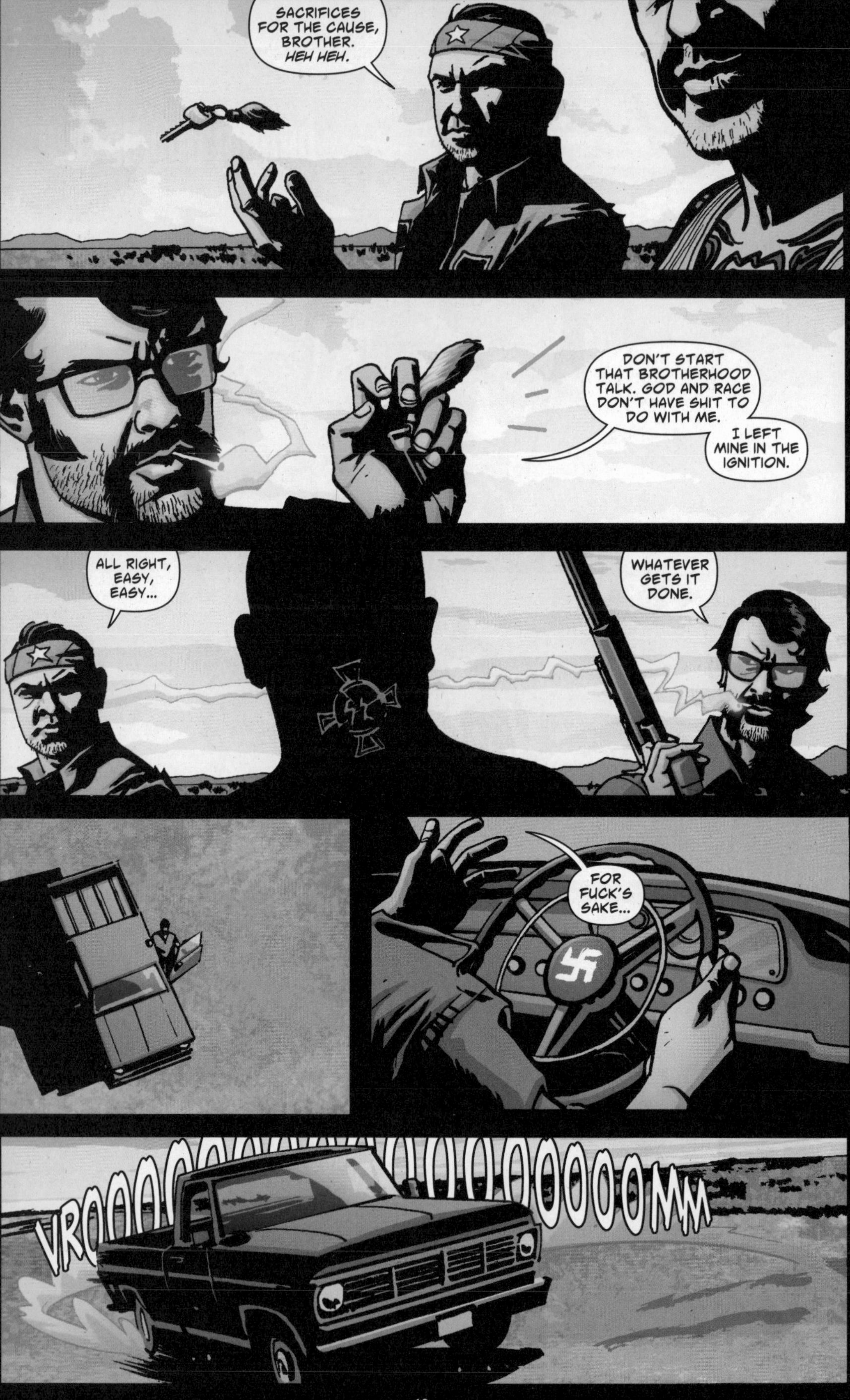
SACRIFICES FOR THE CAUSE, BROTHER. HEH HEH.
DON'T START THAT BROTHERHOOD TALK. GOD AND RACE DON'T HAVE SHIT TO DO WITH ME.
I LEFT MINE IN THE IGNITION.
ALL RIGHT, EASY, EASY...
WHATEVER GETS IT DONE.
FOR FUCK'S SAKE...
VROOOOOOOOOOOOOOOOOOMM

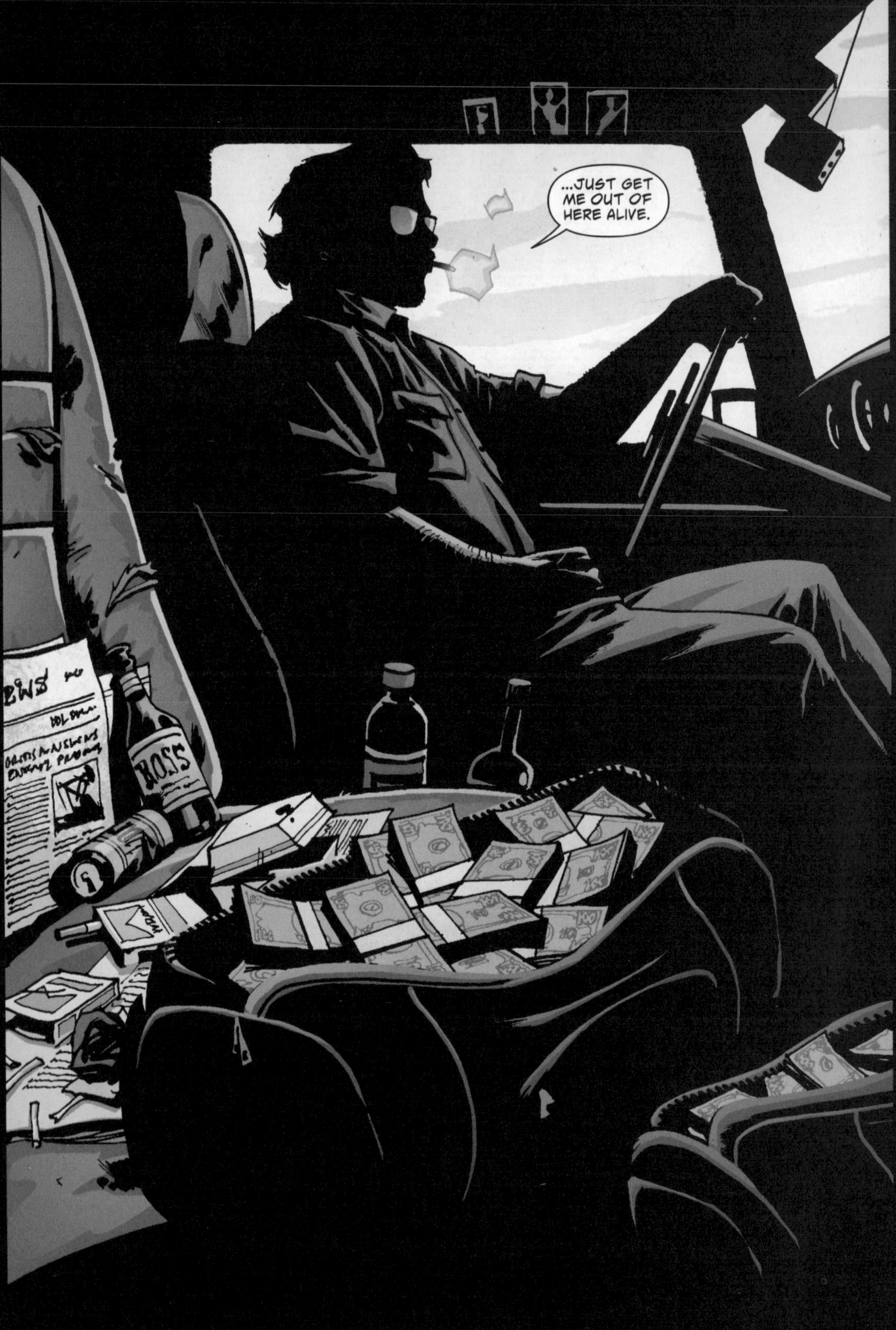
...JUST GET ME OUT OF HERE ALIVE.

…scenes from the G8 summit currently under way in Phoenix, Arizona, with thousands of protestors in bloody conflict with exhausted police officers.

This is the third week the summit's been delayed due to security concerns, with several international delegations held, quite literally, prisoner within their hotel suites…

…some calling it the "slow death of urban America," dozens more blocks of Richmond, Virginia have been abandoned by municipal authorities, with all utilities, 911, and public transit services withdrawn due to massive budget cuts.

Richmond joins a long list of other cities suffering similar fates. Entire neighborboods have been reduced to ghost towns in parts of St. Louis, Chicago, Portland, Boston, and Miami…

…latest in a seemingly endless string of police actions, the USS George Washington carrier strike group moves within fifty miles of the horn of Africa, a part of the world all too familiar with American military intervention.

With close to three-quarters of a million troops on the ground in the Middle East, Congress is faced with the largest war funding bill in U.S. history, one expected to pass unanimously…

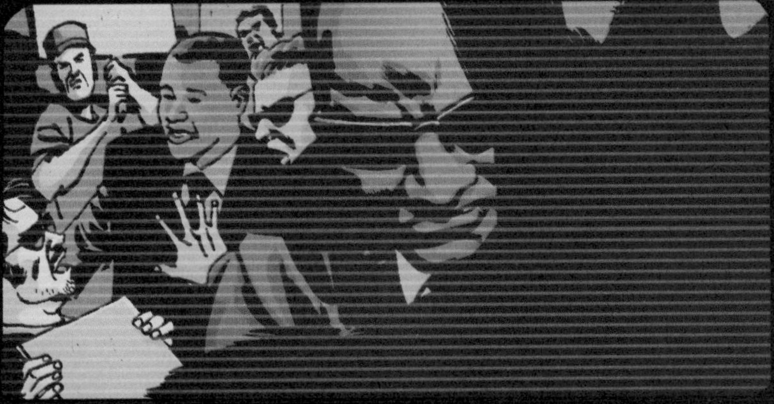

...like this incident from last week, showing the President barely making it aboard Air Force One. The Secret Service has their hands full with numerous threats every time the President makes a public appearance...

...not to mention the now-common practice of assault weapons carried in public. Massive resistance from the NRA and politicians on the Hill have tied law enforcement's hands...

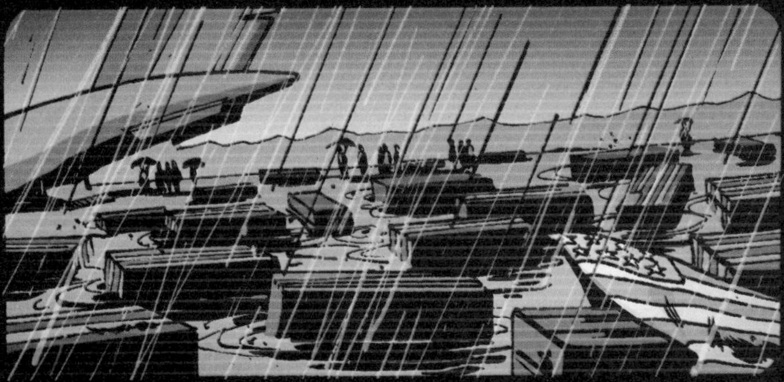

...scenes like this from Fort Conrad, where dozens if not hundreds of bodies of fallen soldiers sit out in the rain, unclaimed and unidentified. Repeated calls to military command have gone unanswered, and the residents of the town are faced with the horrifying thought of having to open the coffins and identify the bodies themselves...

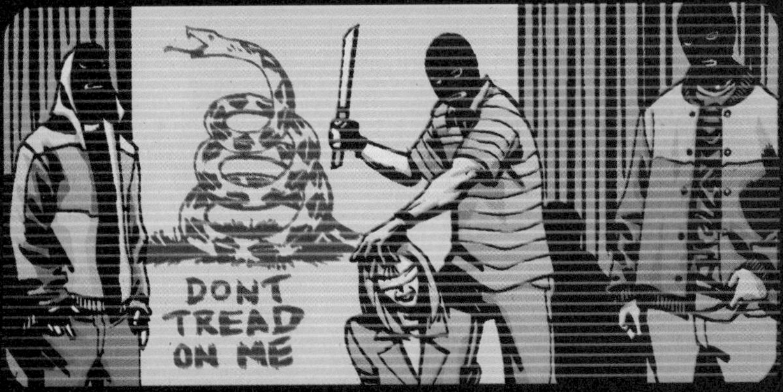
DONT TREAD ON ME

...in an Op Ed article in today's *Times,* decried the administration's clear lack of domestic agenda, noting that fear-mongering and constantly playing the "homeland defense" card is accomplishing nothing but a further disintegration of the fabric of American society.

With a combined thirty-nine years of war on no less than six fronts across the globe, he goes on to wonder "Just what is it that defines us these days? What does America mean – not only to the rest of the world – but to us at home?"

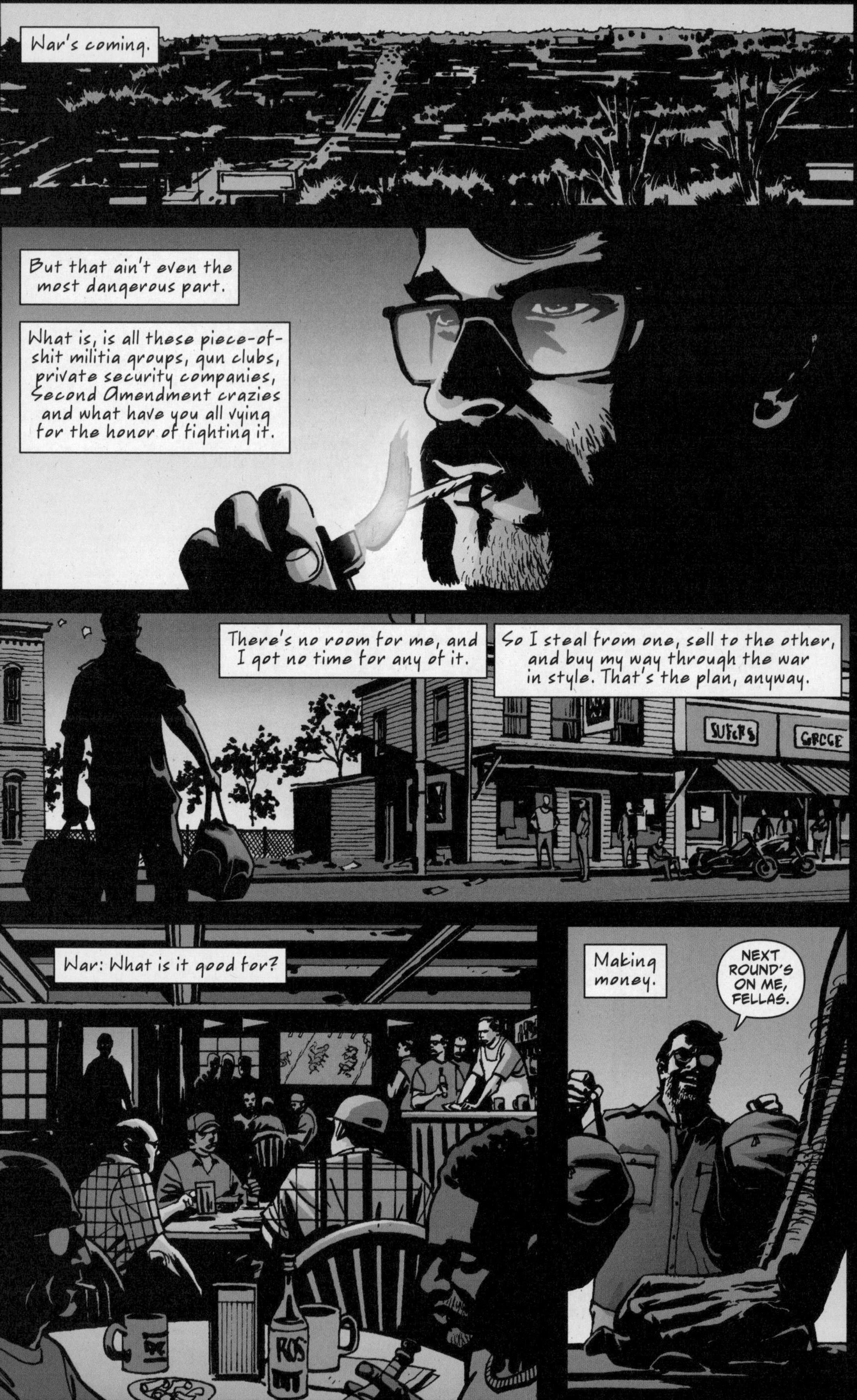
War's coming.
But that ain't even the most dangerous part.
What is, is all these piece-of-shit militia groups, gun clubs, private security companies, Second Amendment crazies and what have you all vying for the honor of fighting it.
There's no room for me, and I got no time for any of it.
So I steal from one, sell to the other, and buy my way through the war in style. That's the plan, anyway.
War: What is it good for?
Making money.
NEXT ROUND'S ON ME, FELLAS.

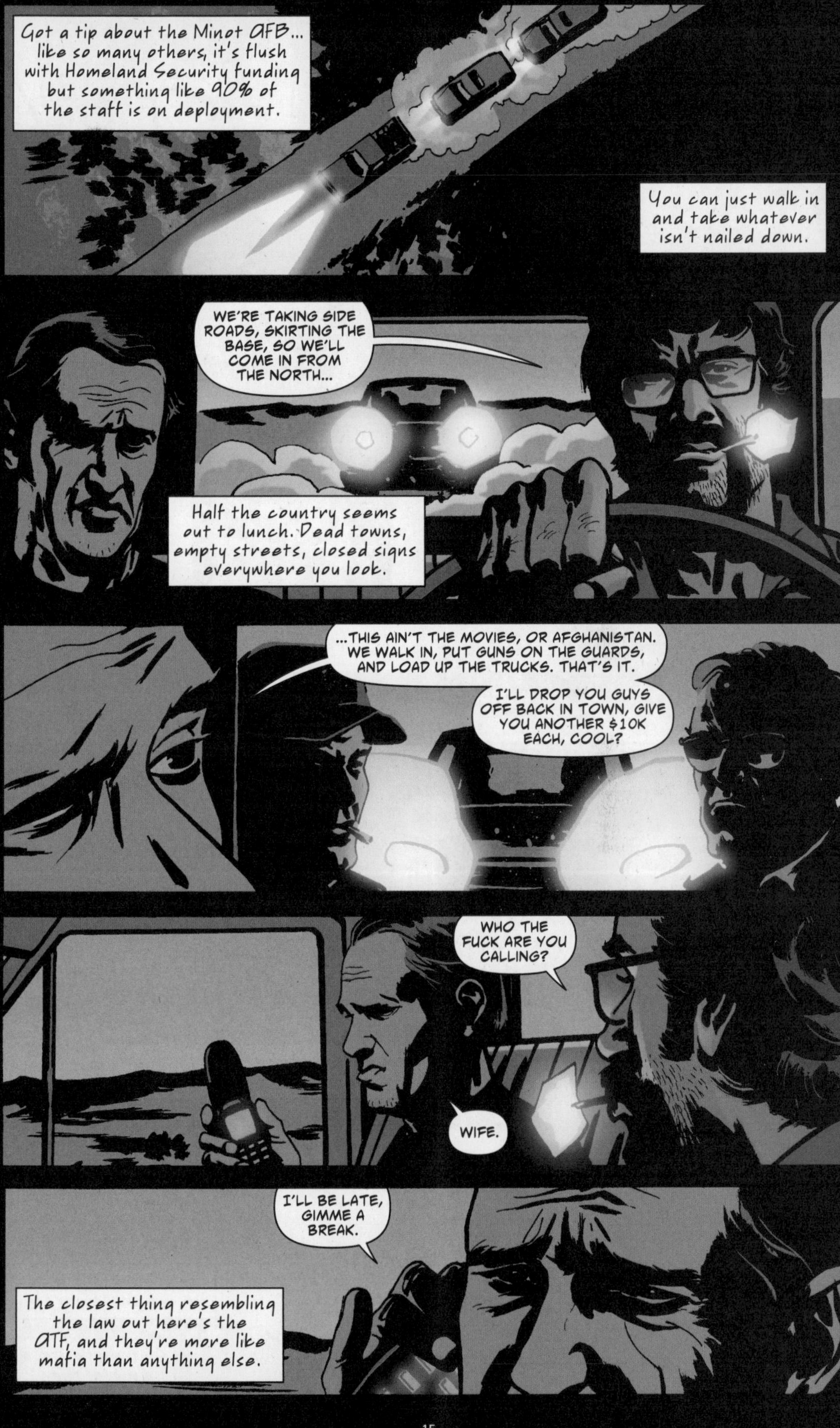
Got a tip about the Minot AFB... like so many others, it's flush with Homeland Security funding but something like 90% of the staff is on deployment.
You can just walk in and take whatever isn't nailed down.
WE'RE TAKING SIDE ROADS, SKIRTING THE BASE, SO WE'LL COME IN FROM THE NORTH...
Half the country seems out to lunch. Dead towns, empty streets, closed signs everywhere you look.
...THIS AIN'T THE MOVIES, OR AFGHANISTAN. WE WALK IN, PUT GUNS ON THE GUARDS, AND LOAD UP THE TRUCKS. THAT'S IT.
I'LL DROP YOU GUYS OFF BACK IN TOWN, GIVE YOU ANOTHER $10K EACH, COOL?
WHO THE FUCK ARE YOU CALLING?
WIFE.
I'LL BE LATE, GIMME A BREAK.
The closest thing resembling the law out here's the ATF, and they're more like mafia than anything else.

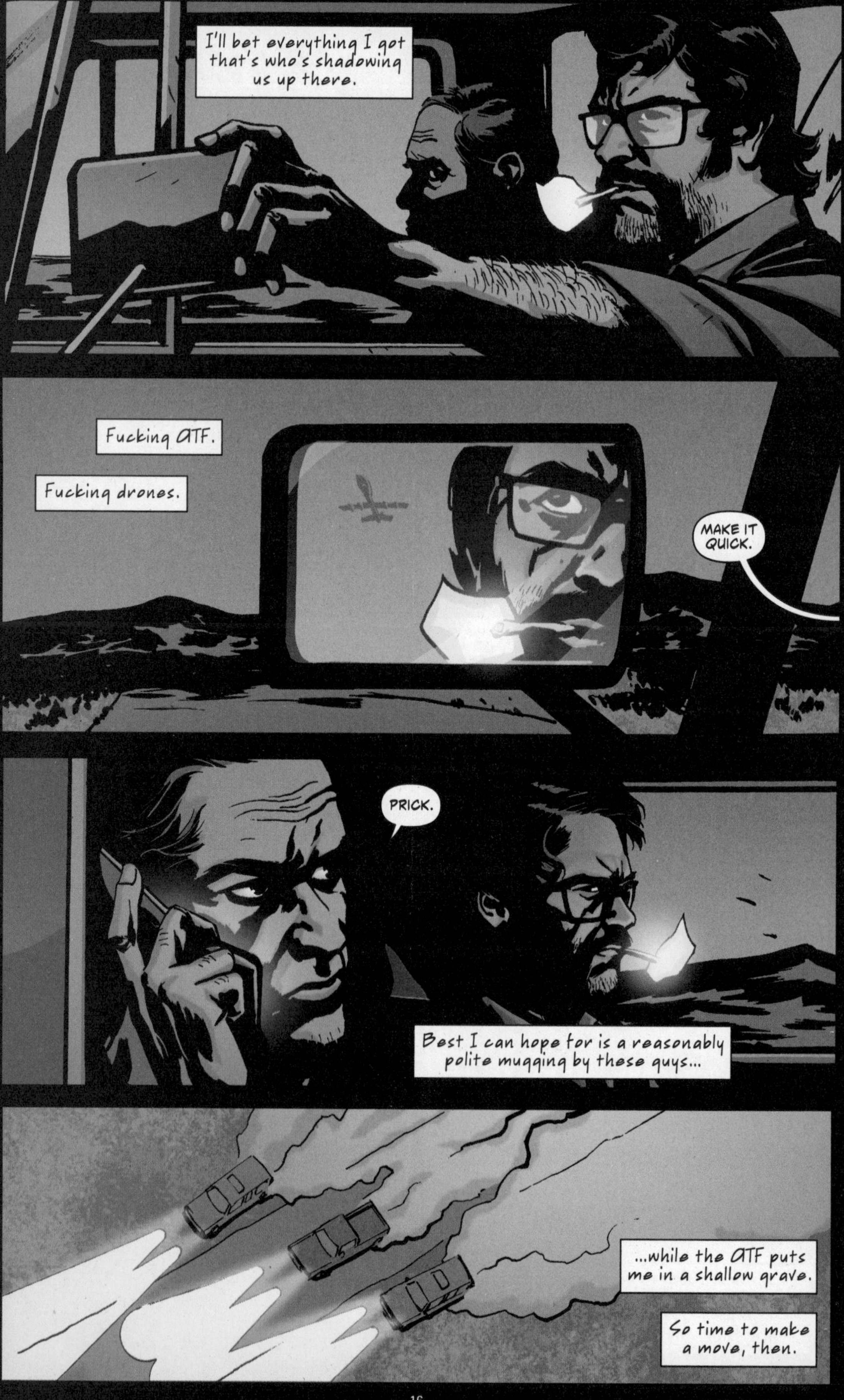
I'll bet everything I got that's who's shadowing us up there.
Fucking ATF.
Fucking drones.
MAKE IT QUICK.
PRICK.
Best I can hope for is a reasonably polite mugging by these guys...
...while the ATF puts me in a shallow grave.
So time to make a move, then.

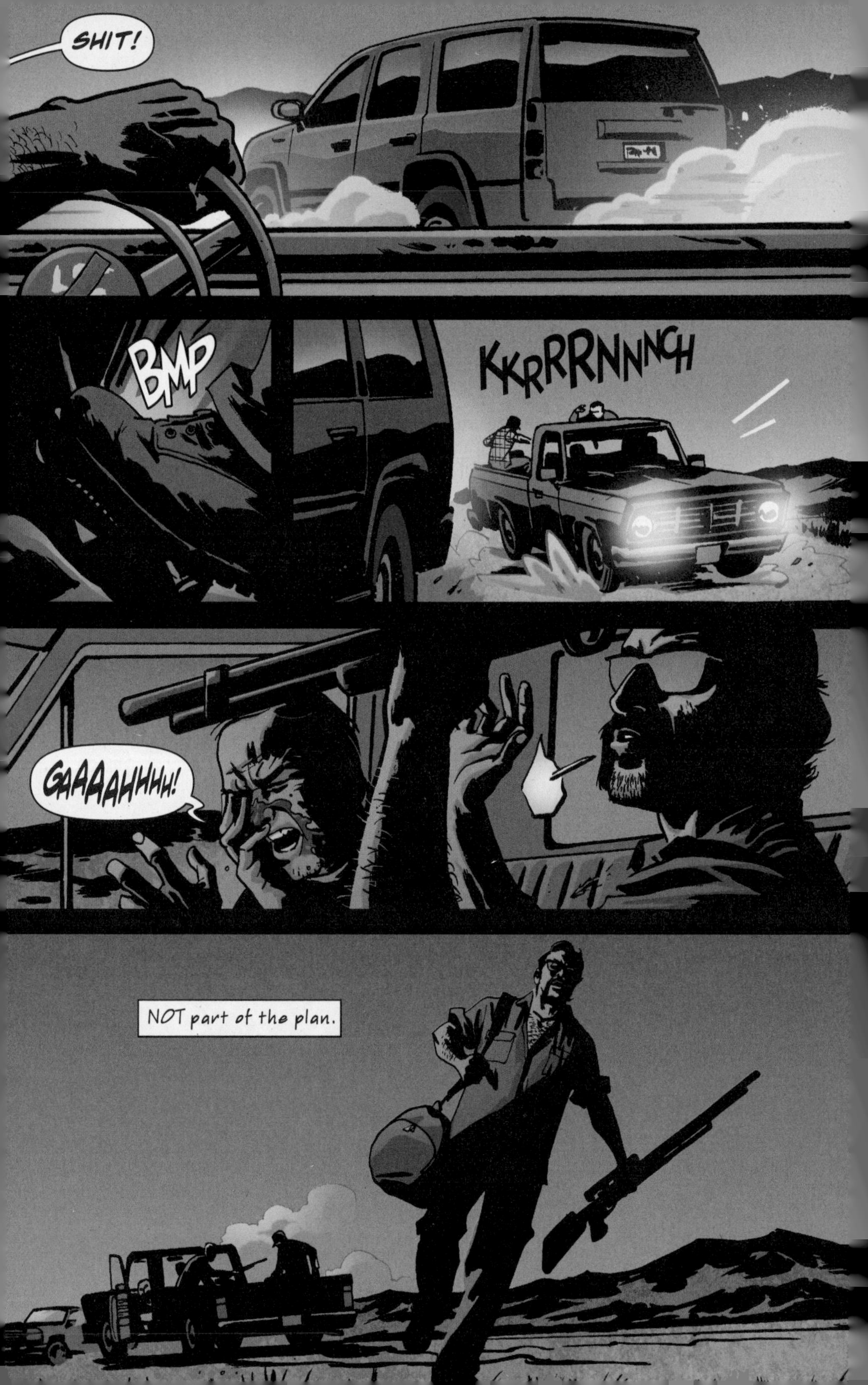
SHIT!
BMP
KKRRRNNNCH
GAAAAHHHH!
NOT part of the plan.

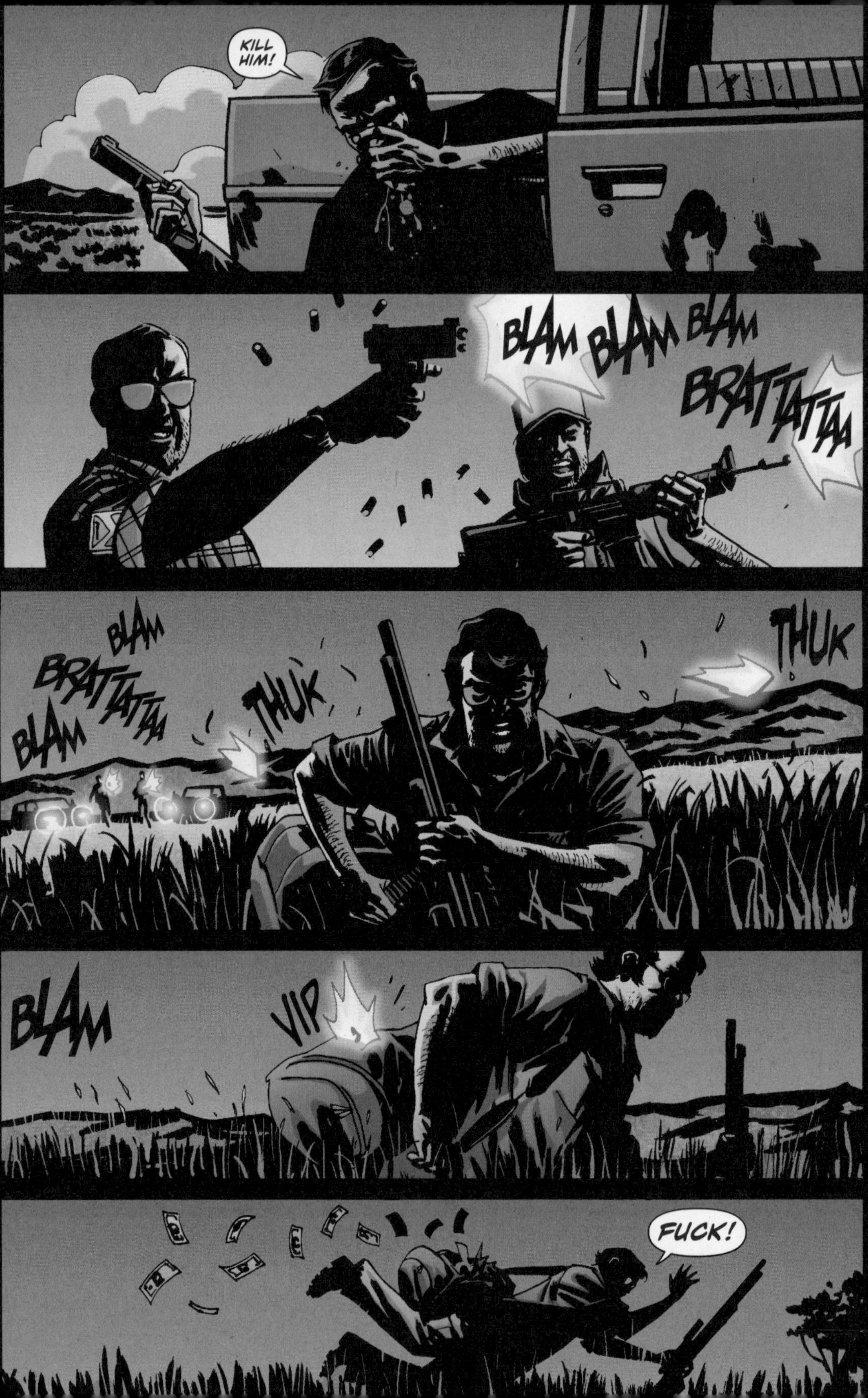
KILL HIM!
BLAM BLAM BLAM
BRATTATTAA
BLAM
BRATTATTAA
BLAM
THUK
THUK
BLAM
VIP
FUCK!

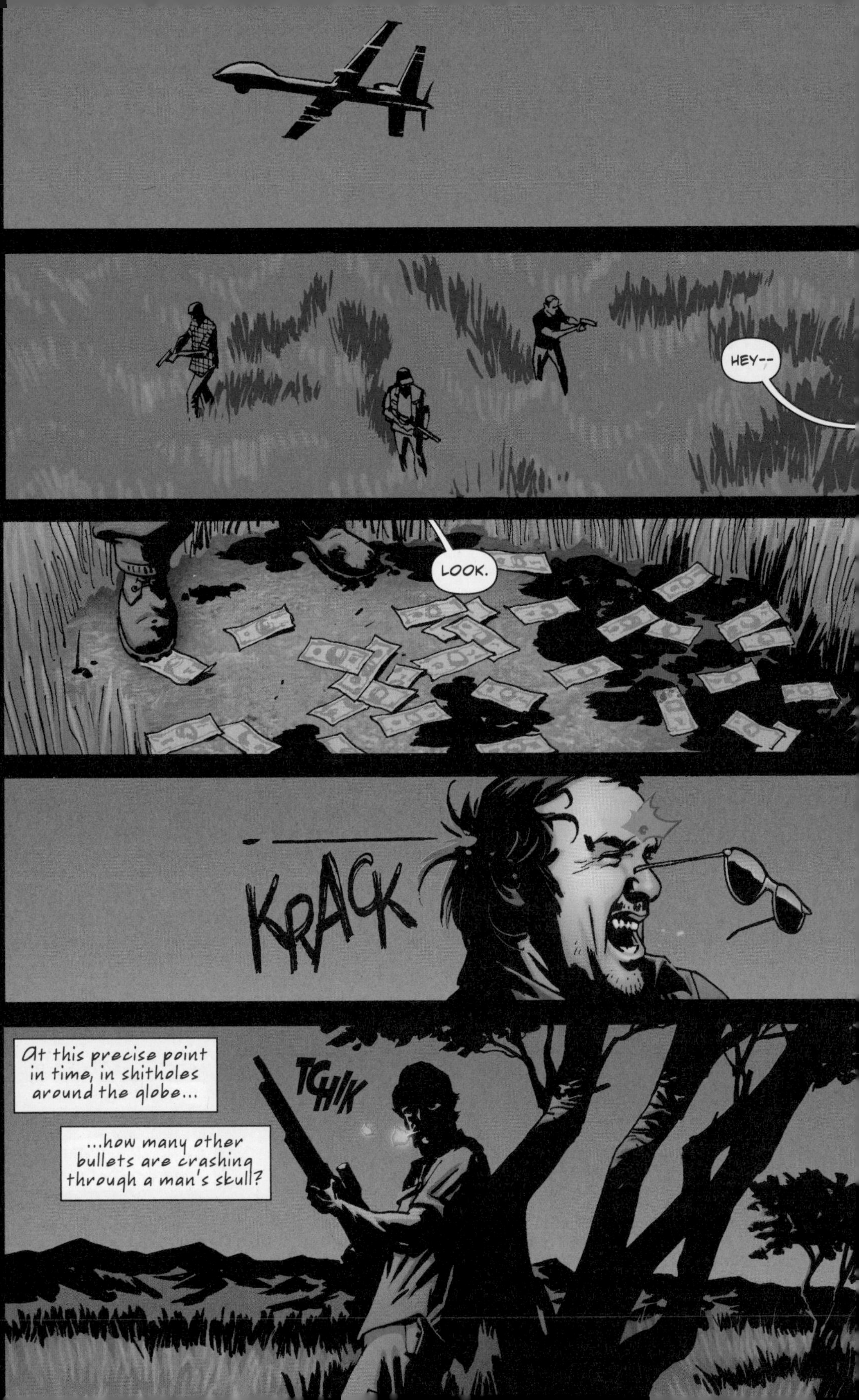
HEY--
LOOK.
KRACK
At this precise point in time, in shitholes around the globe...
TCHIK
...how many other bullets are crashing through a man's skull?

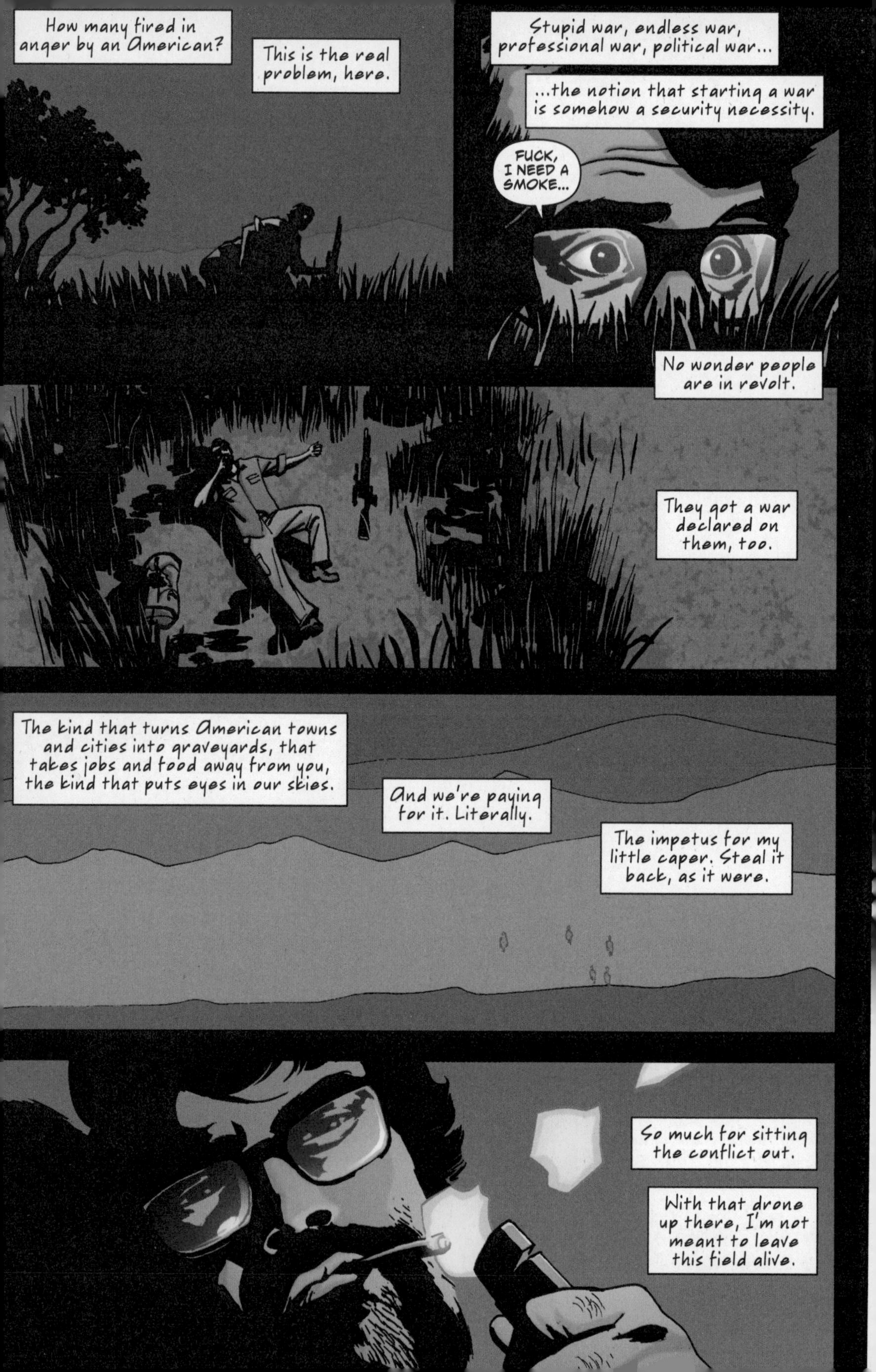

How many fired in anger by an American?
This is the real problem, here.
Stupid war, endless war, professional war, political war...
...the notion that starting a war is somehow a security necessity.
FUCK, I NEED A SMOKE...
No wonder people are in revolt.
They got a war declared on them, too.
The kind that turns American towns and cities into graveyards, that takes jobs and food away from you, the kind that puts eyes in our skies.
And we're paying for it. Literally.
The impetus for my little caper. Steal it back, as it were.
So much for sitting the conflict out.
With that drone up there, I'm not meant to leave this field alive.

…unknown substance found in this peaceful suburbs mail system this morning. At least seven carriers suspected to have been exposed…

BRAMPTON SCHOOL BOMBING

HUNDREDS SUSPECTED KILLED. POSSIBLE "DIRTY" CONTAMINATE HAMPERING RESCUE EFFORTS

…latest in a rash of school bombings that seem to have one thing in common – all serving affluent counties with representatives who voted for the recent round of Pentagon war funding…

SWAT SWAT SWAT

…negotiations having run out, New York City SWAT teams move in on City Hall Park…

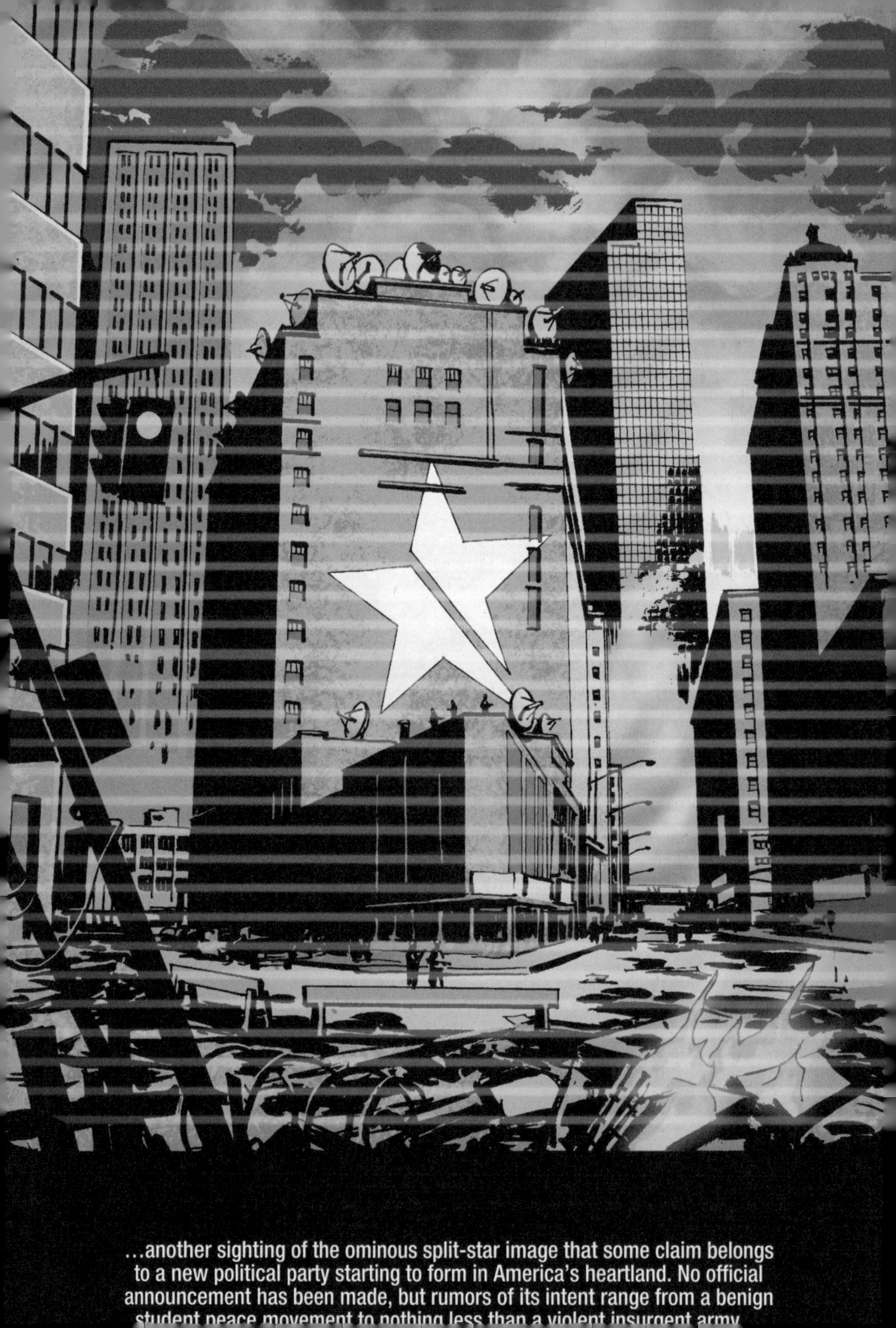

...another sighting of the ominous split-star image that some claim belongs to a new political party starting to form in America's heartland. No official announcement has been made, but rumors of its intent range from a benign student peace movement to nothing less than a violent insurgent army.

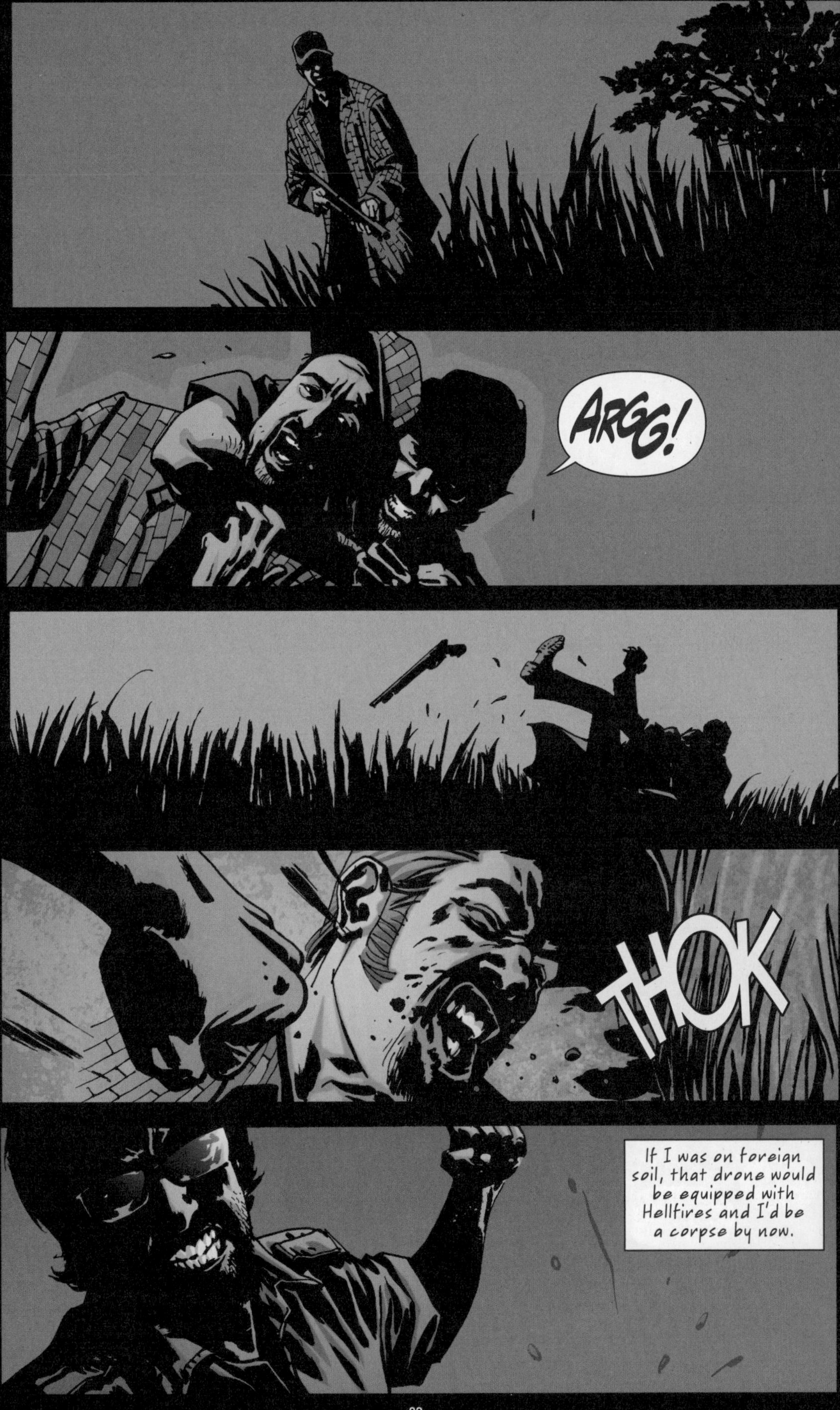
ARGG!
THOK
If I was on foreign soil, that drone would be equipped with Hellfires and I'd be a corpse by now.

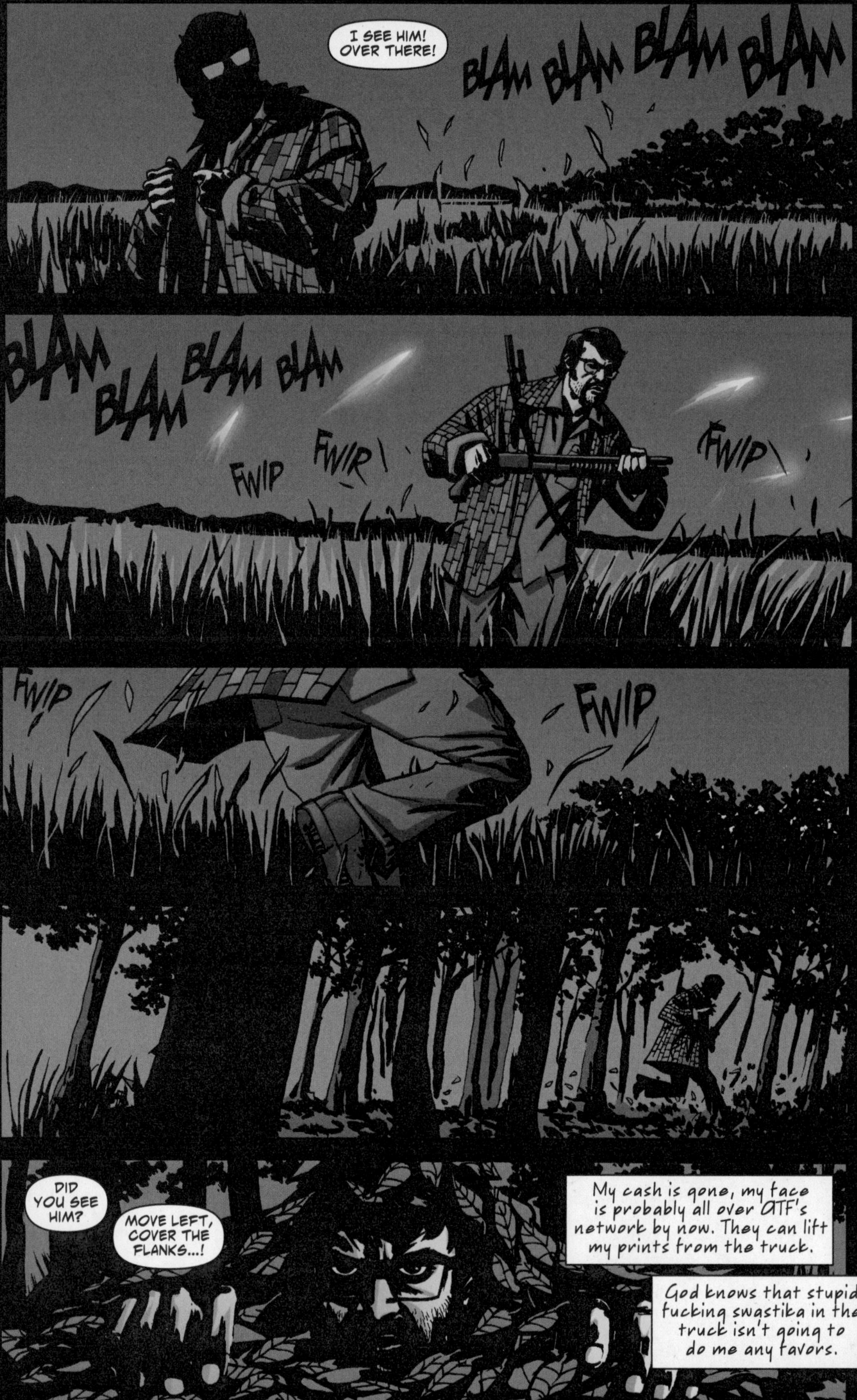

I SEE HIM! OVER THERE!
BLAM BLAM BLAM BLAM
BLAM BLAM BLAM BLAM
FWIP
FWIR
FWIP
FWIP
FWIP
DID YOU SEE HIM?
MOVE LEFT, COVER THE FLANKS...!
My cash is gone, my face is probably all over ATF's network by now. They can lift my prints from the truck.
God knows that stupid fucking swastika in the truck isn't going to do me any favors.

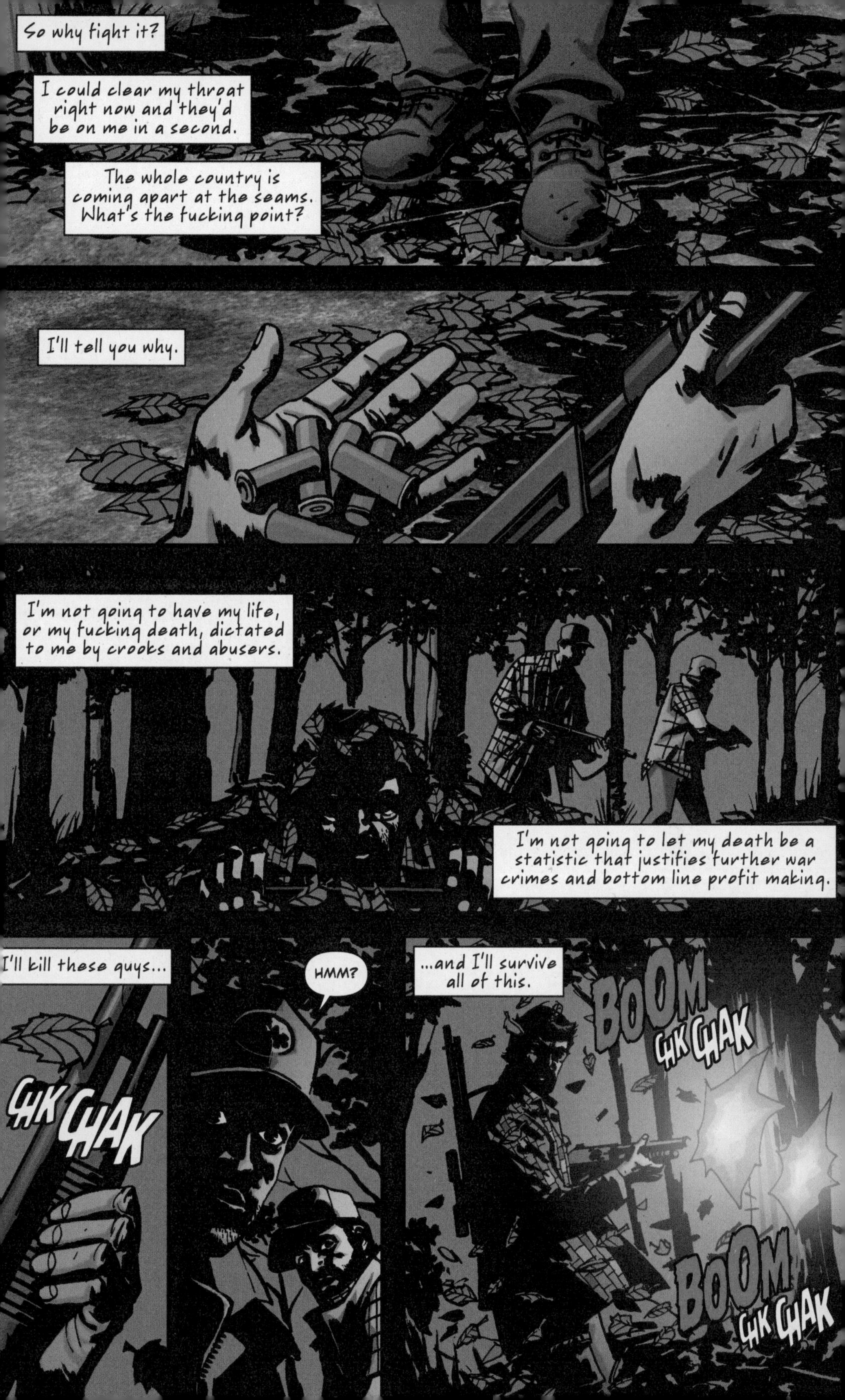
So why fight it?
I could clear my throat right now and they'd be on me in a second.
The whole country is coming apart at the seams. What's the fucking point?
I'll tell you why.
I'm not going to have my life, or my fucking death, dictated to me by crooks and abusers.
I'm not going to let my death be a statistic that justifies further war crimes and bottom line profit making.
I'll kill these guys...
CHK CHAK
HMM?
...and I'll survive all of this.
BOOM
CHK CHAK
BOOM
CHK CHAK

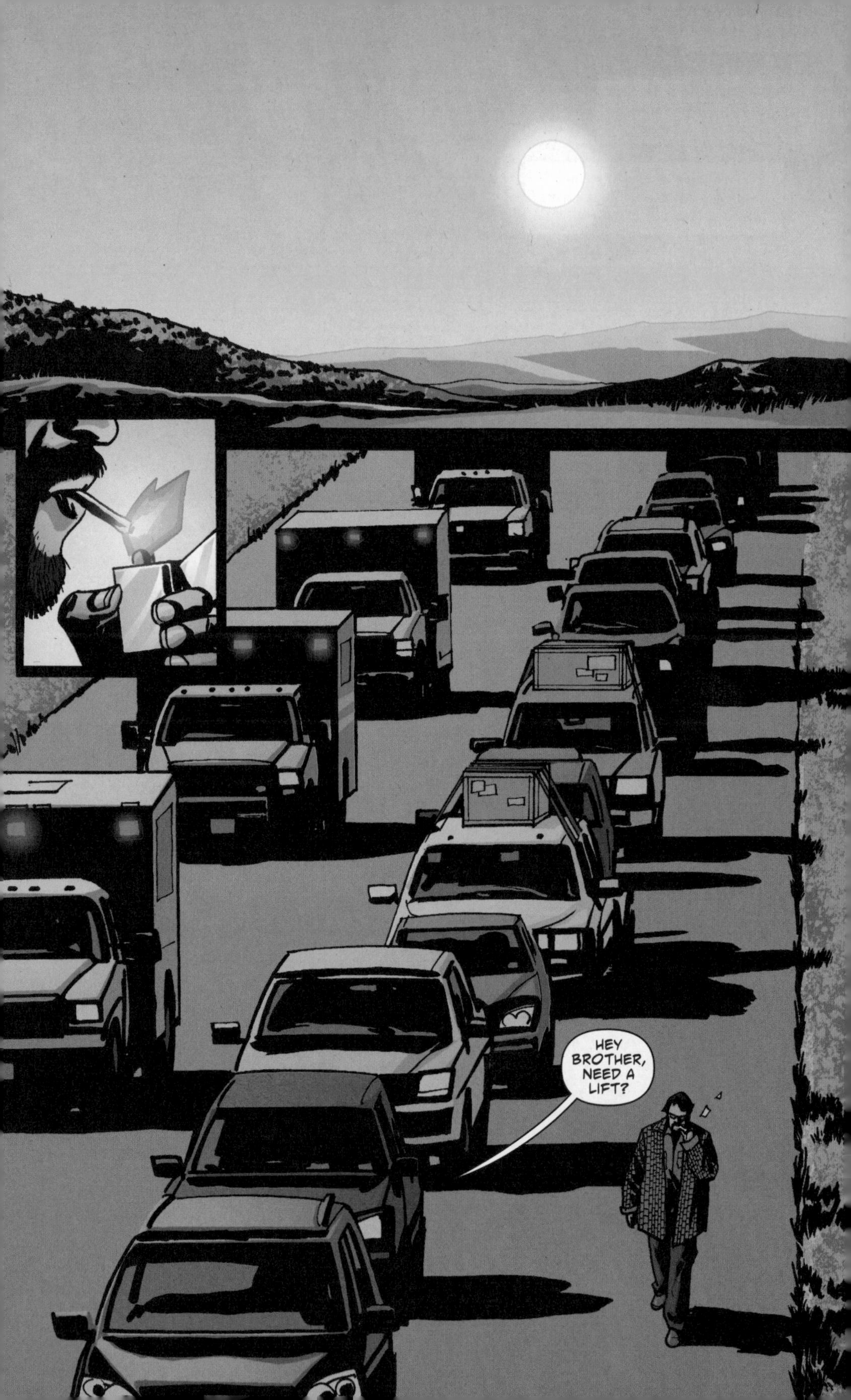
HEY BROTHER, NEED A LIFT?

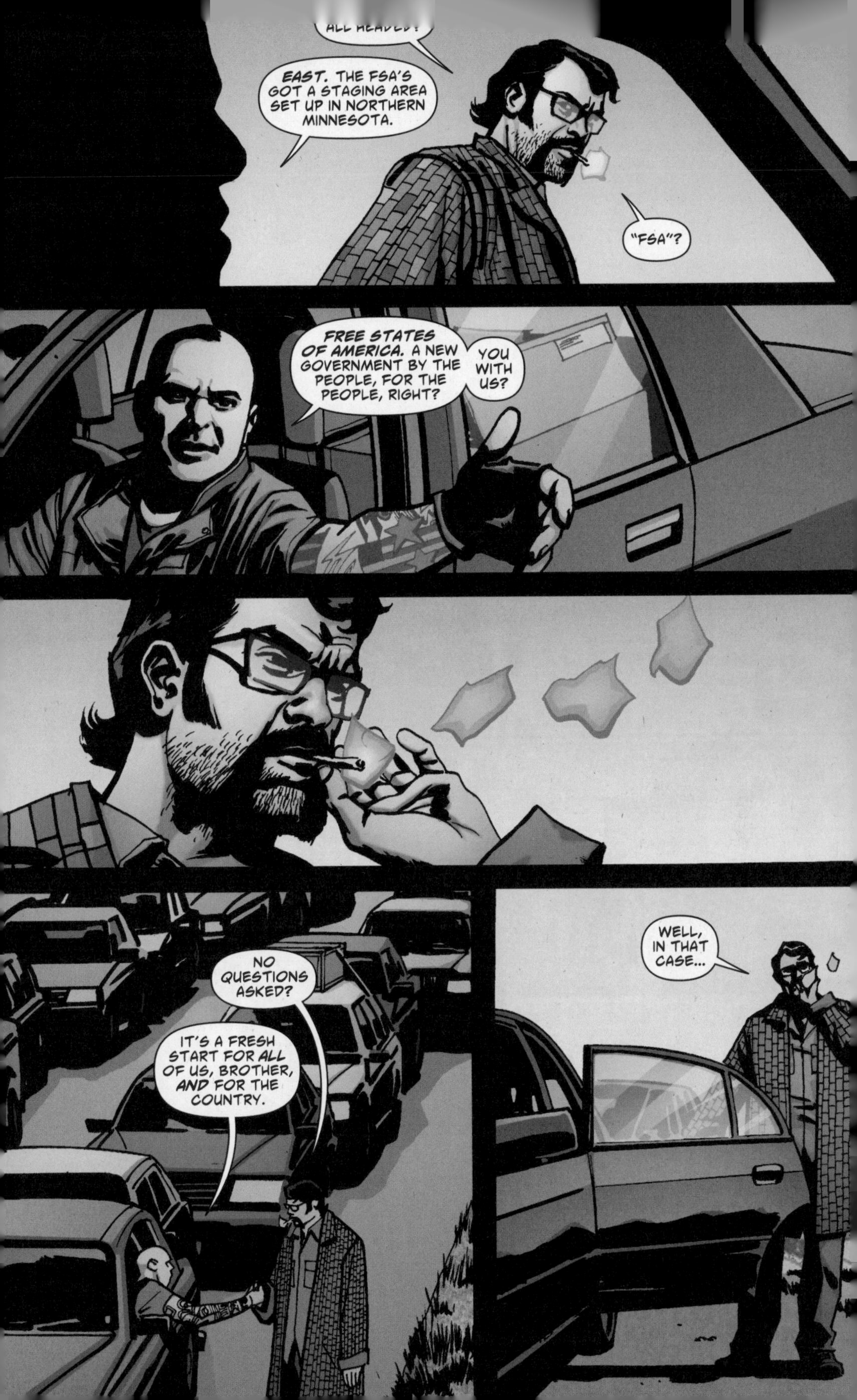
EAST. THE FSA'S GOT A STAGING AREA SET UP IN NORTHERN MINNESOTA.
"FSA"?
FREE STATES OF AMERICA. A NEW GOVERNMENT BY THE PEOPLE, FOR THE PEOPLE, RIGHT?
YOU WITH US?
NO QUESTIONS ASKED?
IT'S A FRESH START FOR ALL OF US, BROTHER, AND FOR THE COUNTRY.
WELL, IN THAT CASE...

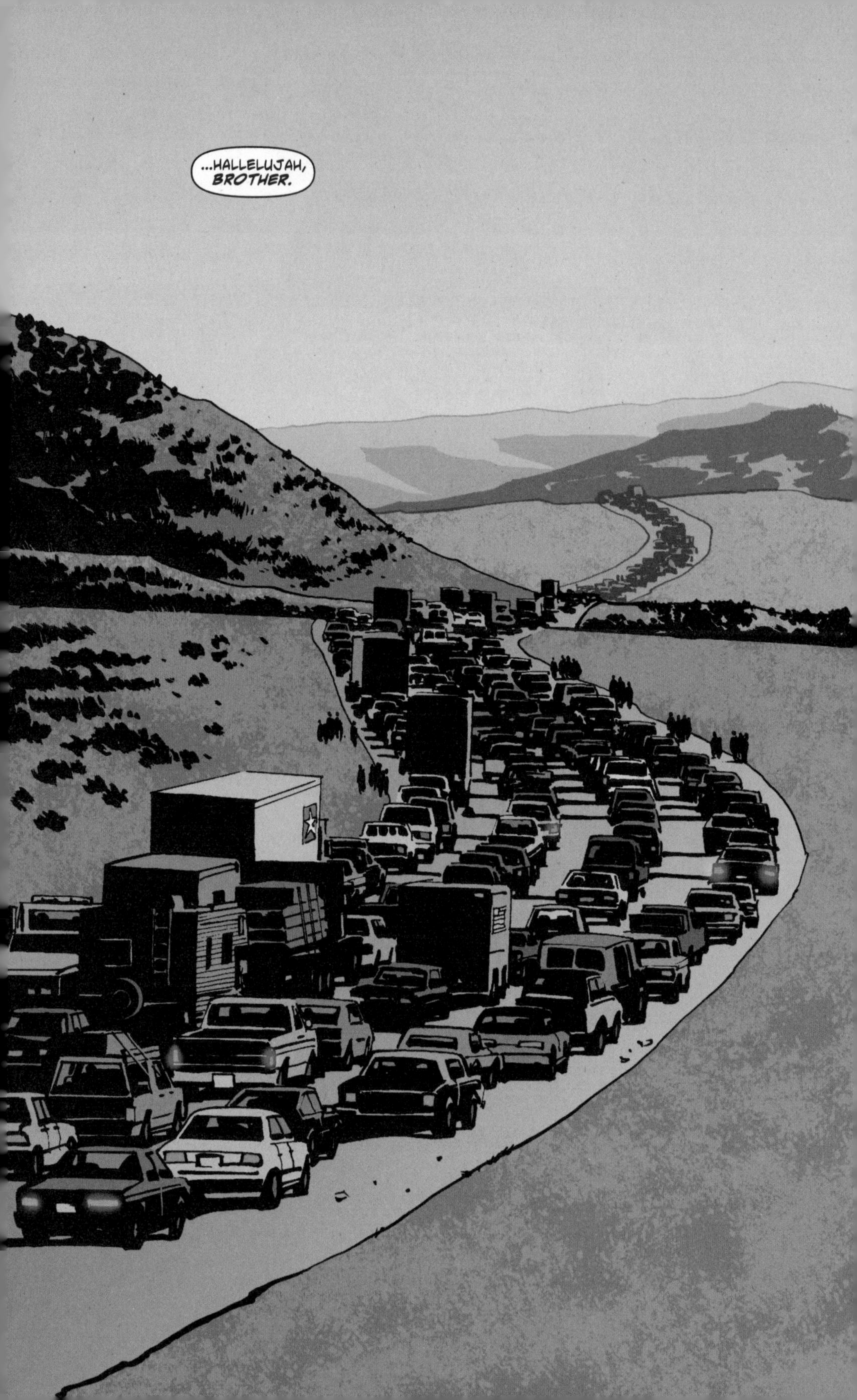
...HALLELUJAH, BROTHER.

DMZ

FREE STATES RISING

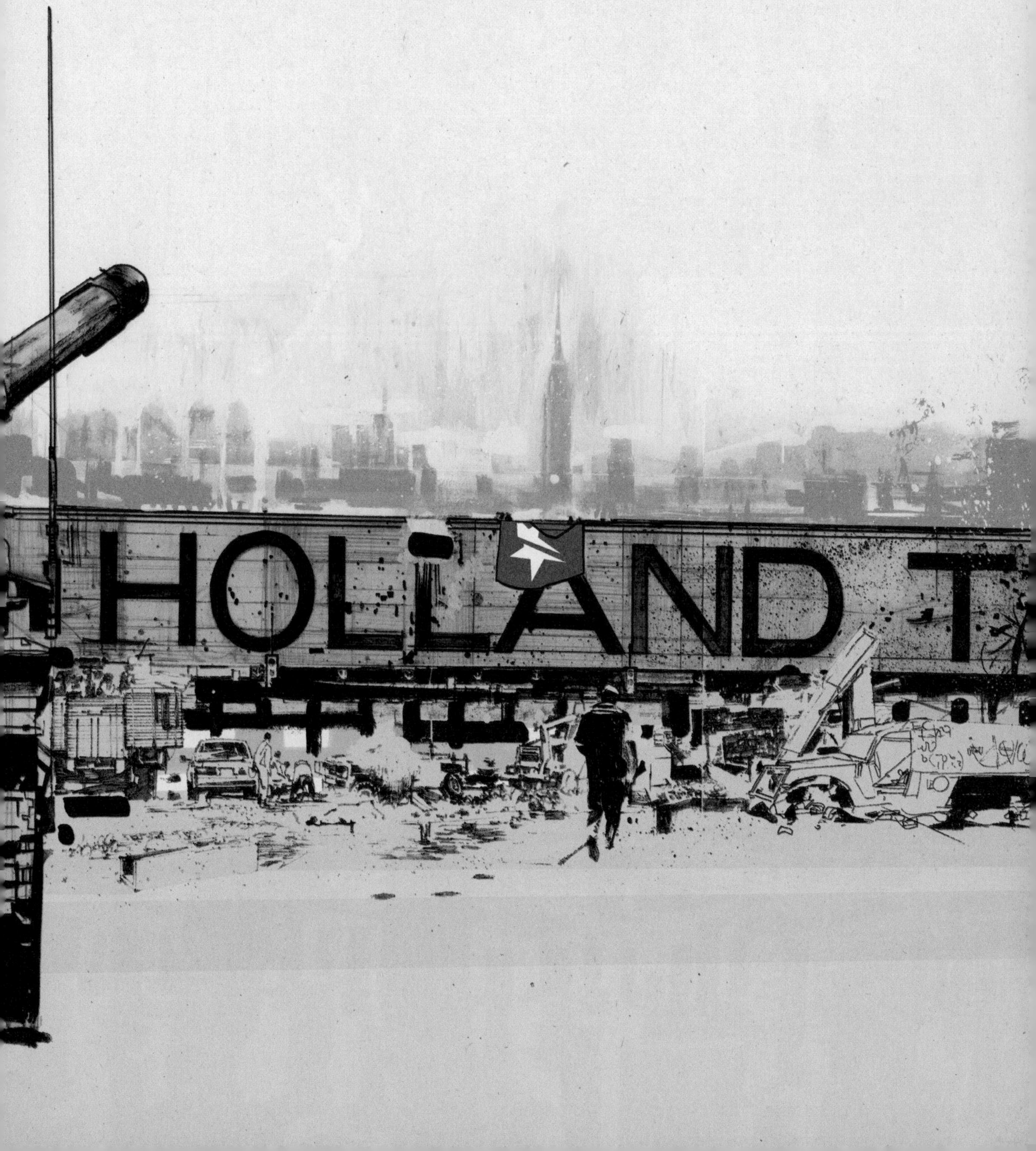
HOLLAND T

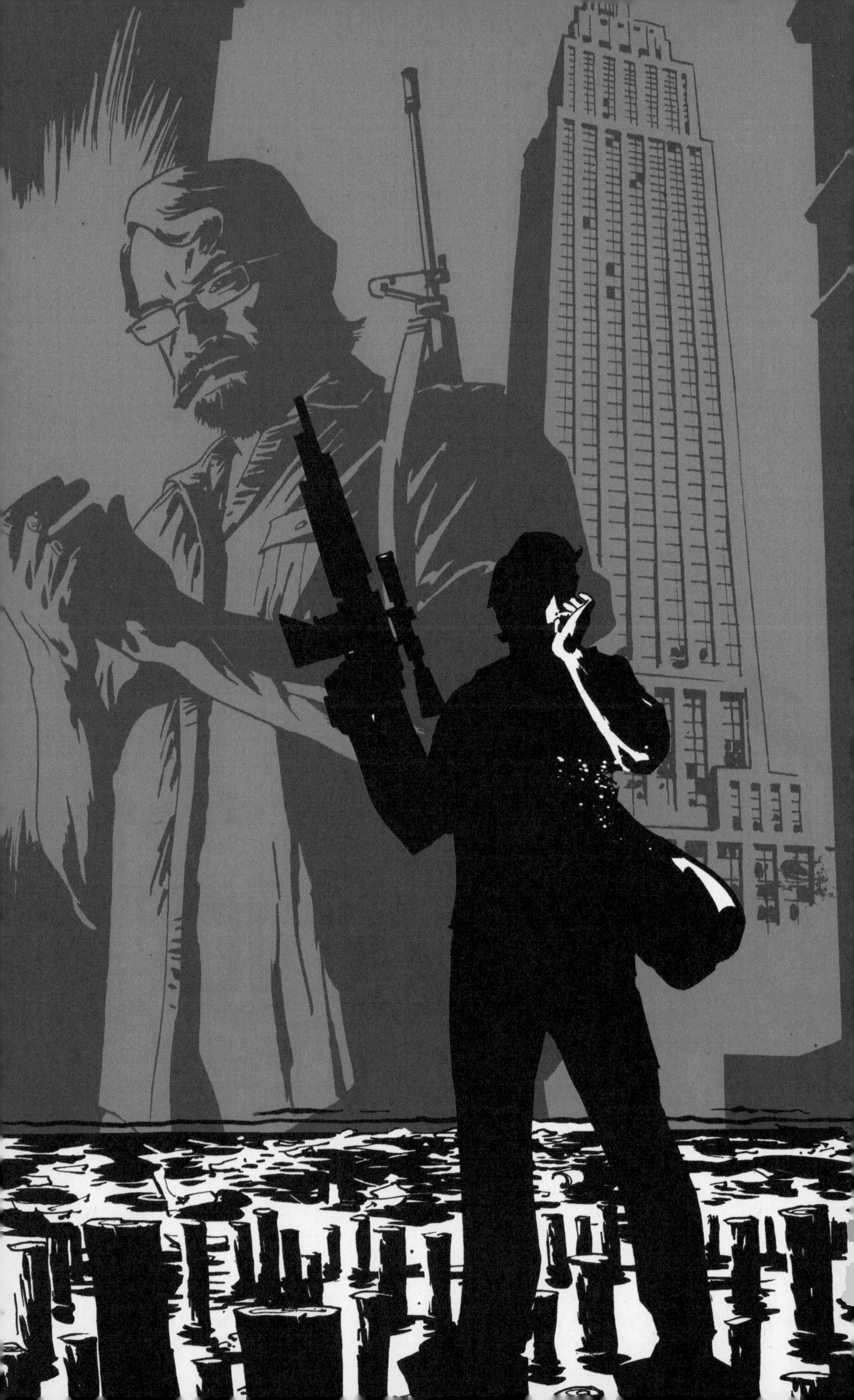

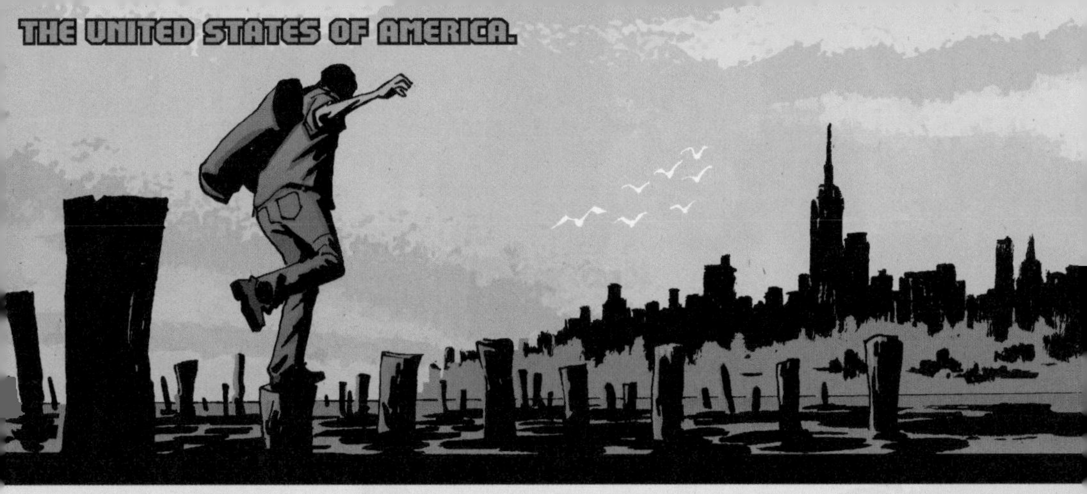
THE UNITED STATES OF AMERICA.

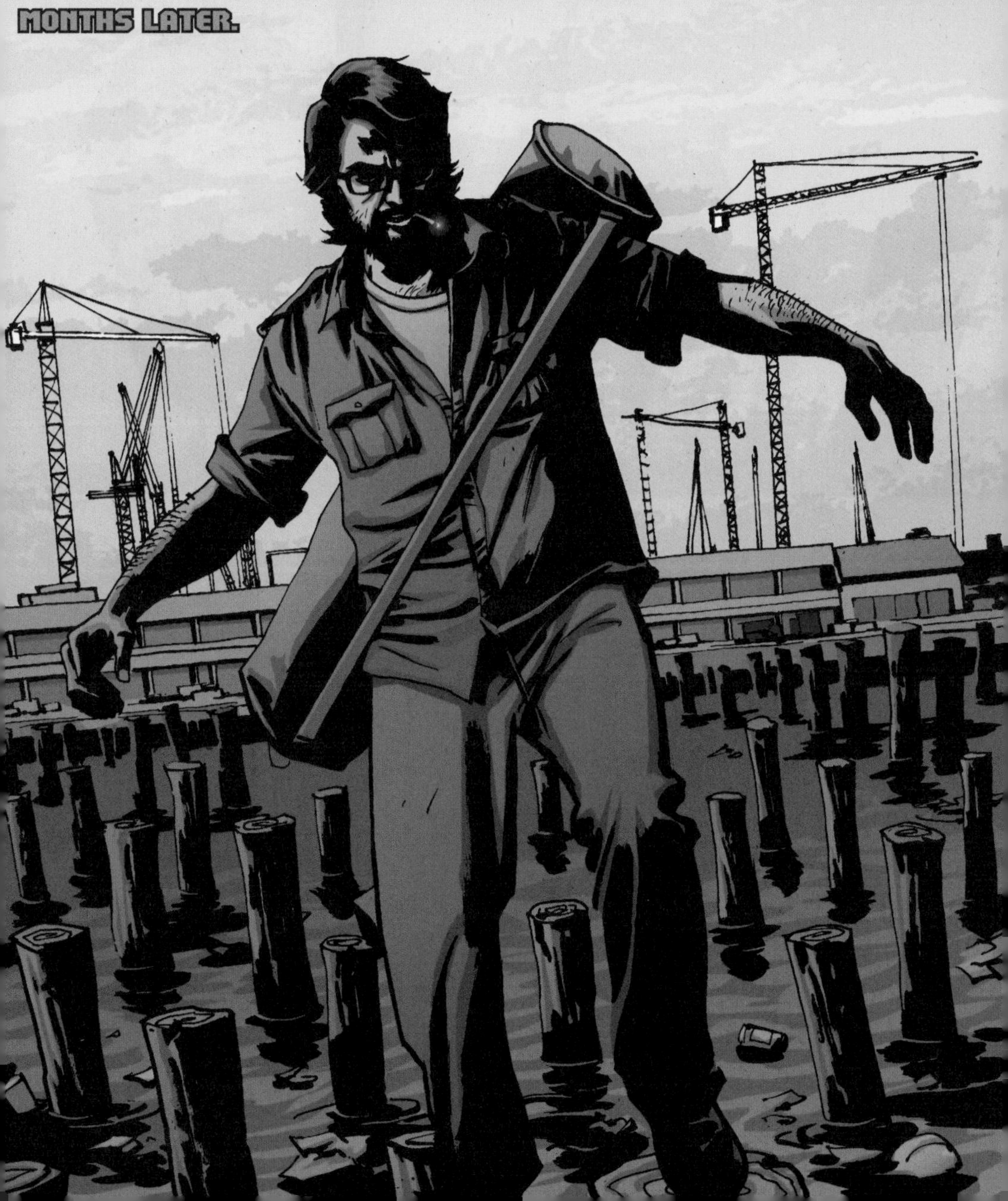
MONTHS LATER.

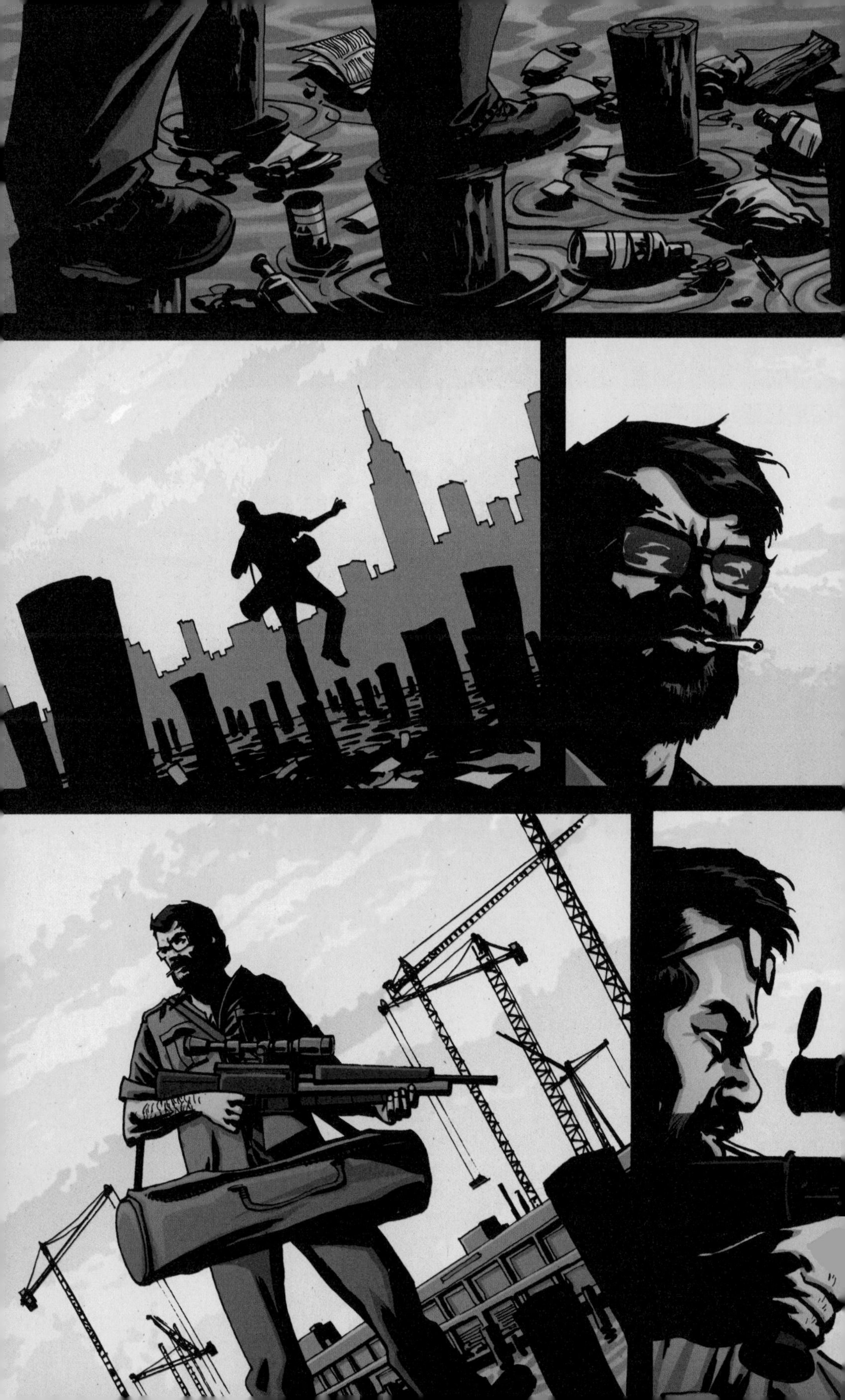

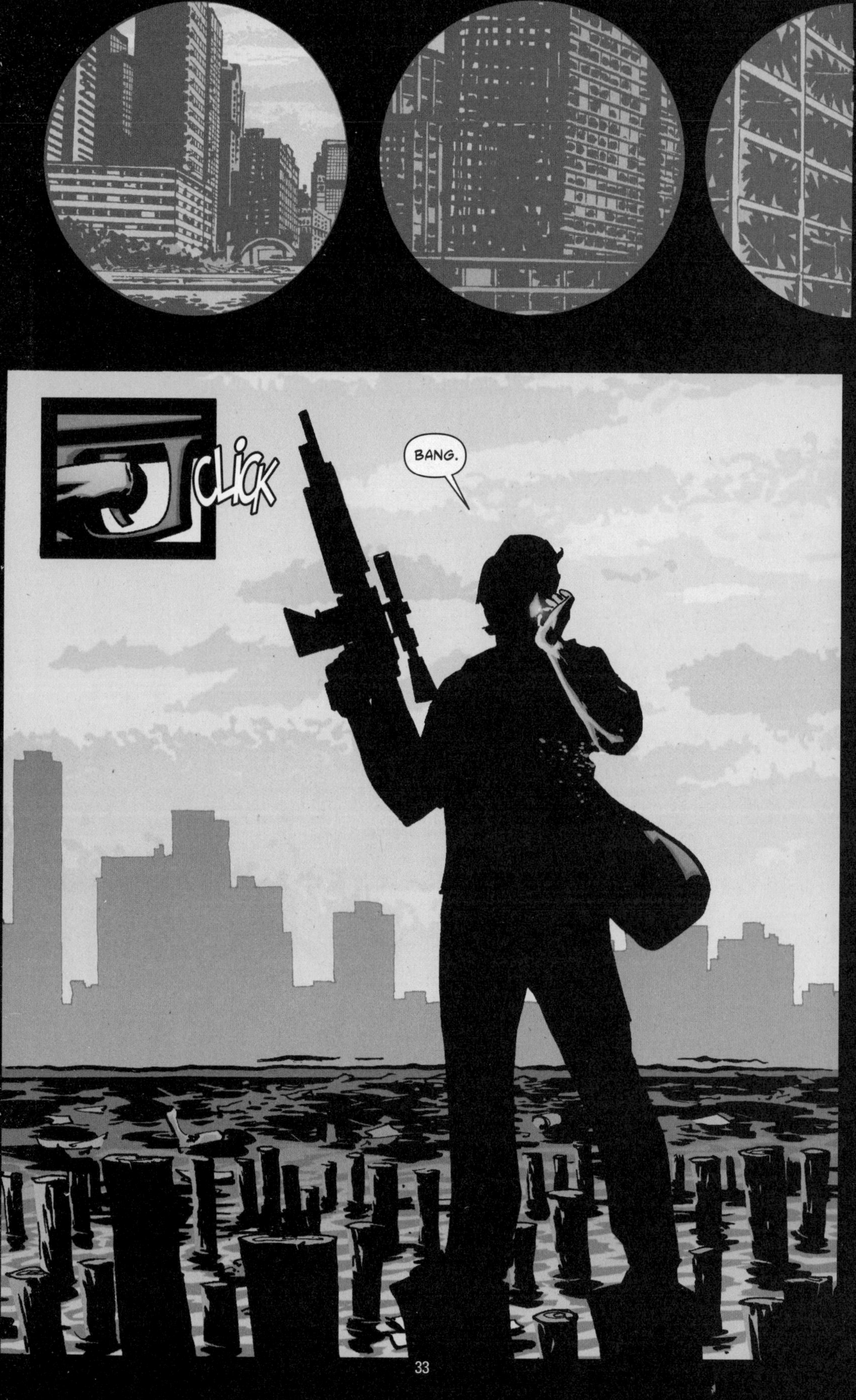
CLICK
BANG.

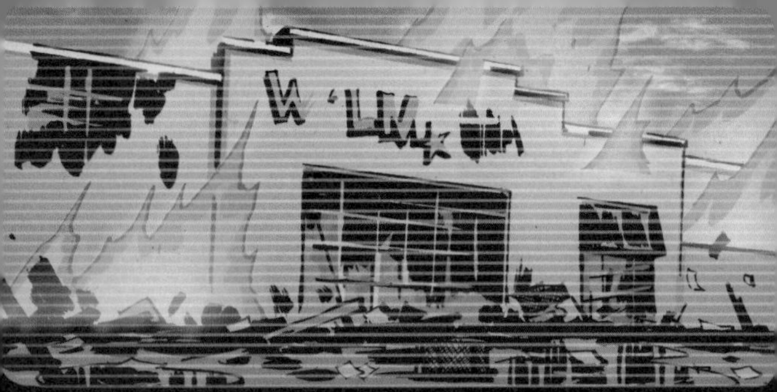

…absolute carnage stretching across four states as elements of the so-called "Free States Army" continue their push east. Residents of the Mid-Atlantic states brace themselves for the arrival of what is, truly, a second American civil war…

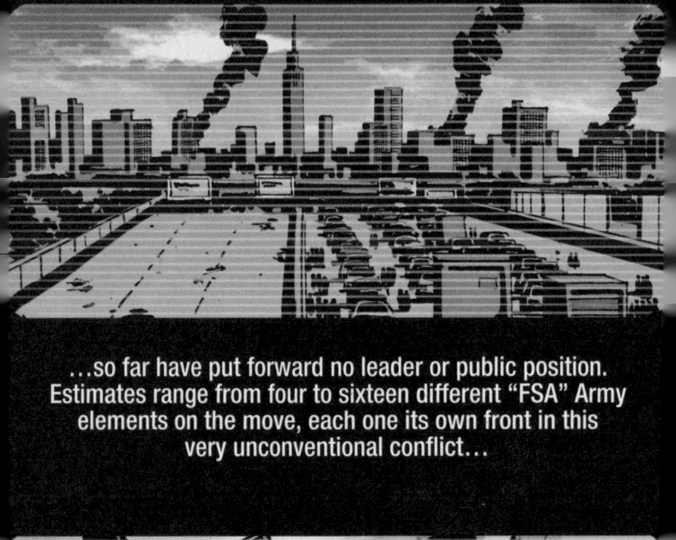

…so far have put forward no leader or public position. Estimates range from four to sixteen different "FSA" Army elements on the move, each one its own front in this very unconventional conflict…

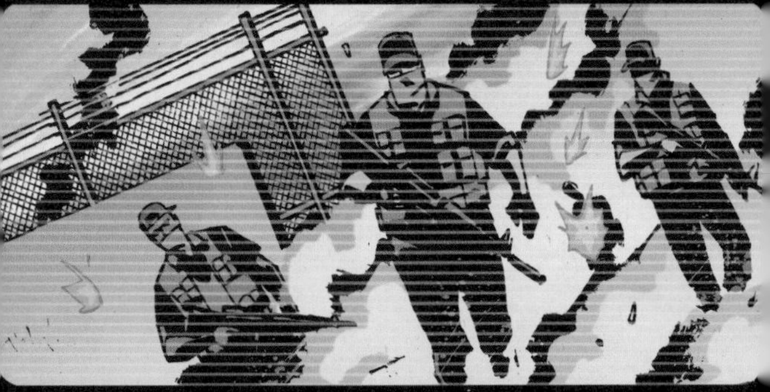

…described as "ripe for the picking," National Guard bases continue to fall and be absorbed by "Free States" insurgents, picking armories clean in the process. Reports that National Guar soldiers are defecting to the rebel ranks re[illegible]ain unverified.

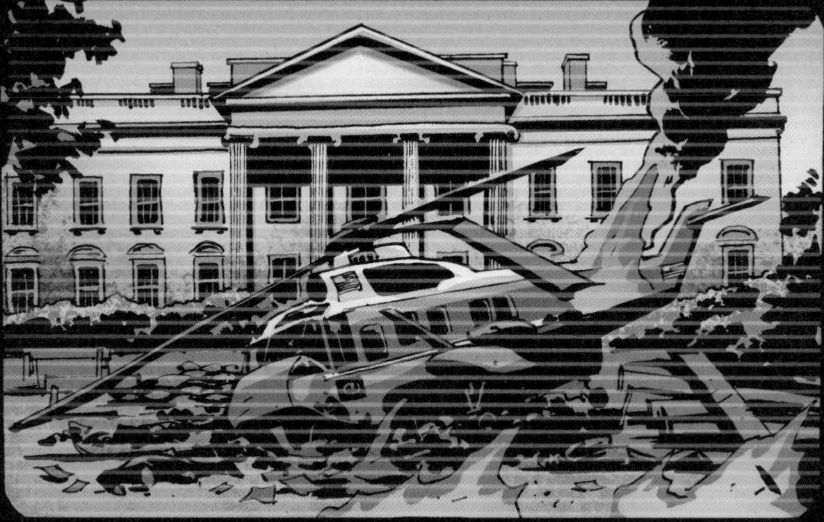

...complete and total silence following the Presidential address...

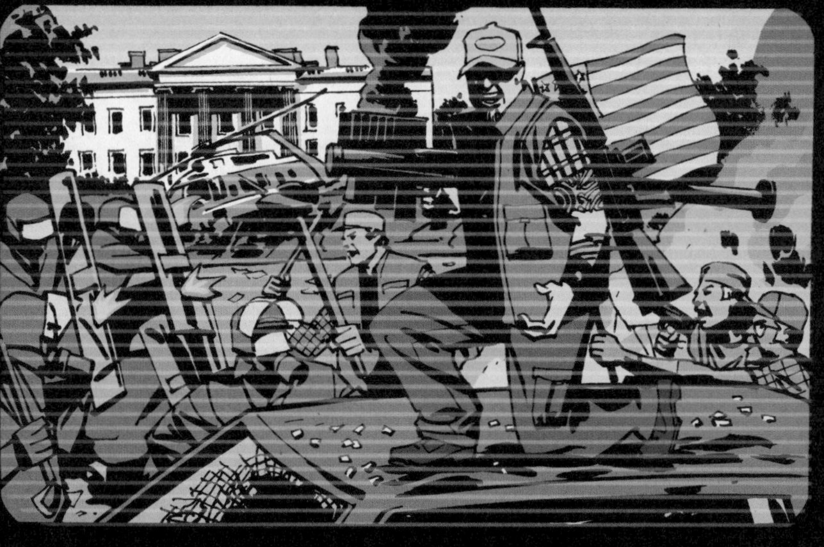

...the twilight of our hallowed union...

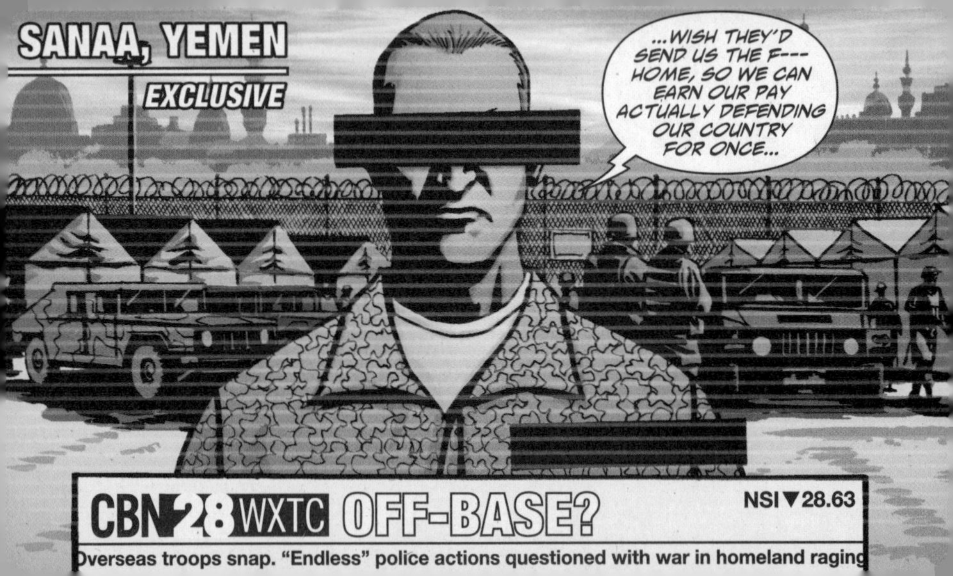

SANAA, YEMEN
EXCLUSIVE
...WISH THEY'D SEND US THE F--- HOME, SO WE CAN EARN OUR PAY ACTUALLY DEFENDING OUR COUNTRY FOR ONCE...
CBN 28 WXTC OFF-BASE?
NSI ▼28.63
Overseas troops snap. "Endless" police actions questioned with war in homeland raging

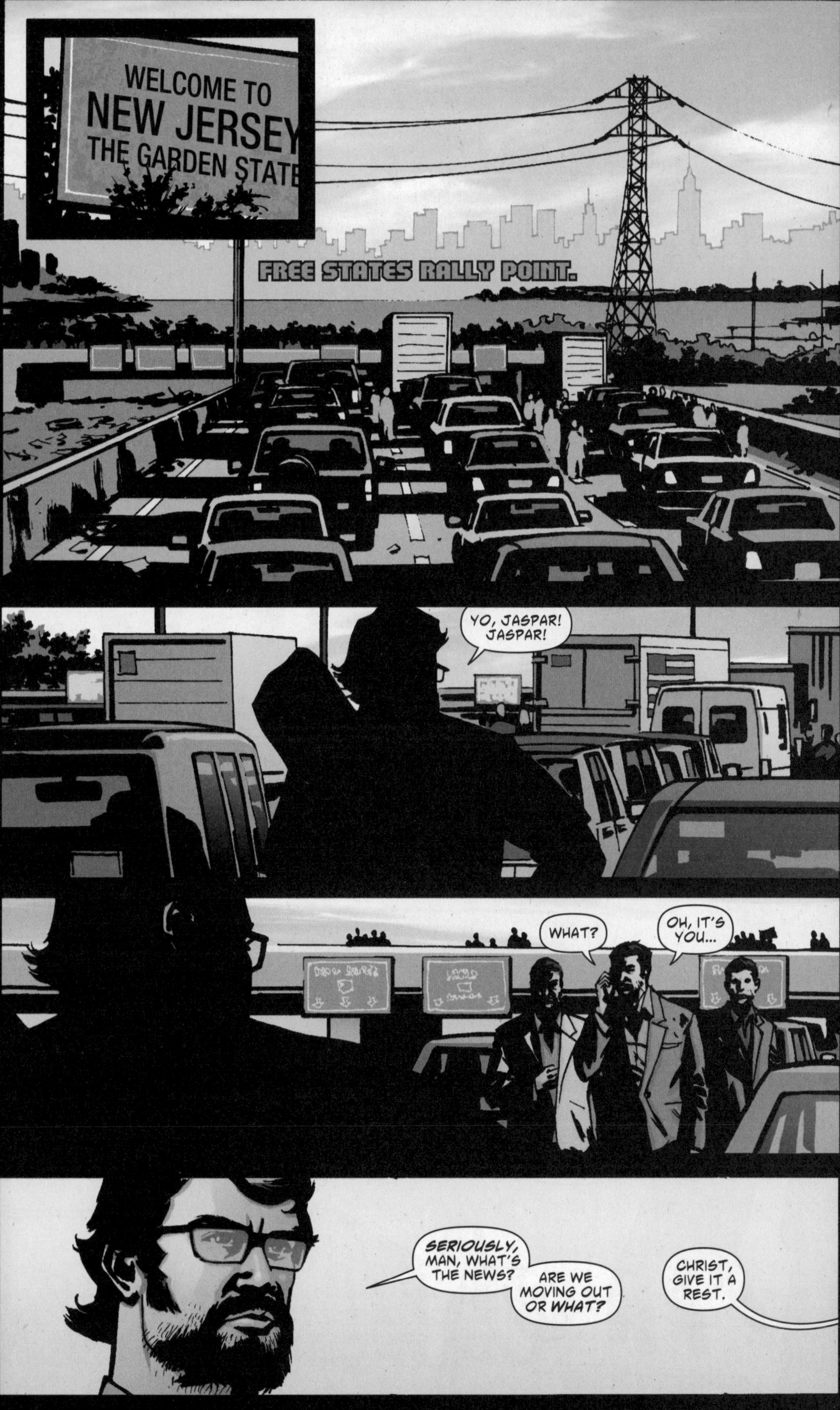
WELCOME TO
NEW JERSEY
THE GARDEN STATE
FREE STATES RALLY POINT.
YO, JASPAR! JASPAR!
WHAT?
OH, IT'S YOU...
SERIOUSLY, MAN, WHAT'S THE NEWS?
ARE WE MOVING OUT OR WHAT?
CHRIST, GIVE IT A REST.

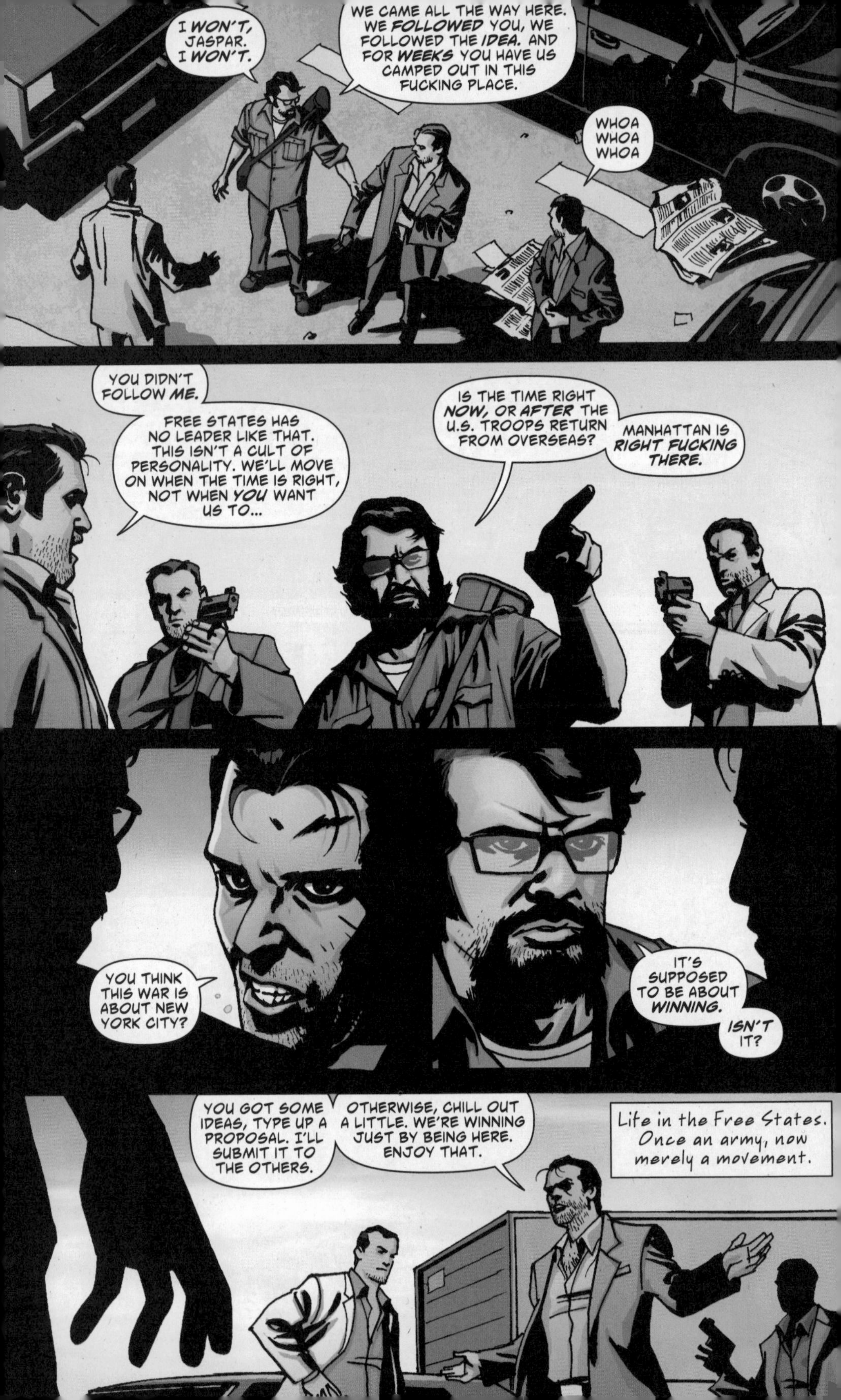

I WON'T, JASPAR. I WON'T.
WE CAME ALL THE WAY HERE. WE FOLLOWED YOU, WE FOLLOWED THE IDEA. AND FOR WEEKS YOU HAVE US CAMPED OUT IN THIS FUCKING PLACE.
WHOA WHOA WHOA
YOU DIDN'T FOLLOW ME.
FREE STATES HAS NO LEADER LIKE THAT. THIS ISN'T A CULT OF PERSONALITY. WE'LL MOVE ON WHEN THE TIME IS RIGHT, NOT WHEN YOU WANT US TO...
IS THE TIME RIGHT NOW, OR AFTER THE U.S. TROOPS RETURN FROM OVERSEAS?
MANHATTAN IS RIGHT FUCKING THERE.
YOU THINK THIS WAR IS ABOUT NEW YORK CITY?
IT'S SUPPOSED TO BE ABOUT WINNING.
ISN'T IT?
YOU GOT SOME IDEAS, TYPE UP A PROPOSAL. I'LL SUBMIT IT TO THE OTHERS.
OTHERWISE, CHILL OUT A LITTLE. WE'RE WINNING JUST BY BEING HERE. ENJOY THAT.
Life in the Free States. Once an army, now merely a movement.

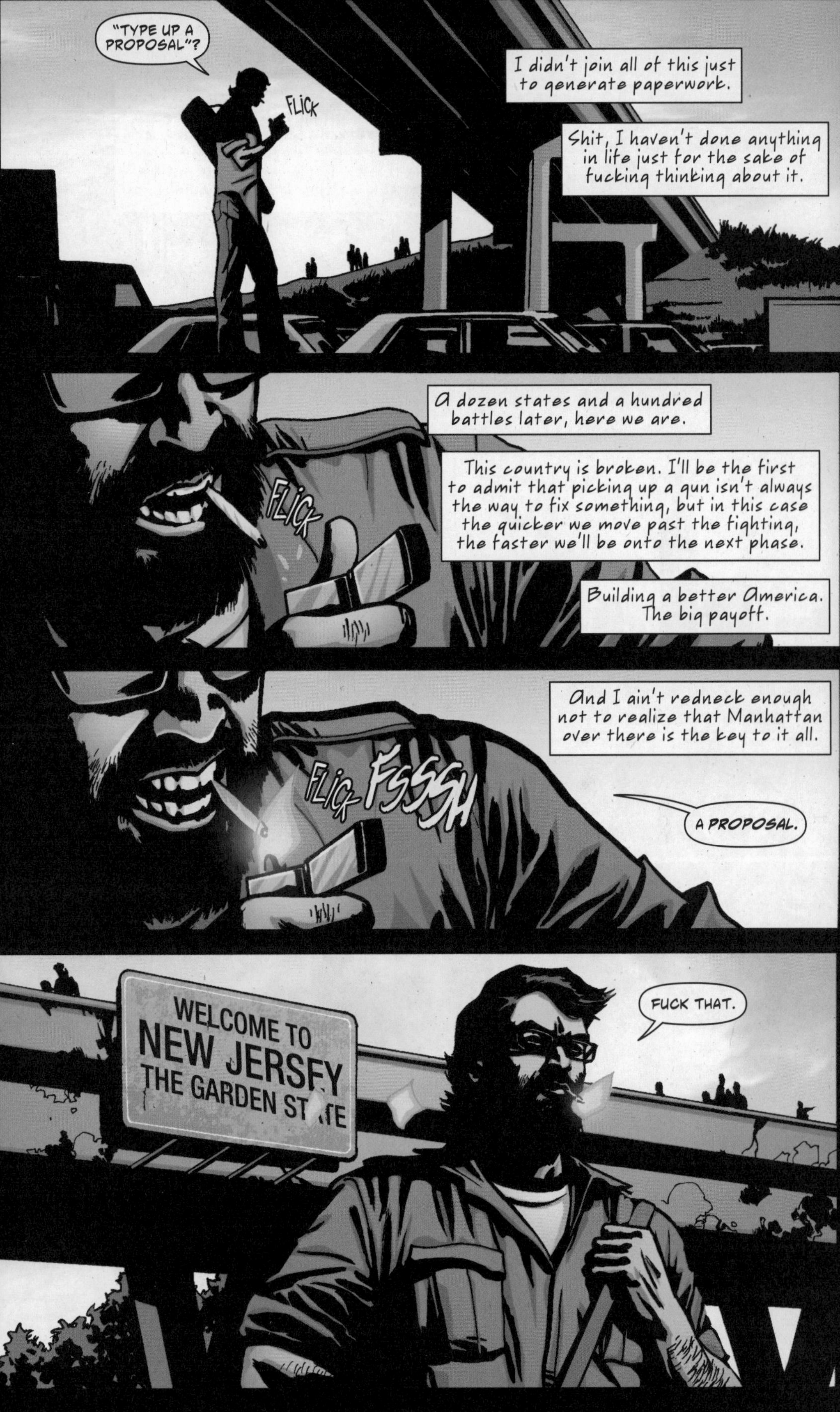
"TYPE UP A PROPOSAL"?
I didn't join all of this just to generate paperwork.
FLICK
Shit, I haven't done anything in life just for the sake of fucking thinking about it.
A dozen states and a hundred battles later, here we are.
This country is broken. I'll be the first to admit that picking up a gun isn't always the way to fix something, but in this case the quicker we move past the fighting, the faster we'll be onto the next phase.
FLICK
Building a better America. The big payoff.
And I ain't redneck enough not to realize that Manhattan over there is the key to it all.
FLICK FSSSH
A PROPOSAL.
WELCOME TO NEW JERSEY THE GARDEN STATE
FUCK THAT.

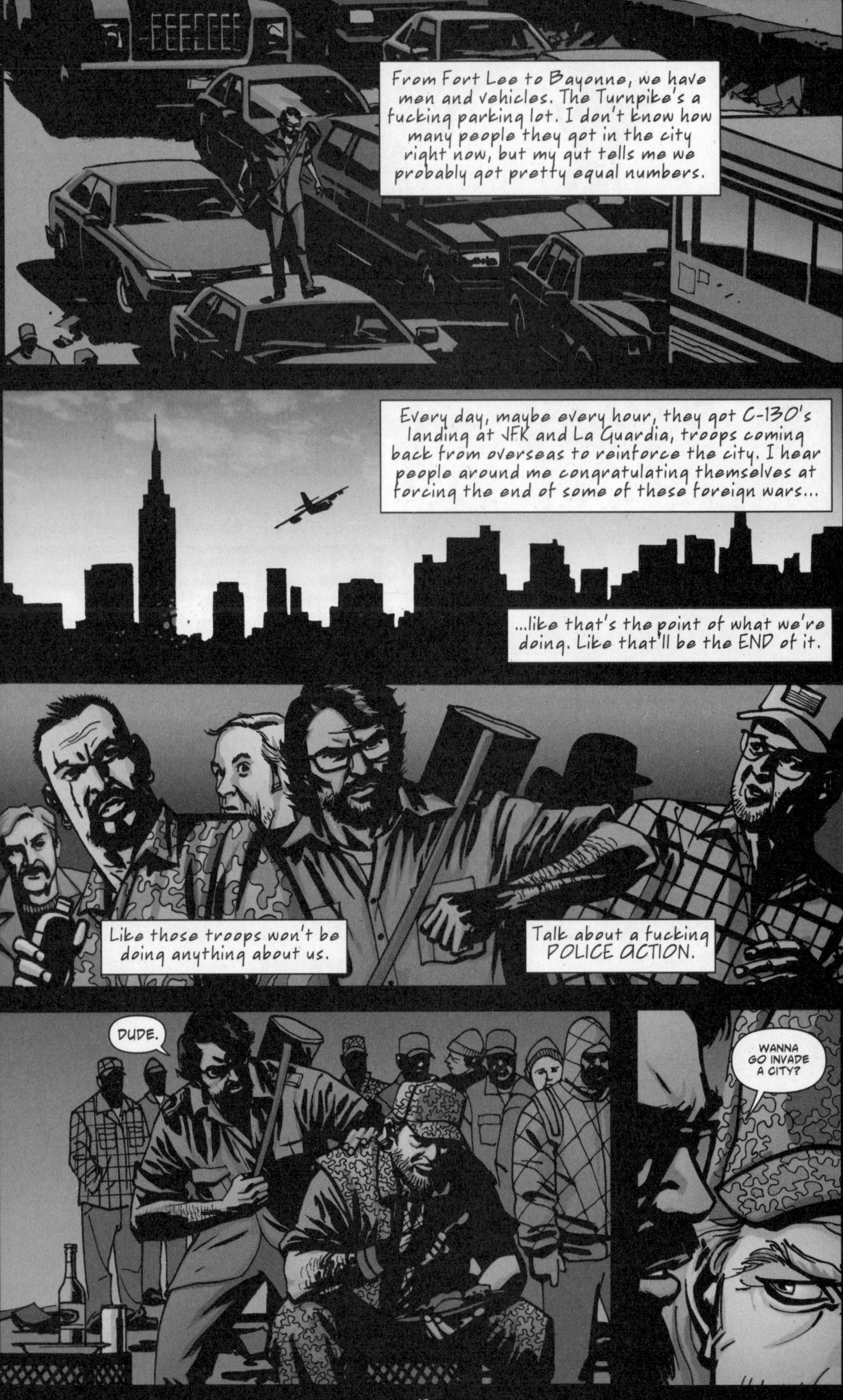
From Fort Lee to Bayonne, we have men and vehicles. The Turnpike's a fucking parking lot. I don't know how many people they got in the city right now, but my gut tells me we probably got pretty equal numbers.
Every day, maybe every hour, they got C-130's landing at JFK and La Guardia, troops coming back from overseas to reinforce the city. I hear people around me congratulating themselves at forcing the end of some of these foreign wars...
...like that's the point of what we're doing. Like that'll be the END of it.
Like those troops won't be doing anything about us.
Talk about a fucking POLICE ACTION.
DUDE.
WANNA GO INVADE A CITY?

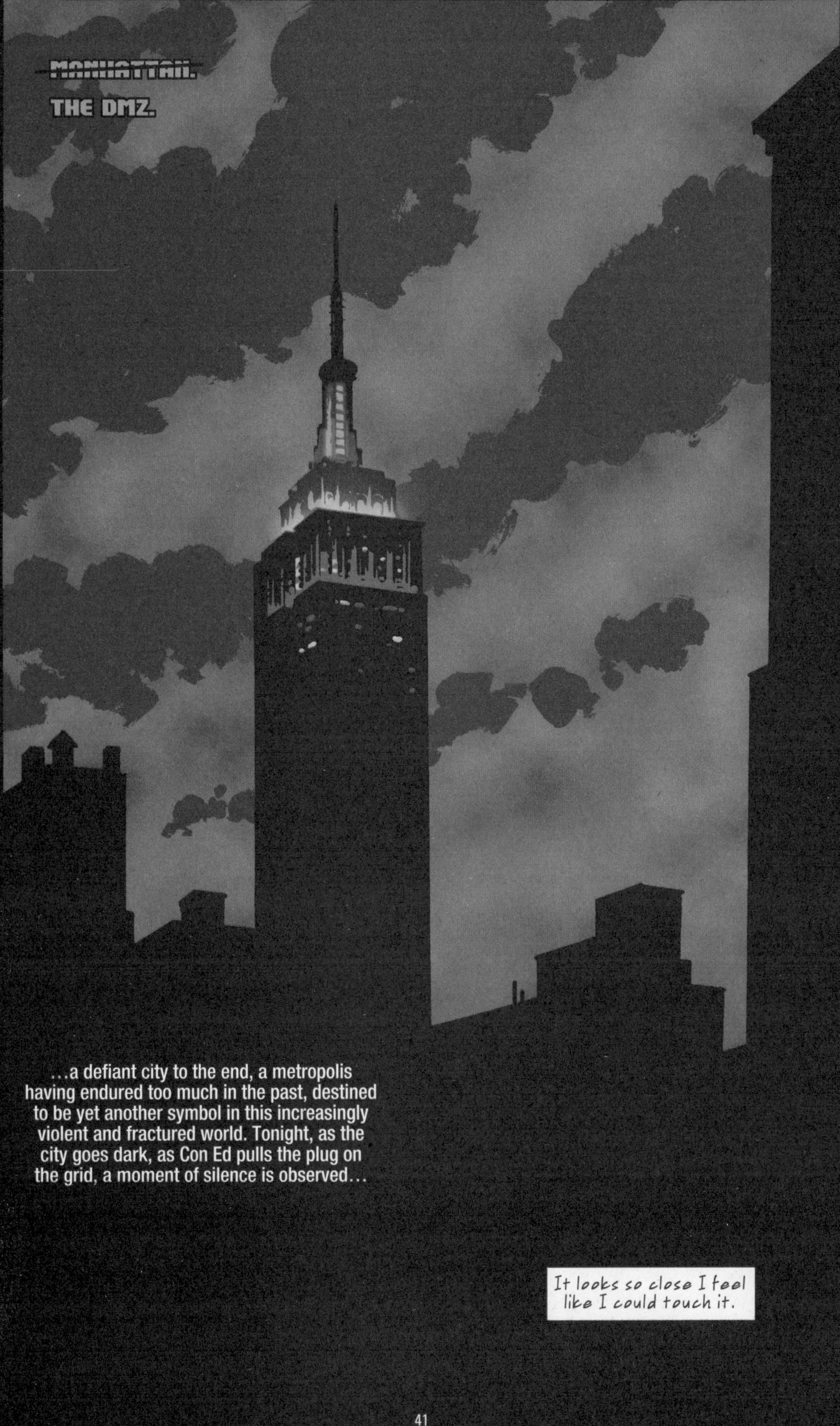

~~MANHATTAN.~~
THE DMZ.
...a defiant city to the end, a metropolis having endured too much in the past, destined to be yet another symbol in this increasingly violent and fractured world. Tonight, as the city goes dark, as Con Ed pulls the plug on the grid, a moment of silence is observed...
It looks so close I feel like I could touch it.

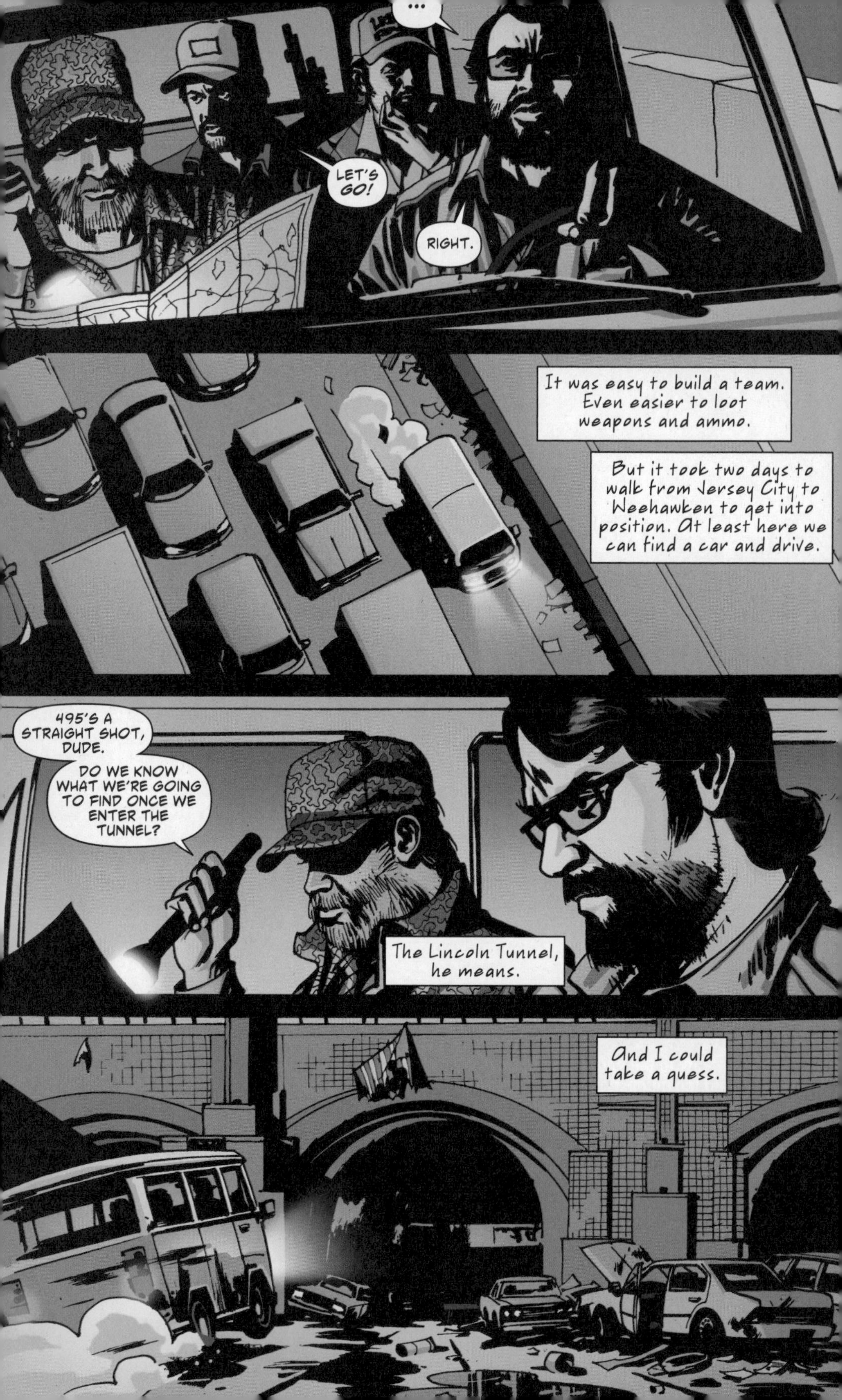
...
LET'S GO!
RIGHT.
It was easy to build a team. Even easier to loot weapons and ammo.
But it took two days to walk from Jersey City to Weehawken to get into position. At least here we can find a car and drive.
495'S A STRAIGHT SHOT, DUDE.
DO WE KNOW WHAT WE'RE GOING TO FIND ONCE WE ENTER THE TUNNEL?
The Lincoln Tunnel, he means.
And I could take a guess.

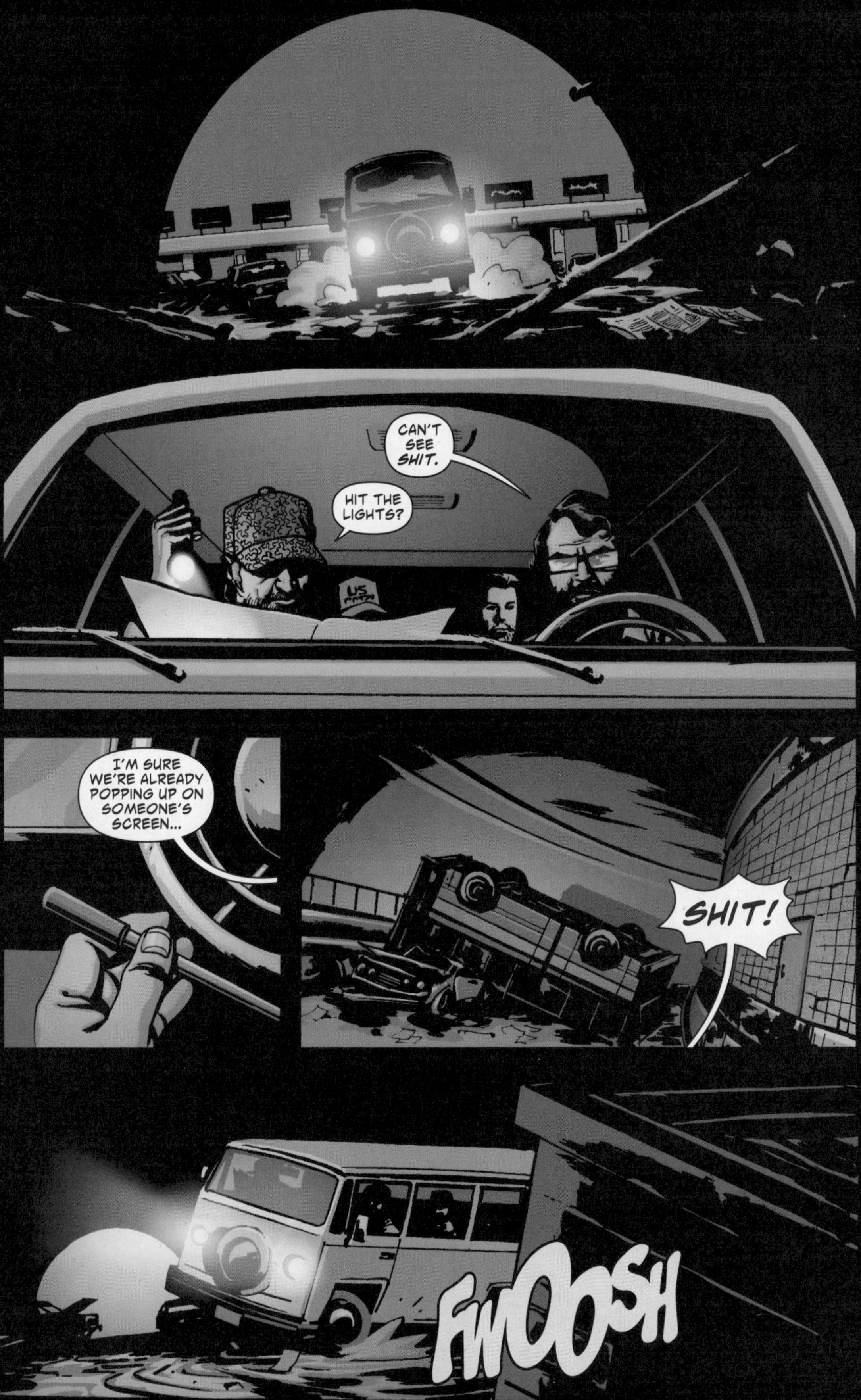

CAN'T SEE SHIT.
HIT THE LIGHTS?
I'M SURE WE'RE ALREADY POPPING UP ON SOMEONE'S SCREEN...
SHIT!
FWOOSH

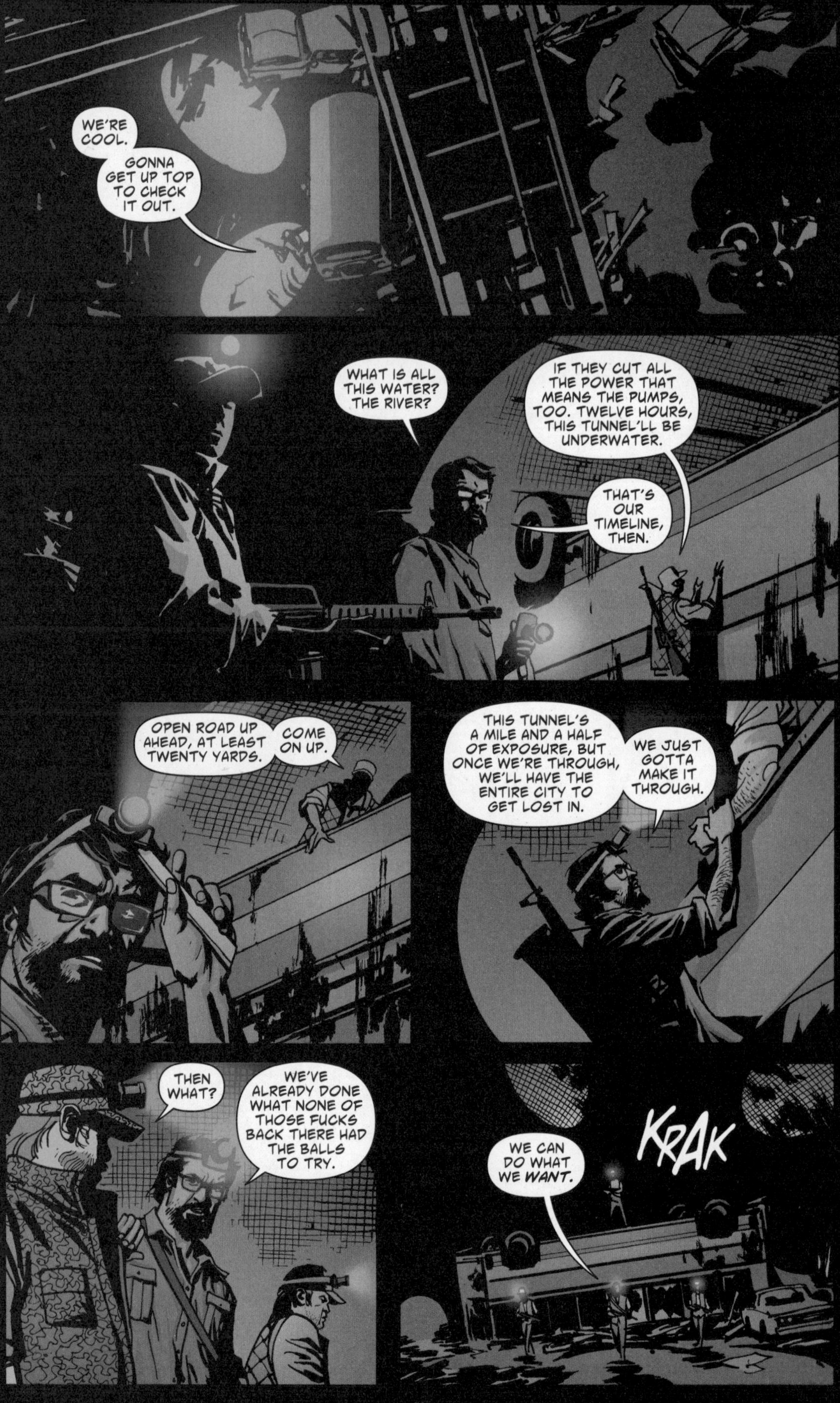
WE'RE COOL.
GONNA GET UP TOP TO CHECK IT OUT.
WHAT IS ALL THIS WATER? THE RIVER?
IF THEY CUT ALL THE POWER THAT MEANS THE PUMPS, TOO. TWELVE HOURS, THIS TUNNEL'LL BE UNDERWATER.
THAT'S OUR TIMELINE, THEN.
OPEN ROAD UP AHEAD, AT LEAST TWENTY YARDS.
COME ON UP.
THIS TUNNEL'S A MILE AND A HALF OF EXPOSURE, BUT ONCE WE'RE THROUGH, WE'LL HAVE THE ENTIRE CITY TO GET LOST IN.
WE JUST GOTTA MAKE IT THROUGH.
THEN WHAT?
WE'VE ALREADY DONE WHAT NONE OF THOSE FUCKS BACK THERE HAD THE BALLS TO TRY.
KRAK
WE CAN DO WHAT WE *WANT*.

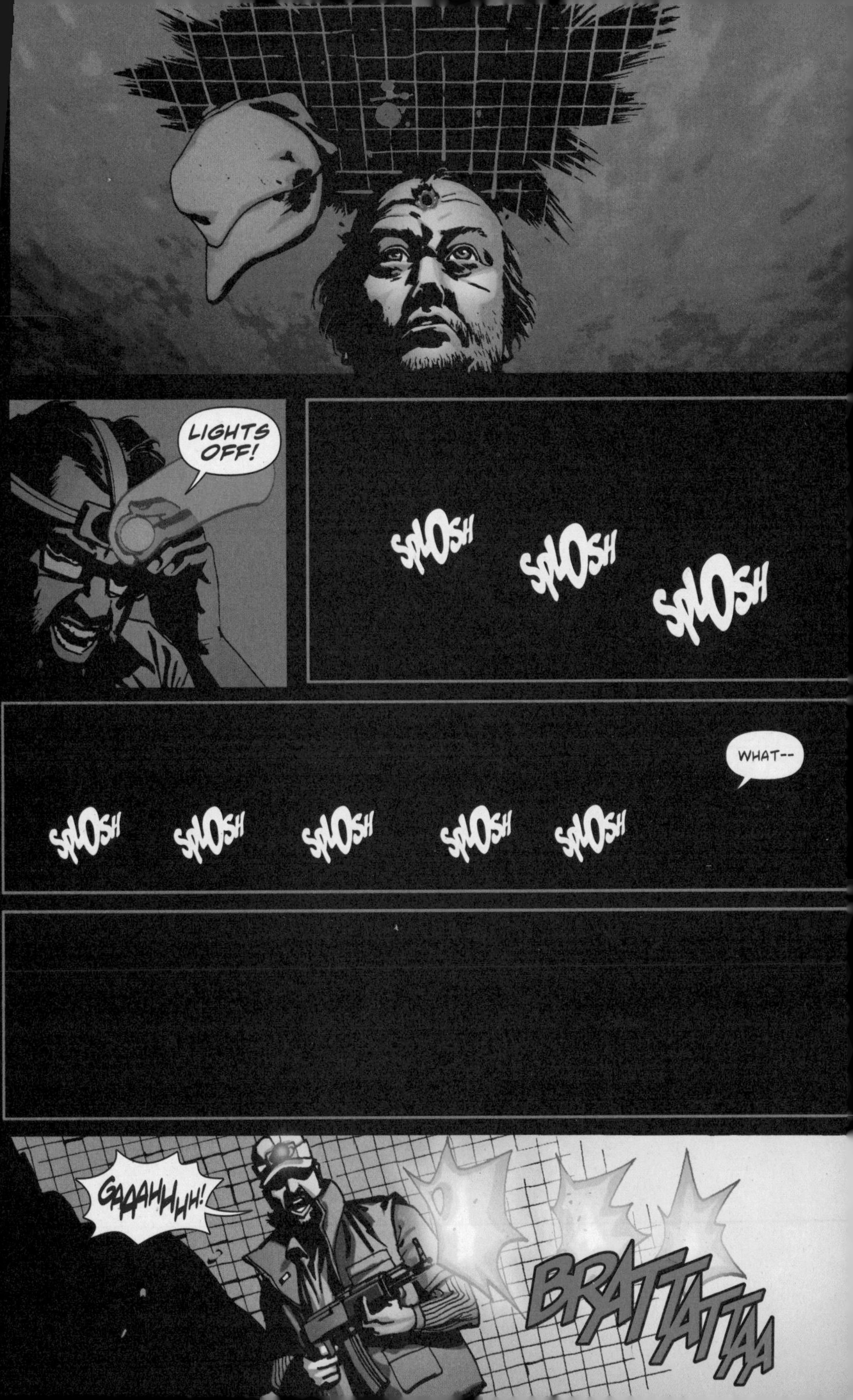
LIGHTS OFF!
SPLOSH
SPLOSH
SPLOSH
SPLOSH
SPLOSH
SPLOSH
SPLOSH
SPLOSH
WHAT--
GAAAHHHH!
BRATTATTAA

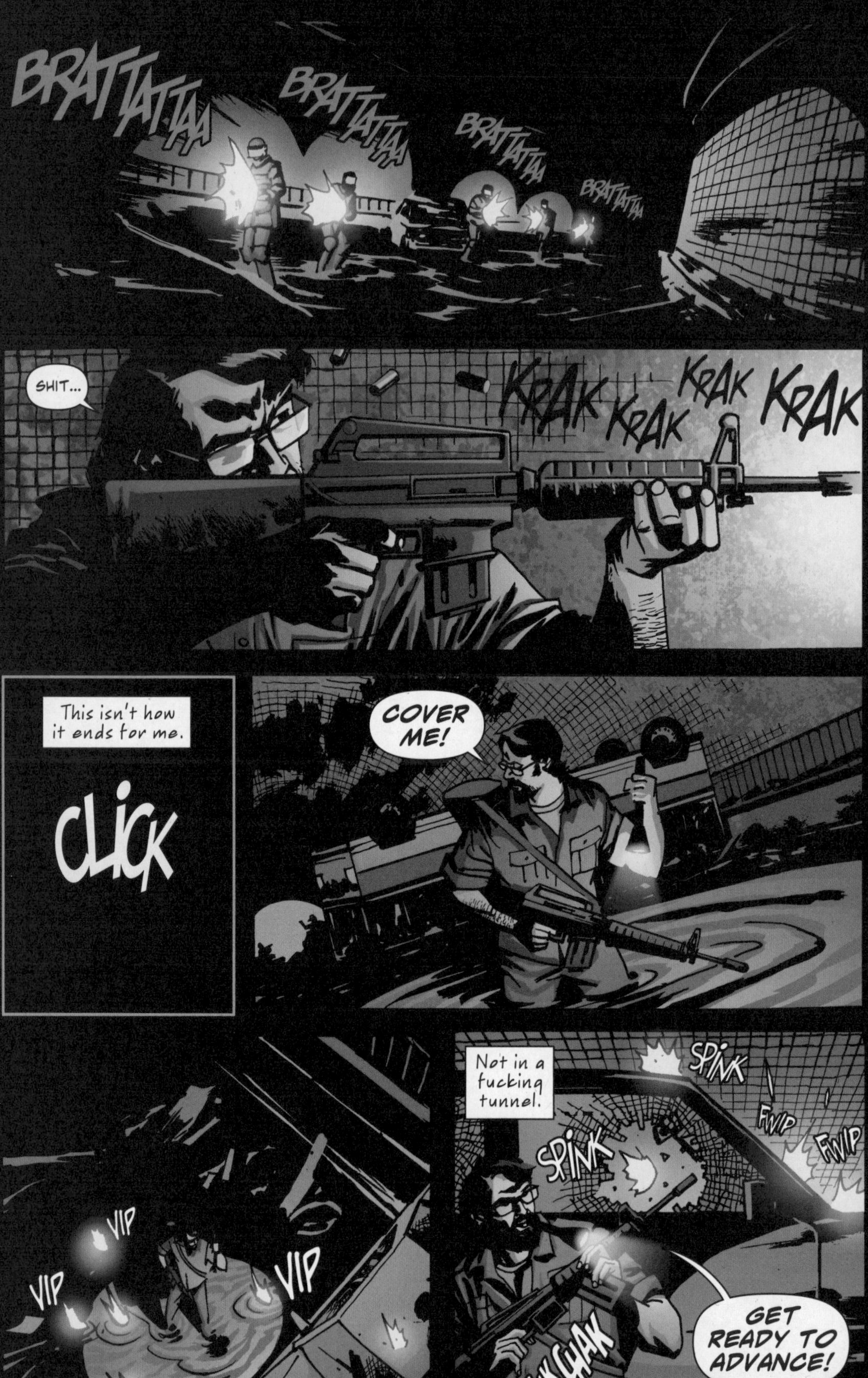
BRATTATTAA
BRATTATTAA
BRATTATTAA
BRATTATTAA
SHIT...
KRAK KRAK KRAK KRAK
This isn't how it ends for me.
CLICK
COVER ME!
VIP
VIP
VIP
VIP
Not in a fucking tunnel.
SPINK
FWIP
FWIP
SPINK
CHK CHAK
GET READY TO ADVANCE!

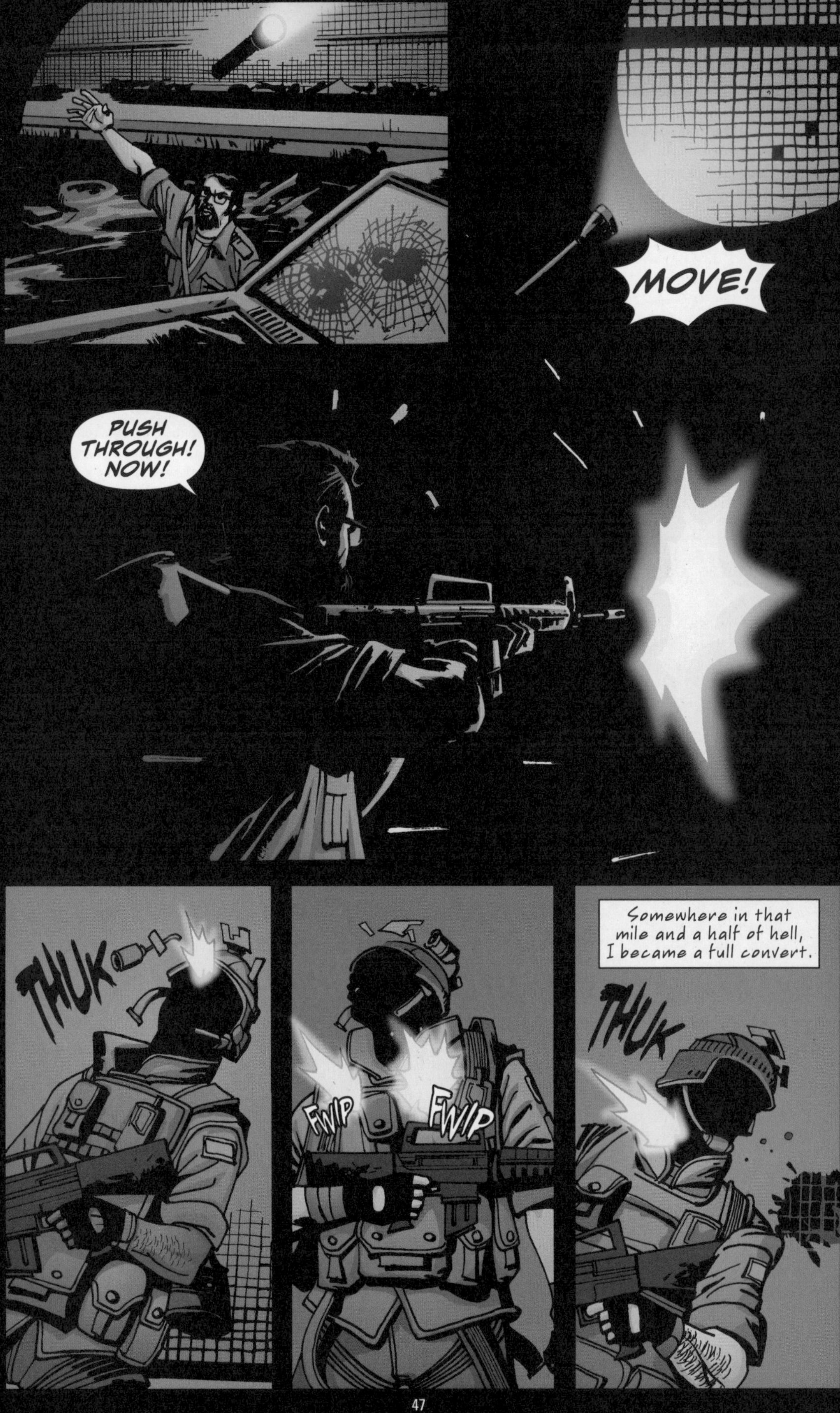
MOVE!
PUSH THROUGH! NOW!
THUK
FWIP
FWIP
Somewhere in that mile and a half of hell, I became a full convert.
THUK

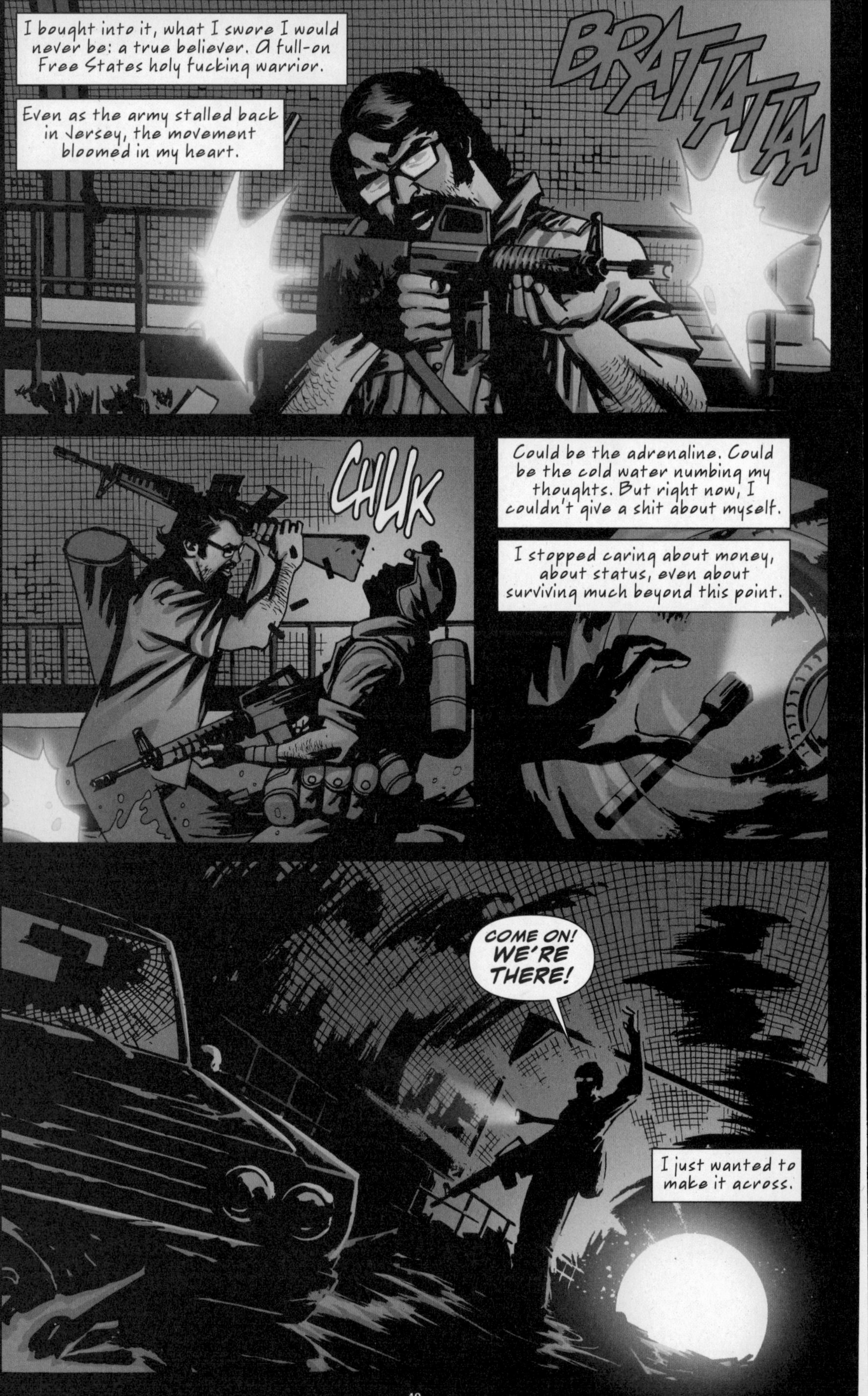
I bought into it, what I swore I would never be: a true believer. A full-on Free States holy fucking warrior.
Even as the army stalled back in Jersey, the movement bloomed in my heart.
BRATTATTAA
CHUK
Could be the adrenaline. Could be the cold water numbing my thoughts. But right now, I couldn't give a shit about myself.
I stopped caring about money, about status, even about surviving much beyond this point.
COME ON! WE'RE THERE!
I just wanted to make it across.

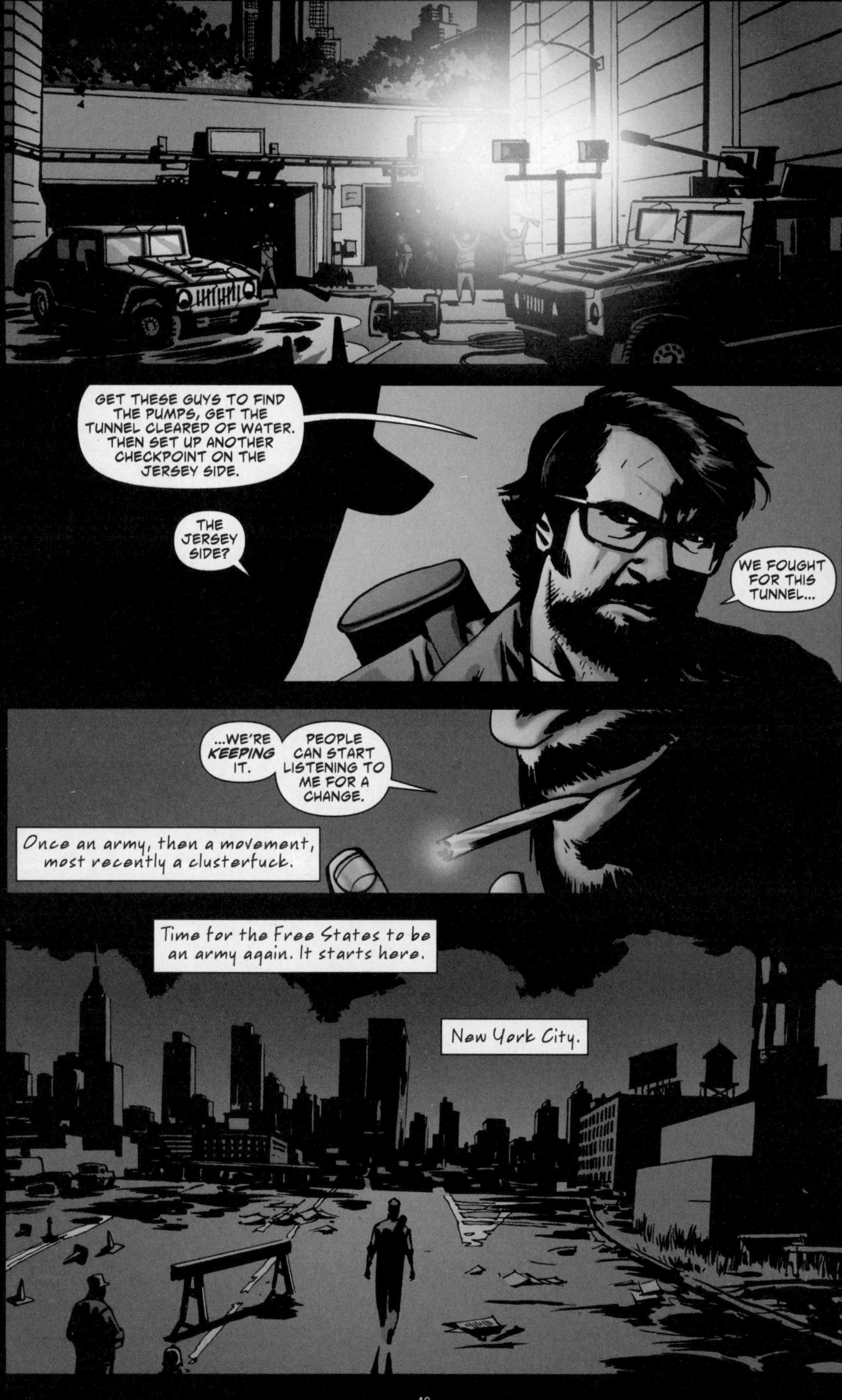

GET THESE GUYS TO FIND THE PUMPS, GET THE TUNNEL CLEARED OF WATER. THEN SET UP ANOTHER CHECKPOINT ON THE JERSEY SIDE.
THE JERSEY SIDE?
WE FOUGHT FOR THIS TUNNEL...
...WE'RE KEEPING IT.
PEOPLE CAN START LISTENING TO ME FOR A CHANGE.
Once an army, then a movement, most recently a clusterfuck.
Time for the Free States to be an army again. It starts here.
New York City.

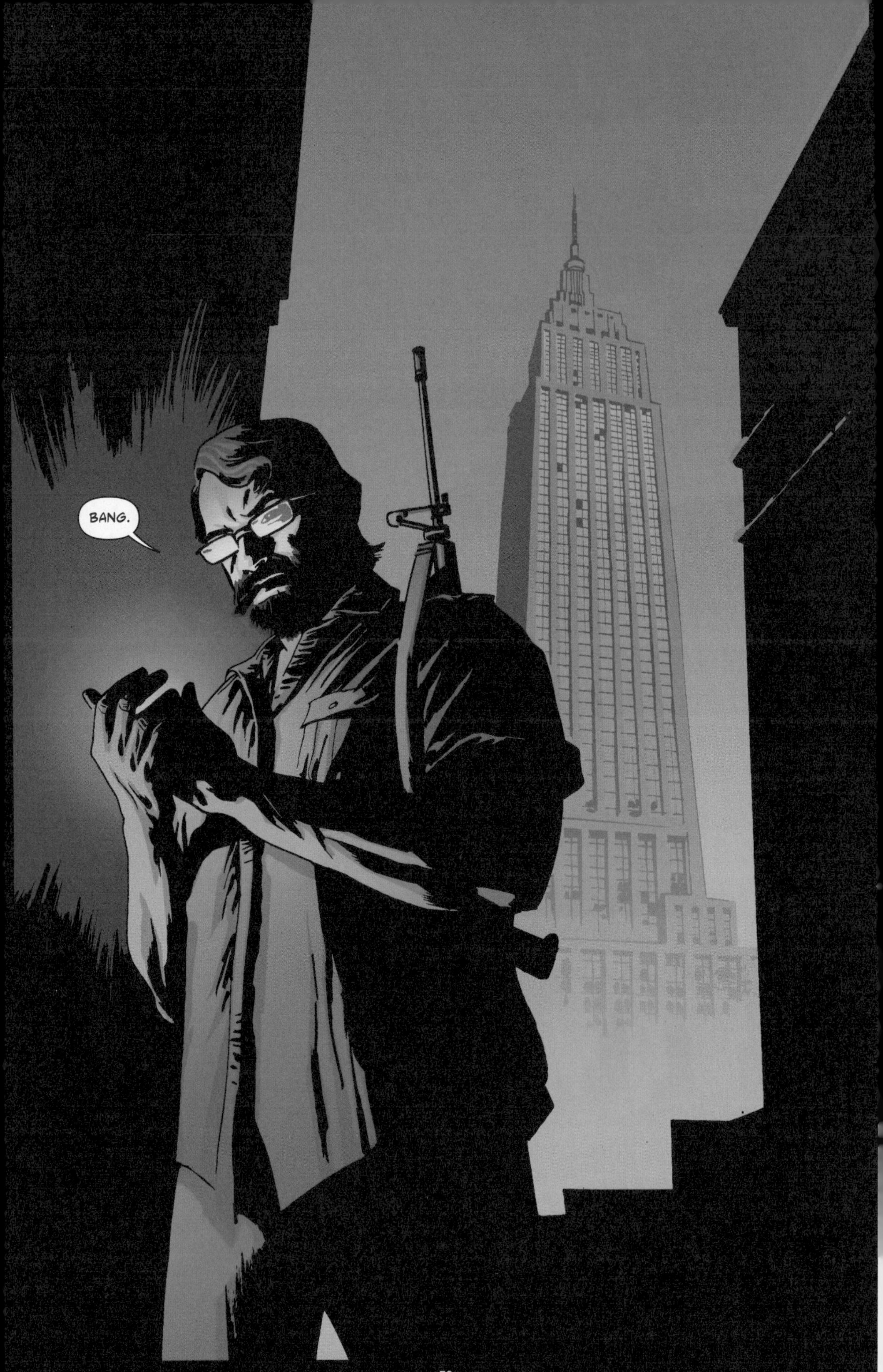
BANG.

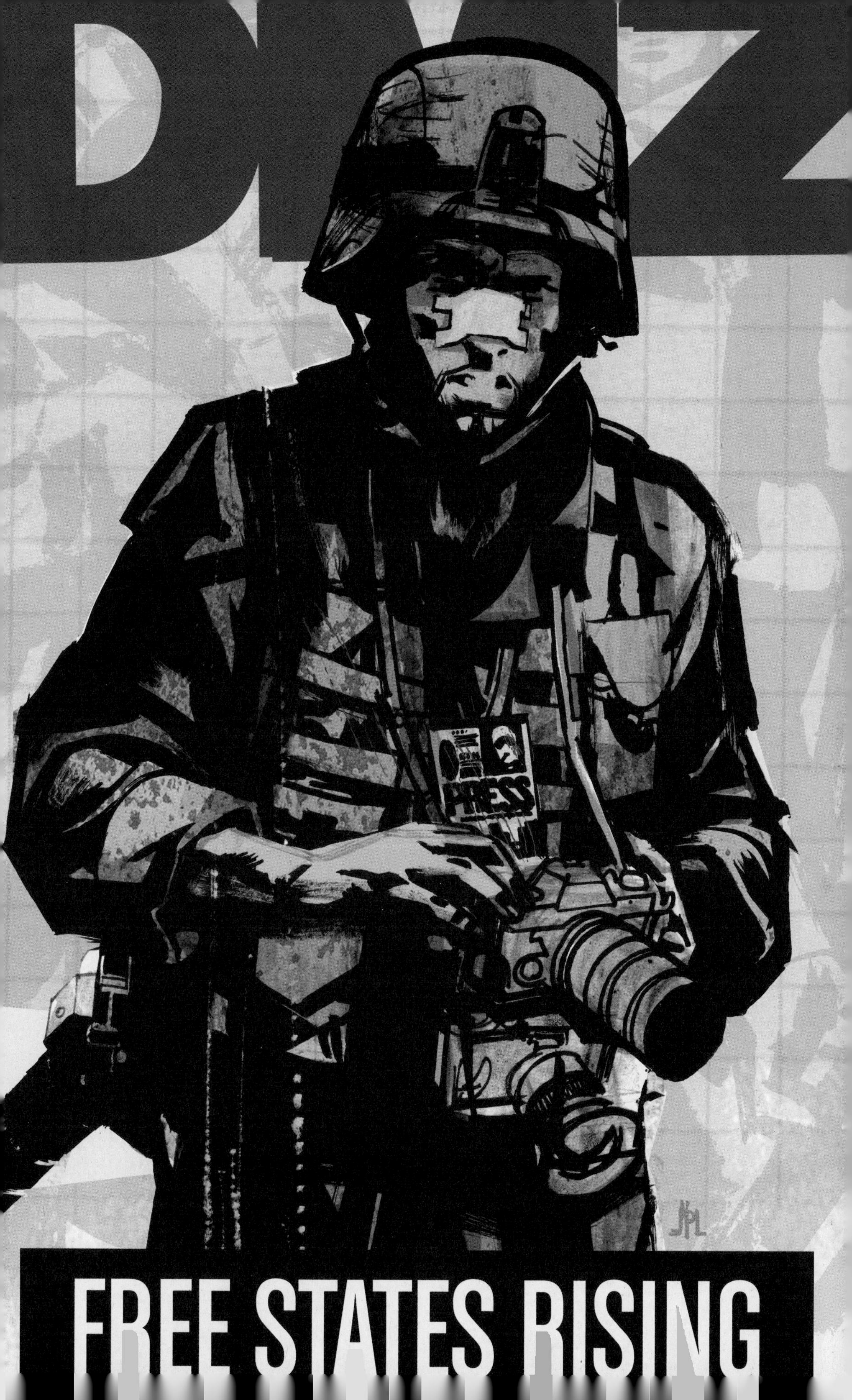
PRESS
JPL
FREE STATES RISING

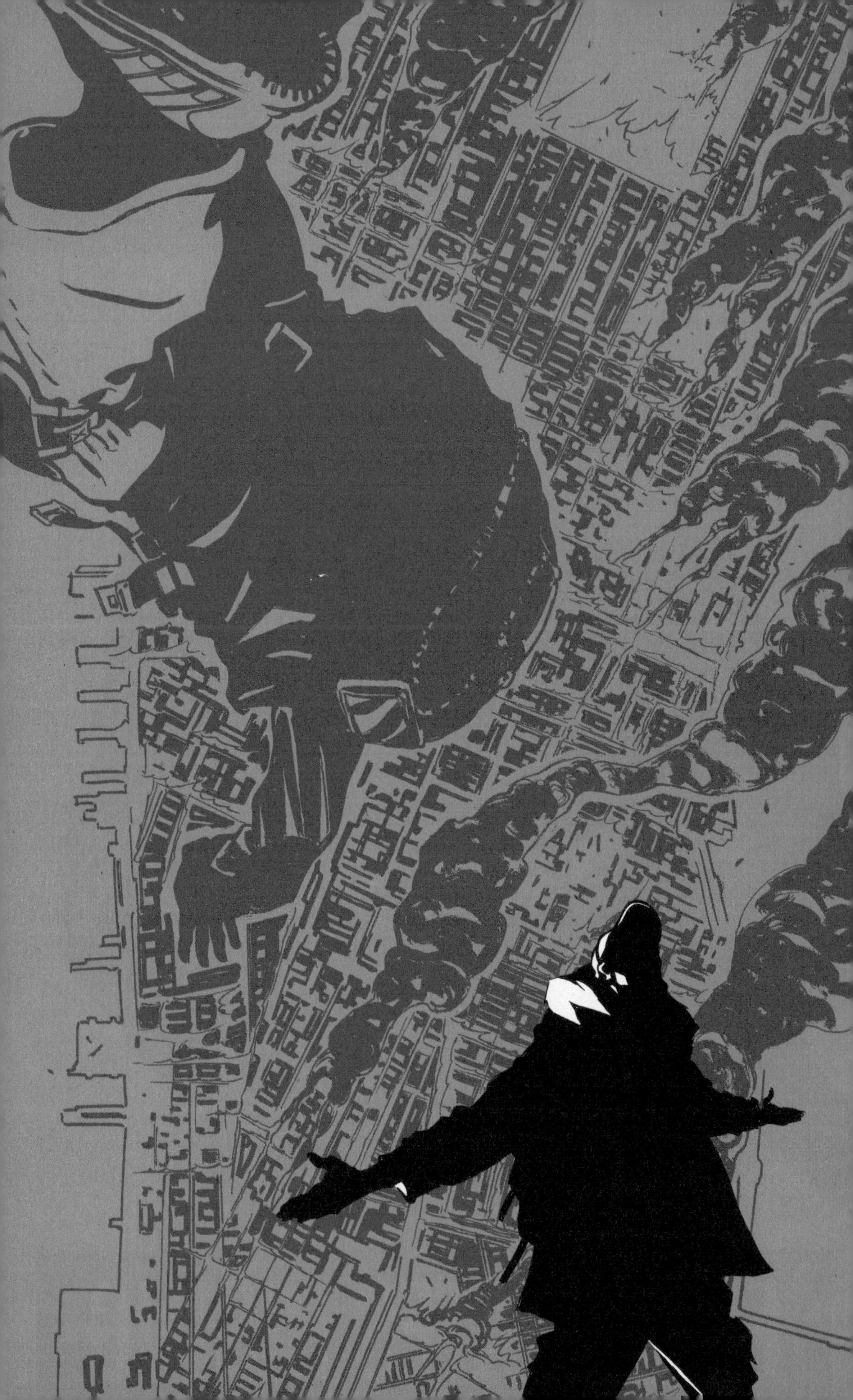

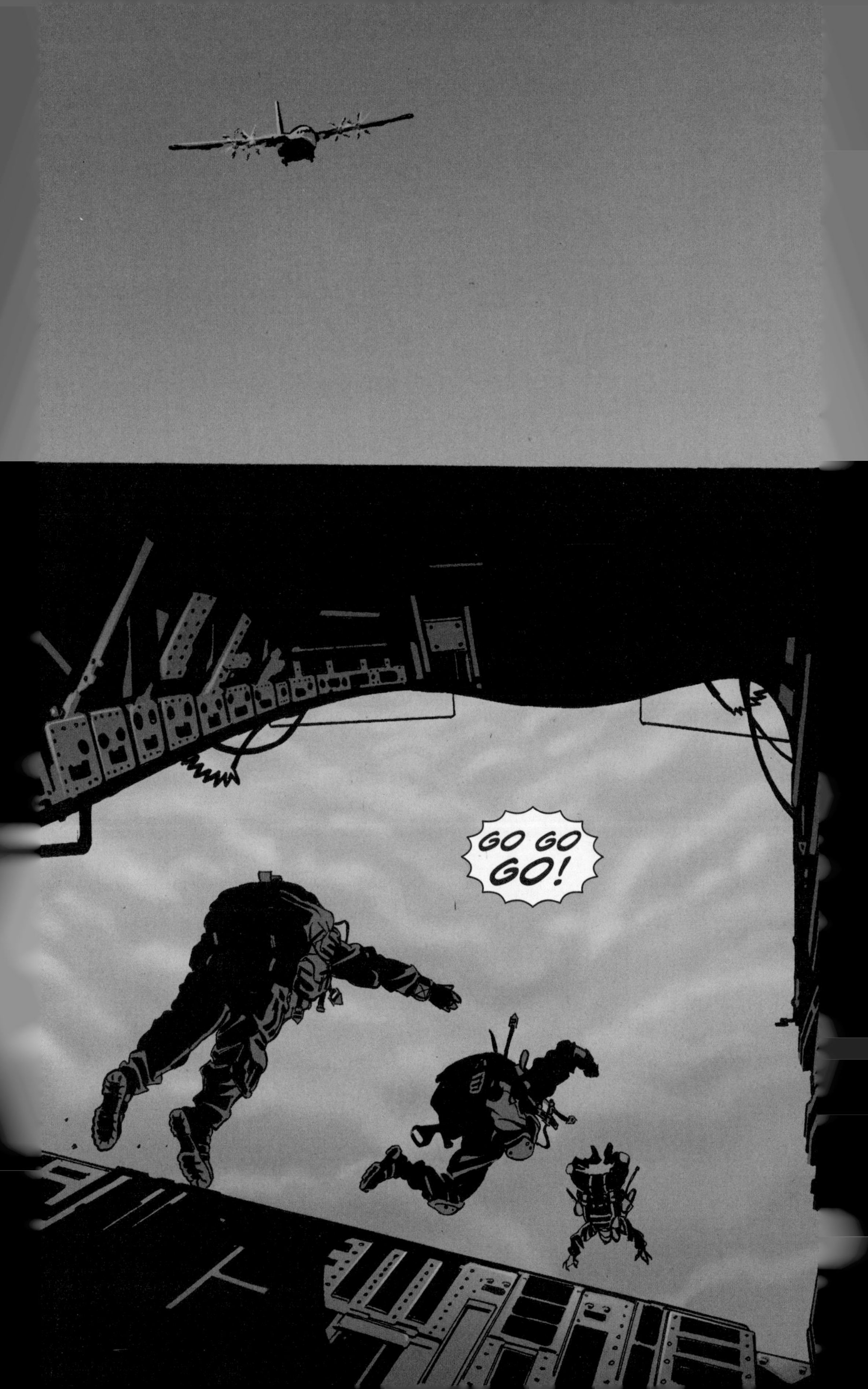
GO GO GO!

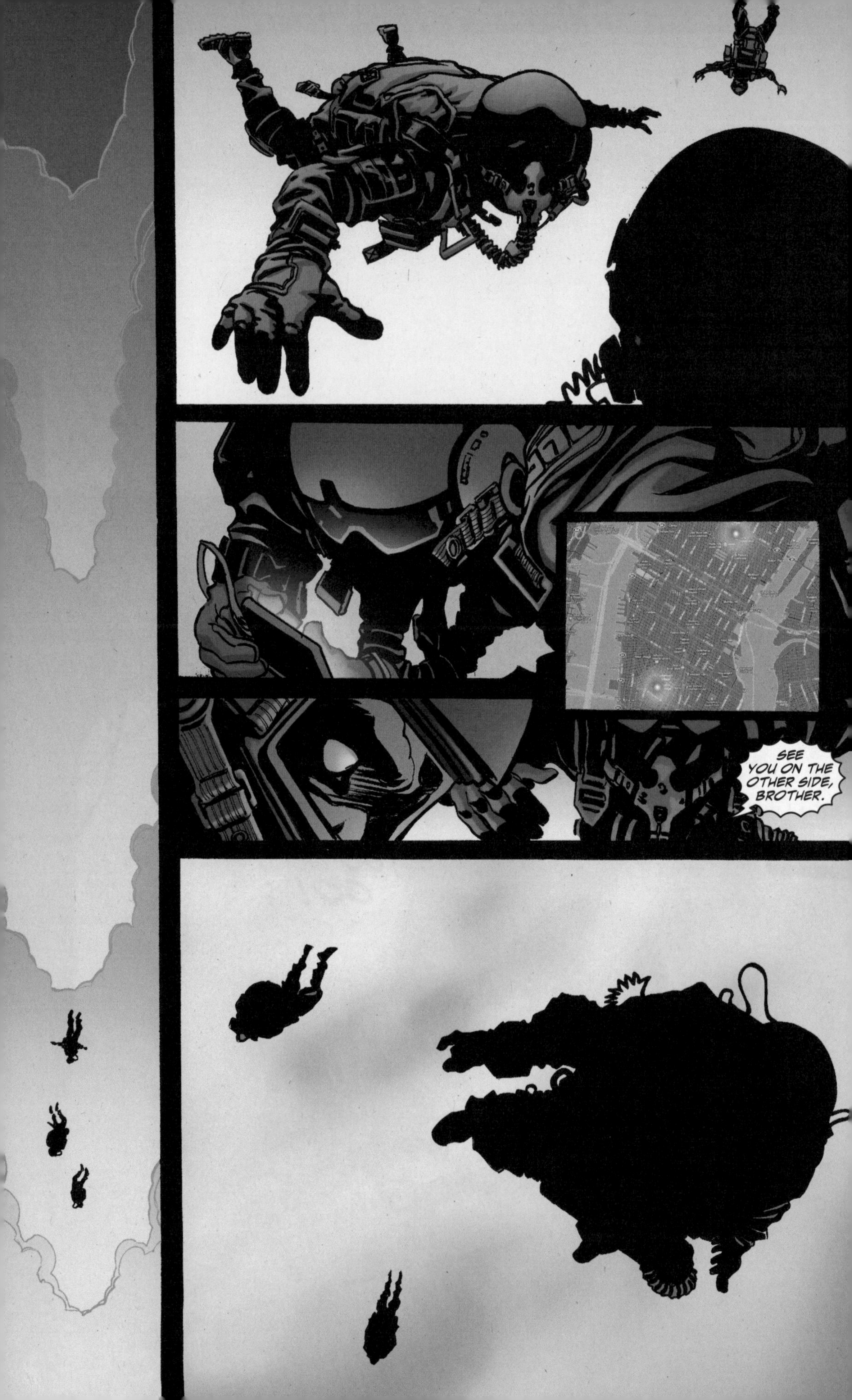
SEE YOU ON THE OTHER SIDE, BROTHER.

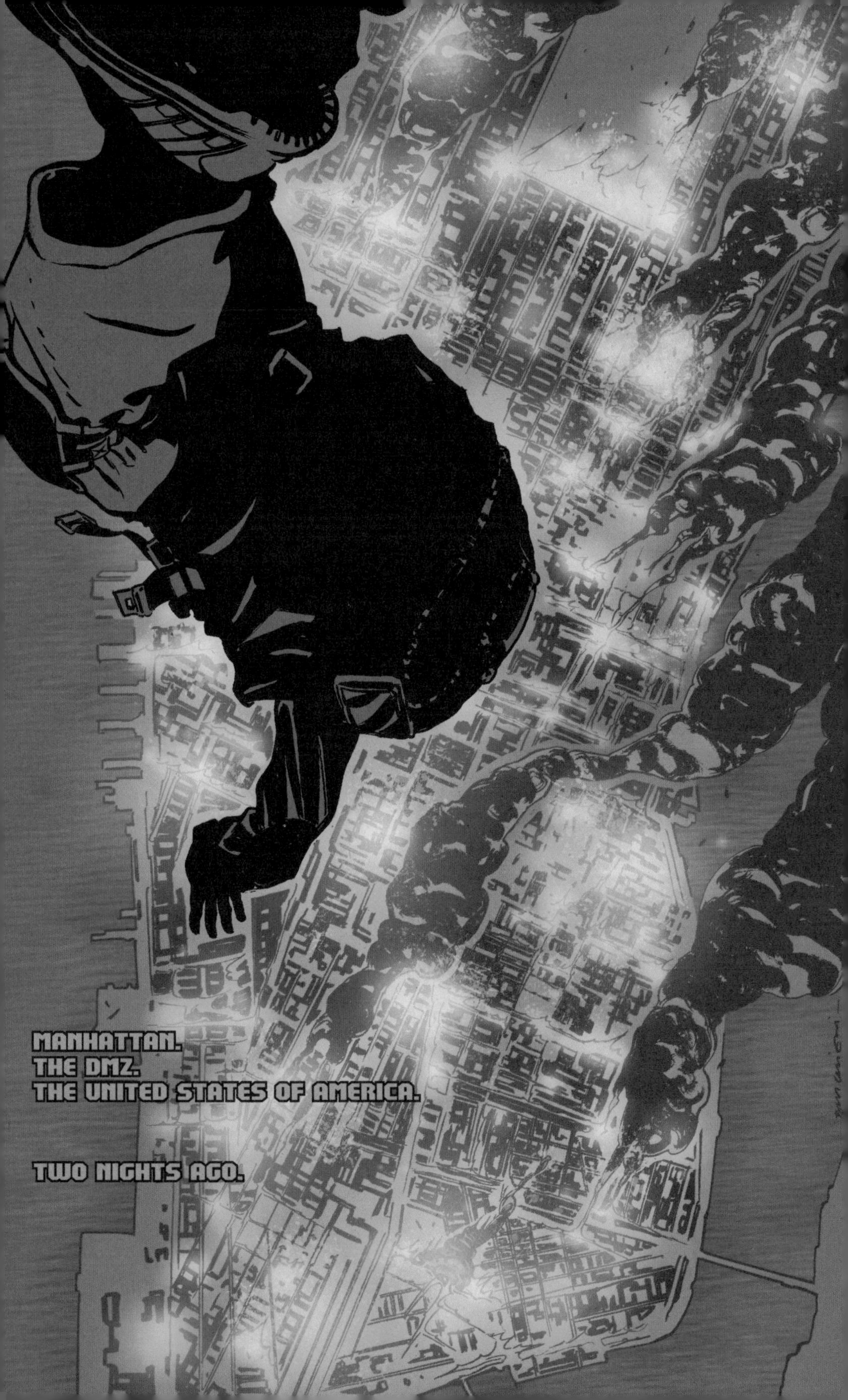
MANHATTAN.
THE DMZ.
THE UNITED STATES OF AMERICA.
TWO NIGHTS AGO.

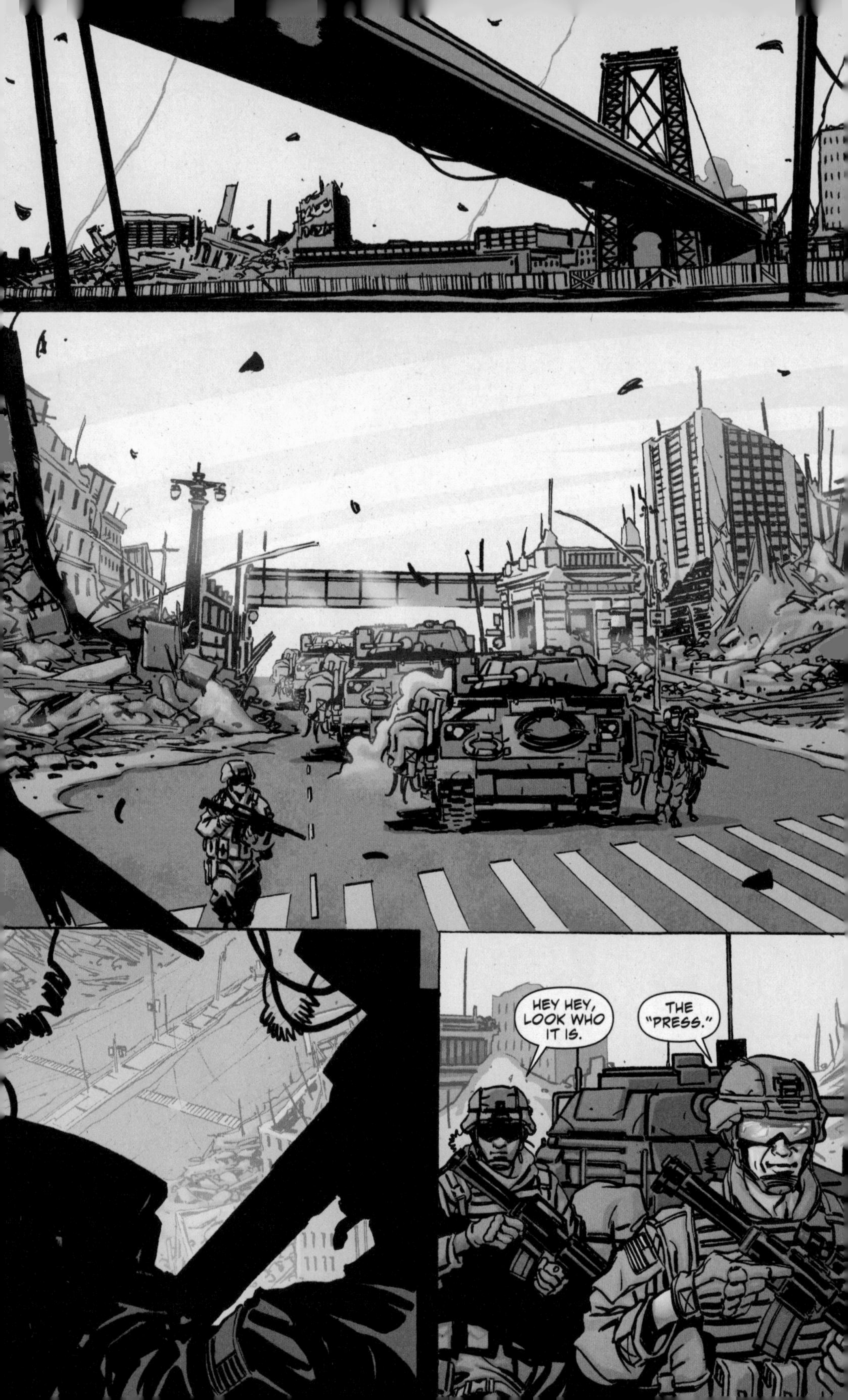
HEY HEY, LOOK WHO IT IS.
THE "PRESS."

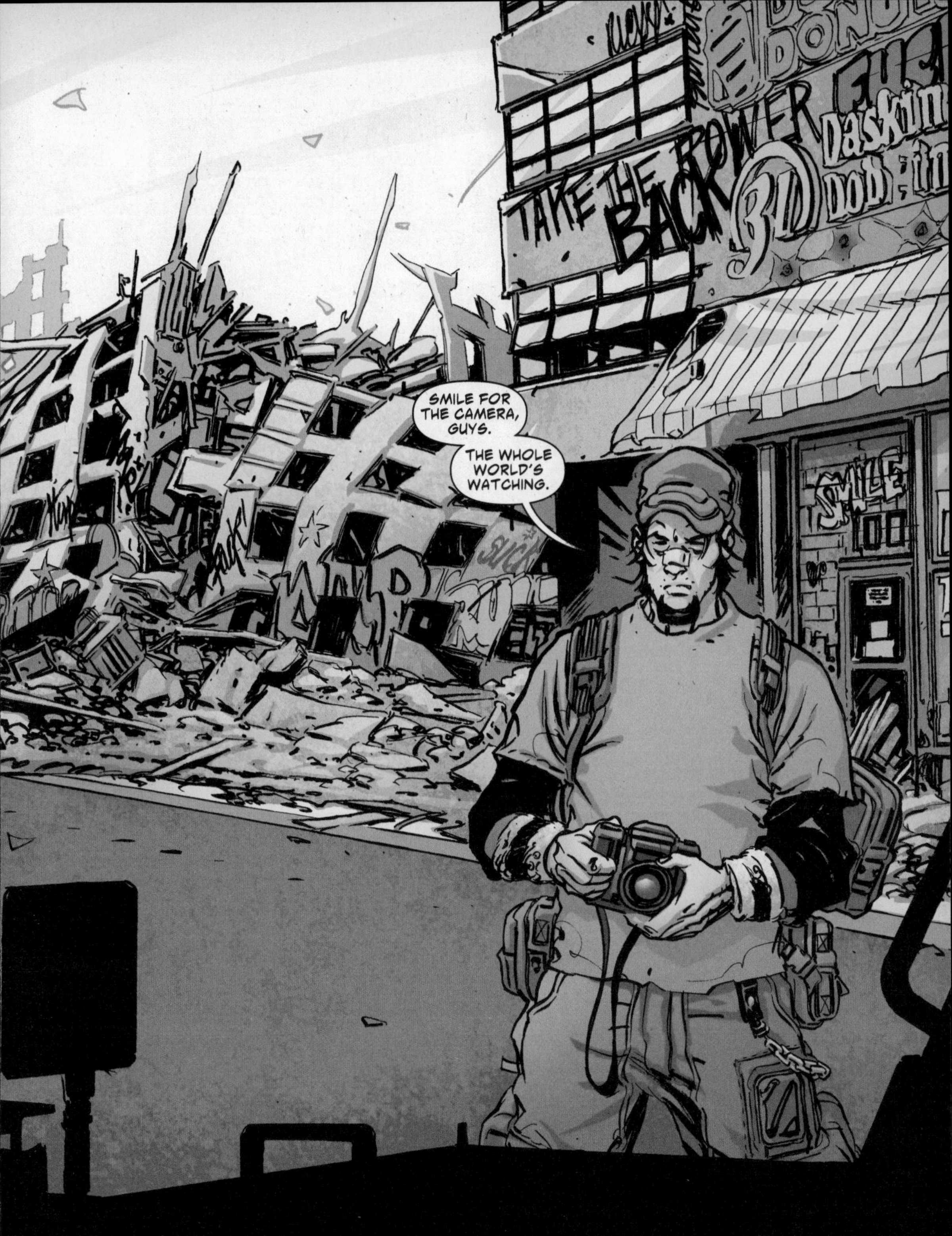
TAKE THE POWER BACK
SMILE FOR THE CAMERA, GUYS.
THE WHOLE WORLD'S WATCHING.
SMILE

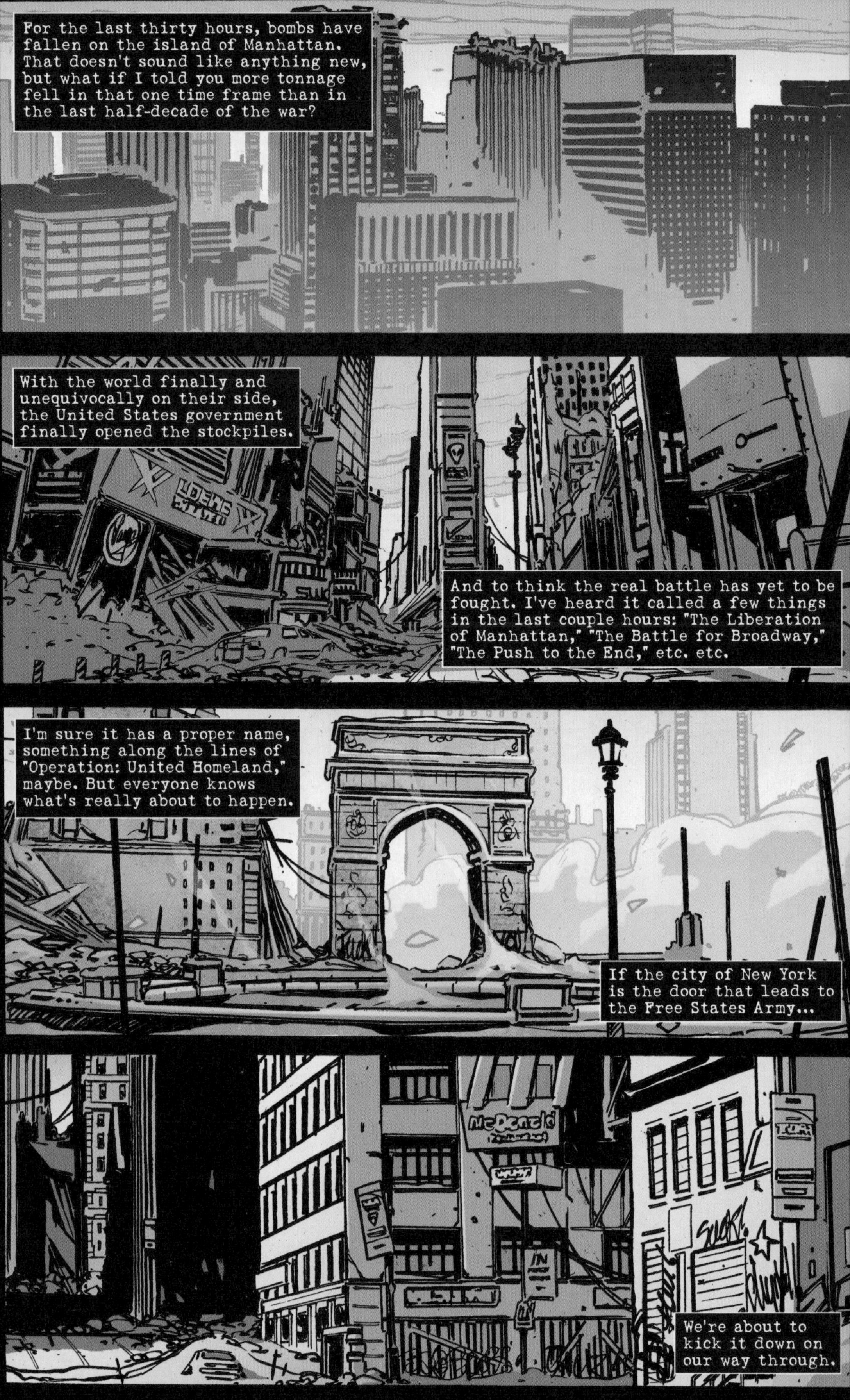

For the last thirty hours, bombs have fallen on the island of Manhattan. That doesn't sound like anything new, but what if I told you more tonnage fell in that one time frame than in the last half-decade of the war?
With the world finally and unequivocally on their side, the United States government finally opened the stockpiles.
LOEWS
And to think the real battle has yet to be fought. I've heard it called a few things in the last couple hours: "The Liberation of Manhattan," "The Battle for Broadway," "The Push to the End," etc. etc.
I'm sure it has a proper name, something along the lines of "Operation: United Homeland," maybe. But everyone knows what's really about to happen.
If the city of New York is the door that leads to the Free States Army...
We're about to kick it down on our way through.

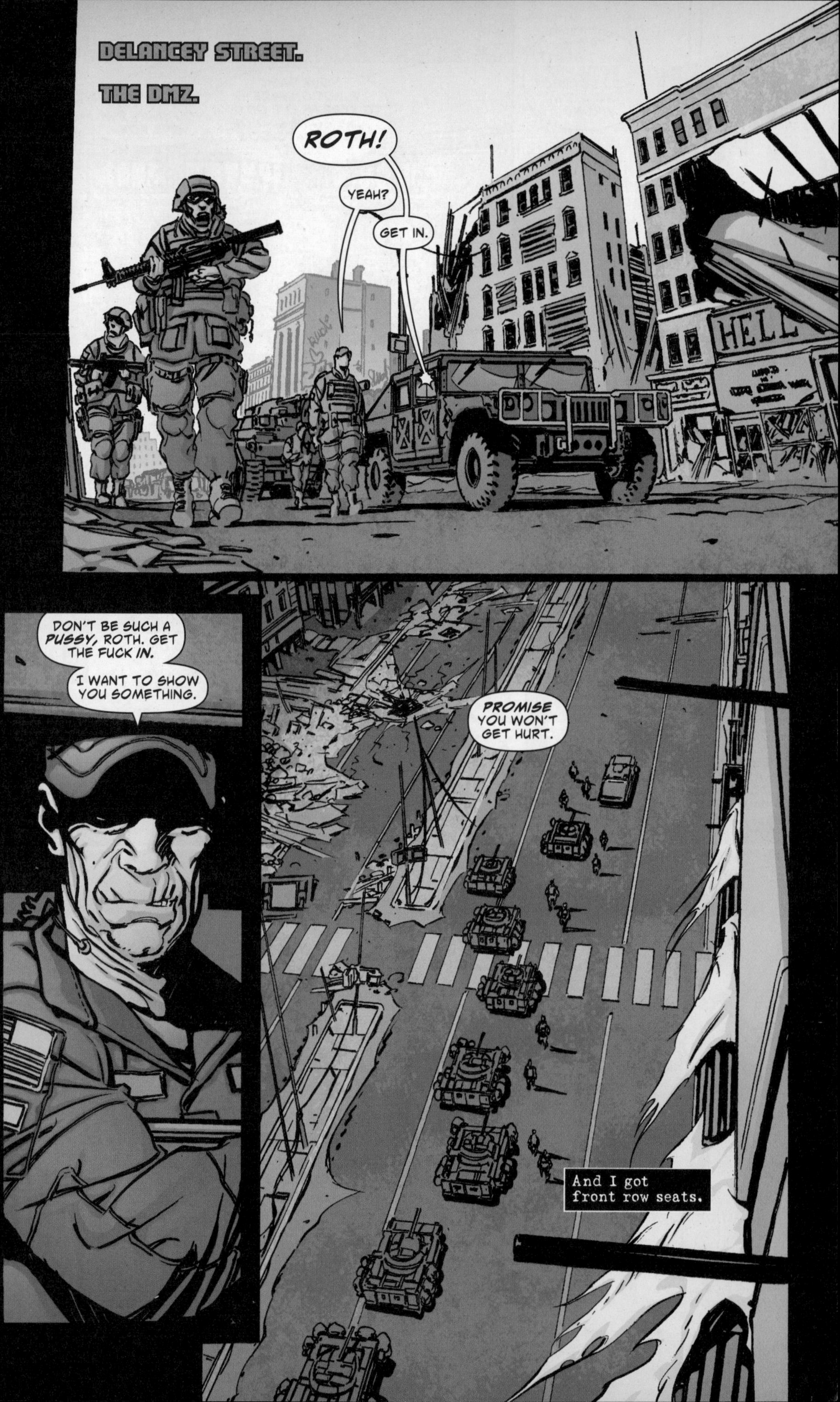
DELANCEY STREET.
THE DMZ.
ROTH!
YEAH?
GET IN.
HELL
DON'T BE SUCH A PUSSY, ROTH. GET THE FUCK IN.
I WANT TO SHOW YOU SOMETHING.
PROMISE YOU WON'T GET HURT.
And I got front row seats.

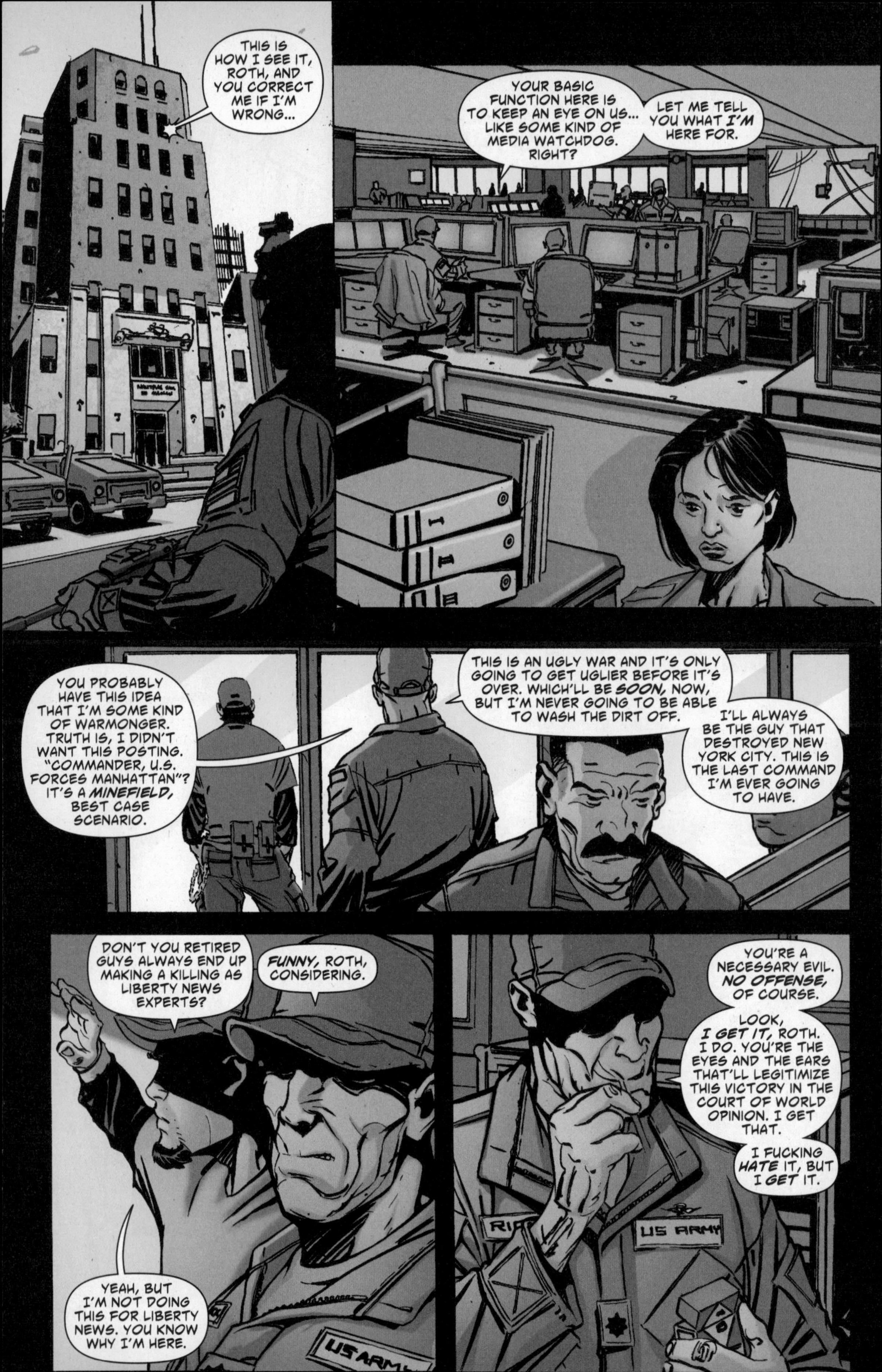
THIS IS HOW I SEE IT, ROTH, AND YOU CORRECT ME IF I'M WRONG...
YOUR BASIC FUNCTION HERE IS TO KEEP AN EYE ON US... LIKE SOME KIND OF MEDIA WATCHDOG. RIGHT?
LET ME TELL YOU WHAT *I'M* HERE FOR.
YOU PROBABLY HAVE THIS IDEA THAT I'M SOME KIND OF WARMONGER. TRUTH IS, I DIDN'T WANT THIS POSTING. "COMMANDER, U.S. FORCES MANHATTAN"? IT'S A *MINEFIELD,* BEST CASE SCENARIO.
THIS IS AN UGLY WAR AND IT'S ONLY GOING TO GET UGLIER BEFORE IT'S OVER. WHICH'LL BE *SOON,* NOW, BUT I'M NEVER GOING TO BE ABLE TO WASH THE DIRT OFF.
I'LL ALWAYS BE THE GUY THAT DESTROYED NEW YORK CITY. THIS IS THE LAST COMMAND I'M EVER GOING TO HAVE.
DON'T YOU RETIRED GUYS ALWAYS END UP MAKING A KILLING AS LIBERTY NEWS EXPERTS?
FUNNY, ROTH, CONSIDERING.
YEAH, BUT I'M NOT DOING THIS FOR LIBERTY NEWS. YOU KNOW WHY I'M HERE.
US ARMY
YOU'RE A NECESSARY EVIL. ***NO OFFENSE,*** OF COURSE.
LOOK, ***I GET IT,*** ROTH. I DO. YOU'RE THE EYES AND THE EARS THAT'LL LEGITIMIZE THIS VICTORY IN THE COURT OF WORLD OPINION. I GET THAT.
I FUCKING ***HATE*** IT, BUT I ***GET*** IT.
US ARMY

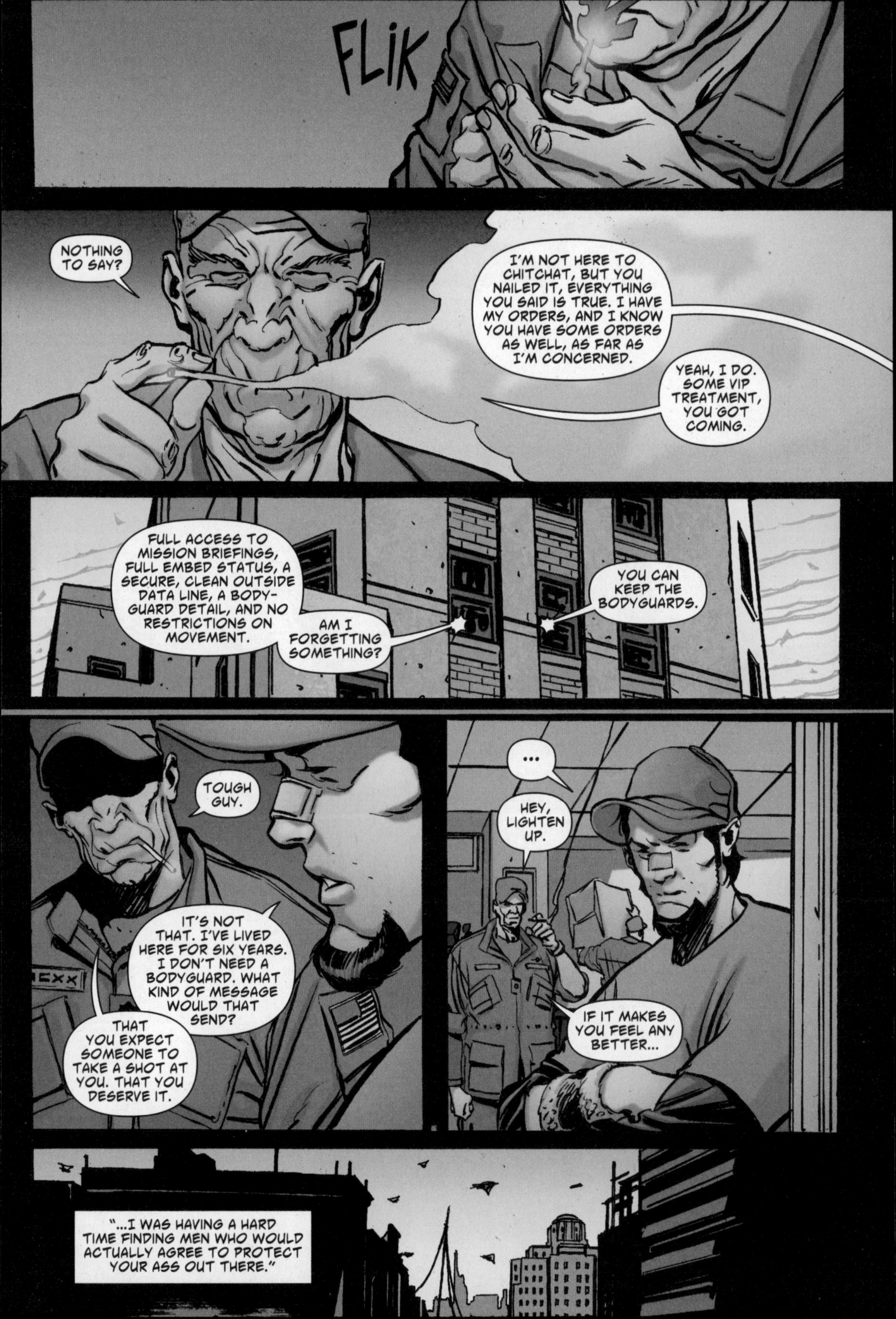
FLIK
NOTHING TO SAY?
I'M NOT HERE TO CHITCHAT, BUT YOU NAILED IT, EVERYTHING YOU SAID IS TRUE. I HAVE MY ORDERS, AND I KNOW YOU HAVE SOME ORDERS AS WELL, AS FAR AS I'M CONCERNED.
YEAH, I DO. SOME VIP TREATMENT, YOU GOT COMING.
FULL ACCESS TO MISSION BRIEFINGS, FULL EMBED STATUS, A SECURE, CLEAN OUTSIDE DATA LINE, A BODY-GUARD DETAIL, AND NO RESTRICTIONS ON MOVEMENT.
AM I FORGETTING SOMETHING?
YOU CAN KEEP THE BODYGUARDS.
TOUGH GUY.
IT'S NOT THAT. I'VE LIVED HERE FOR SIX YEARS. I DON'T NEED A BODYGUARD. WHAT KIND OF MESSAGE WOULD THAT SEND?
THAT YOU EXPECT SOMEONE TO TAKE A SHOT AT YOU. THAT YOU DESERVE IT.
...
HEY, LIGHTEN UP.
IF IT MAKES YOU FEEL ANY BETTER...
"...I WAS HAVING A HARD TIME FINDING MEN WHO WOULD ACTUALLY AGREE TO PROTECT YOUR ASS OUT THERE."

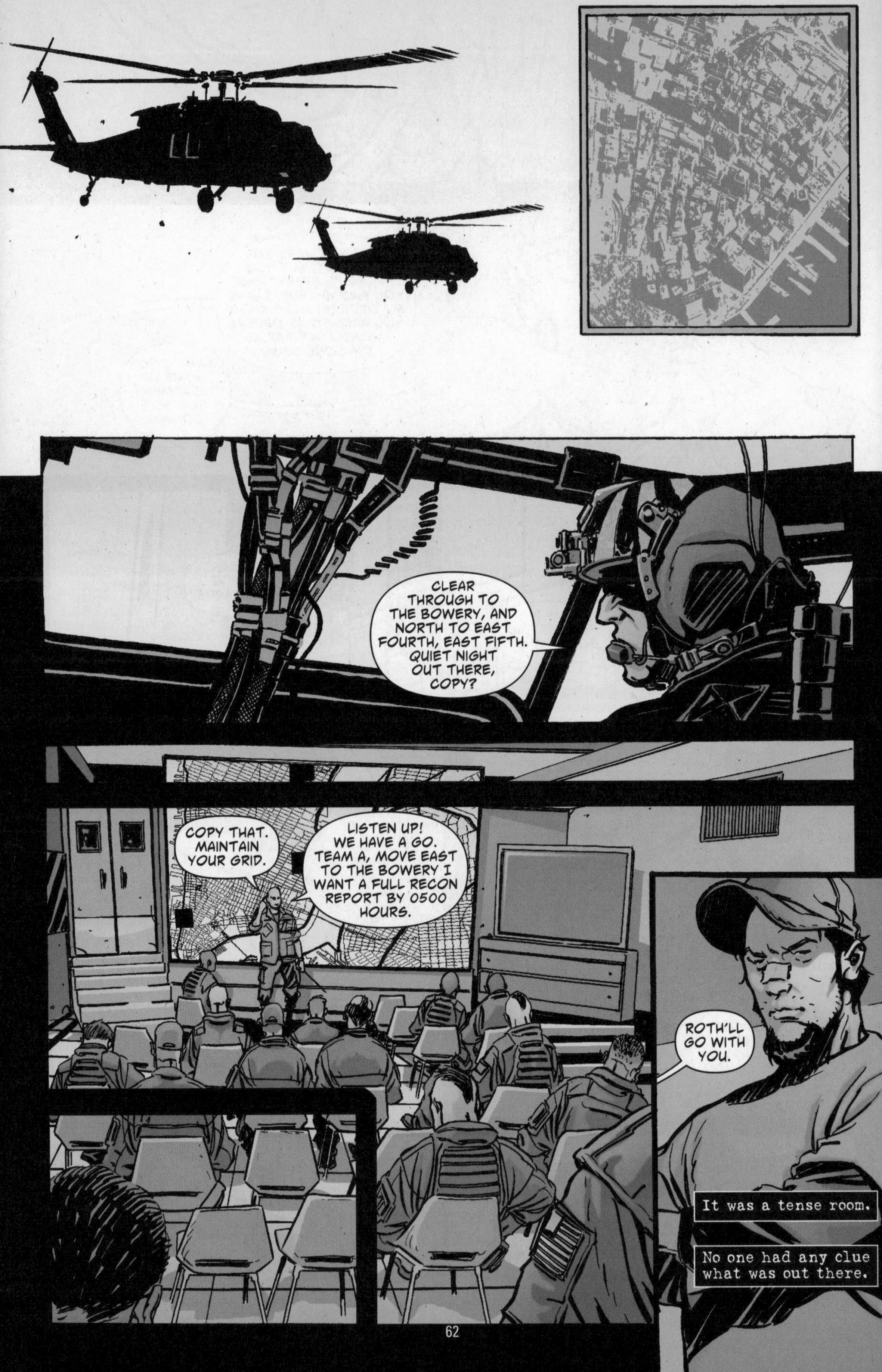
CLEAR THROUGH TO THE BOWERY, AND NORTH TO EAST FOURTH, EAST FIFTH. QUIET NIGHT OUT THERE, COPY?
COPY THAT. MAINTAIN YOUR GRID.
LISTEN UP! WE HAVE A GO. TEAM A, MOVE EAST TO THE BOWERY I WANT A FULL RECON REPORT BY 0500 HOURS.
ROTH'LL GO WITH YOU.
It was a tense room.
No one had any clue what was out there.

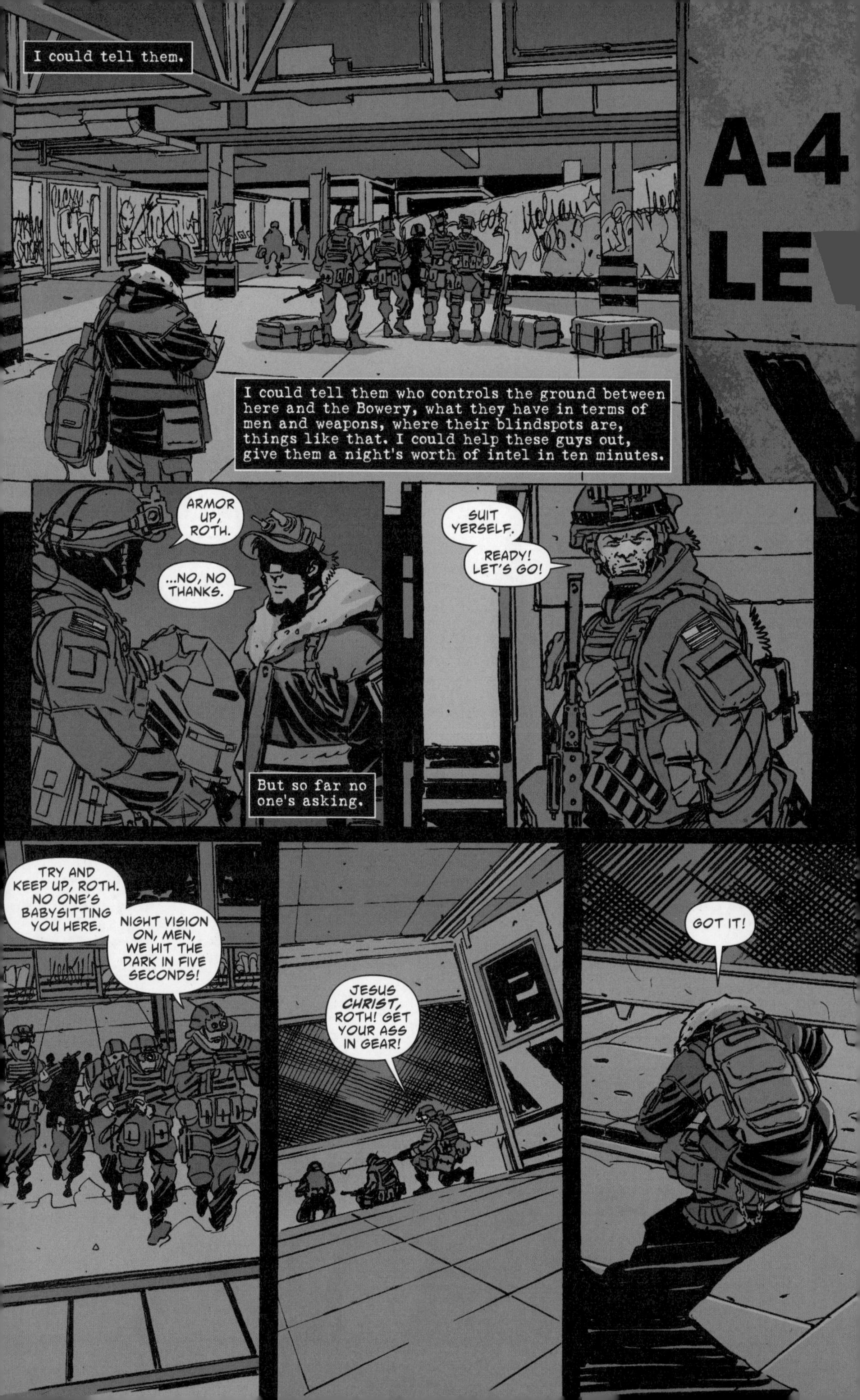

I could tell them.
A-4
LE
I could tell them who controls the ground between here and the Bowery, what they have in terms of men and weapons, where their blindspots are, things like that. I could help these guys out, give them a night's worth of intel in ten minutes.
ARMOR UP, ROTH.
...NO, NO THANKS.
But so far no one's asking.
SUIT YERSELF.
READY! LET'S GO!
TRY AND KEEP UP, ROTH. NO ONE'S BABYSITTING YOU HERE.
NIGHT VISION ON, MEN, WE HIT THE DARK IN FIVE SECONDS!
JESUS CHRIST, ROTH! GET YOUR ASS IN GEAR!
GOT IT!

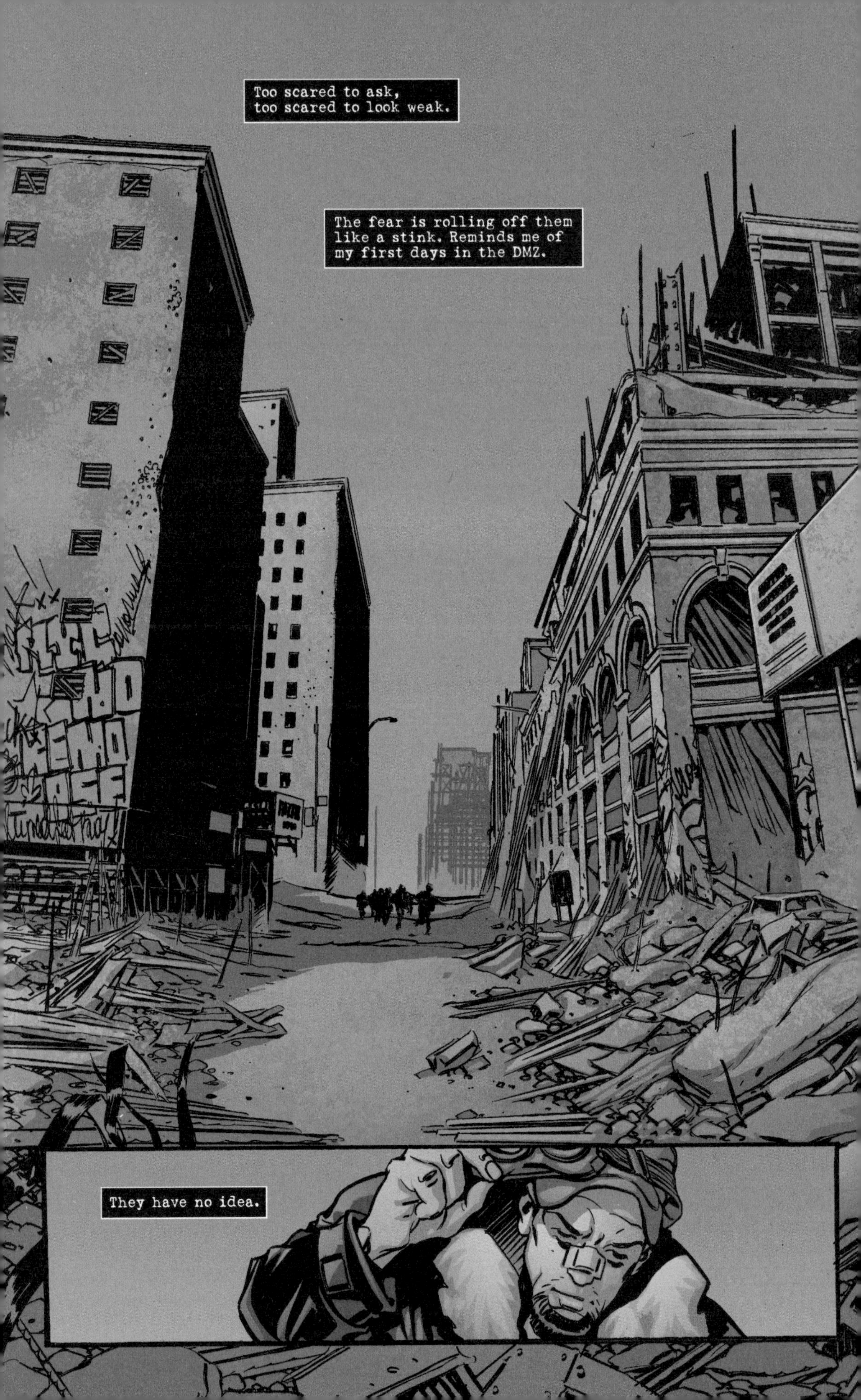
Too scared to ask, too scared to look weak.
The fear is rolling off them like a stink. Reminds me of my first days in the DMZ.
They have no idea.

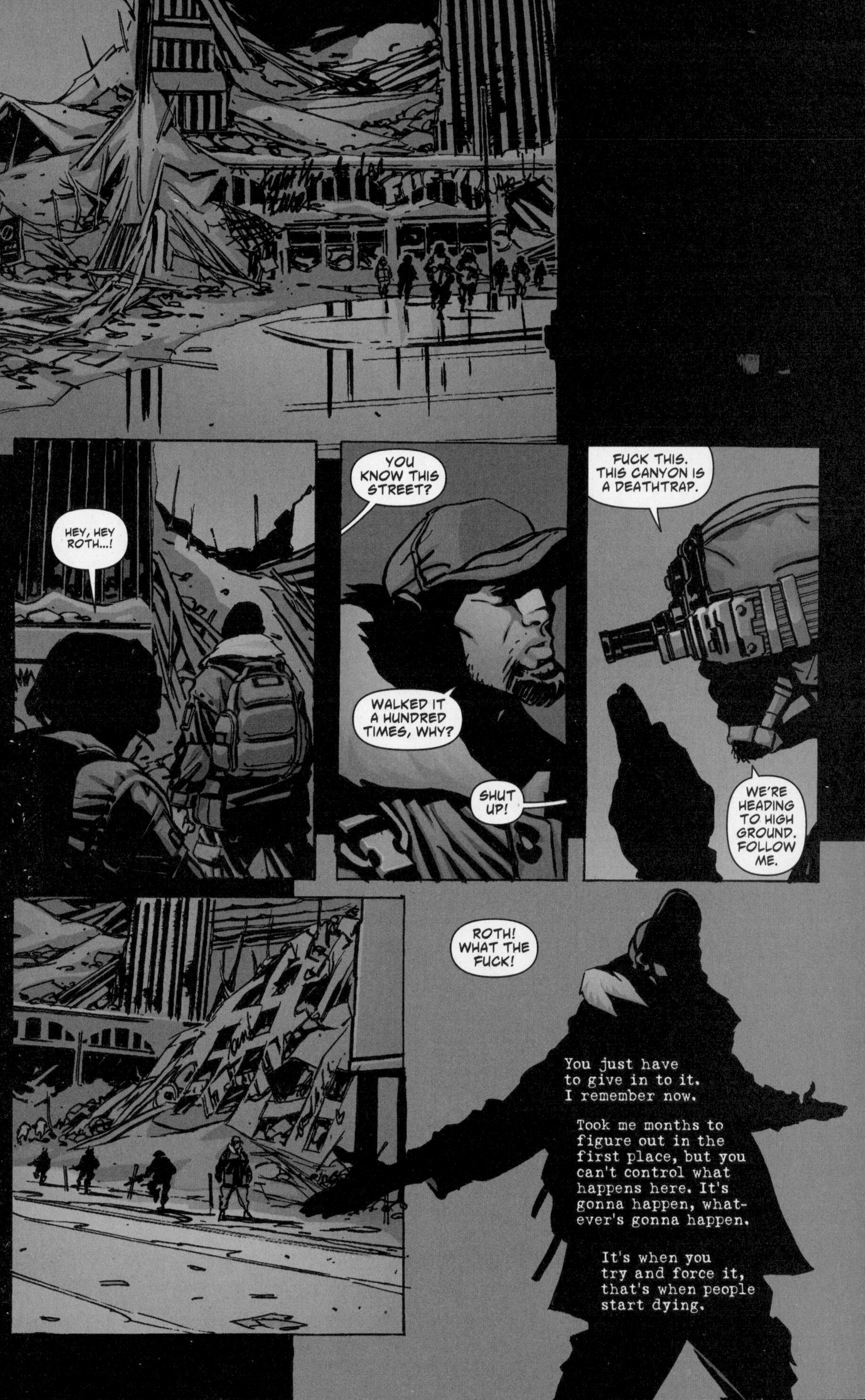
HEY, HEY ROTH...!
YOU KNOW THIS STREET?
WALKED IT A HUNDRED TIMES, WHY?
SHUT UP!
FUCK THIS. THIS CANYON IS A DEATHTRAP.
WE'RE HEADING TO HIGH GROUND. FOLLOW ME.
ROTH! WHAT THE FUCK!
You just have to give in to it. I remember now.
Took me months to figure out in the first place, but you can't control what happens here. It's gonna happen, whatever's gonna happen.
It's when you try and force it, that's when people start dying.

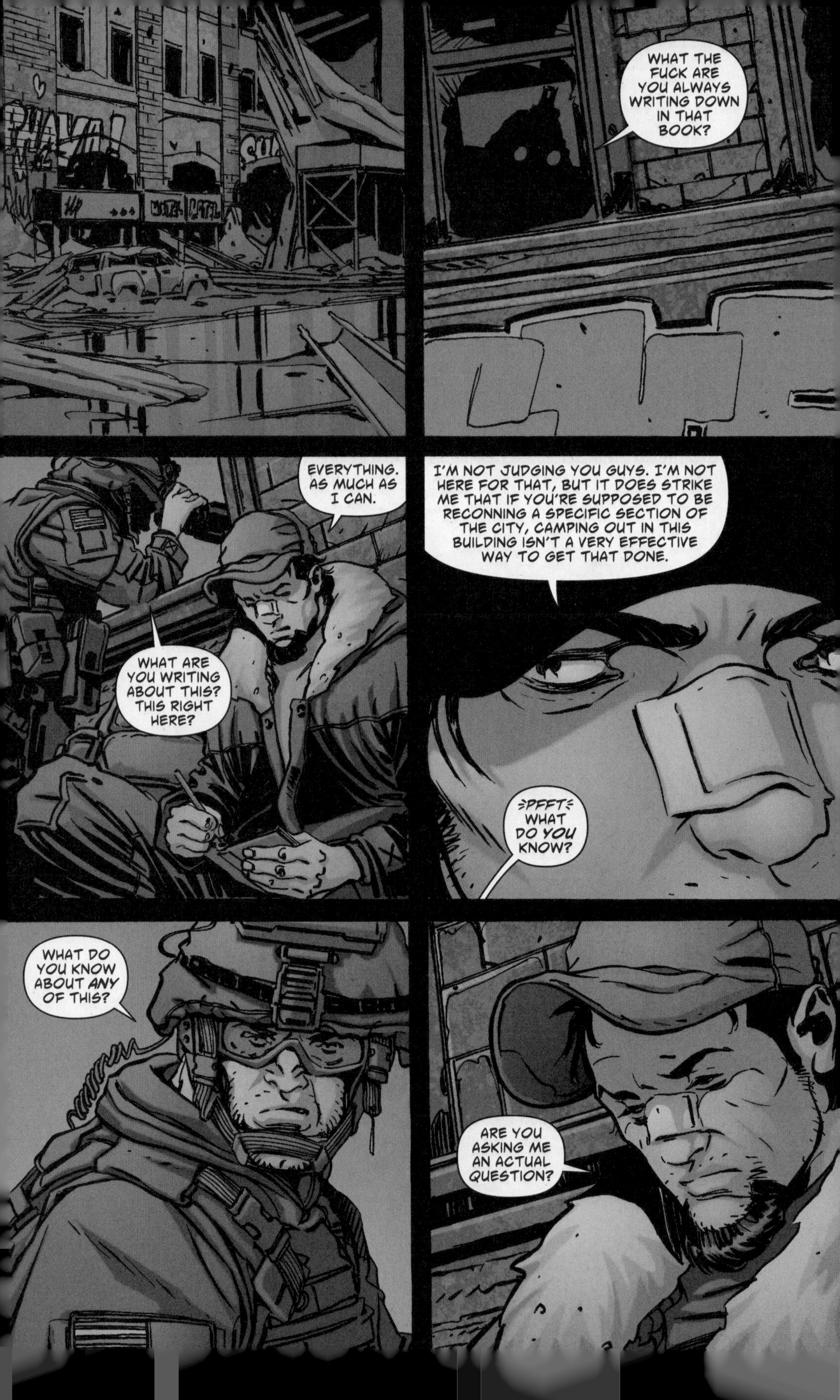
WHAT THE FUCK ARE YOU ALWAYS WRITING DOWN IN THAT BOOK?
EVERYTHING. AS MUCH AS I CAN.
WHAT ARE YOU WRITING ABOUT THIS? THIS RIGHT HERE?
I'M NOT JUDGING YOU GUYS. I'M NOT HERE FOR THAT, BUT IT DOES STRIKE ME THAT IF YOU'RE SUPPOSED TO BE RECONNING A SPECIFIC SECTION OF THE CITY, CAMPING OUT IN THIS BUILDING ISN'T A VERY EFFECTIVE WAY TO GET THAT DONE.
PFFT WHAT DO YOU KNOW?
WHAT DO YOU KNOW ABOUT ANY OF THIS?
ARE YOU ASKING ME AN ACTUAL QUESTION?

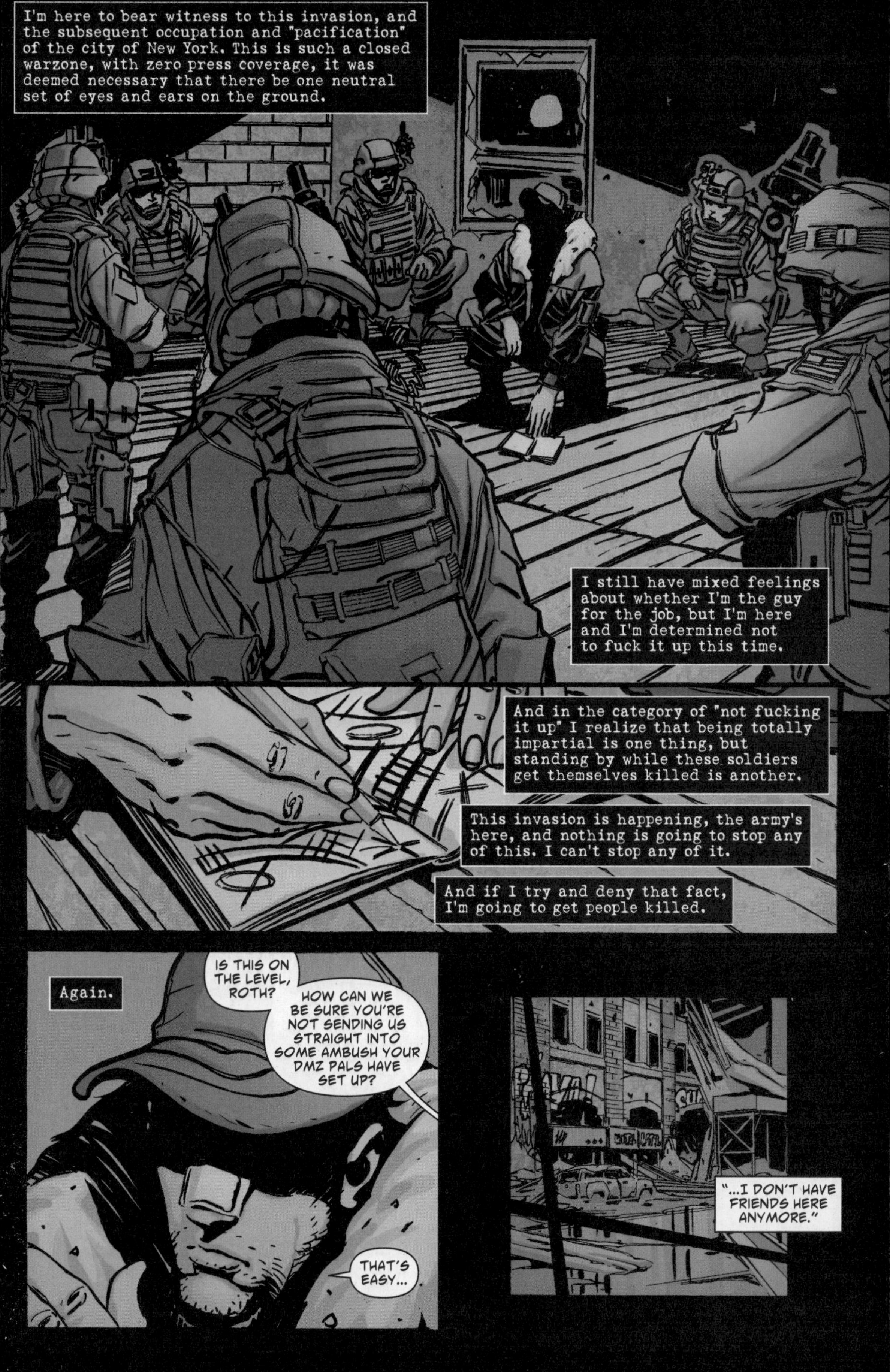
I'm here to bear witness to this invasion, and the subsequent occupation and "pacification" of the city of New York. This is such a closed warzone, with zero press coverage, it was deemed necessary that there be one neutral set of eyes and ears on the ground.
I still have mixed feelings about whether I'm the guy for the job, but I'm here and I'm determined not to fuck it up this time.
And in the category of "not fucking it up" I realize that being totally impartial is one thing, but standing by while these soldiers get themselves killed is another.
This invasion is happening, the army's here, and nothing is going to stop any of this. I can't stop any of it.
And if I try and deny that fact, I'm going to get people killed.
Again.
IS THIS ON THE LEVEL, ROTH?
HOW CAN WE BE SURE YOU'RE NOT SENDING US STRAIGHT INTO SOME AMBUSH YOUR DMZ PALS HAVE SET UP?
THAT'S EASY...
"...I DON'T HAVE FRIENDS HERE ANYMORE."

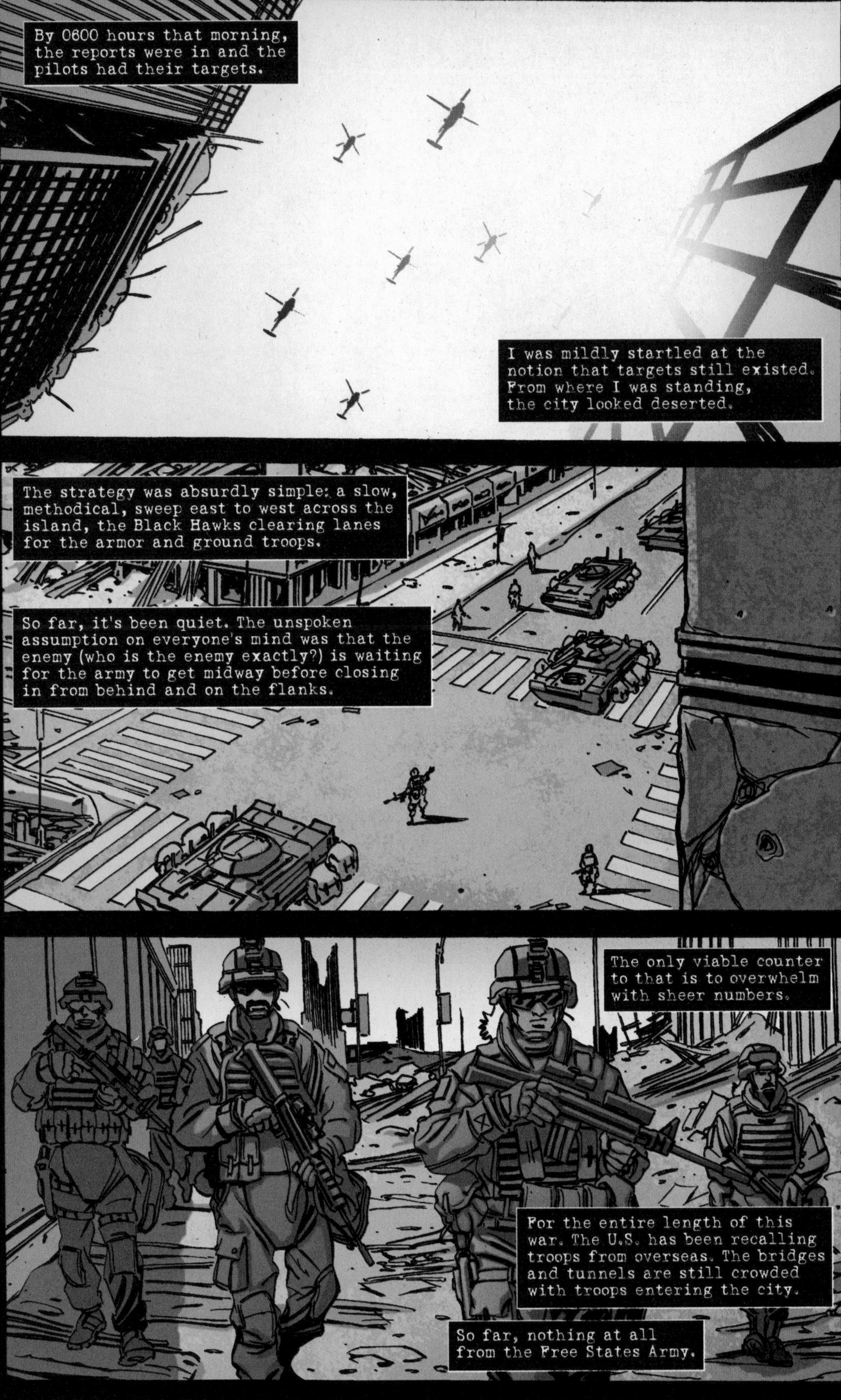
By 0600 hours that morning, the reports were in and the pilots had their targets.
I was mildly startled at the notion that targets still existed. From where I was standing, the city looked deserted.
The strategy was absurdly simple: a slow, methodical, sweep east to west across the island, the Black Hawks clearing lanes for the armor and ground troops.
So far, it's been quiet. The unspoken assumption on everyone's mind was that the enemy (who is the enemy exactly?) is waiting for the army to get midway before closing in from behind and on the flanks.
The only viable counter to that is to overwhelm with sheer numbers.
For the entire length of this war. The U.S. has been recalling troops from overseas. The bridges and tunnels are still crowded with troops entering the city.
So far, nothing at all from the Free States Army.

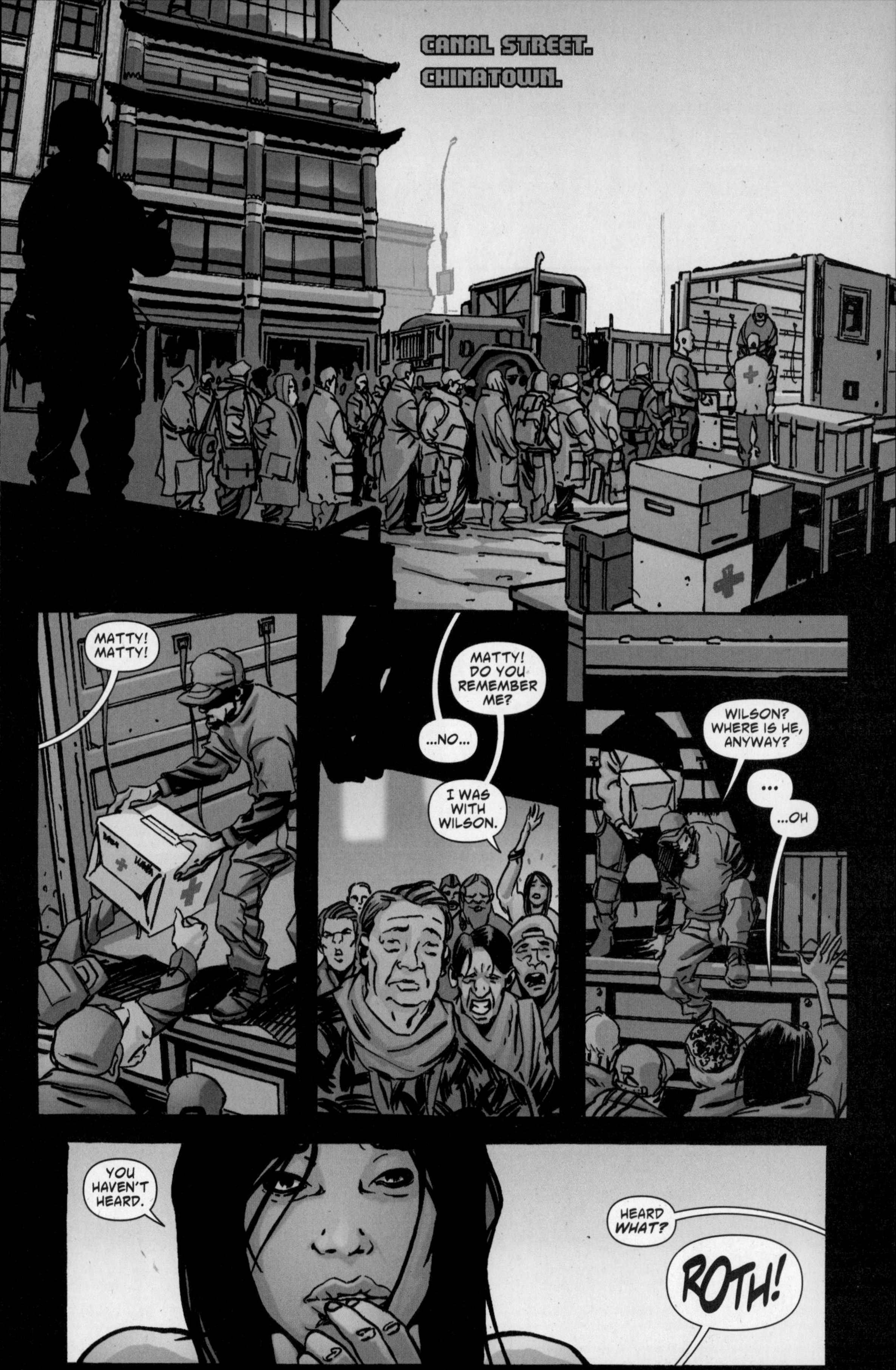
CANAL STREET.
CHINATOWN.
MATTY! MATTY!
MATTY! DO YOU REMEMBER ME?
...NO...
I WAS WITH WILSON.
WILSON? WHERE IS HE, ANYWAY?
...
...OH
YOU HAVEN'T HEARD.
HEARD WHAT?
ROTH!

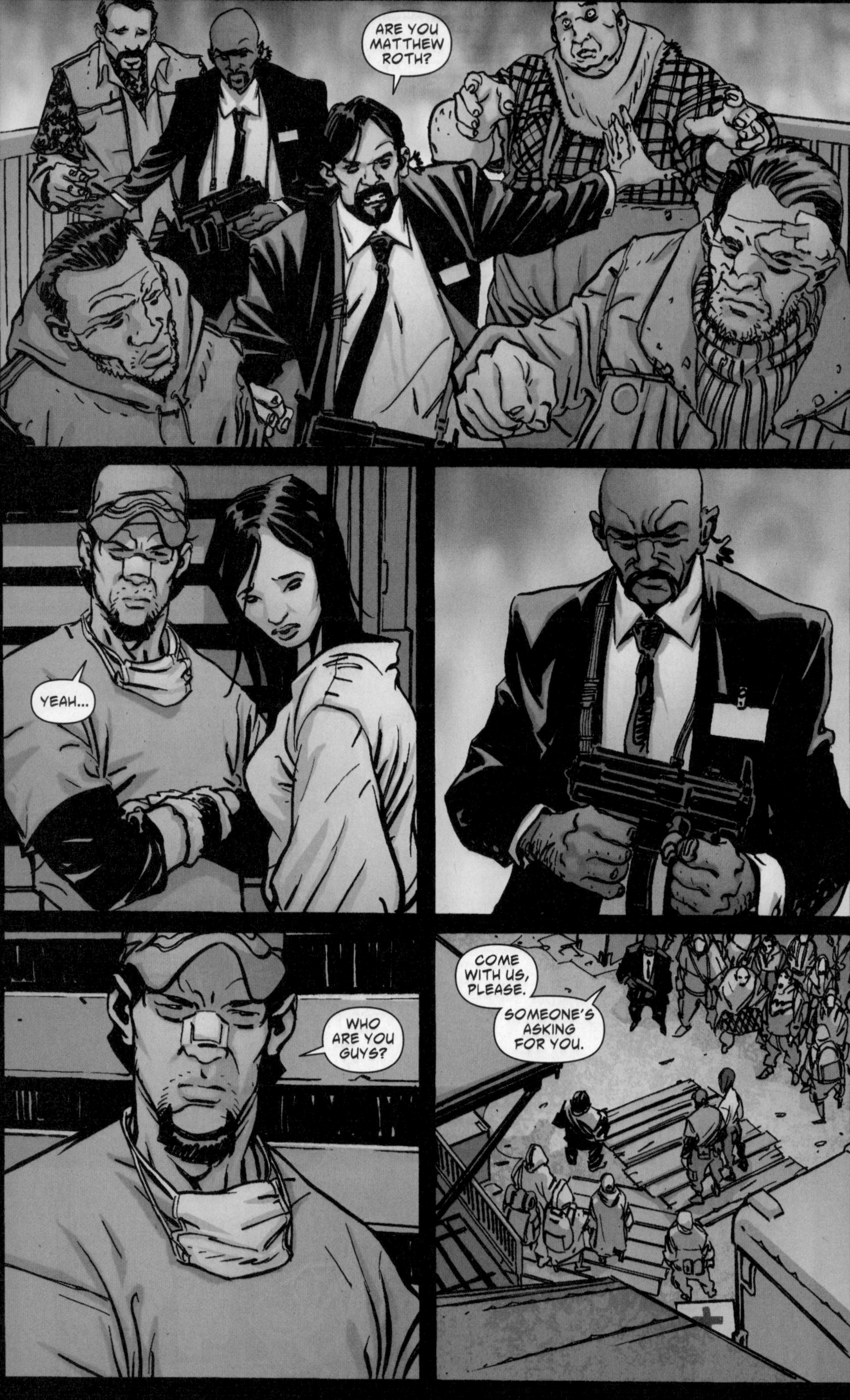
ARE YOU MATTHEW ROTH?
YEAH...
WHO ARE YOU GUYS?
COME WITH US, PLEASE.
SOMEONE'S ASKING FOR YOU.

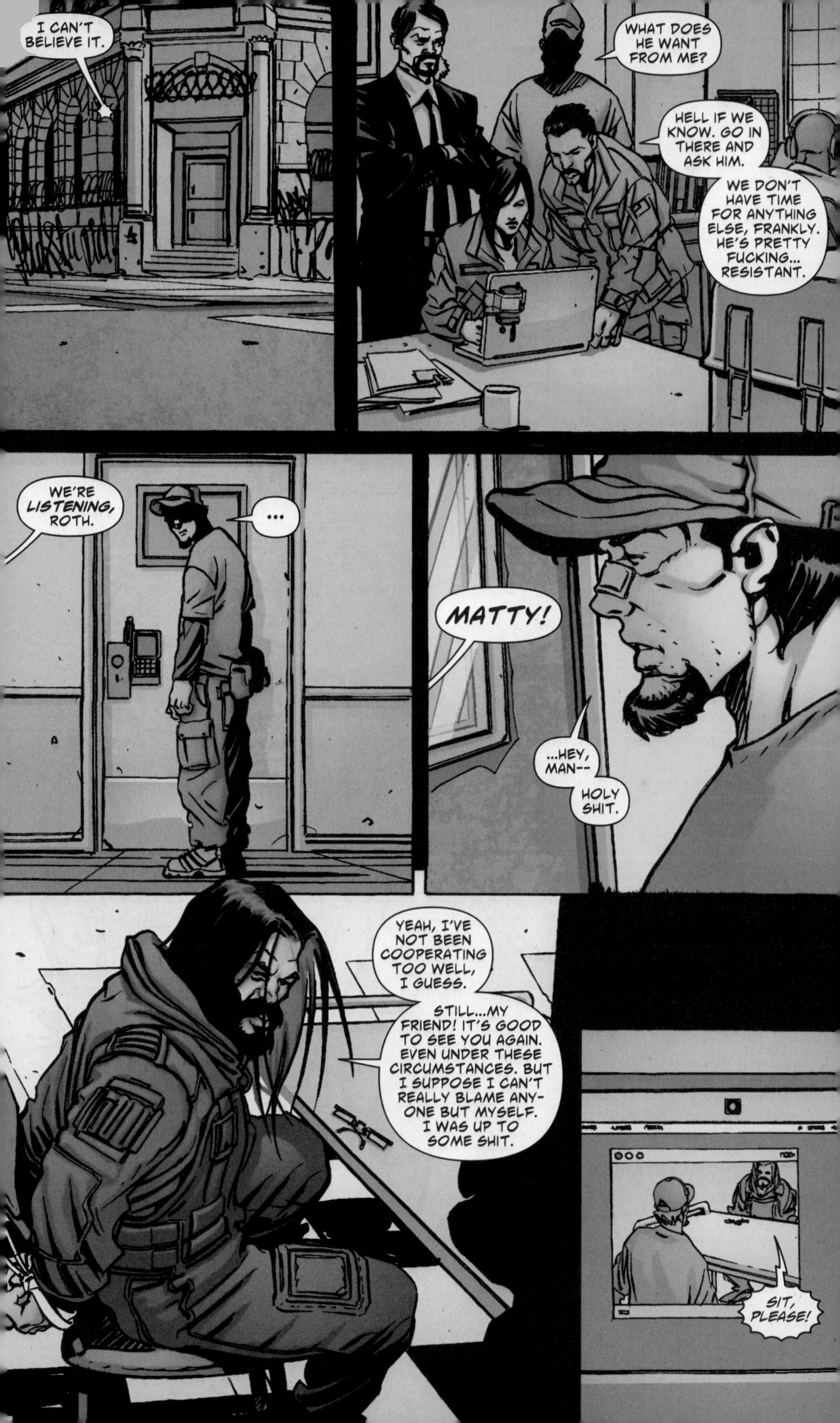
I CAN'T BELIEVE IT.
WHAT DOES HE WANT FROM ME?
HELL IF WE KNOW. GO IN THERE AND ASK HIM.
WE DON'T HAVE TIME FOR ANYTHING ELSE, FRANKLY. HE'S PRETTY FUCKING... RESISTANT.
WE'RE LISTENING, ROTH.
...
MATTY!
...HEY, MAN--
HOLY SHIT.
YEAH, I'VE NOT BEEN COOPERATING TOO WELL, I GUESS.
STILL...MY FRIEND! IT'S GOOD TO SEE YOU AGAIN. EVEN UNDER THESE CIRCUMSTANCES. BUT I SUPPOSE I CAN'T REALLY BLAME ANY-ONE BUT MYSELF. I WAS UP TO SOME SHIT.
SIT, PLEASE!

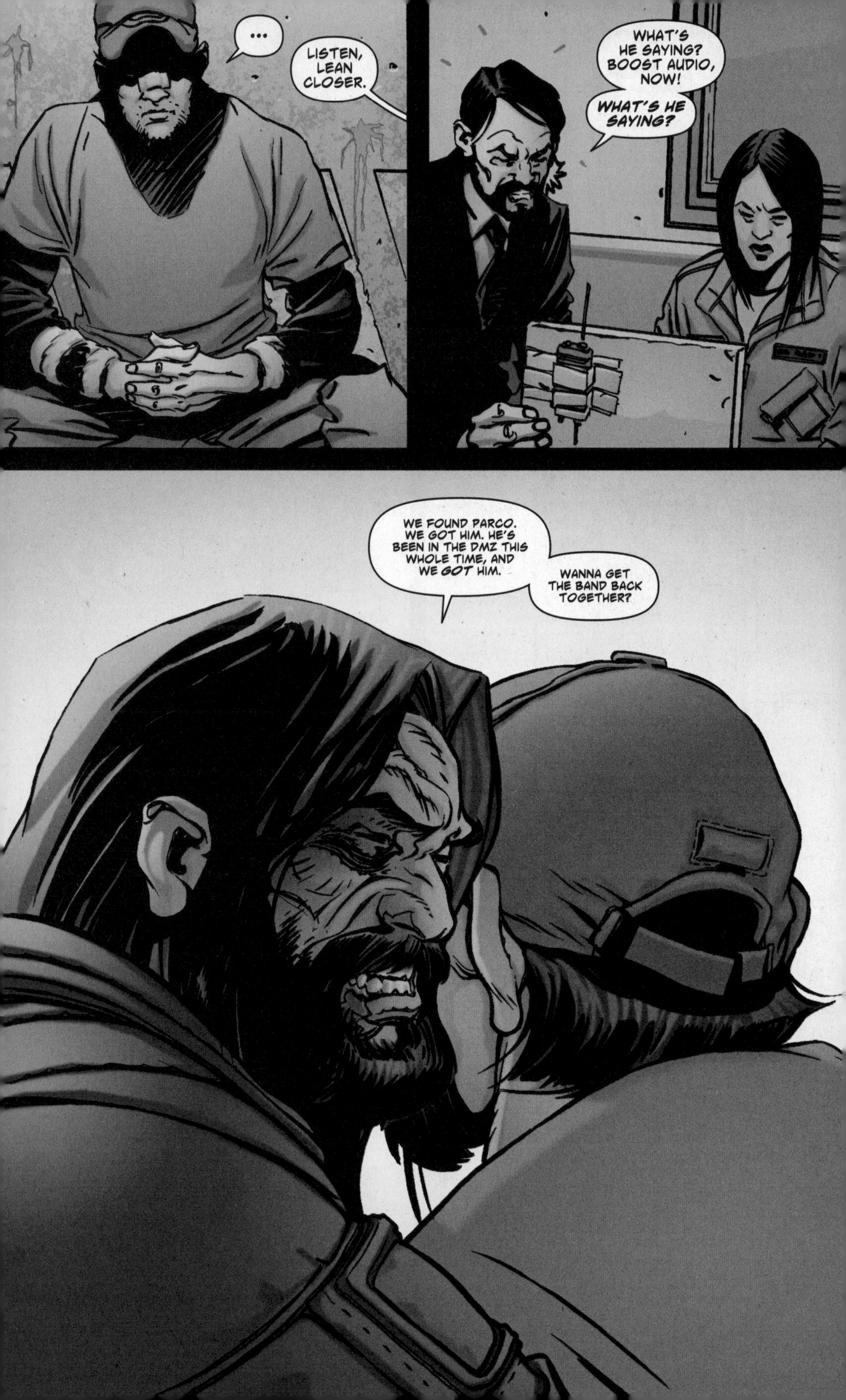
...
LISTEN, LEAN CLOSER.
WHAT'S HE SAYING? BOOST AUDIO, NOW!
WHAT'S HE SAYING?
WE FOUND PARCO. WE GOT HIM. HE'S BEEN IN THE DMZ THIS WHOLE TIME, AND WE *GOT* HIM.
WANNA GET THE BAND BACK TOGETHER?

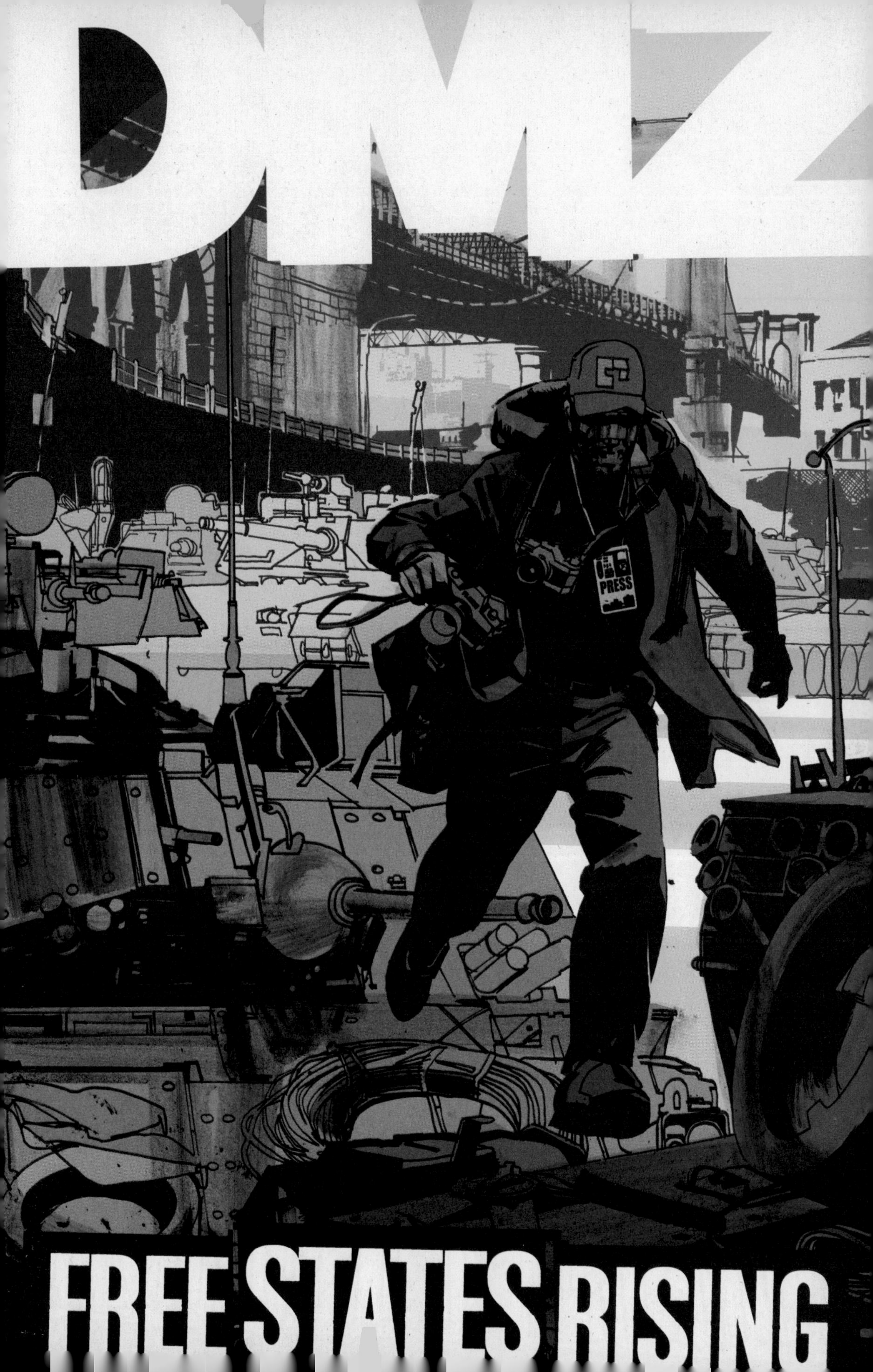
DMZ
PRESS
FREE STATES RISING

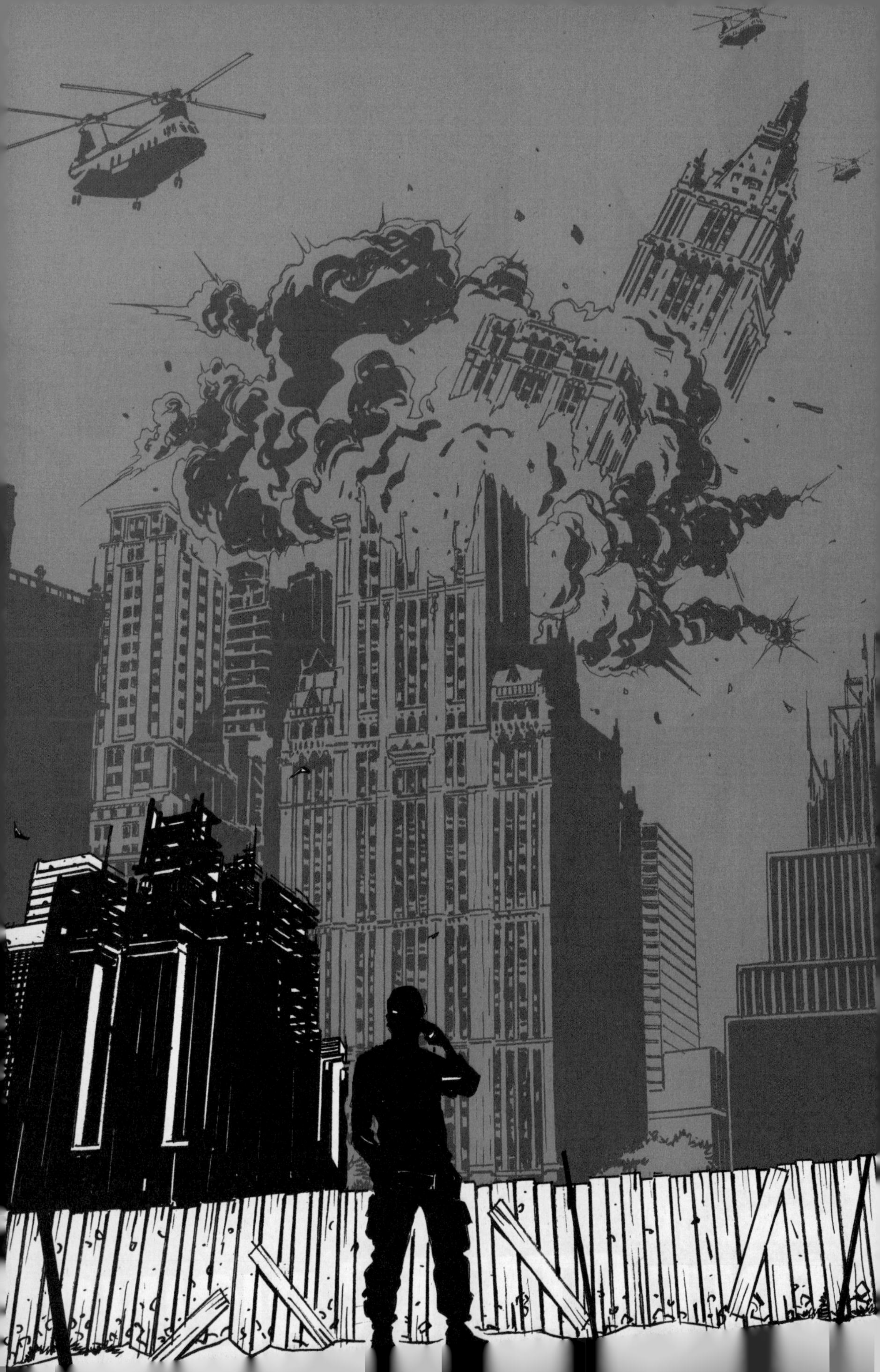

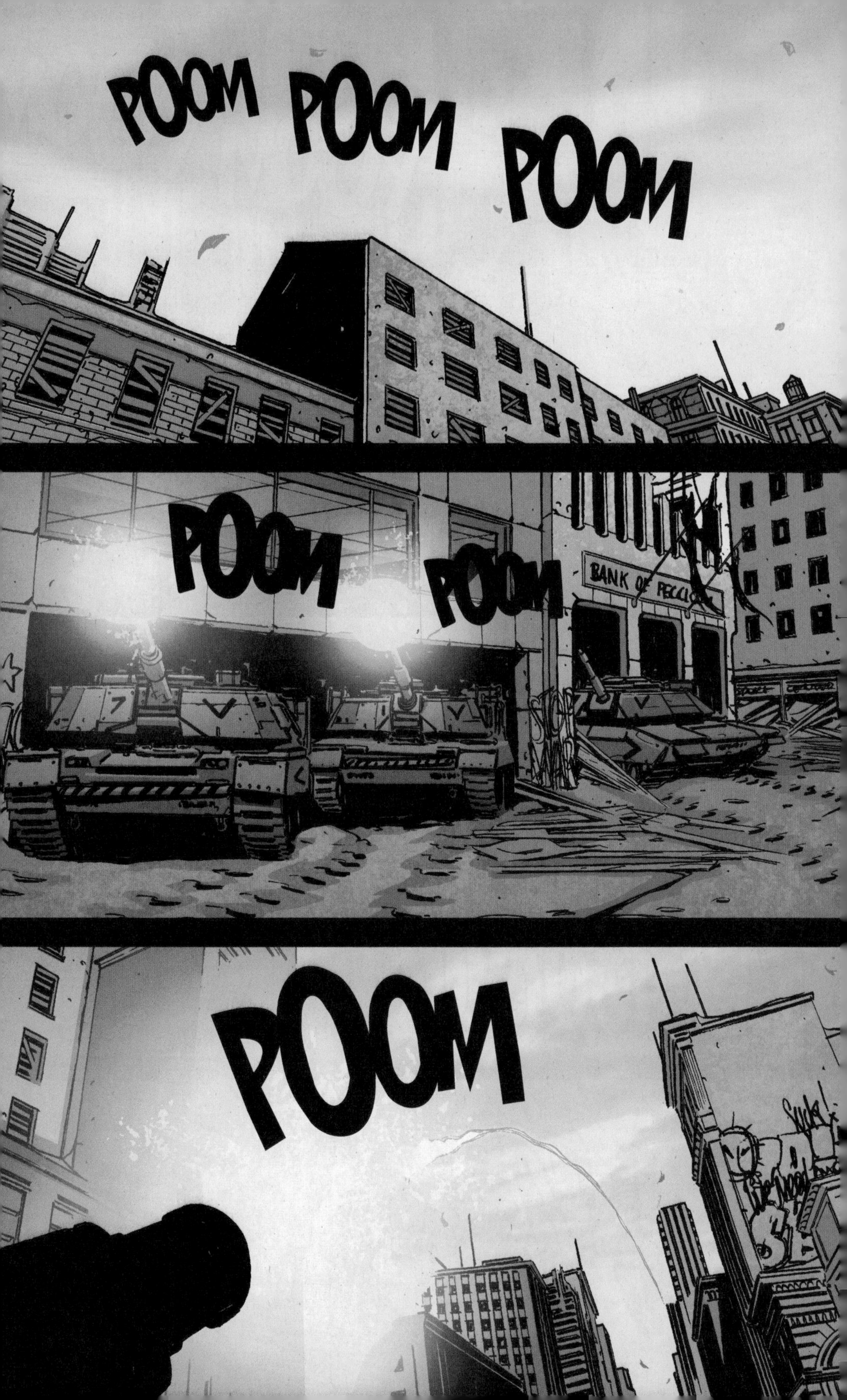
POOM POOM POOM
POOM
POOM
BANK OF
POOM

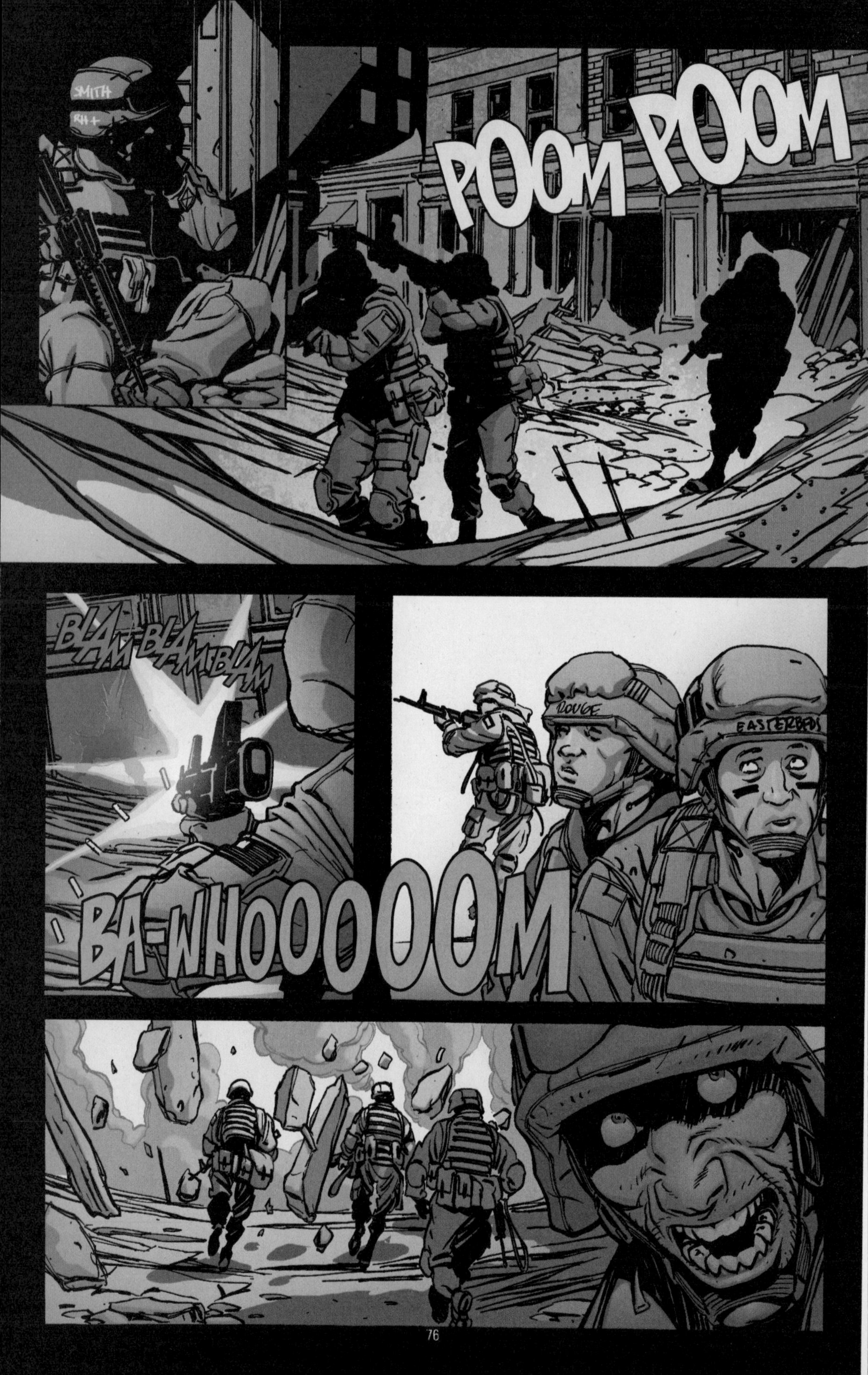
SMITH
RH+
POOM POOM
BLAM BLAM BLAM
BA-WHOOOOOOM
ROUGE
EASTERBEDS

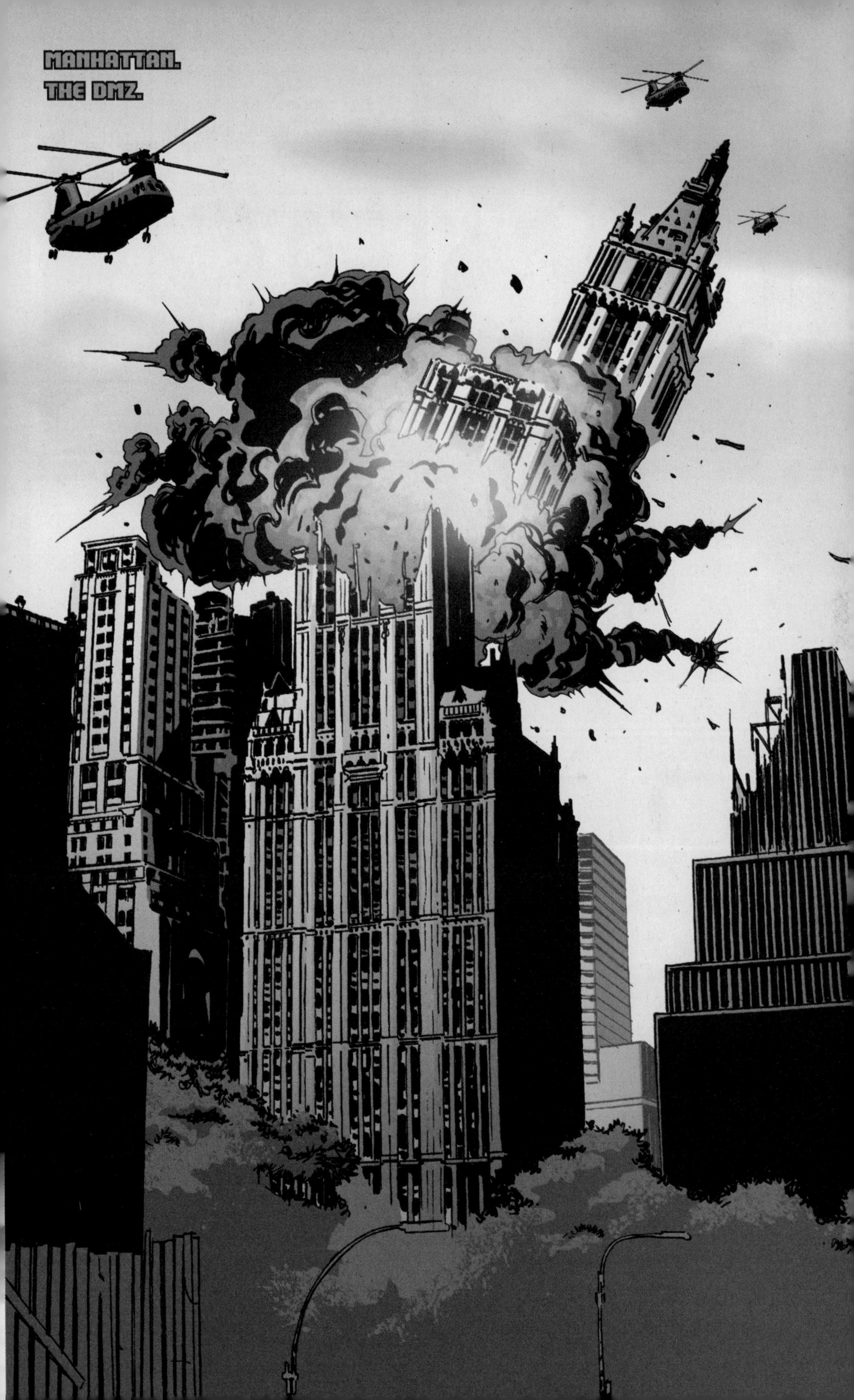
MANHATTAN.
THE DMZ.

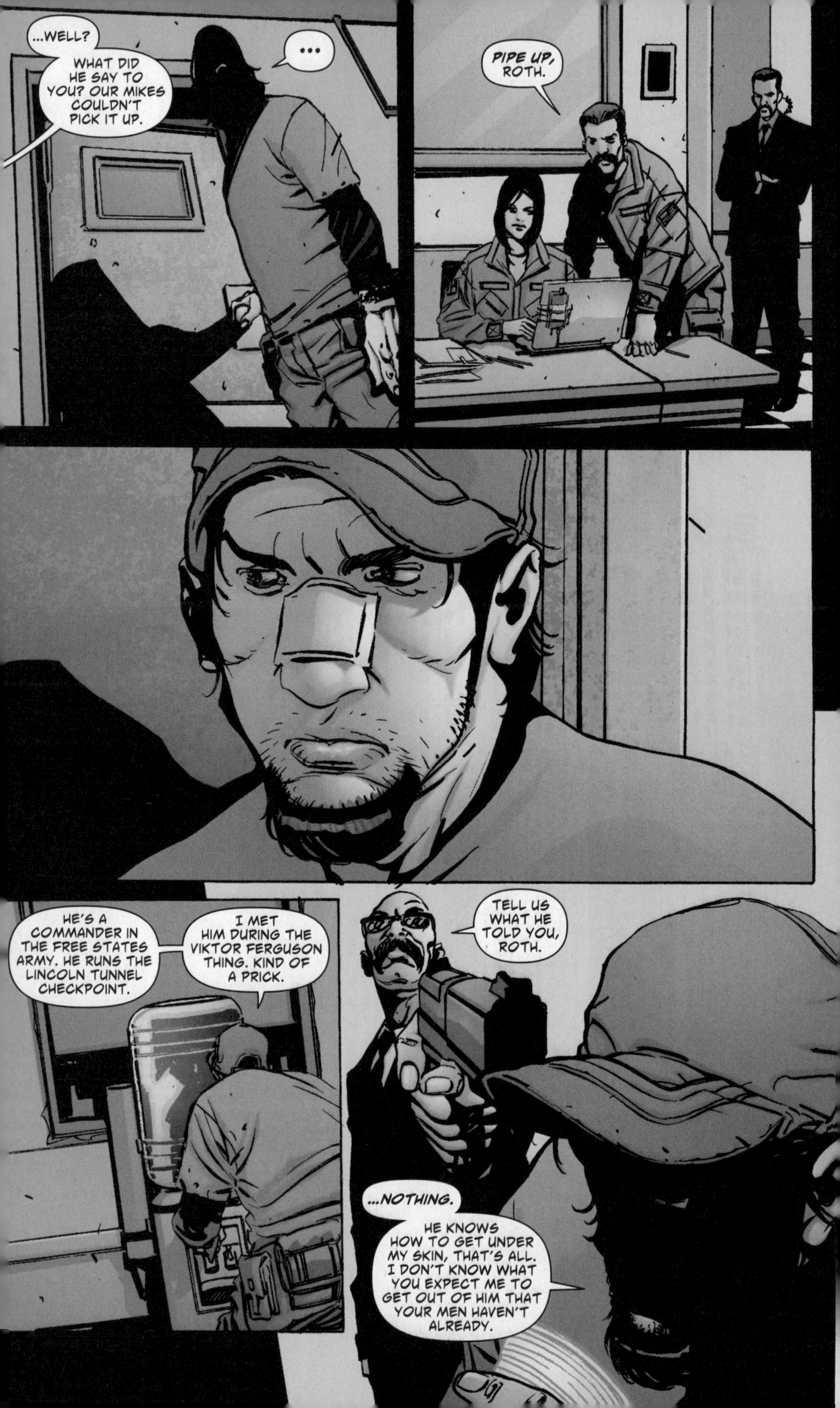
...WELL?
WHAT DID HE SAY TO YOU? OUR MIKES COULDN'T PICK IT UP.
...
PIPE UP, ROTH.
HE'S A COMMANDER IN THE FREE STATES ARMY. HE RUNS THE LINCOLN TUNNEL CHECKPOINT.
I MET HIM DURING THE VIKTOR FERGUSON THING. KIND OF A PRICK.
TELL US WHAT HE TOLD YOU, ROTH.
...NOTHING.
HE KNOWS HOW TO GET UNDER MY SKIN, THAT'S ALL. I DON'T KNOW WHAT YOU EXPECT ME TO GET OUT OF HIM THAT YOUR MEN HAVEN'T ALREADY.

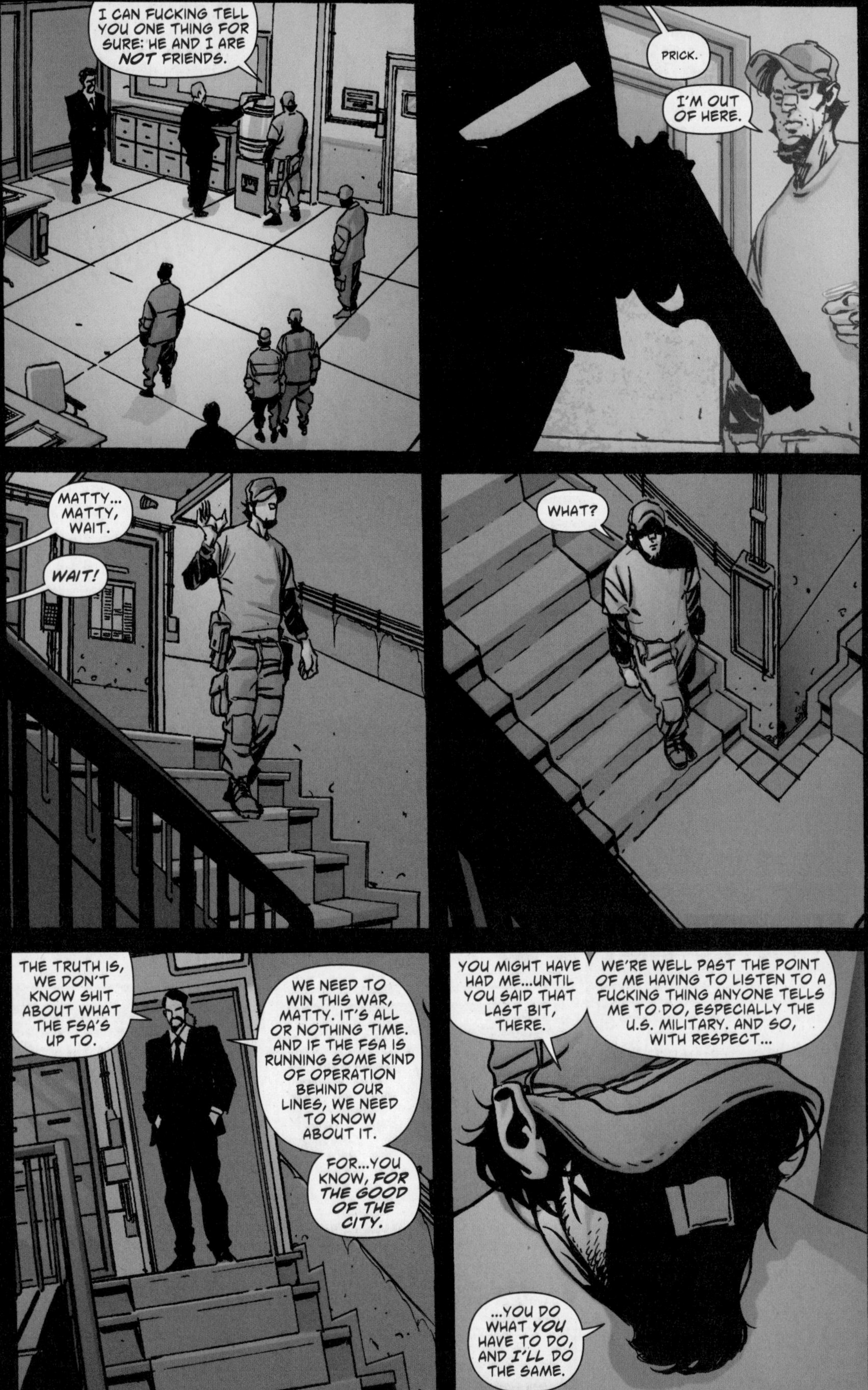
I CAN FUCKING TELL YOU ONE THING FOR SURE: HE AND I ARE NOT FRIENDS.
PRICK.
I'M OUT OF HERE.
MATTY... MATTY, WAIT.
WAIT!
WHAT?
THE TRUTH IS, WE DON'T KNOW SHIT ABOUT WHAT THE FSA'S UP TO.
WE NEED TO WIN THIS WAR, MATTY. IT'S ALL OR NOTHING TIME. AND IF THE FSA IS RUNNING SOME KIND OF OPERATION BEHIND OUR LINES, WE NEED TO KNOW ABOUT IT.
FOR...YOU KNOW, FOR THE GOOD OF THE CITY.
YOU MIGHT HAVE HAD ME...UNTIL YOU SAID THAT LAST BIT, THERE.
WE'RE WELL PAST THE POINT OF ME HAVING TO LISTEN TO A FUCKING THING ANYONE TELLS ME TO DO, ESPECIALLY THE U.S. MILITARY. AND SO, WITH RESPECT...
...YOU DO WHAT YOU HAVE TO DO, AND I'LL DO THE SAME.

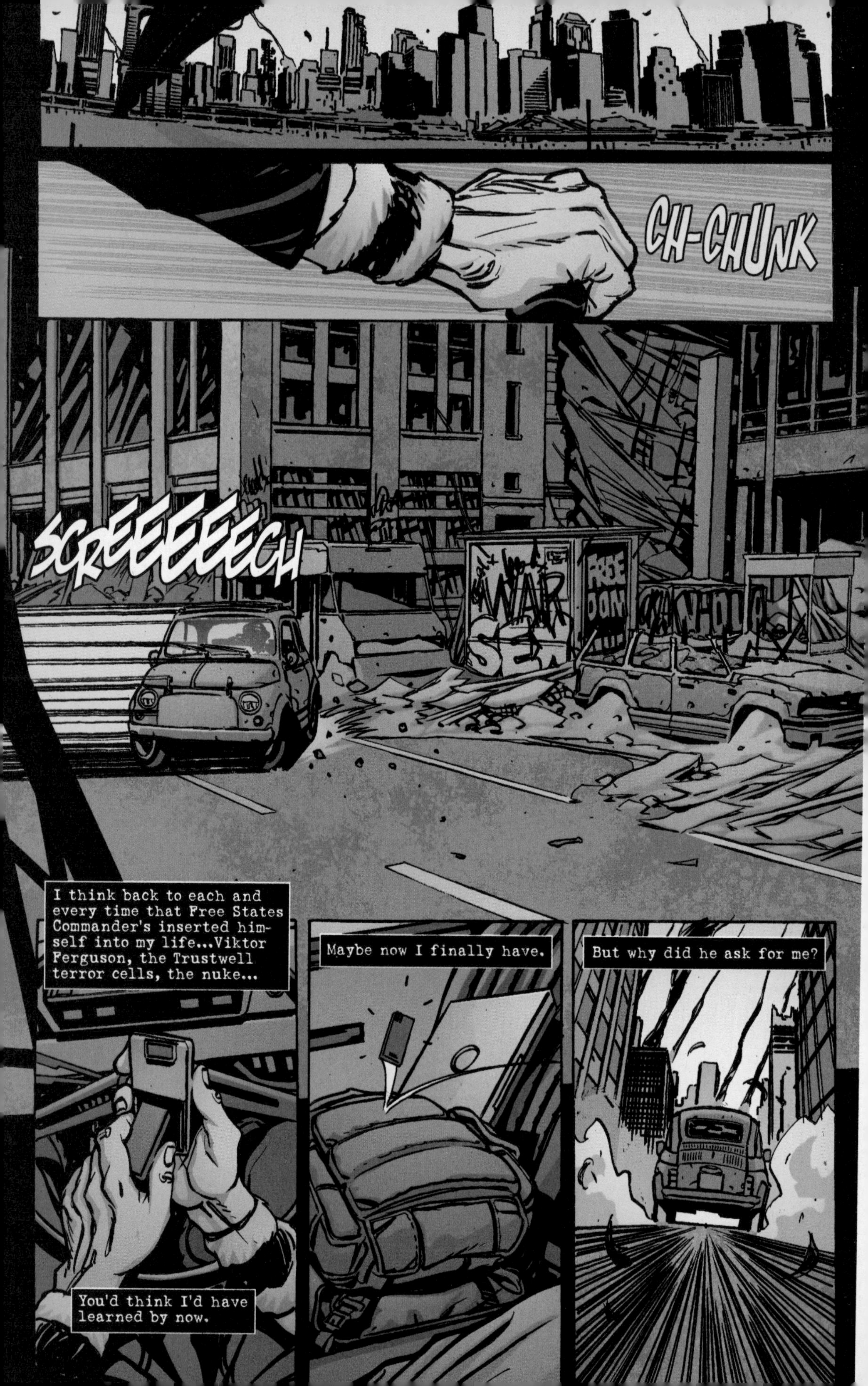
CH-CHUNK
SCREEEEEECH
WAR
FREE DOM
I think back to each and every time that Free States Commander's inserted himself into my life...Viktor Ferguson, the Trustwell terror cells, the nuke...
You'd think I'd have learned by now.
Maybe now I finally have.
But why did he ask for me?

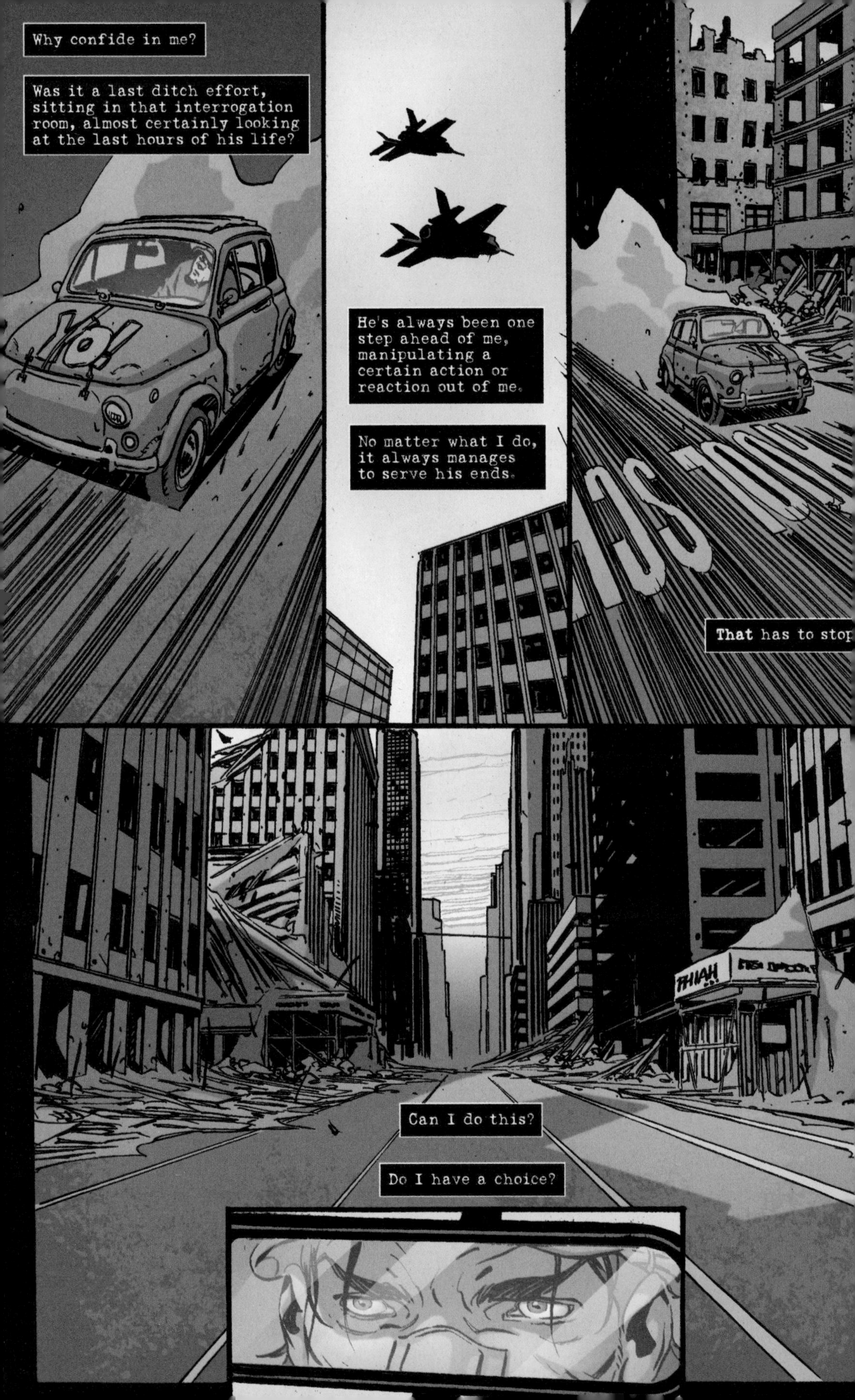
Why confide in me?
Was it a last ditch effort, sitting in that interrogation room, almost certainly looking at the last hours of his life?
Yo!
He's always been one step ahead of me, manipulating a certain action or reaction out of me.
No matter what I do, it always manages to serve his ends.
That has to stop
Can I do this?
Do I have a choice?

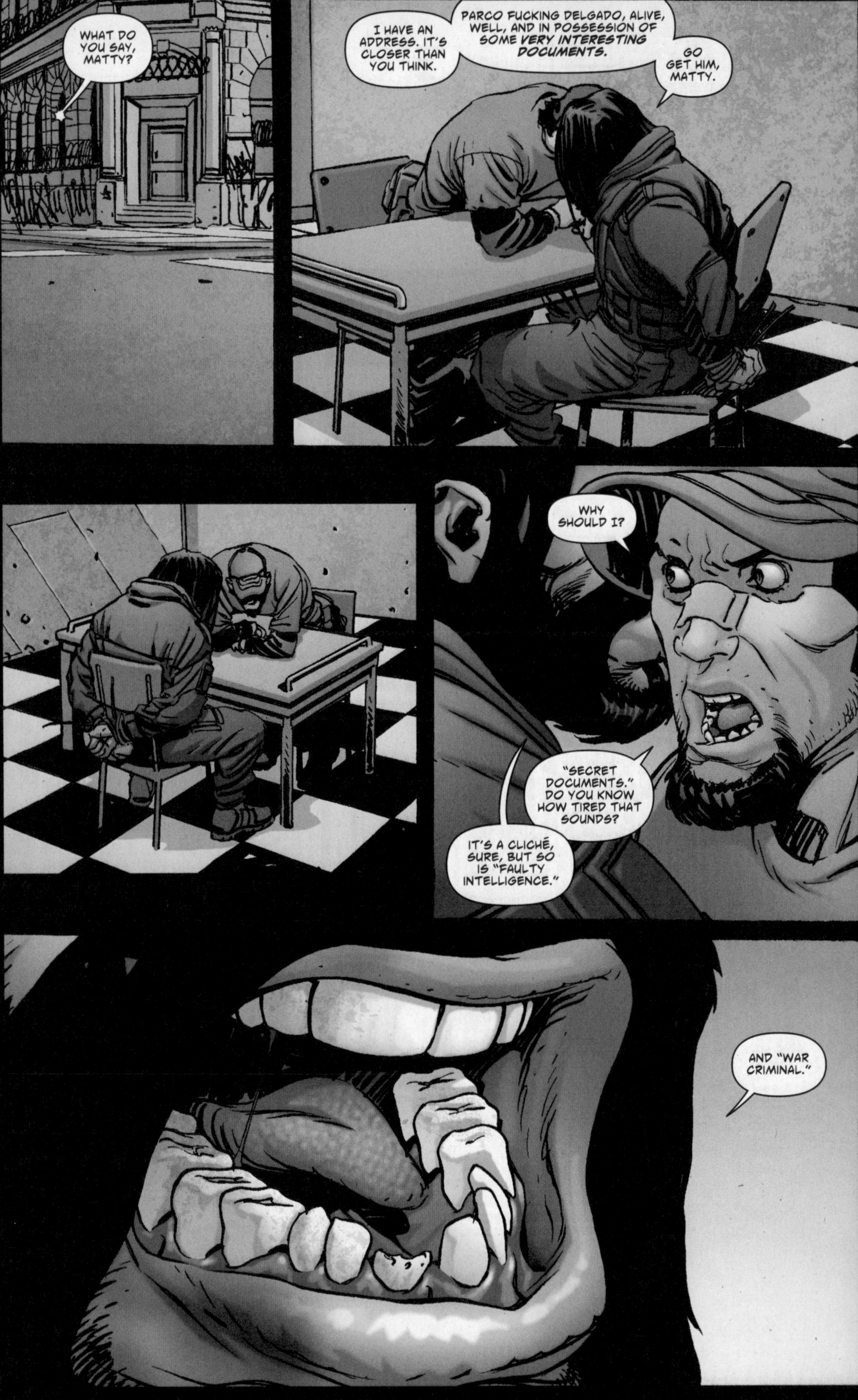
WHAT DO YOU SAY, MATTY?
I HAVE AN ADDRESS. IT'S CLOSER THAN YOU THINK.
PARCO FUCKING DELGADO, ALIVE, WELL, AND IN POSSESSION OF SOME VERY INTERESTING DOCUMENTS.
GO GET HIM, MATTY.
WHY SHOULD I?
"SECRET DOCUMENTS." DO YOU KNOW HOW TIRED THAT SOUNDS?
IT'S A CLICHÉ, SURE, BUT SO IS "FAULTY INTELLIGENCE."
AND "WAR CRIMINAL."

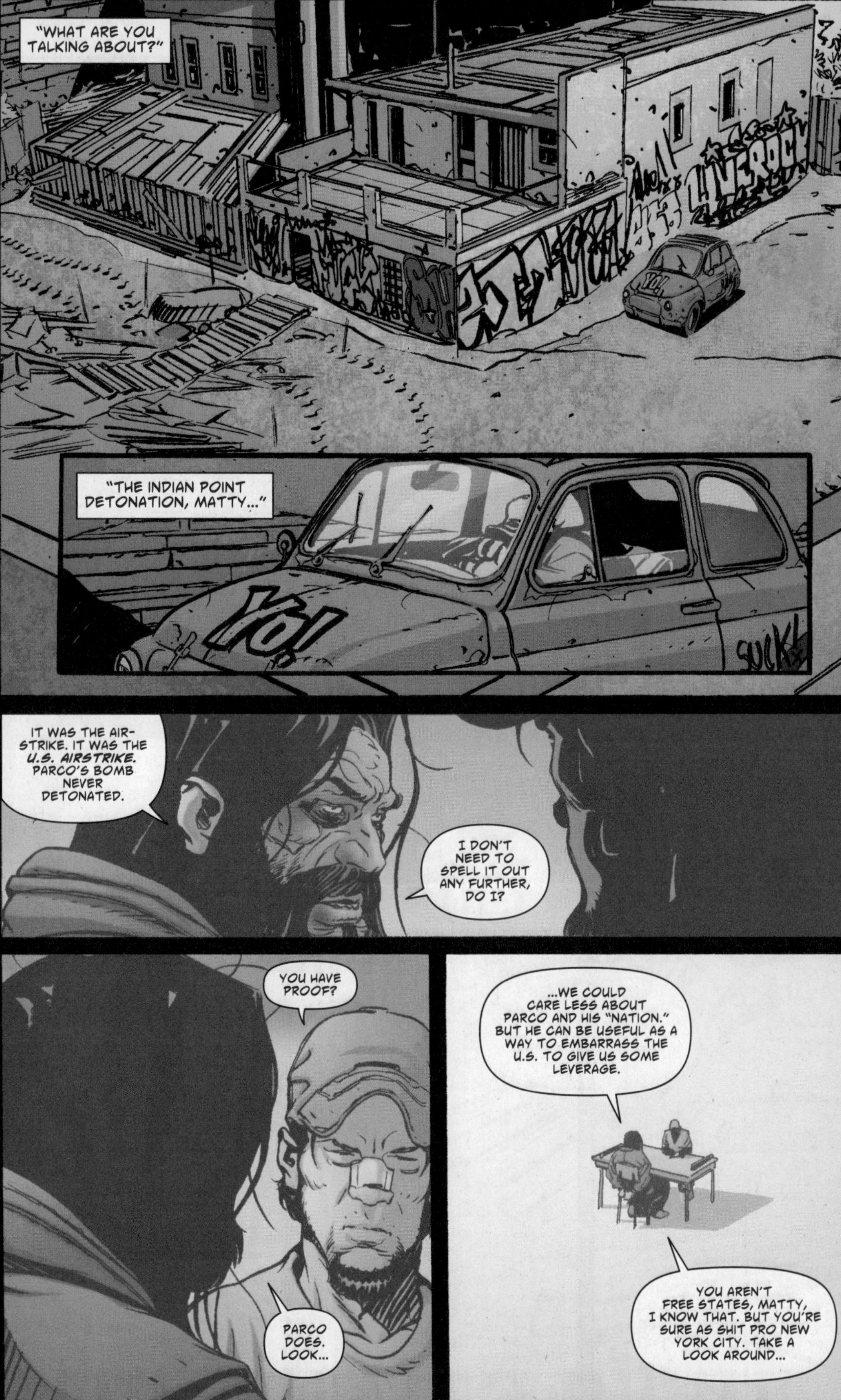
"WHAT ARE YOU TALKING ABOUT?"
YO!
"THE INDIAN POINT DETONATION, MATTY..."
YO!
SUCK!
IT WAS THE AIR-STRIKE. IT WAS THE U.S. AIRSTRIKE. PARCO'S BOMB NEVER DETONATED.
I DON'T NEED TO SPELL IT OUT ANY FURTHER, DO I?
YOU HAVE PROOF?
PARCO DOES. LOOK...
...WE COULD CARE LESS ABOUT PARCO AND HIS "NATION." BUT HE CAN BE USEFUL AS A WAY TO EMBARRASS THE U.S. TO GIVE US SOME LEVERAGE.
YOU AREN'T FREE STATES, MATTY, I KNOW THAT. BUT YOU'RE SURE AS SHIT PRO NEW YORK CITY. TAKE A LOOK AROUND...

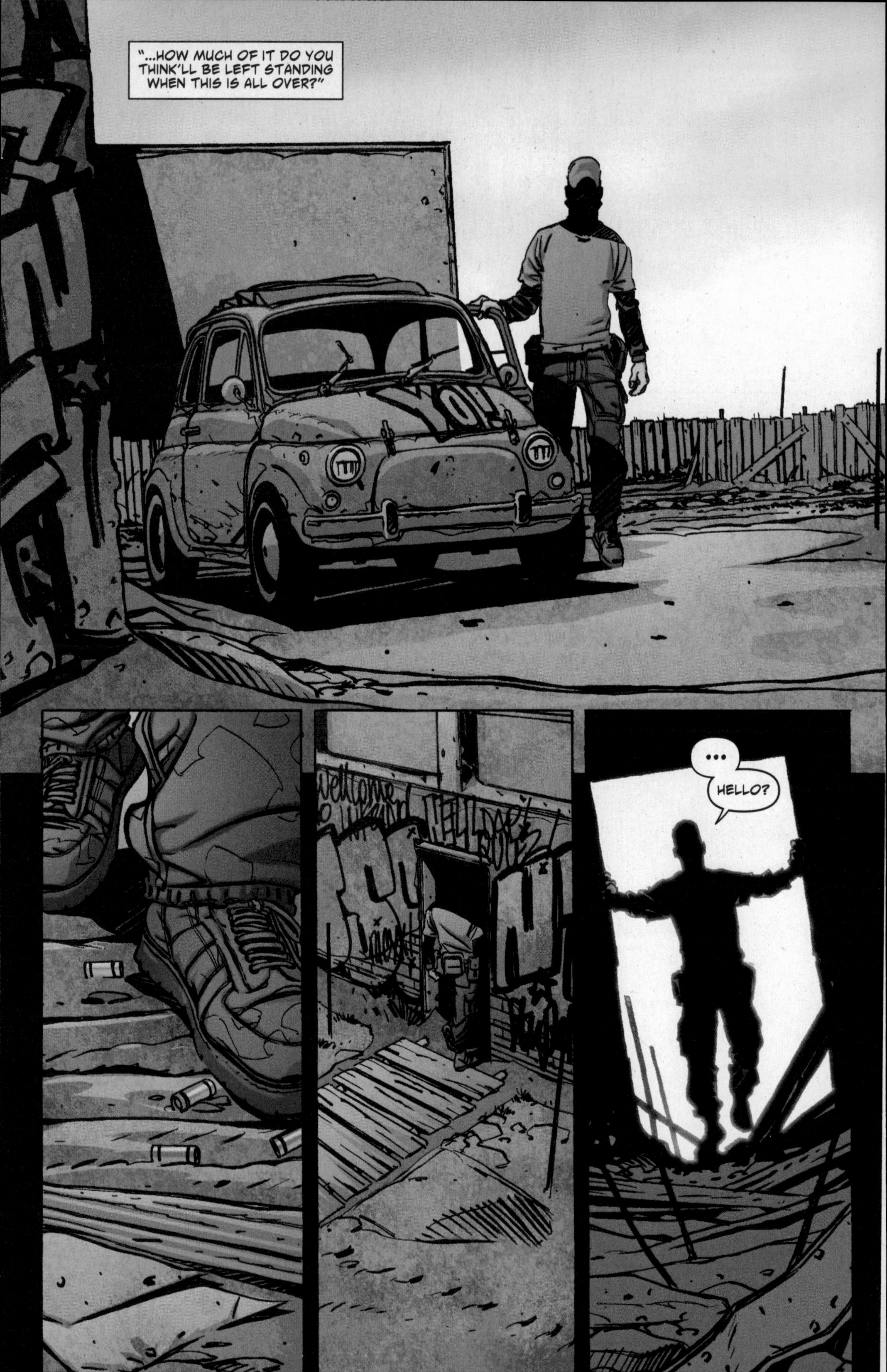
"...HOW MUCH OF IT DO YOU THINK'LL BE LEFT STANDING WHEN THIS IS ALL OVER?"
...
HELLO?

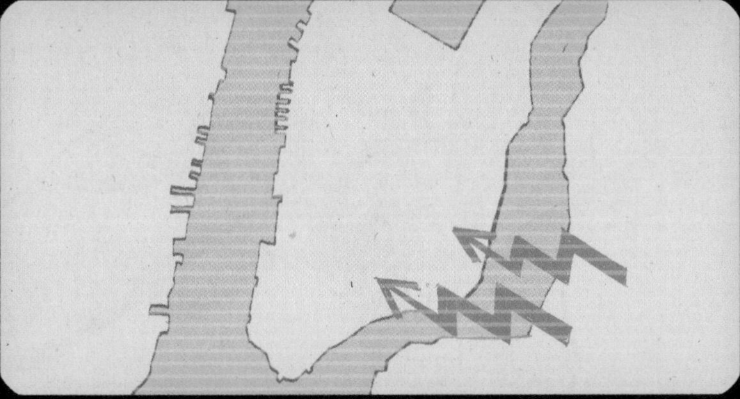

...day four of the Battle for Manhattan, as the massive column of American troops continues to pour into the island, its defenders still reeling from the air campaign, offering little to no resistance...

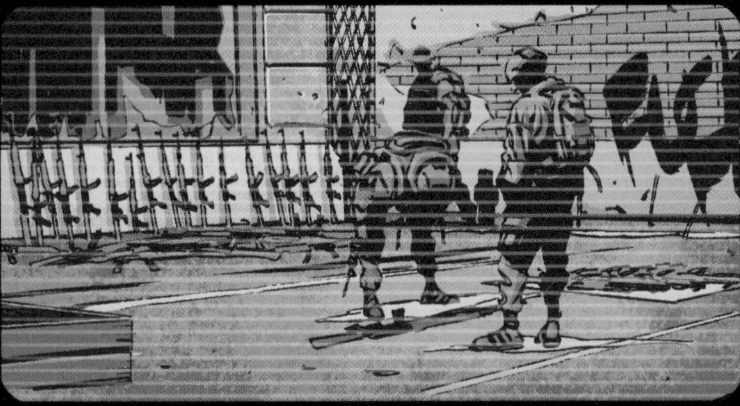

...massive arms caches discovered, foreign-manufactured automatic weapons and ammunition, serial numbers rerportedly filed off. For more speculation on possible countries of origin, we take you to...

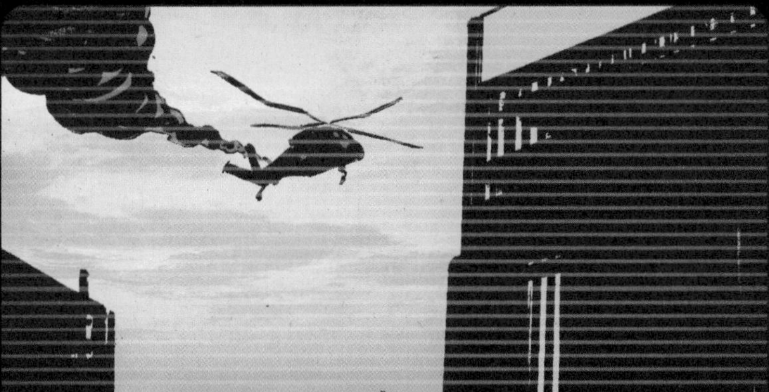

...not without risk, and pockets of insurgent activity must still be rooted out. The President, speaking from American Command aboard Air Force One, promised a swift end to this final battle, and a thorough one...

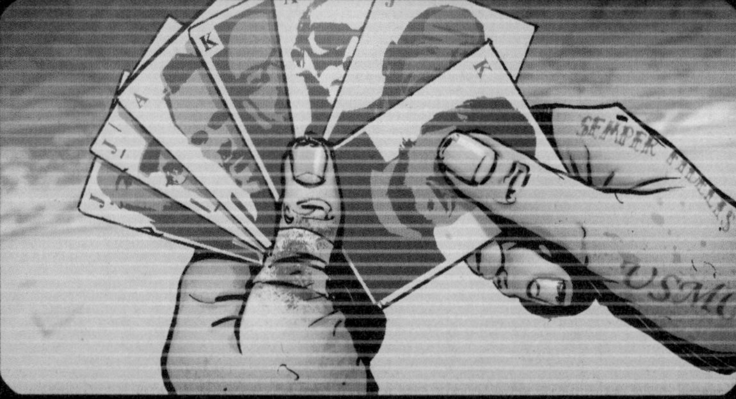
SEMPER
USMC

...sort of barbarity we have come to associate...

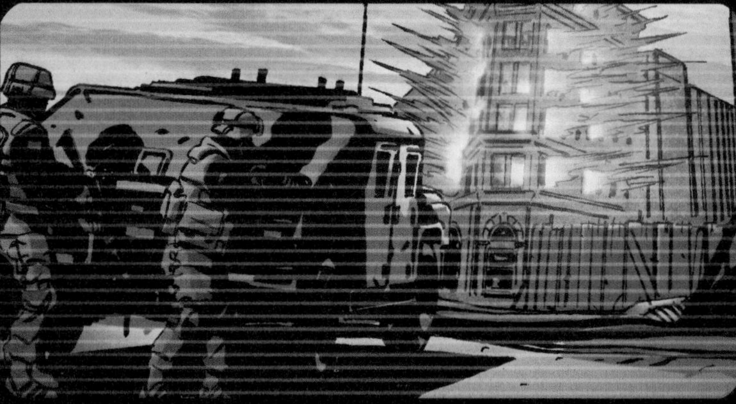

"...this is an operation based on pragmatism rather than emotion," the commander was quoted as saying. "My soldiers are not here to be tourists, and for the duration of this operation, Manhattan is not an American city but a field of battle..."

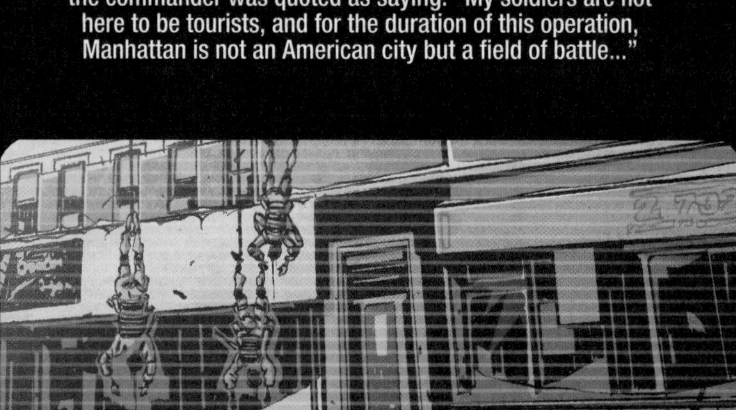
C'MON OLIVER

...almost unprecedented war, pitting a country against itself on an epic scale. It's impossible to predict how history will judge this conflict, but however it does, it will be tinged with a profound sadness that I suspect we've only begun to realize...

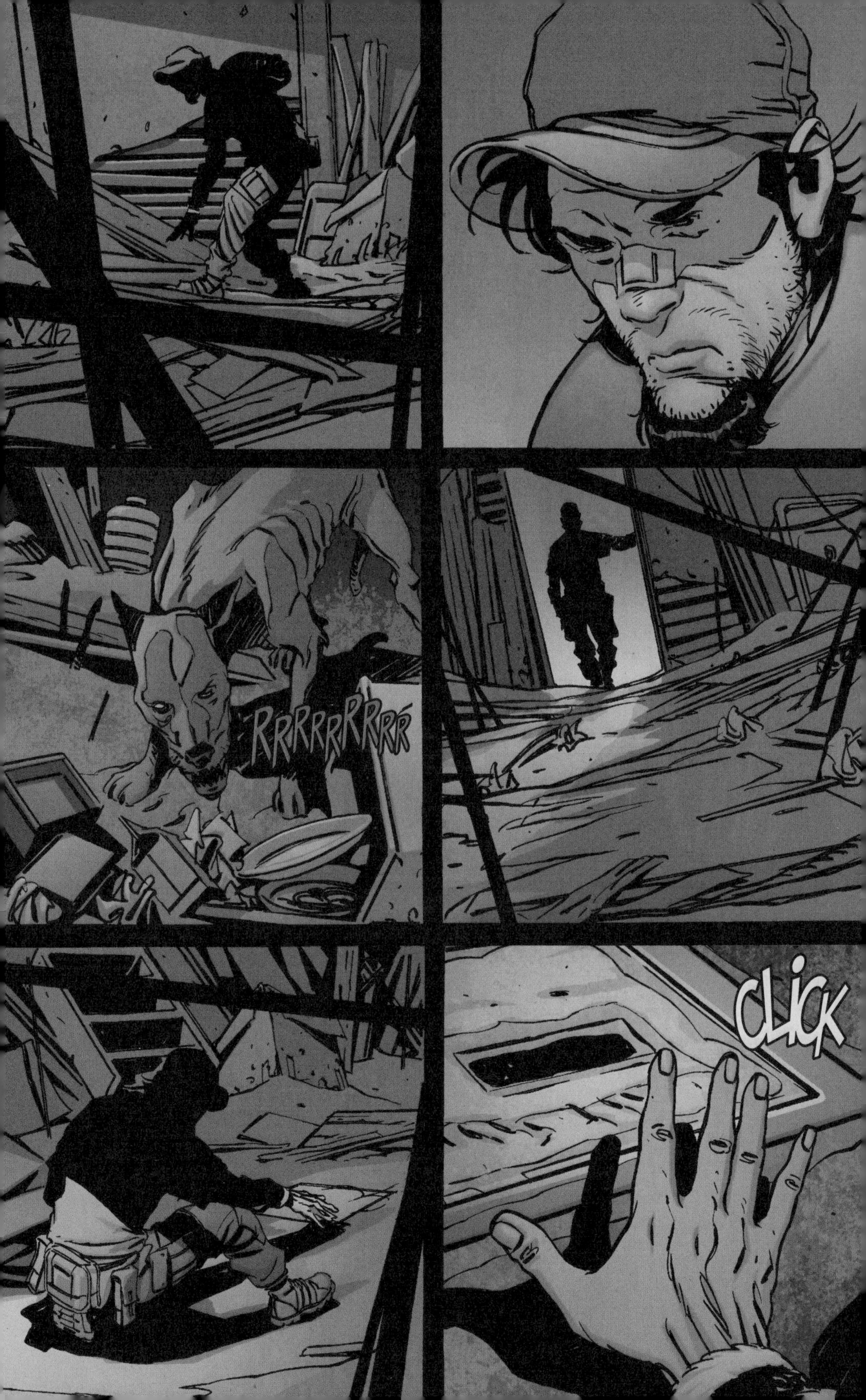
RRRRRRRRR
CLICK

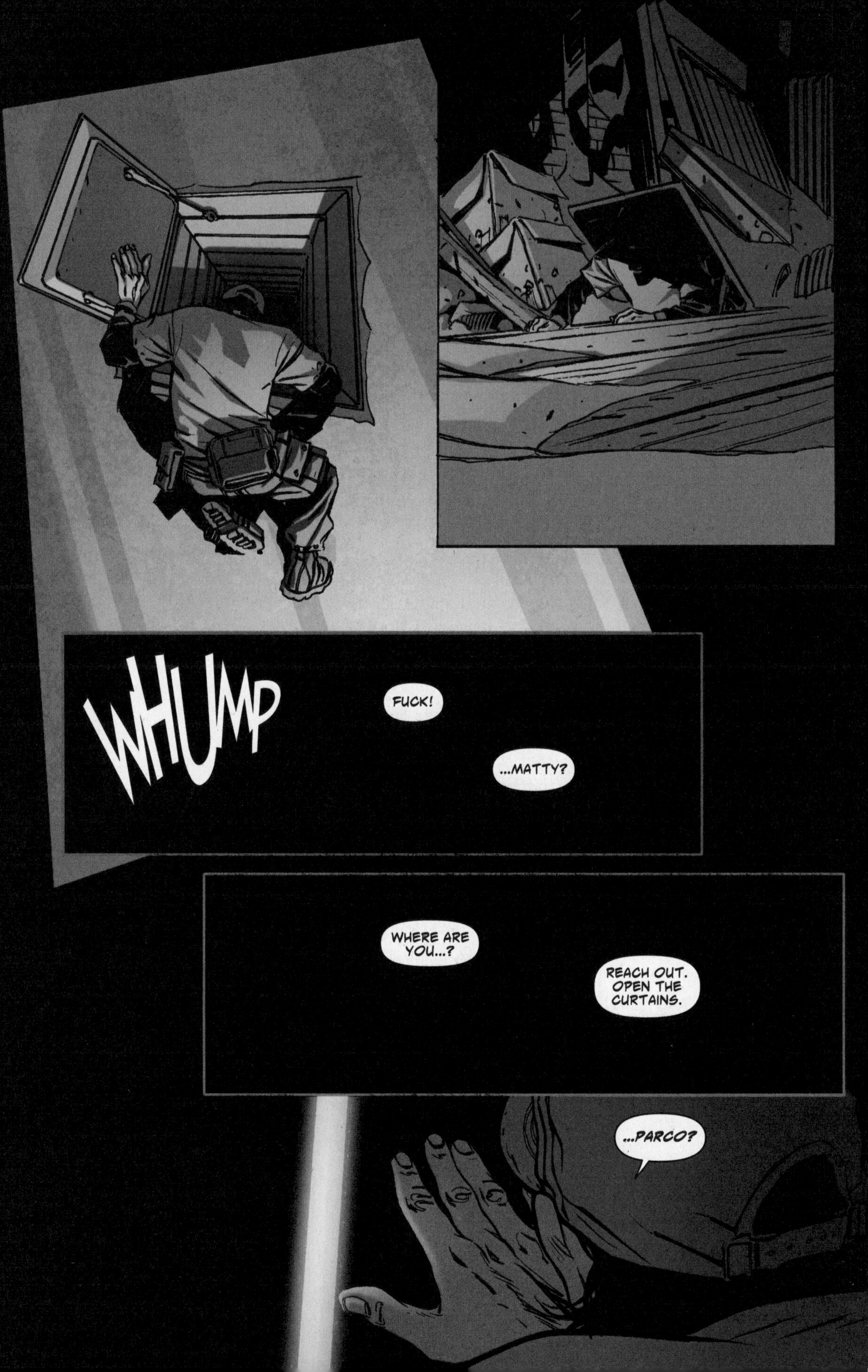
WHUMP
FUCK!
...MATTY?
WHERE ARE YOU...?
REACH OUT. OPEN THE CURTAINS.
...PARCO?

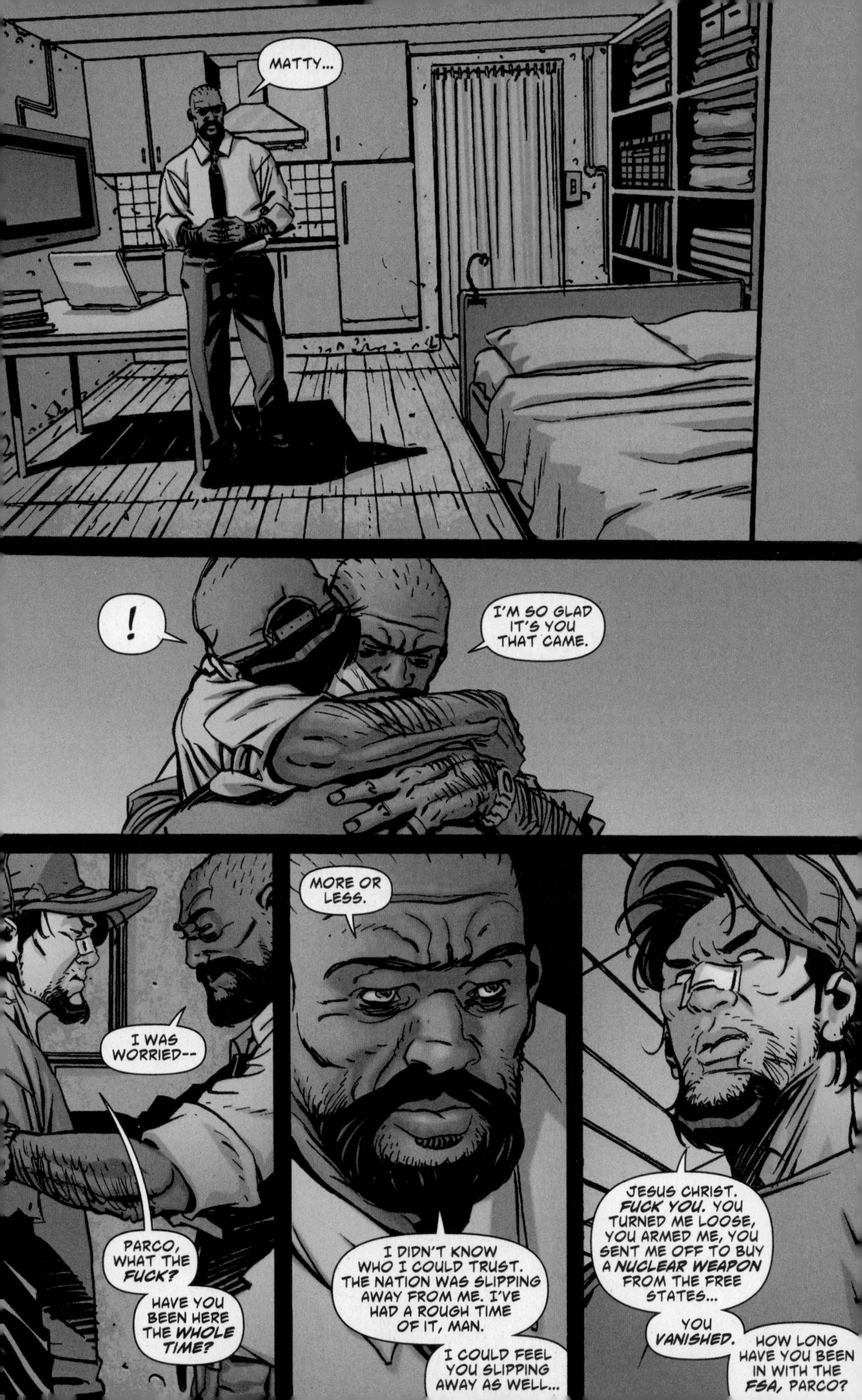
MATTY...
!
I'M SO GLAD IT'S YOU THAT CAME.
I WAS WORRIED--
PARCO, WHAT THE FUCK?
HAVE YOU BEEN HERE THE WHOLE TIME?
MORE OR LESS.
I DIDN'T KNOW WHO I COULD TRUST. THE NATION WAS SLIPPING AWAY FROM ME. I'VE HAD A ROUGH TIME OF IT, MAN.
I COULD FEEL YOU SLIPPING AWAY AS WELL...
JESUS CHRIST. FUCK YOU. YOU TURNED ME LOOSE, YOU ARMED ME, YOU SENT ME OFF TO BUY A NUCLEAR WEAPON FROM THE FREE STATES...
YOU VANISHED.
HOW LONG HAVE YOU BEEN IN WITH THE FSA, PARCO?

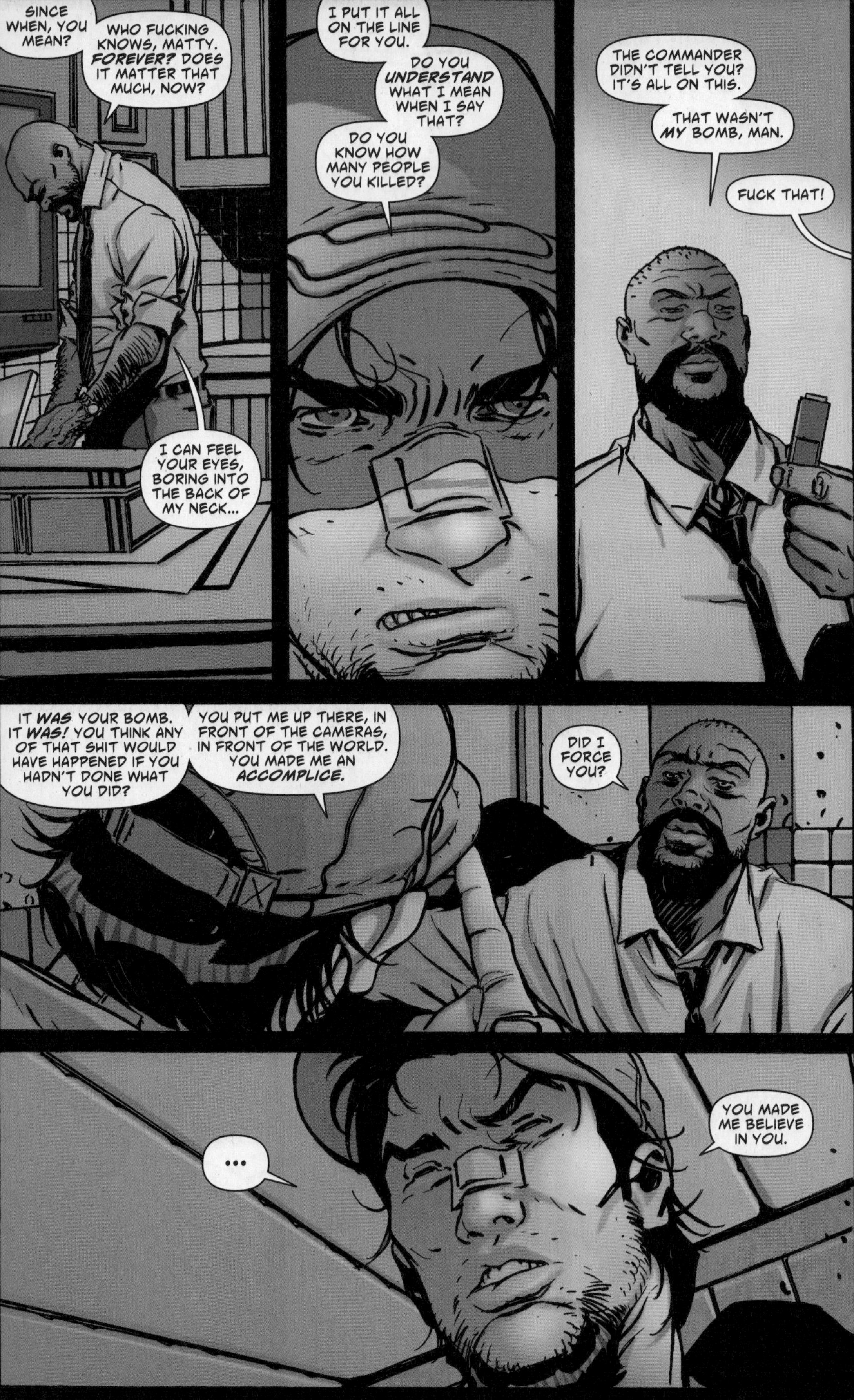
SINCE WHEN, YOU MEAN?
WHO FUCKING KNOWS, MATTY. FOREVER? DOES IT MATTER THAT MUCH, NOW?
I CAN FEEL YOUR EYES, BORING INTO THE BACK OF MY NECK...
I PUT IT ALL ON THE LINE FOR YOU.
DO YOU UNDERSTAND WHAT I MEAN WHEN I SAY THAT?
DO YOU KNOW HOW MANY PEOPLE YOU KILLED?
THE COMMANDER DIDN'T TELL YOU? IT'S ALL ON THIS.
THAT WASN'T MY BOMB, MAN.
FUCK THAT!
IT WAS YOUR BOMB. IT WAS! YOU THINK ANY OF THAT SHIT WOULD HAVE HAPPENED IF YOU HADN'T DONE WHAT YOU DID?
YOU PUT ME UP THERE, IN FRONT OF THE CAMERAS, IN FRONT OF THE WORLD. YOU MADE ME AN ACCOMPLICE.
DID I FORCE YOU?
...
YOU MADE ME BELIEVE IN YOU.

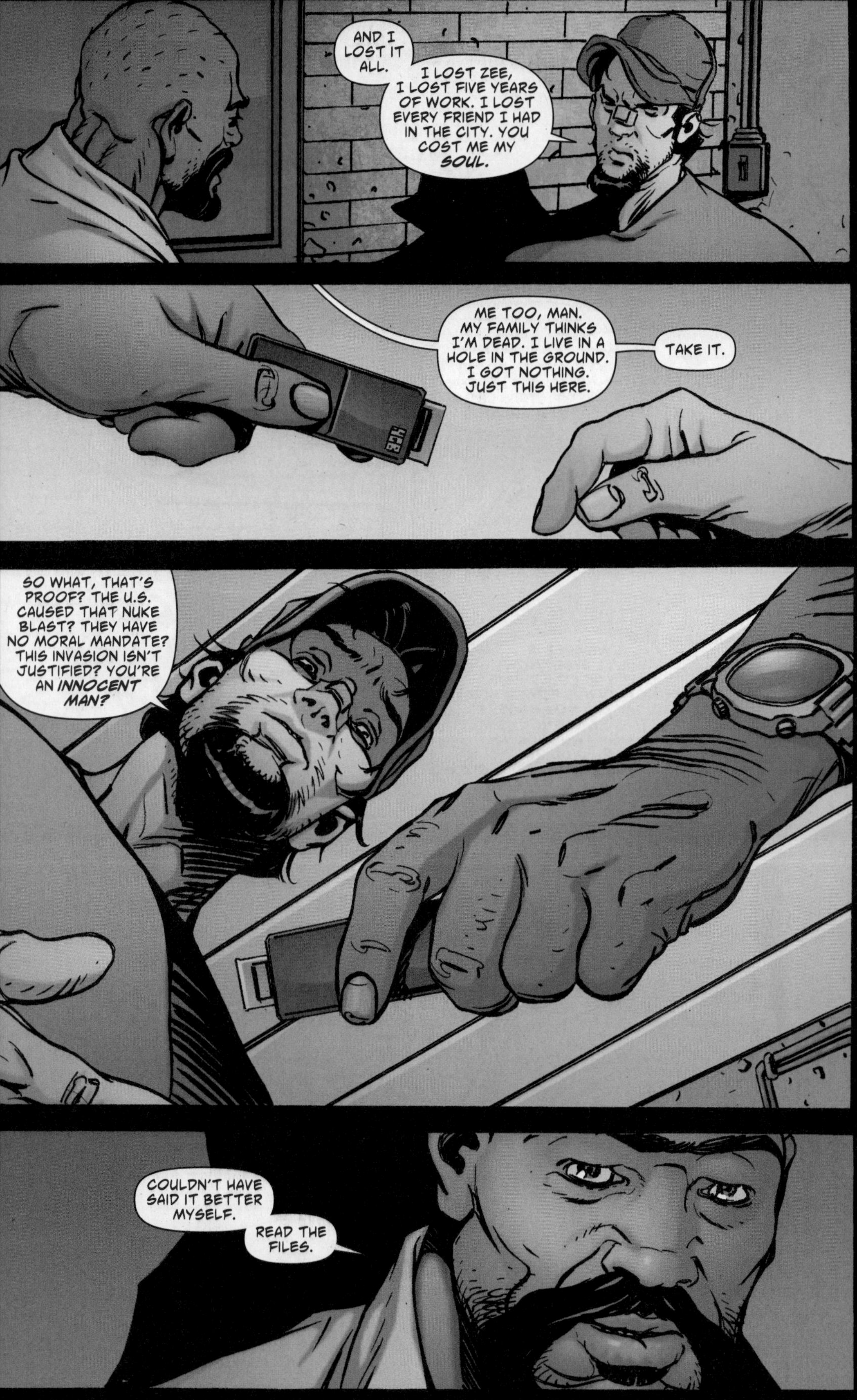
AND I LOST IT ALL.
I LOST ZEE, I LOST FIVE YEARS OF WORK. I LOST EVERY FRIEND I HAD IN THE CITY. YOU COST ME MY SOUL.
ME TOO, MAN. MY FAMILY THINKS I'M DEAD. I LIVE IN A HOLE IN THE GROUND. I GOT NOTHING. JUST THIS HERE.
TAKE IT.
SO WHAT, THAT'S PROOF? THE U.S. CAUSED THAT NUKE BLAST? THEY HAVE NO MORAL MANDATE? THIS INVASION ISN'T JUSTIFIED? YOU'RE AN INNOCENT MAN?
COULDN'T HAVE SAID IT BETTER MYSELF.
READ THE FILES.

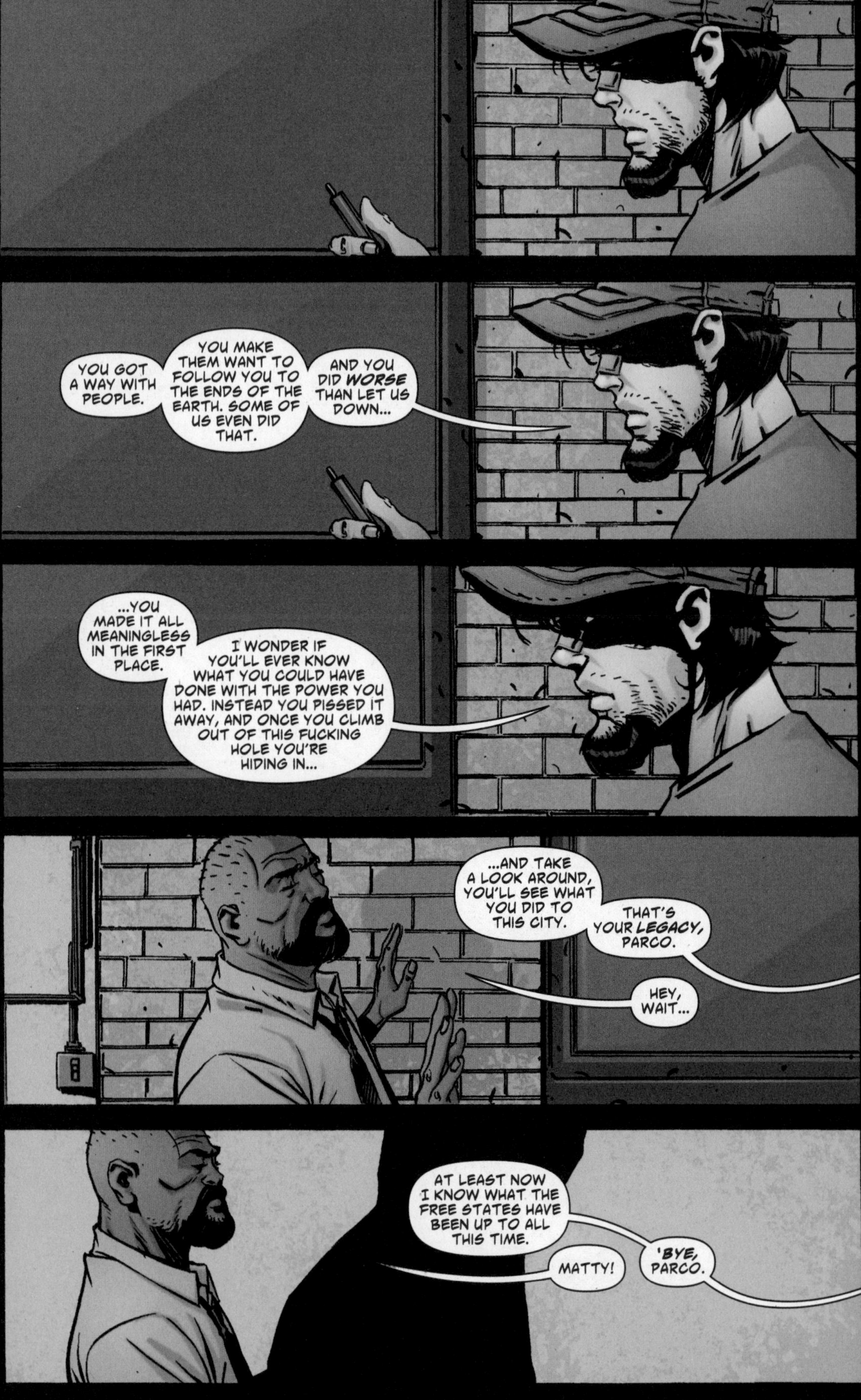
YOU GOT A WAY WITH PEOPLE.
YOU MAKE THEM WANT TO FOLLOW YOU TO THE ENDS OF THE EARTH. SOME OF US EVEN DID THAT.
AND YOU DID *WORSE* THAN LET US DOWN...
...YOU MADE IT ALL MEANINGLESS IN THE FIRST PLACE.
I WONDER IF YOU'LL EVER KNOW WHAT YOU COULD HAVE DONE WITH THE POWER YOU HAD. INSTEAD YOU PISSED IT AWAY, AND ONCE YOU CLIMB OUT OF THIS FUCKING HOLE YOU'RE HIDING IN...
...AND TAKE A LOOK AROUND, YOU'LL SEE WHAT YOU DID TO THIS CITY.
THAT'S YOUR *LEGACY*, PARCO.
HEY, WAIT...
AT LEAST NOW I KNOW WHAT THE FREE STATES HAVE BEEN UP TO ALL THIS TIME.
'*BYE*, PARCO.
MATTY!

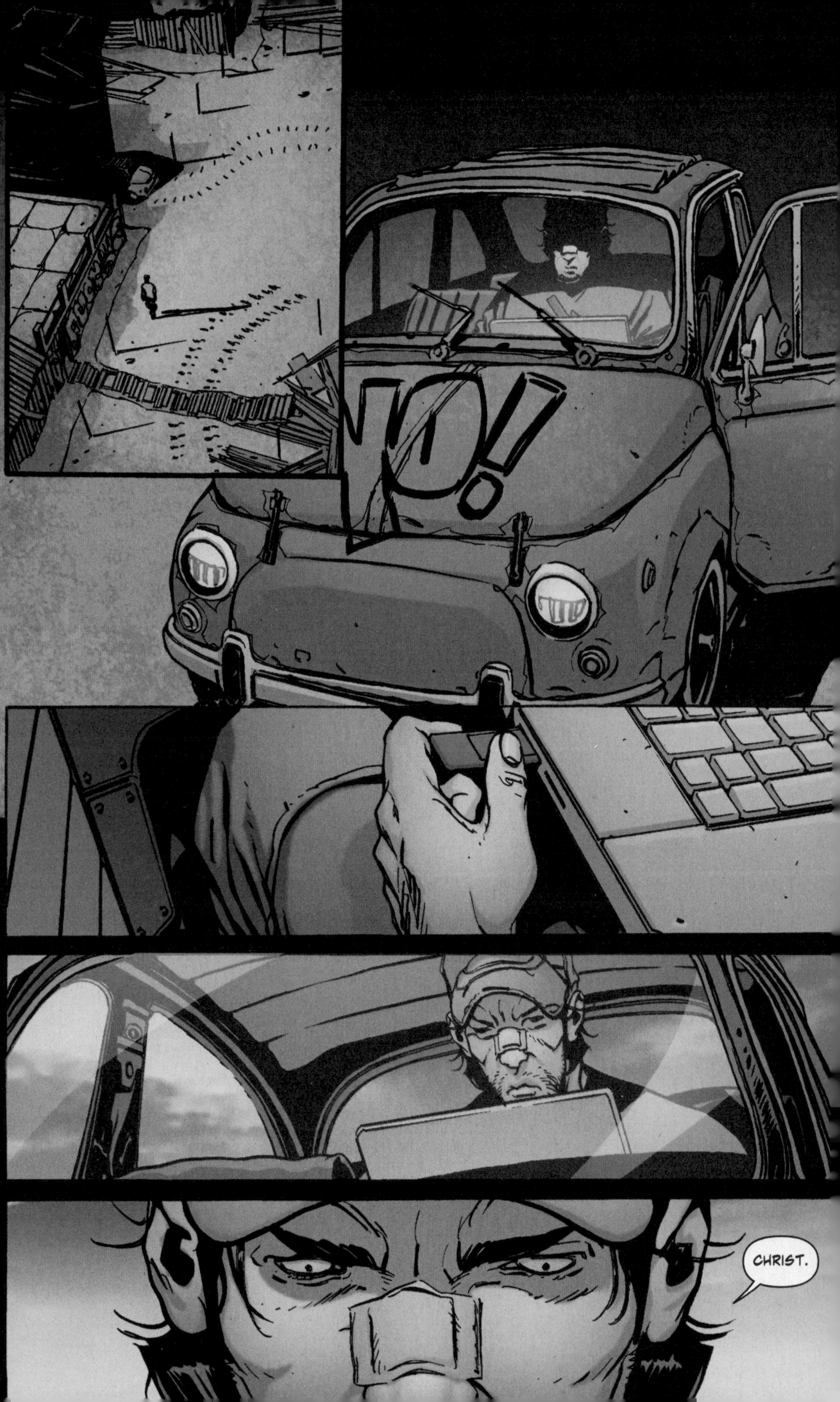
NO!
CHRIST.

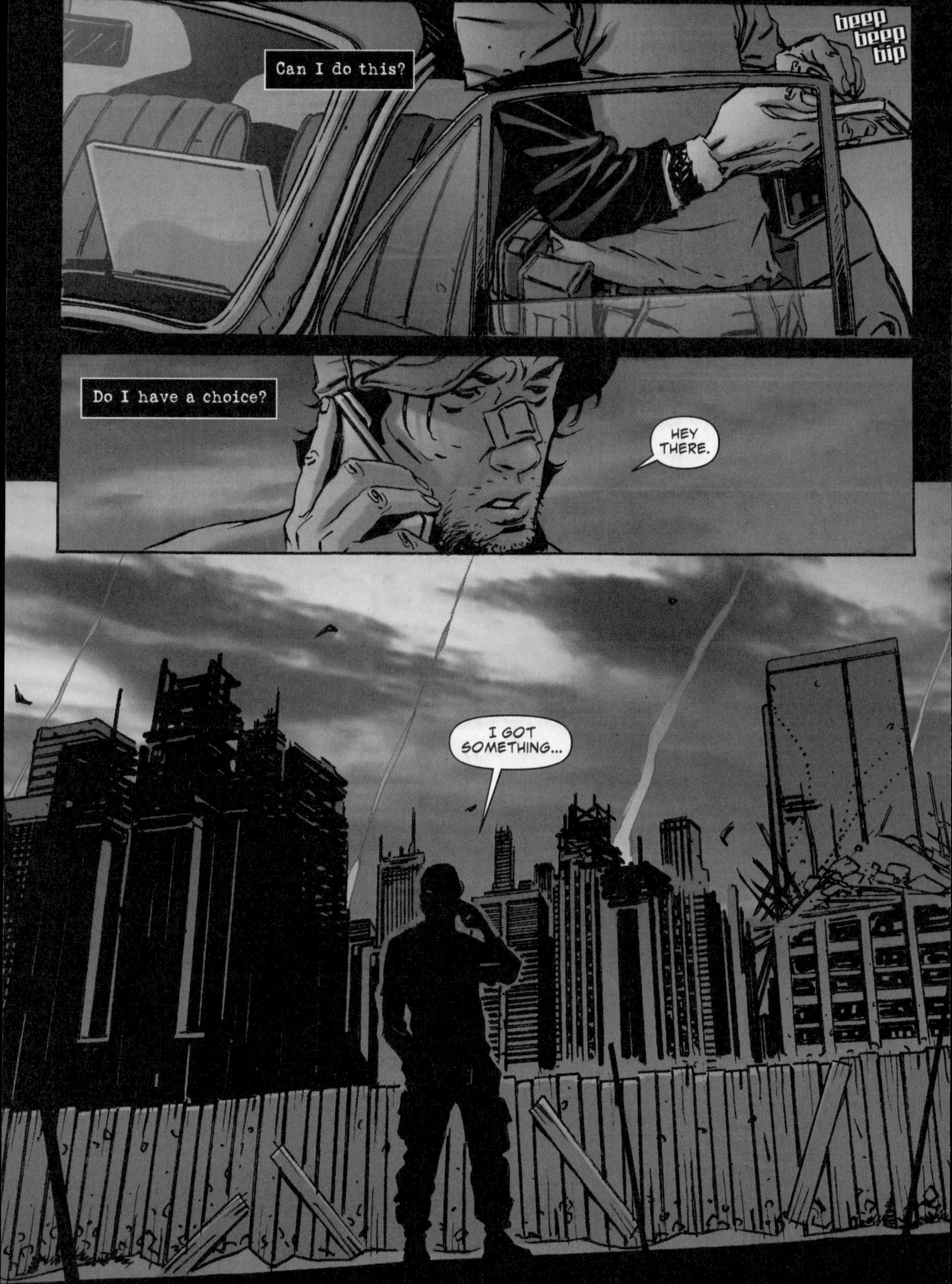
beep beep bip
Can I do this?
Do I have a choice?
HEY THERE.
I GOT SOMETHING...

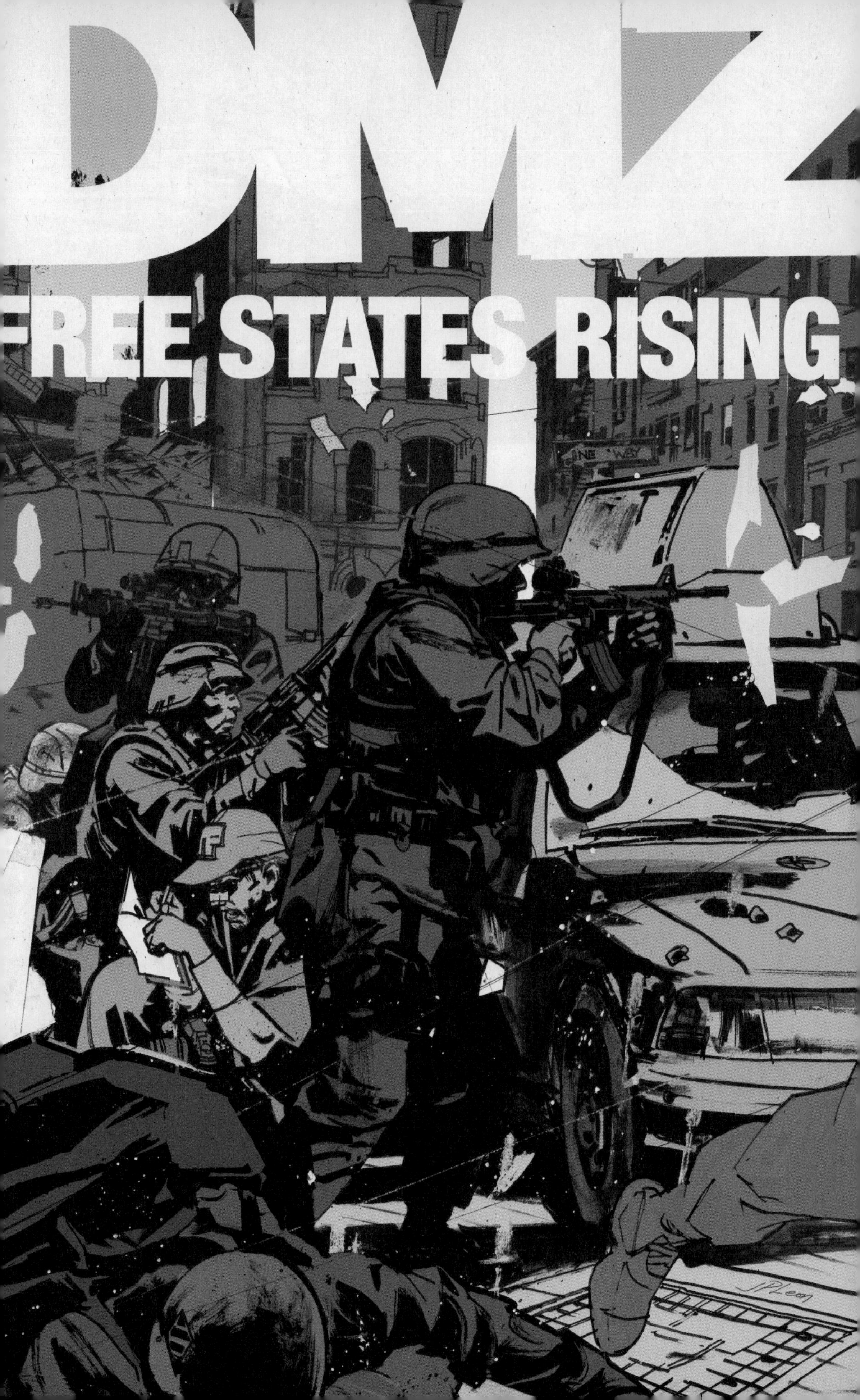
DMZ
FREE STATES RISING

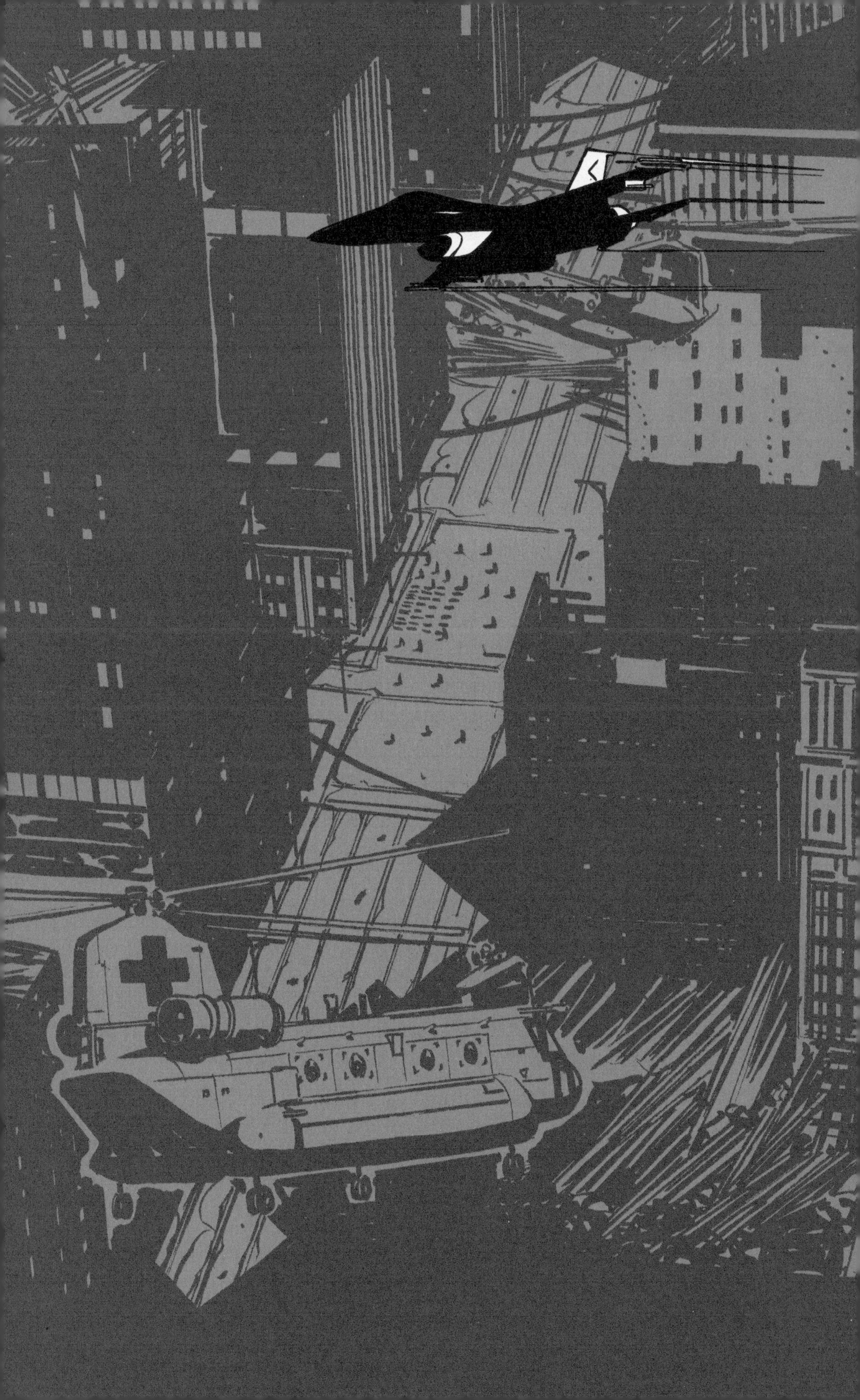

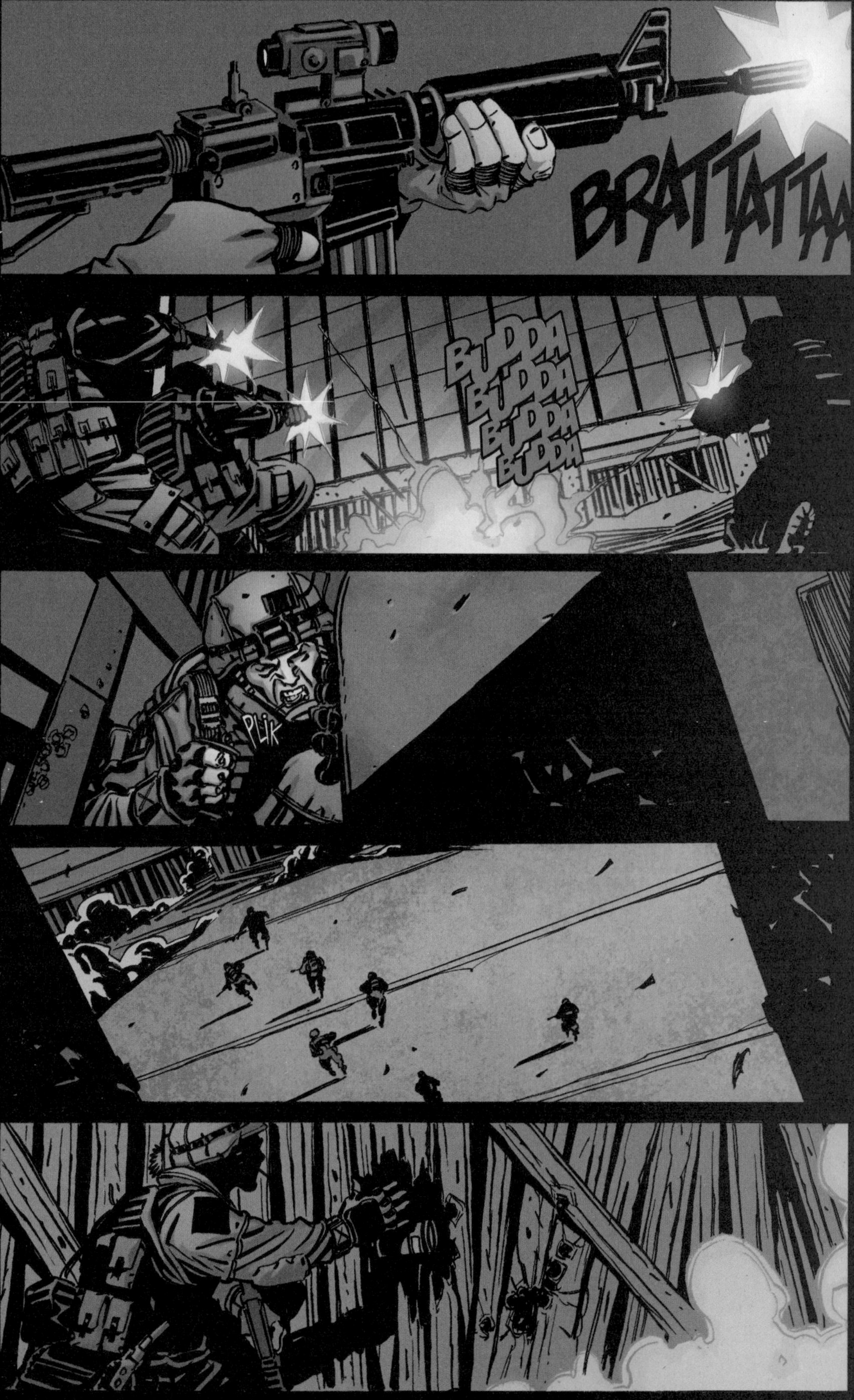
BRATTATTAA
BUDDA BUDDA BUDDA BUDDA BUDDA
PLIK

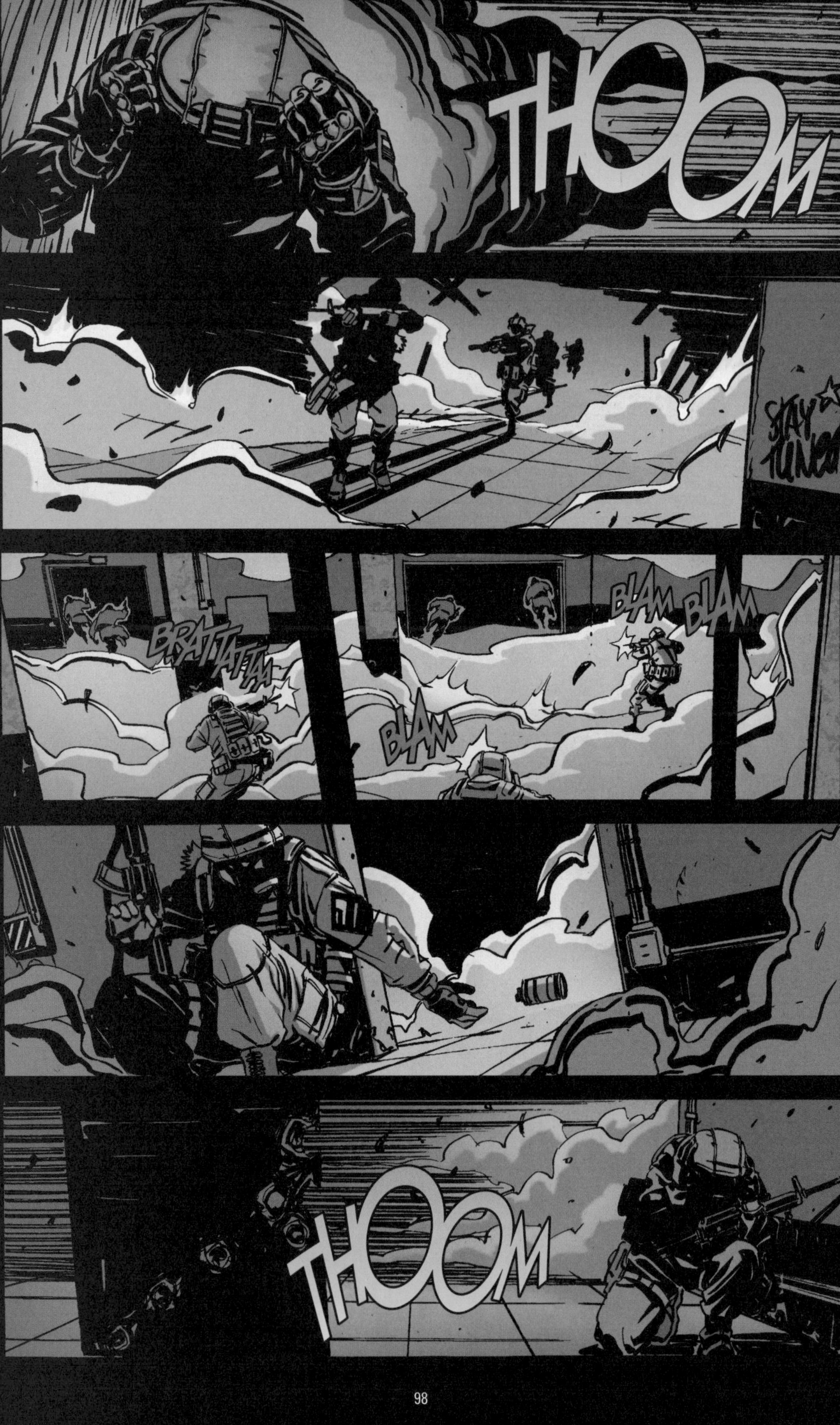
THOOM
STAY
BRATTATTAA
BLAM BLAM
BLAM
THOOM

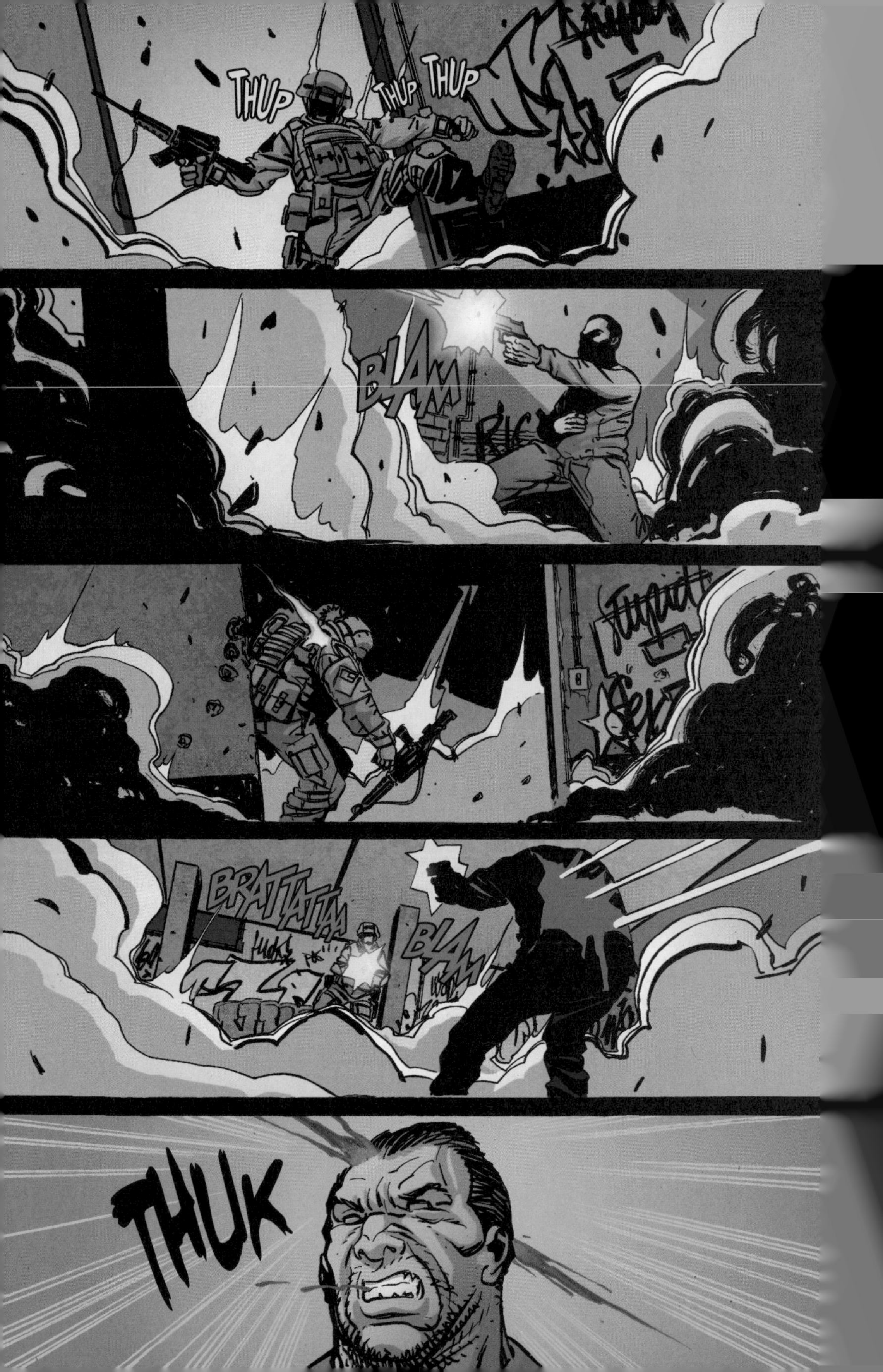
THUP
THUP THUP
BLAM
BRATTATTAA
BLAM
THUK

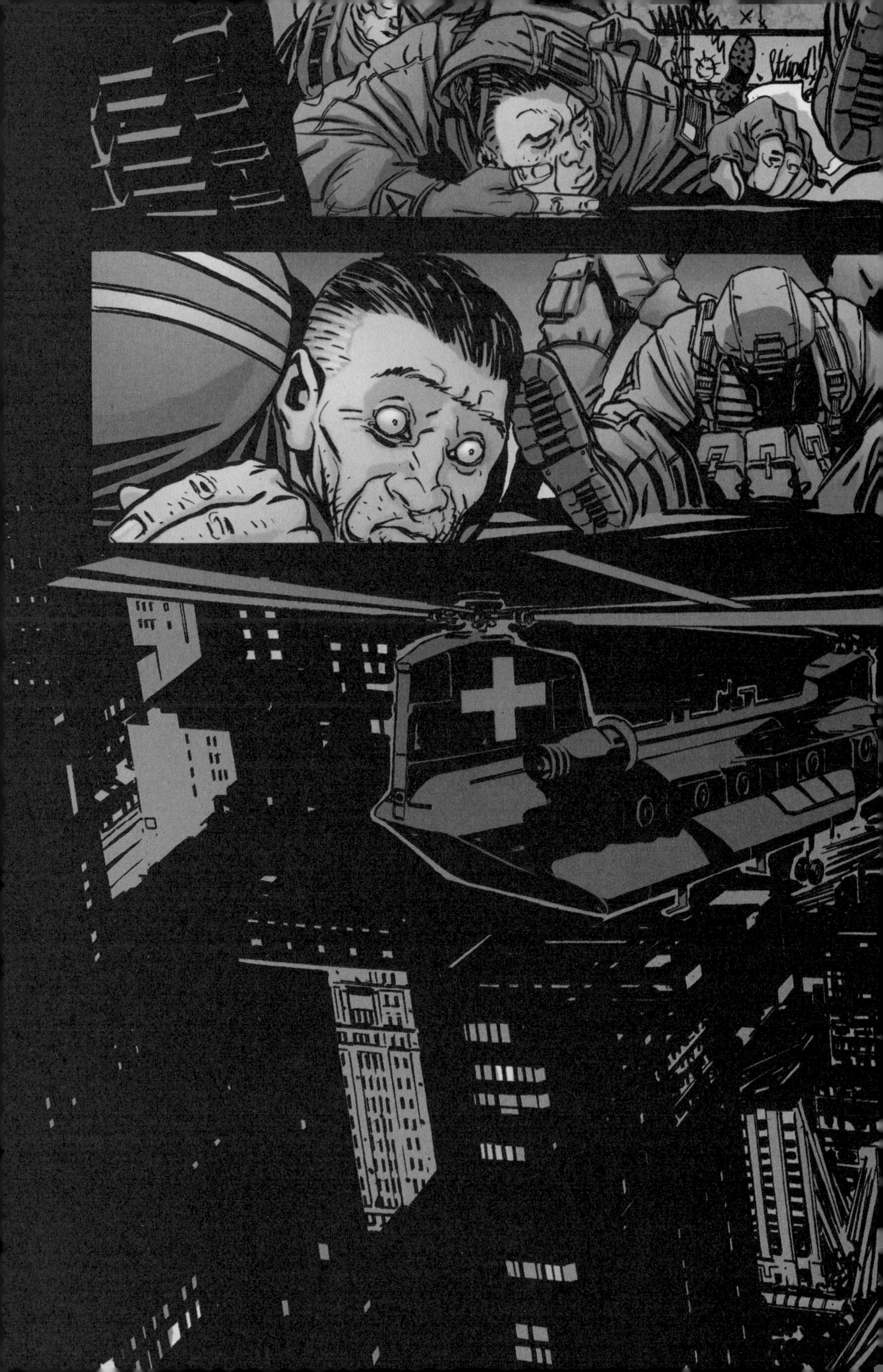

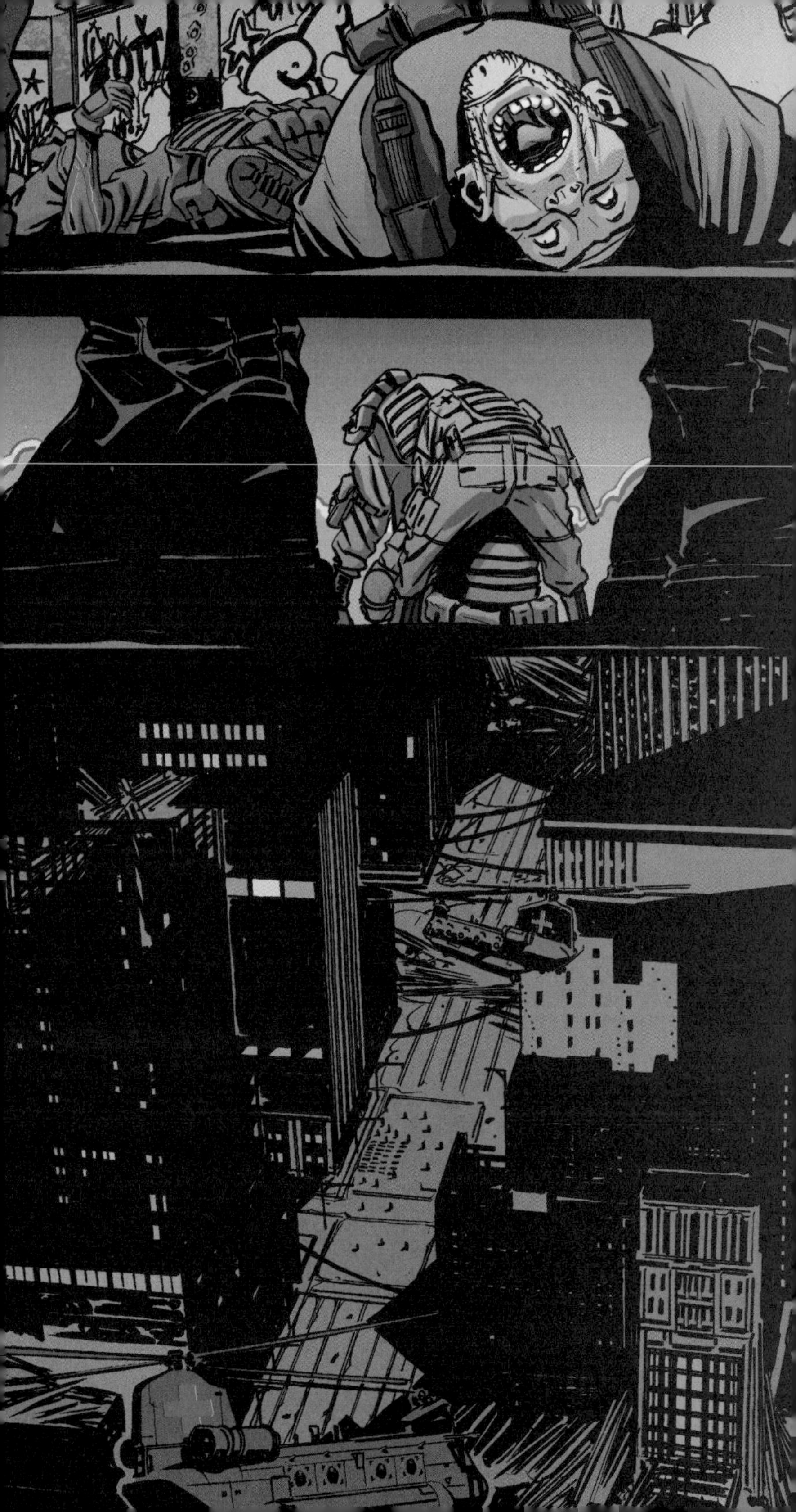

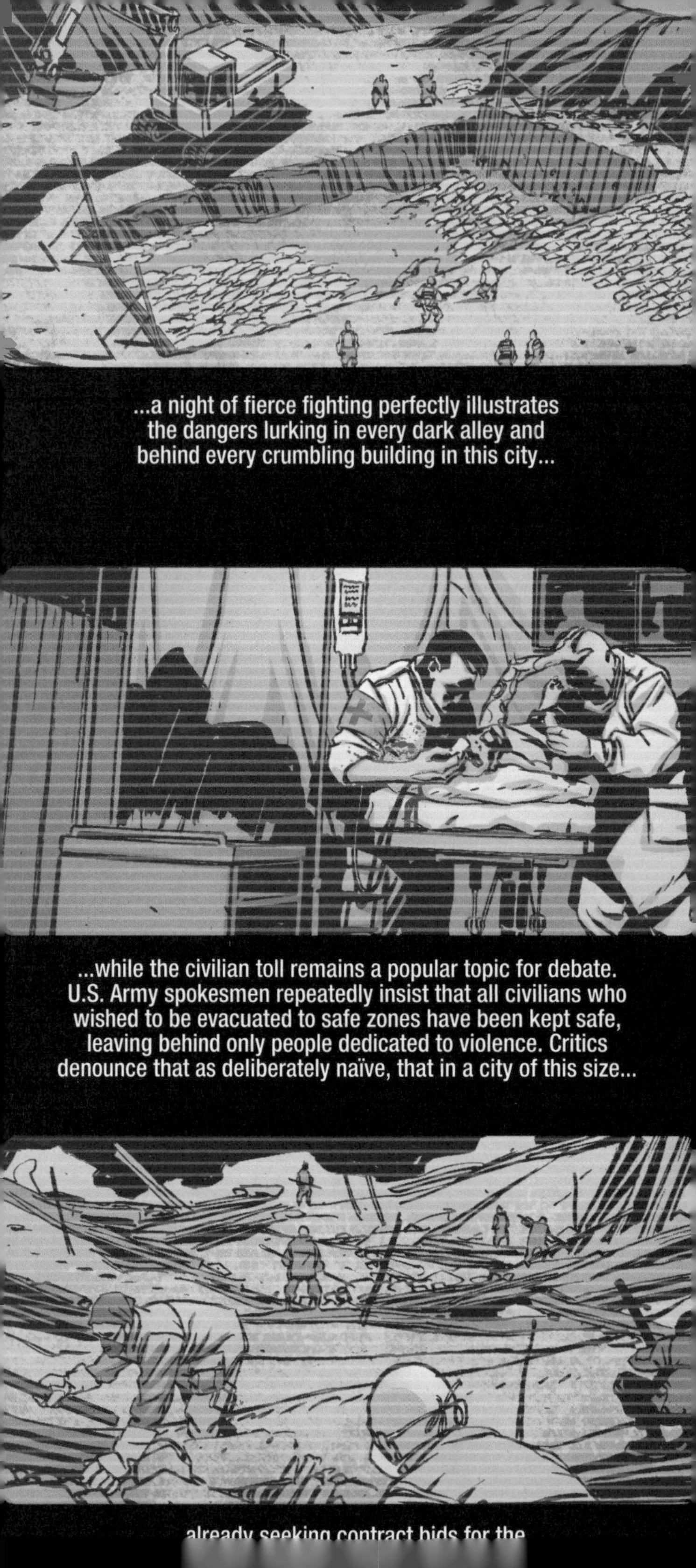
...a night of fierce fighting perfectly illustrates the dangers lurking in every dark alley and behind every crumbling building in this city...
...while the civilian toll remains a popular topic for debate. U.S. Army spokesmen repeatedly insist that all civilians who wished to be evacuated to safe zones have been kept safe, leaving behind only people dedicated to violence. Critics denounce that as deliberately naïve, that in a city of this size...
already seeking contract bids for the

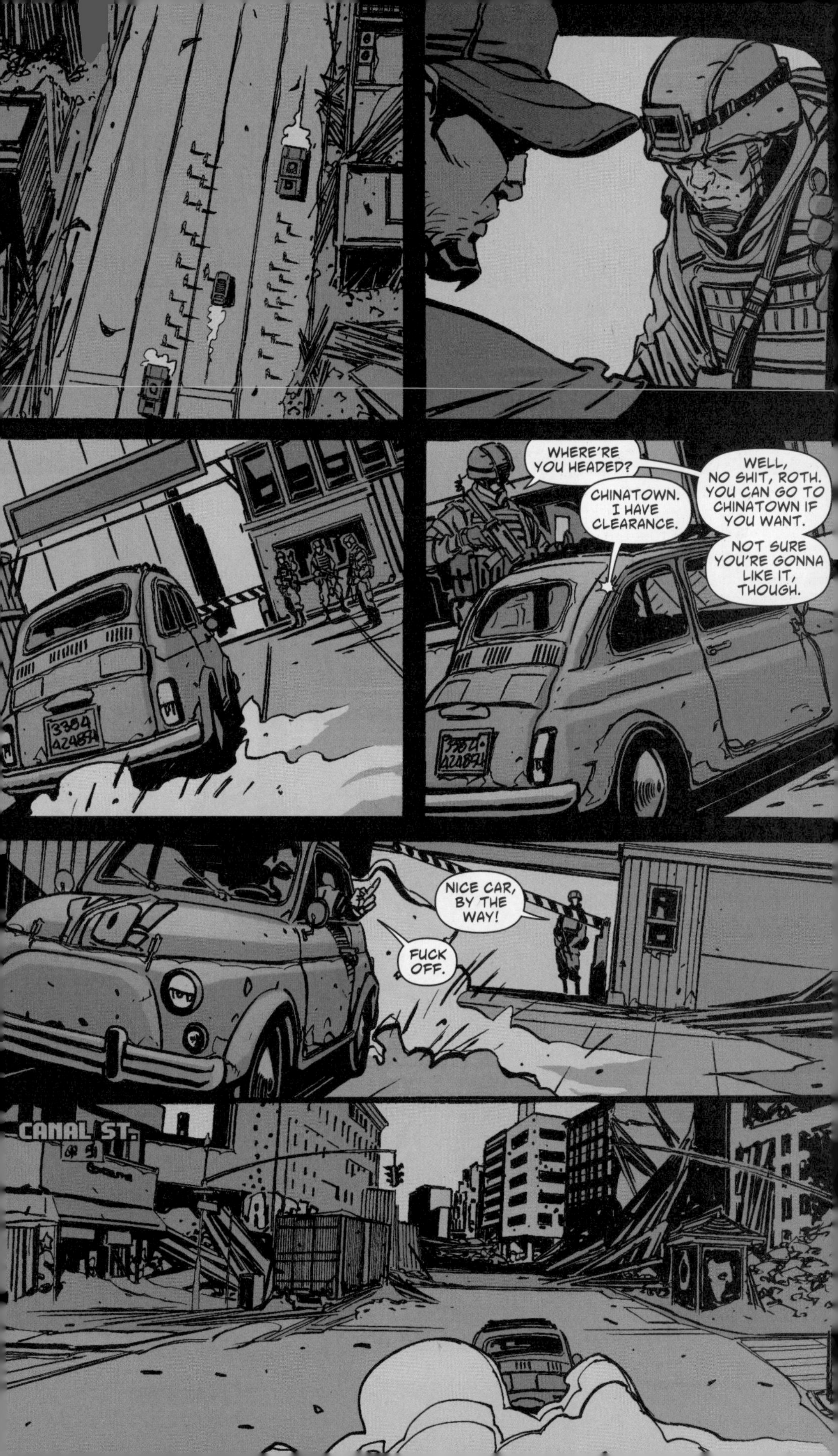
WHERE'RE YOU HEADED?
CHINATOWN. I HAVE CLEARANCE.
WELL, NO SHIT, ROTH. YOU CAN GO TO CHINATOWN IF YOU WANT.
NOT SURE YOU'RE GONNA LIKE IT, THOUGH.
YO!
NICE CAR, BY THE WAY!
FUCK OFF.
CANAL ST.

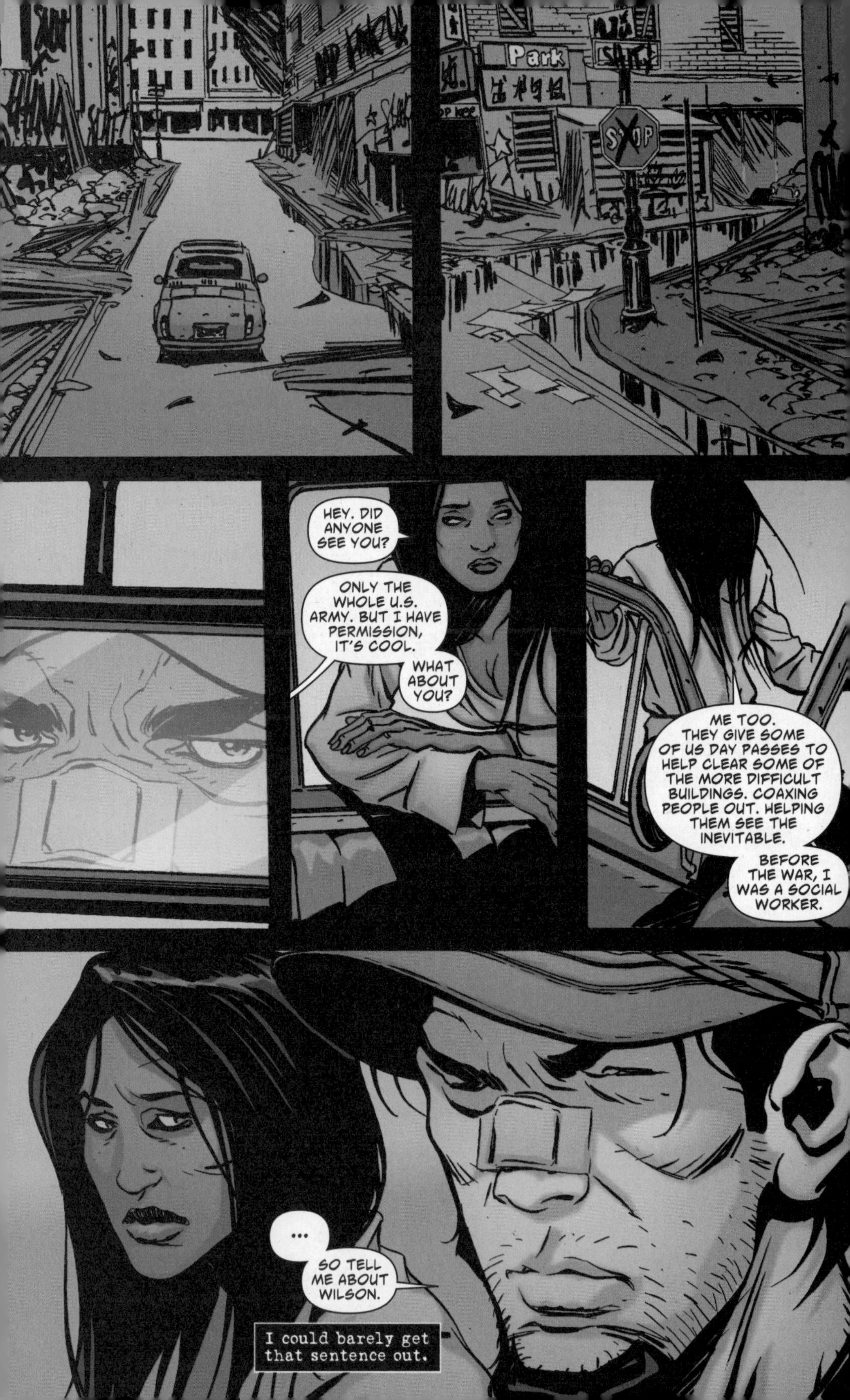
Park
STOP
HEY. DID ANYONE SEE YOU?
ONLY THE WHOLE U.S. ARMY. BUT I HAVE PERMISSION, IT'S COOL.
WHAT ABOUT YOU?
ME TOO. THEY GIVE SOME OF US DAY PASSES TO HELP CLEAR SOME OF THE MORE DIFFICULT BUILDINGS. COAXING PEOPLE OUT. HELPING THEM SEE THE INEVITABLE.
BEFORE THE WAR, I WAS A SOCIAL WORKER.
...
SO TELL ME ABOUT WILSON.
I could barely get that sentence out.

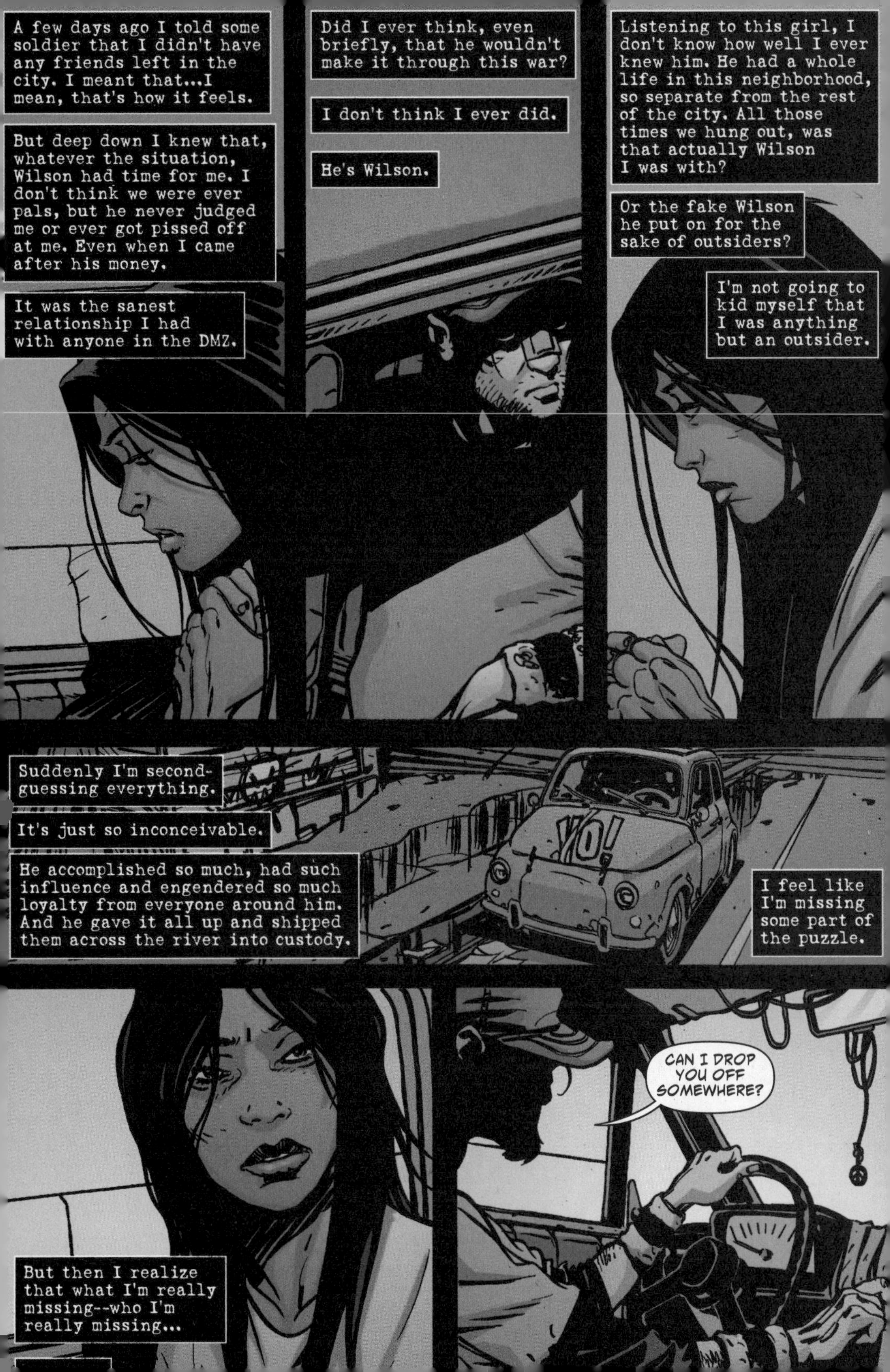
A few days ago I told some soldier that I didn't have any friends left in the city. I meant that...I mean, that's how it feels.
But deep down I knew that, whatever the situation, Wilson had time for me. I don't think we were ever pals, but he never judged me or ever got pissed off at me. Even when I came after his money.
It was the sanest relationship I had with anyone in the DMZ.
Did I ever think, even briefly, that he wouldn't make it through this war?
I don't think I ever did.
He's Wilson.
Listening to this girl, I don't know how well I ever knew him. He had a whole life in this neighborhood, so separate from the rest of the city. All those times we hung out, was that actually Wilson I was with?
Or the fake Wilson he put on for the sake of outsiders?
I'm not going to kid myself that I was anything but an outsider.
Suddenly I'm second-guessing everything.
It's just so inconceivable.
He accomplished so much, had such influence and engendered so much loyalty from everyone around him. And he gave it all up and shipped them across the river into custody.
YO!
I feel like I'm missing some part of the puzzle.
But then I realize that what I'm really missing--who I'm really missing...
CAN I DROP YOU OFF SOMEWHERE?

...begins today, the United States of America vs. Trustwell Incorporated, a private security firm charged with, among other things, the assassination of former U.N. Ambassador Gunnarsson...

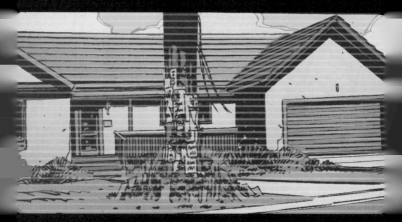

...ong-awaited settlement was reached today in the matter of PFC Chris Steve...d the wrongful death suit filed by his family. Stevens was charged with – a...eventually found innocent of – lethal participation in the day 204 Massacre..

...but not before he was dropped to his death by members of his own unit, allegedly in retaliation for his testimony about that horrific day...

...debuting at number one on both the French

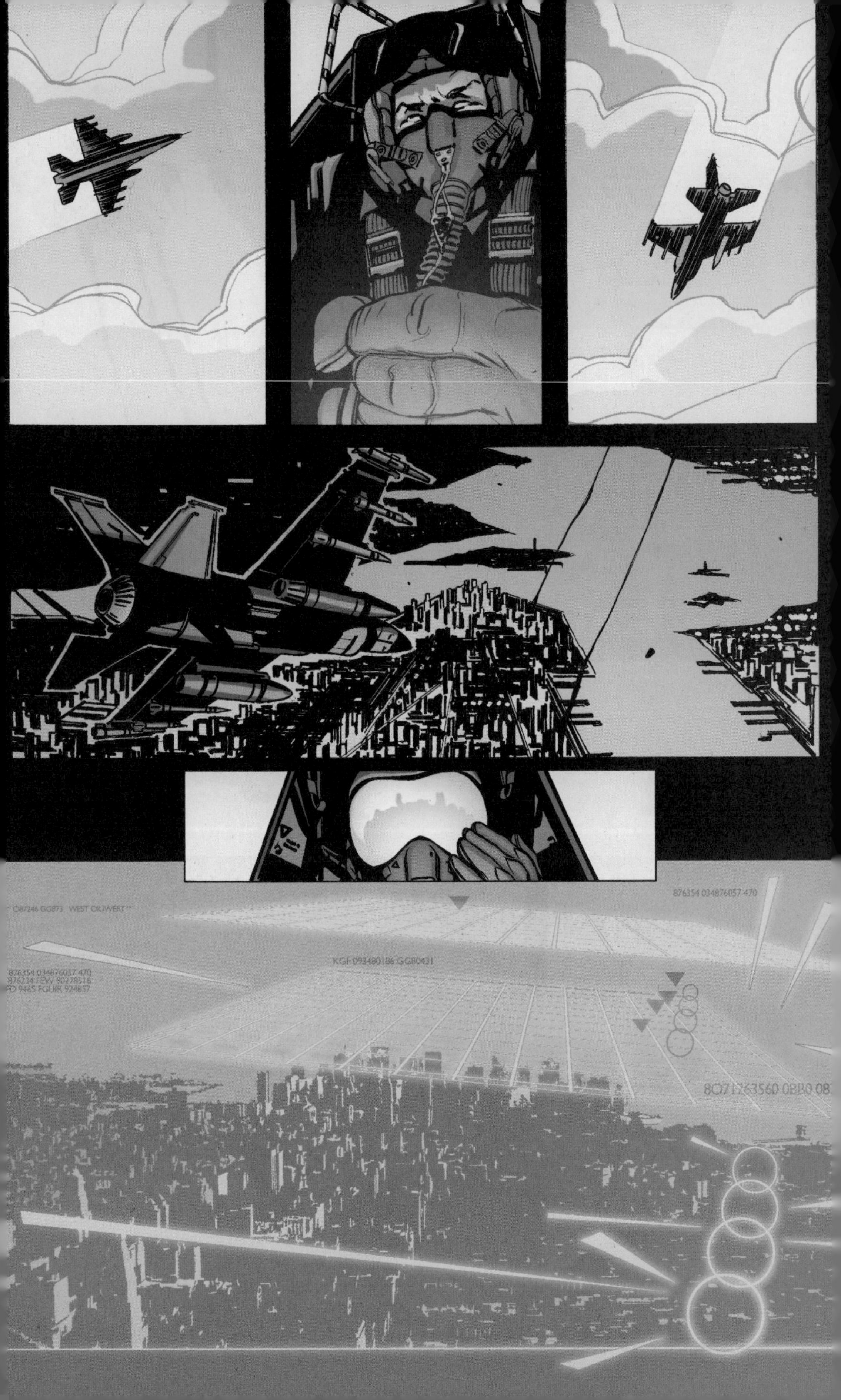

876354 034876057 470
O87246 GG873 WEST OIUWERT
KGF 093480186 GG80431
876354 034876057 470
876234 FEW 90278516
FD 9465 FGUIR 924857
8071263560 0BB0 08

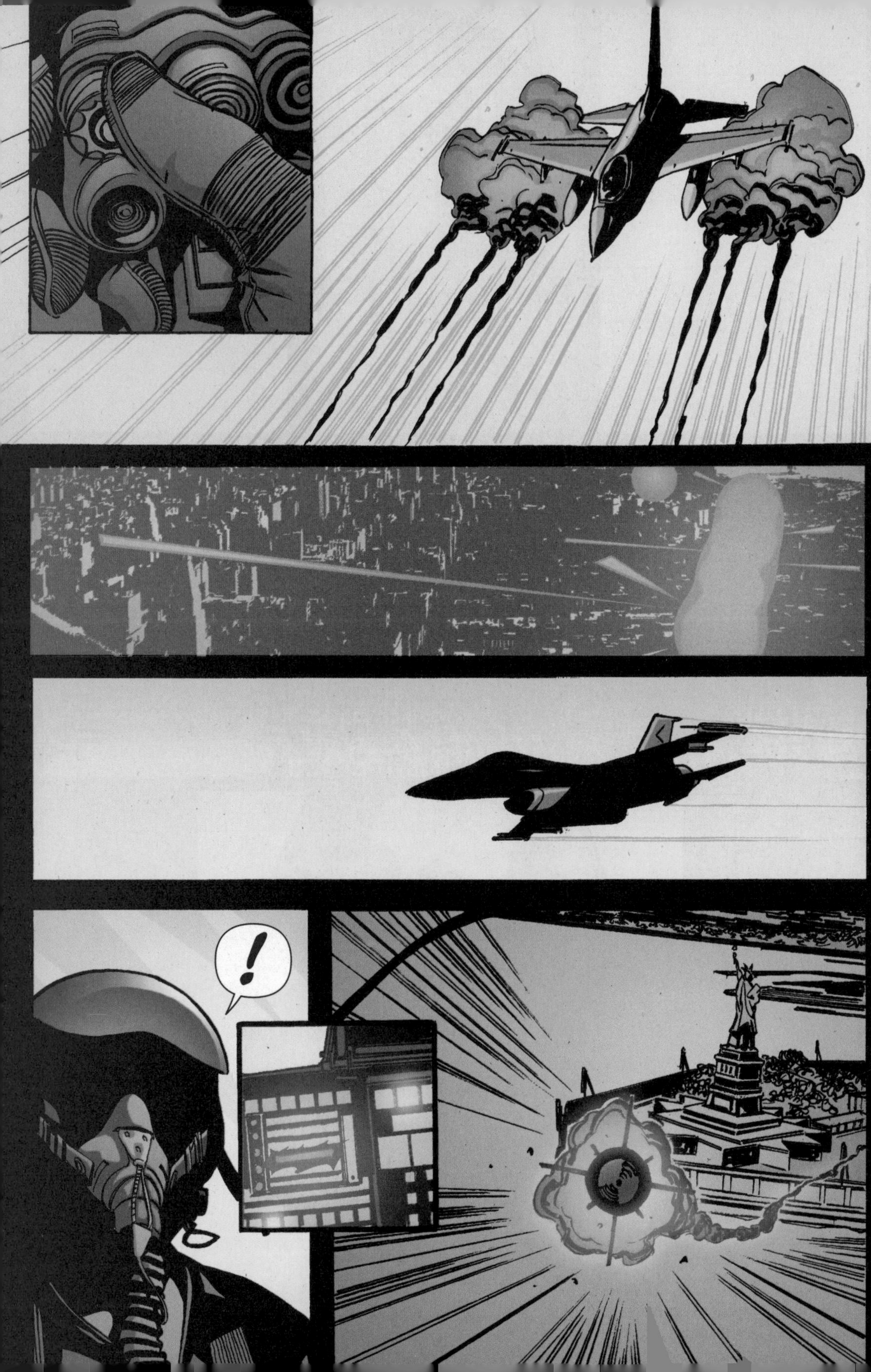
!

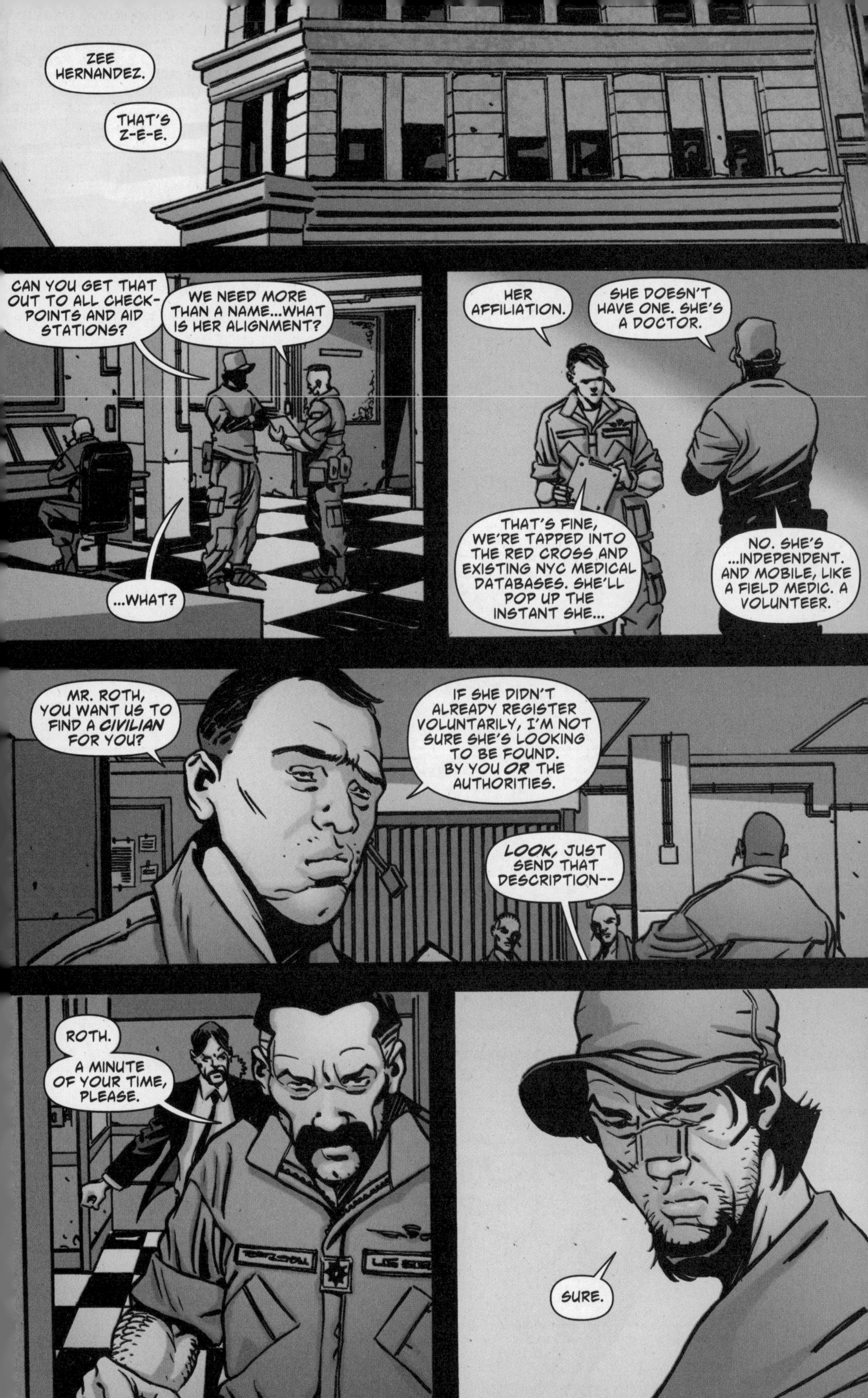
ZEE HERNANDEZ.
THAT'S Z-E-E.
CAN YOU GET THAT OUT TO ALL CHECK-POINTS AND AID STATIONS?
WE NEED MORE THAN A NAME...WHAT IS HER ALIGNMENT?
...WHAT?
HER AFFILIATION.
SHE DOESN'T HAVE ONE. SHE'S A DOCTOR.
THAT'S FINE, WE'RE TAPPED INTO THE RED CROSS AND EXISTING NYC MEDICAL DATABASES. SHE'LL POP UP THE INSTANT SHE...
NO. SHE'S ...INDEPENDENT. AND MOBILE, LIKE A FIELD MEDIC. A VOLUNTEER.
MR. ROTH, YOU WANT US TO FIND A *CIVILIAN* FOR YOU?
IF SHE DIDN'T ALREADY REGISTER VOLUNTARILY, I'M NOT SURE SHE'S LOOKING TO BE FOUND. BY YOU *OR* THE AUTHORITIES.
LOOK, JUST SEND THAT DESCRIPTION--
ROTH.
A MINUTE OF YOUR TIME, PLEASE.
SURE.

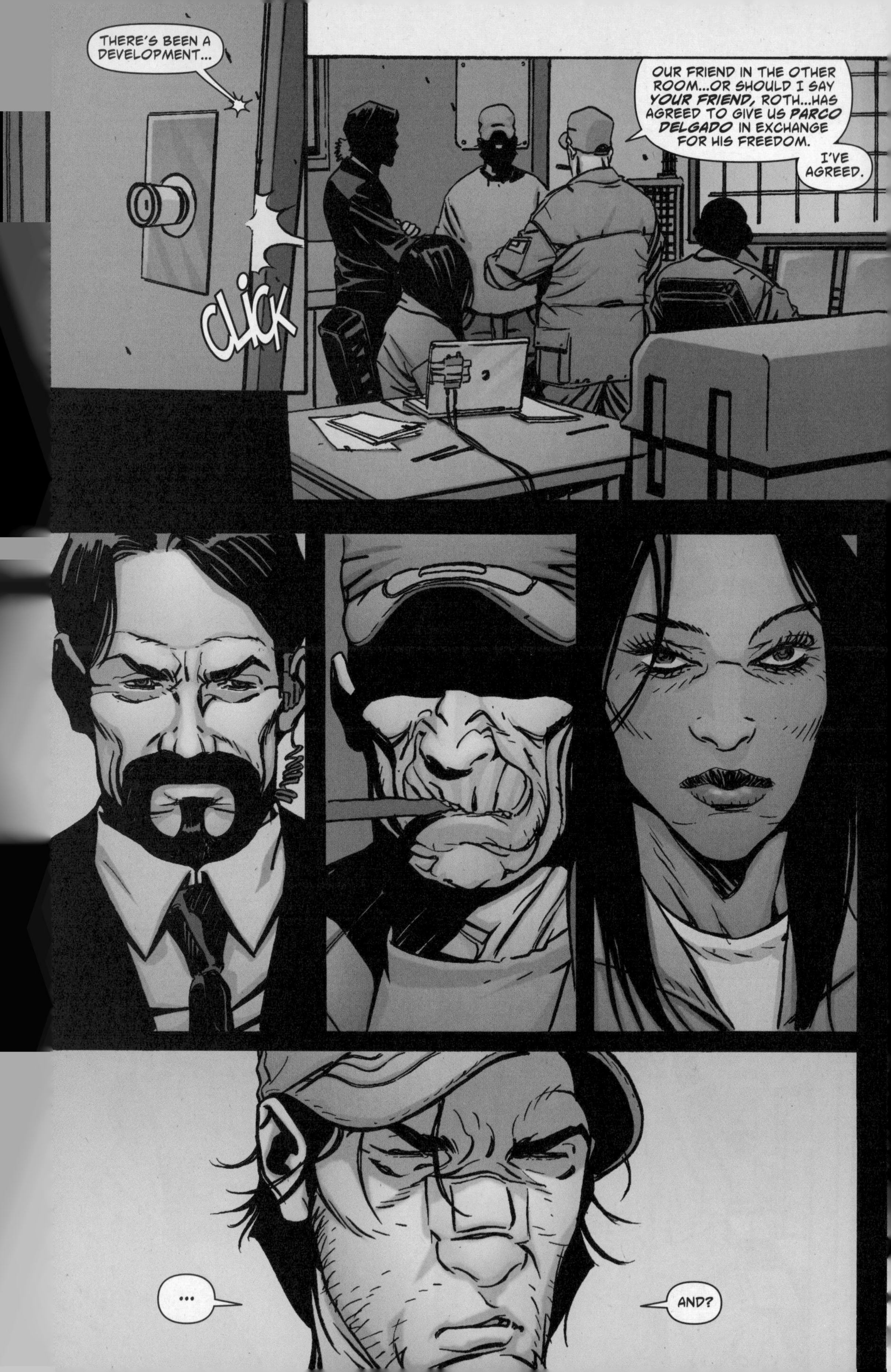

THERE'S BEEN A DEVELOPMENT...
CLICK
OUR FRIEND IN THE OTHER ROOM...OR SHOULD I SAY YOUR FRIEND, ROTH...HAS AGREED TO GIVE US PARCO DELGADO IN EXCHANGE FOR HIS FREEDOM.
I'VE AGREED.
...
AND?

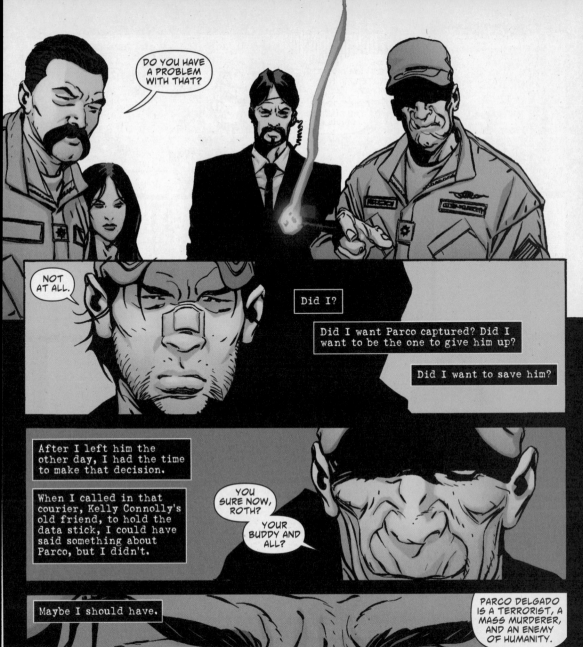

DO YOU HAVE A PROBLEM WITH THAT?

NOT AT ALL.

Did I?

Did I want Parco captured? Did I want to be the one to give him up?

Did I want to save him?

After I left him the other day, I had the time to make that decision.

When I called in that courier, Kelly Connolly's old friend, to hold the data stick, I could have said something about Parco, but I didn't.

YOU SURE NOW, ROTH? YOUR BUDDY AND ALL?

Maybe I should have.

PARCO DELGADO IS A TERRORIST, A MASS MURDERER, AND AN ENEMY OF HUMANITY.

SIR.

What the hell is the Commander up to?

THAT HE IS. I HAVE A TEAM IN PLACE AS OF TEN MINUTES AGO, READY TO MOVE IN--

HELLO? YOU HAVE A GO. YOU MAY EXECUTE.

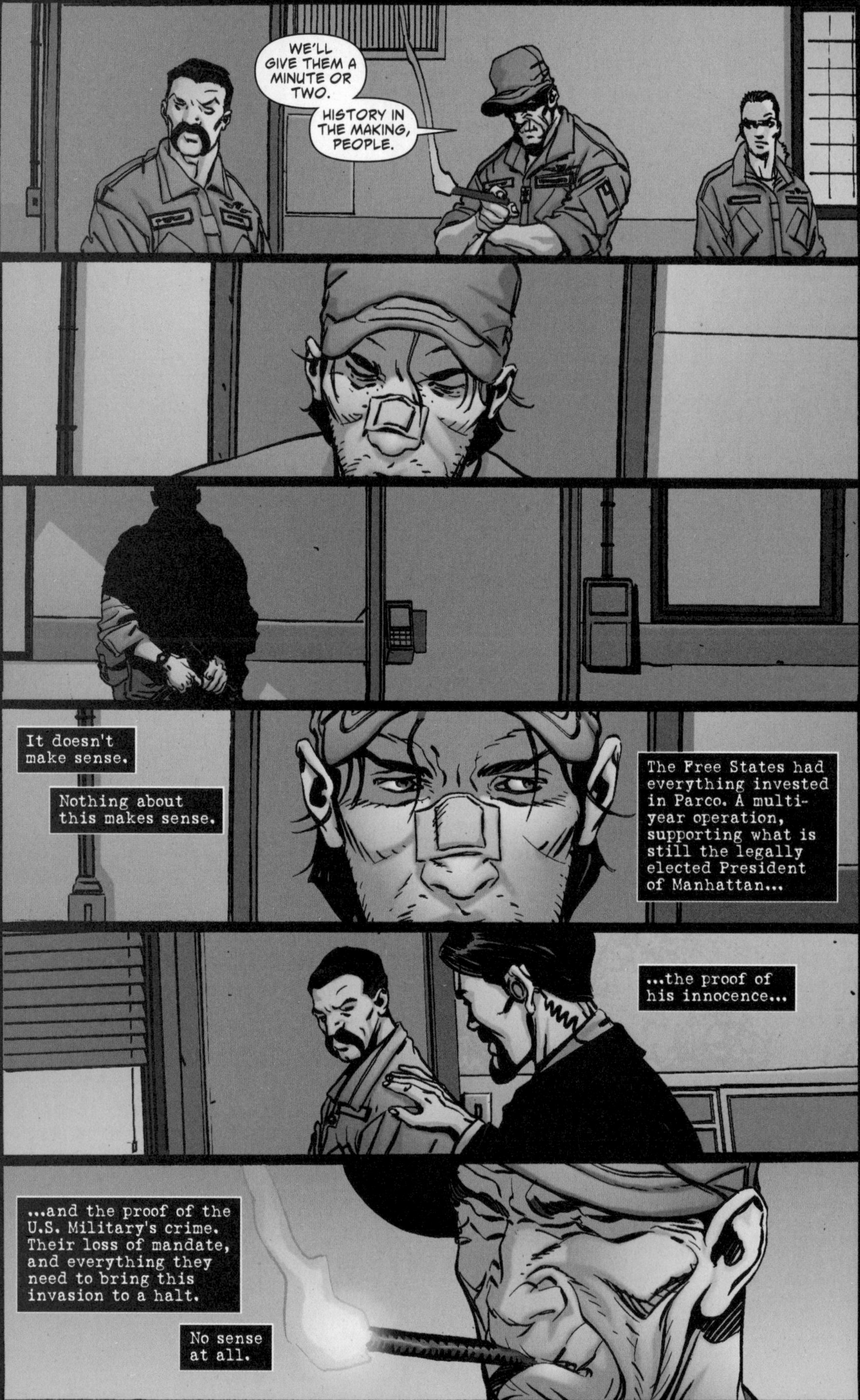
WE'LL GIVE THEM A MINUTE OR TWO.
HISTORY IN THE MAKING, PEOPLE.
It doesn't make sense.
Nothing about this makes sense.
The Free States had everything invested in Parco. A multi-year operation, supporting what is still the legally elected President of Manhattan...
...the proof of his innocence...
...and the proof of the U.S. Military's crime. Their loss of mandate, and everything they need to bring this invasion to a halt.
No sense at all.

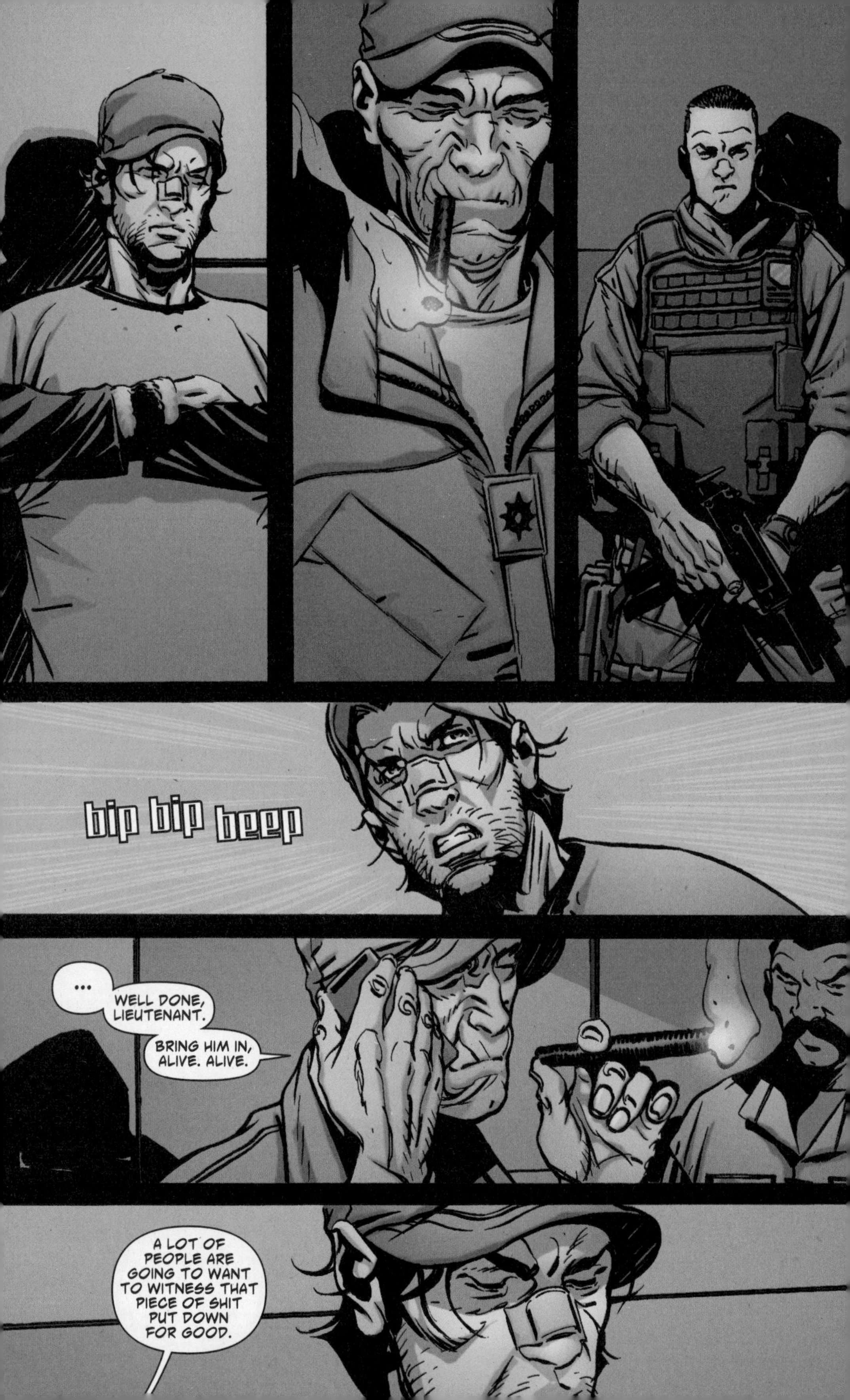
bip bip beep
...
WELL DONE, LIEUTENANT.
BRING HIM IN, ALIVE. ALIVE.
A LOT OF PEOPLE ARE GOING TO WANT TO WITNESS THAT PIECE OF SHIT PUT DOWN FOR GOOD.

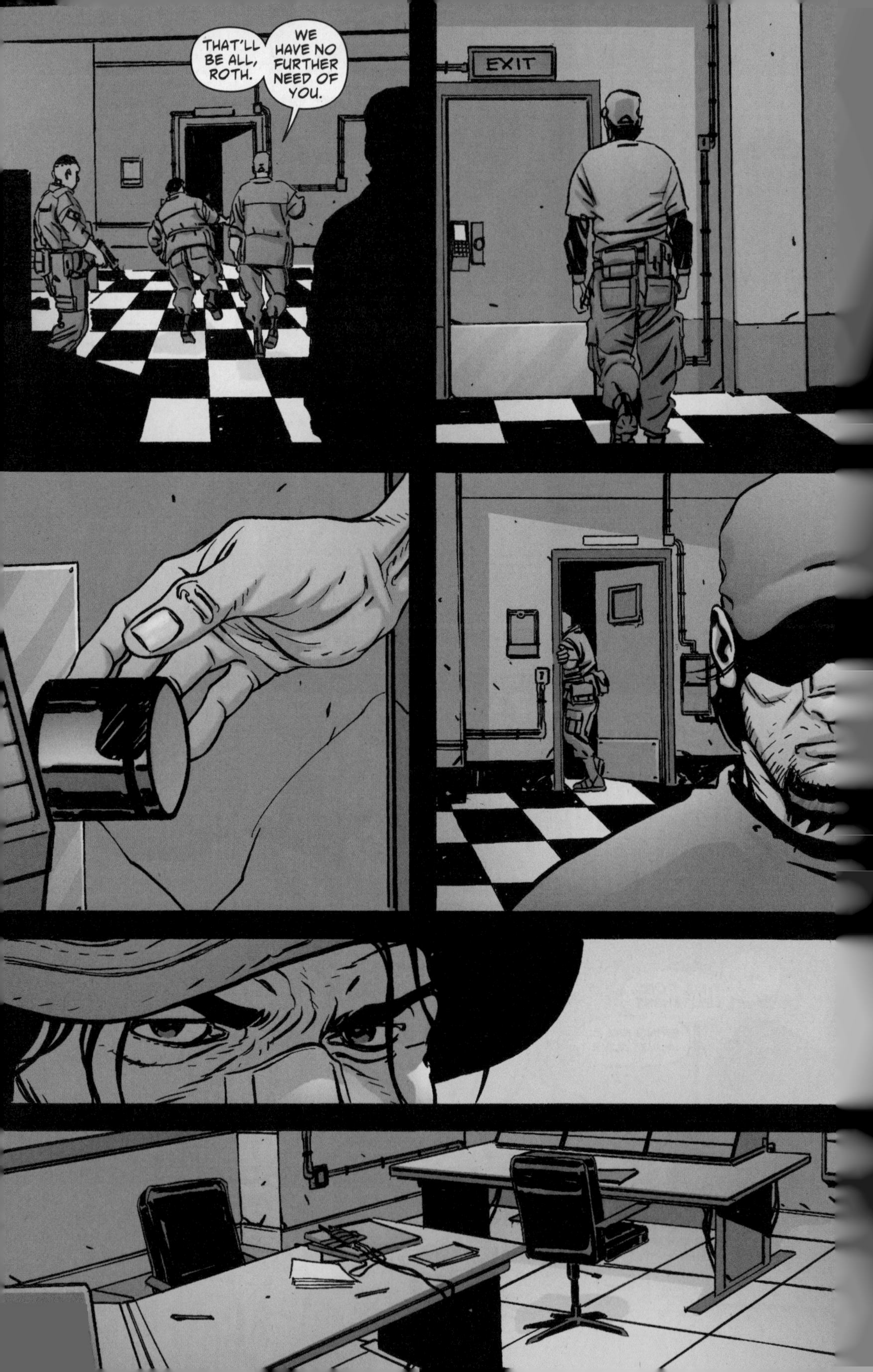
THAT'LL BE ALL, ROTH.
WE HAVE NO FURTHER NEED OF YOU.
EXIT

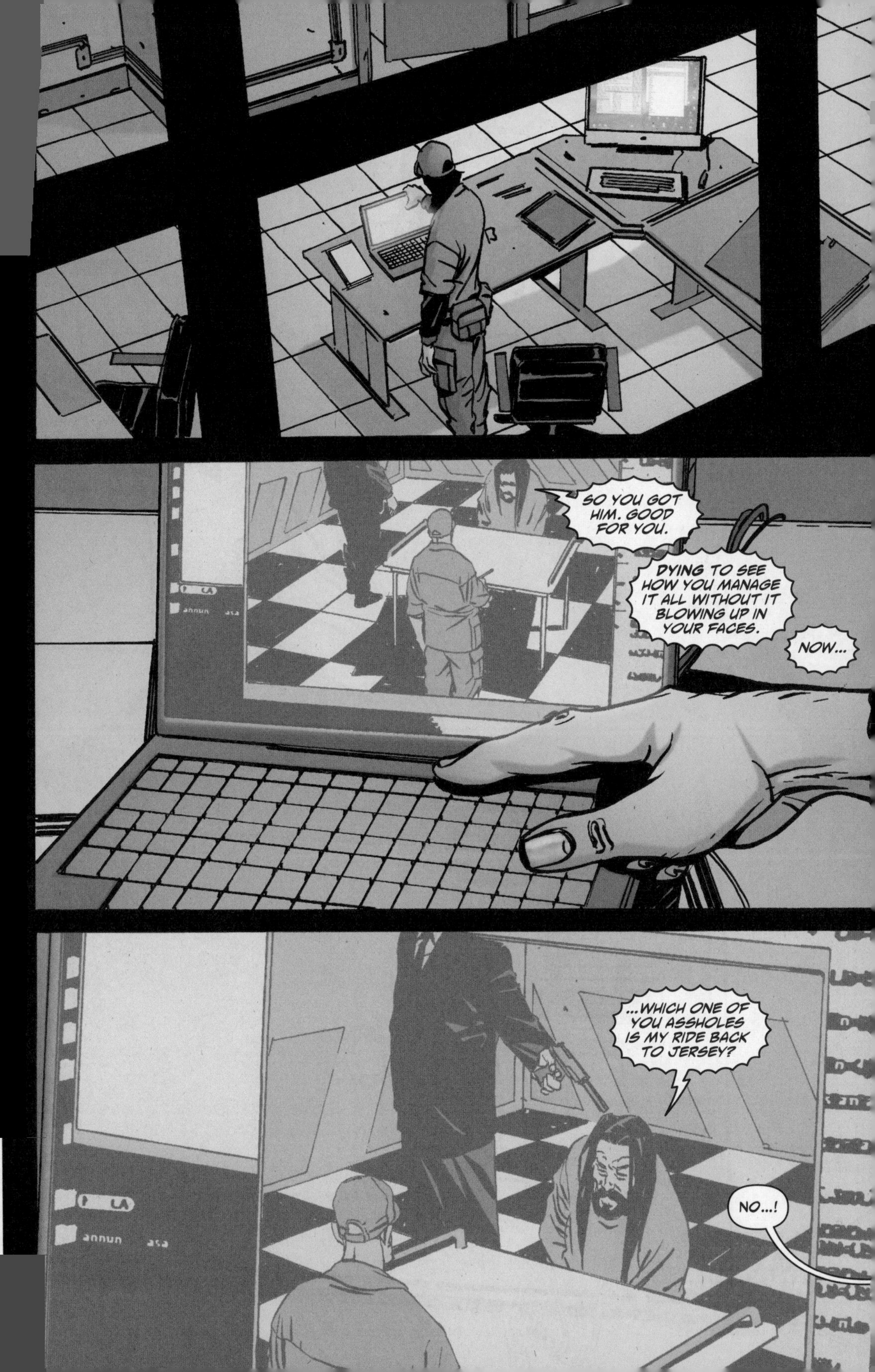
SO YOU GOT HIM. GOOD FOR YOU.
DYING TO SEE HOW YOU MANAGE IT ALL WITHOUT IT BLOWING UP IN YOUR FACES.
NOW...
...WHICH ONE OF YOU ASSHOLES IS MY RIDE BACK TO JERSEY?
NO...!

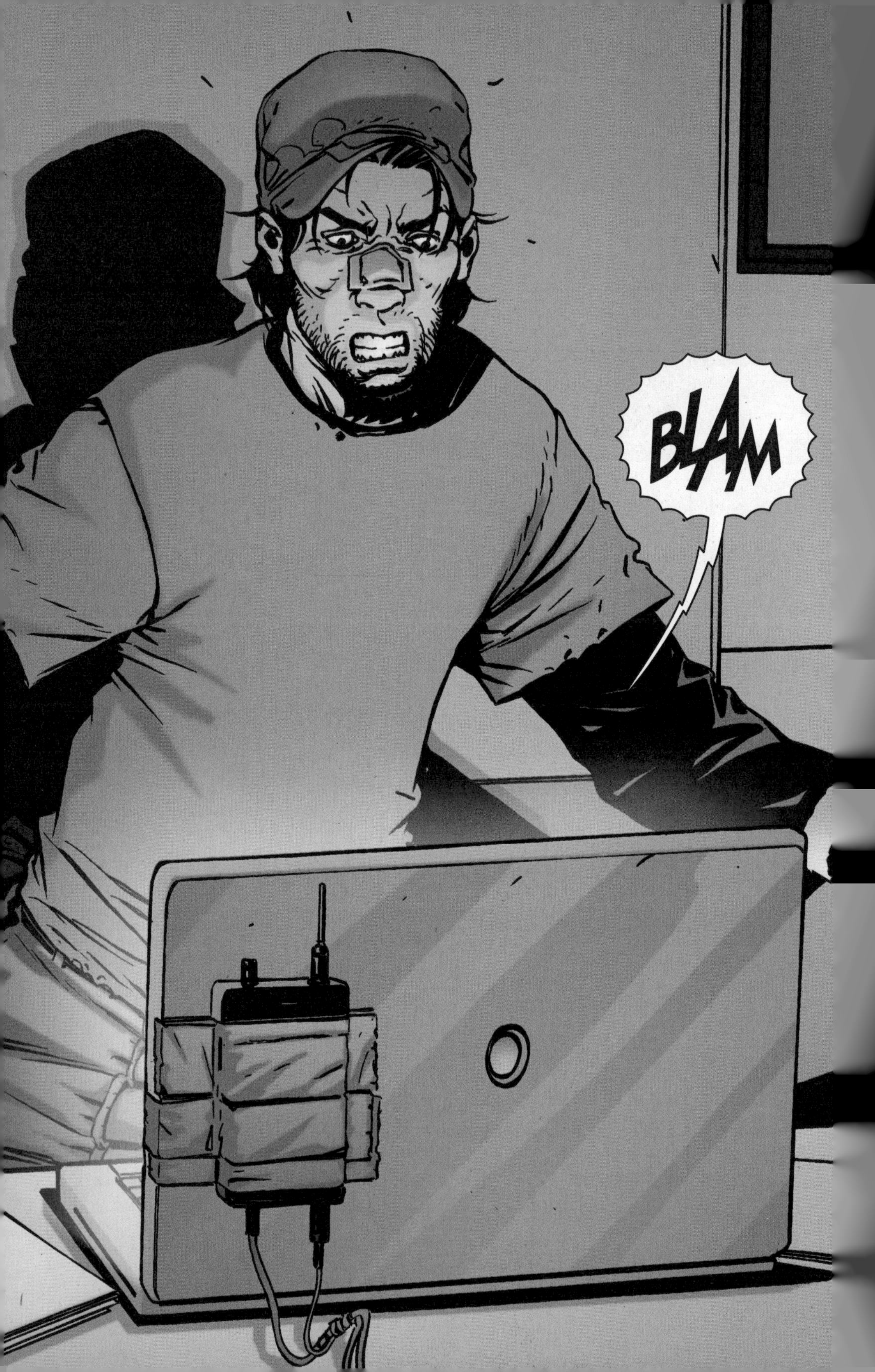
BLAM

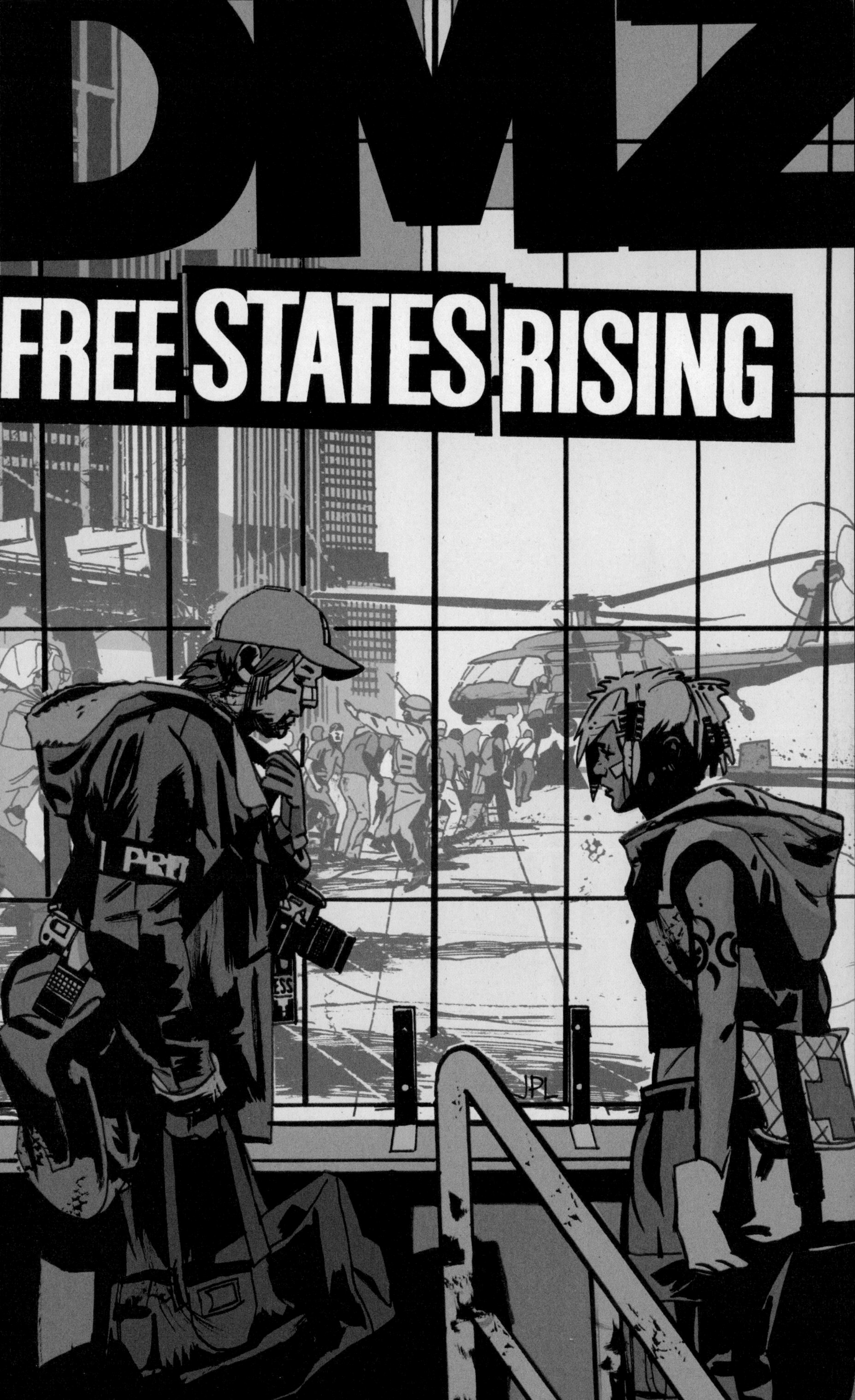
DMZ
FREE STATES RISING
JPL

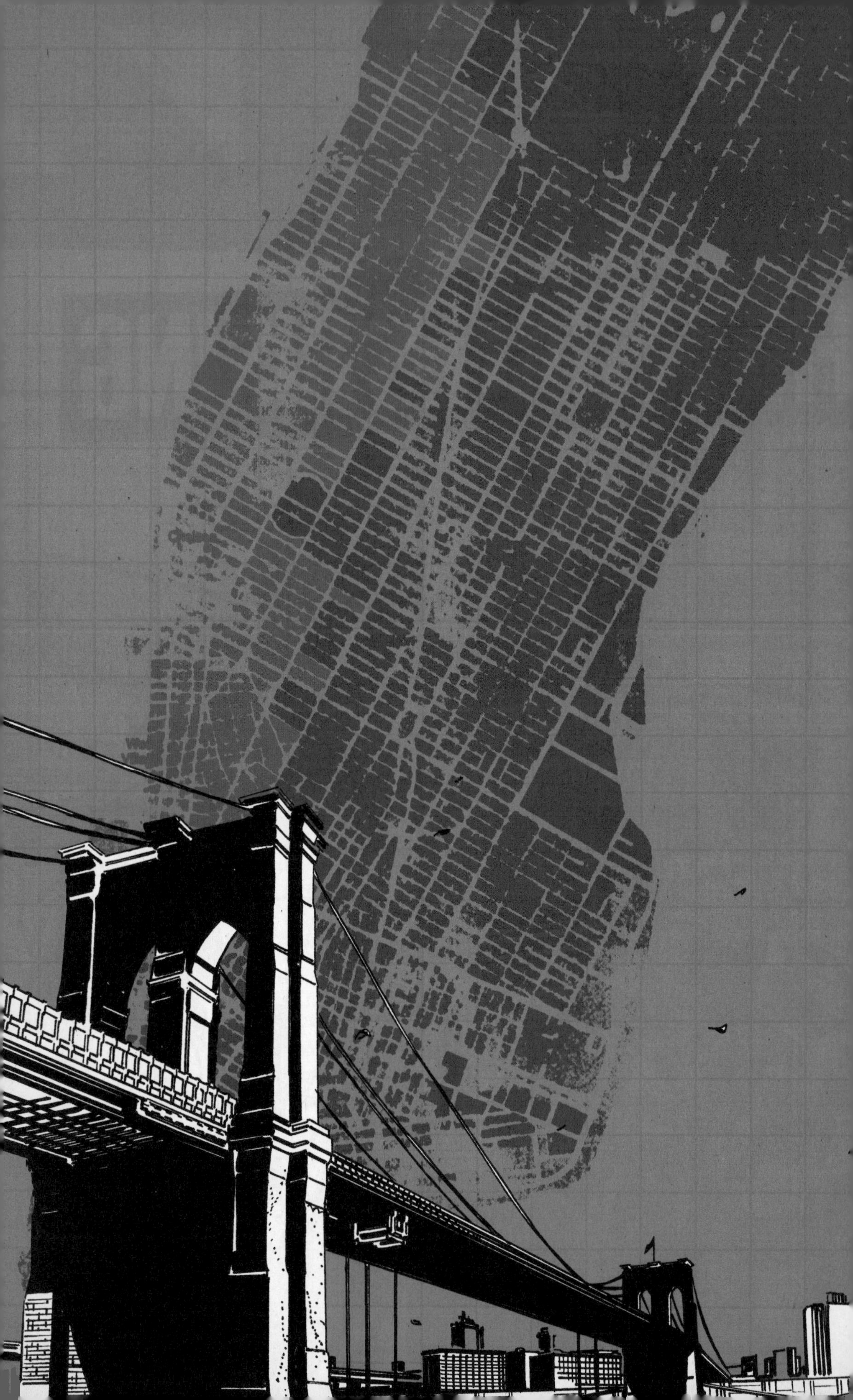

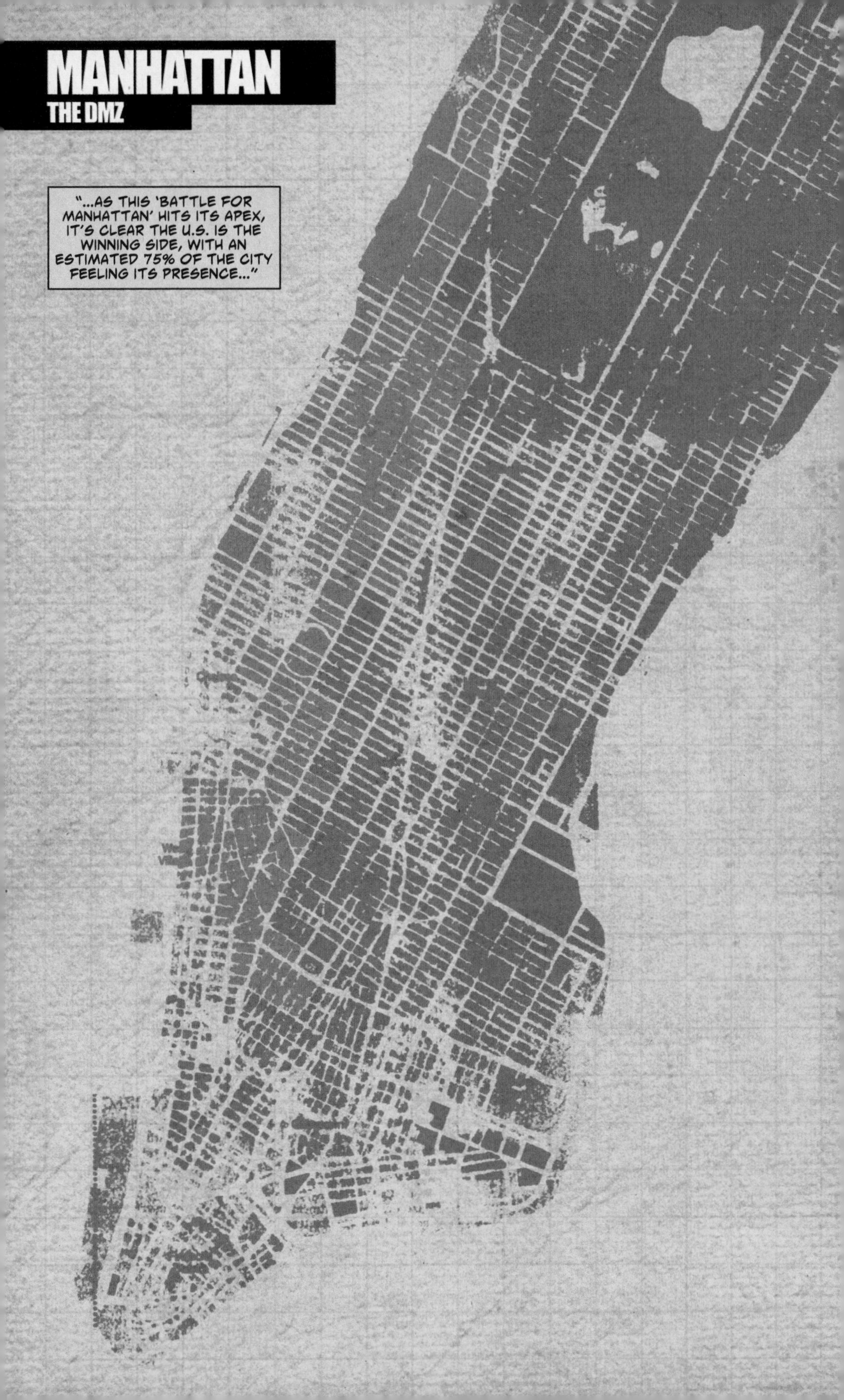
MANHATTAN
THE DMZ
"...AS THIS 'BATTLE FOR MANHATTAN' HITS ITS APEX, IT'S CLEAR THE U.S. IS THE WINNING SIDE, WITH AN ESTIMATED 75% OF THE CITY FEELING ITS PRESENCE..."

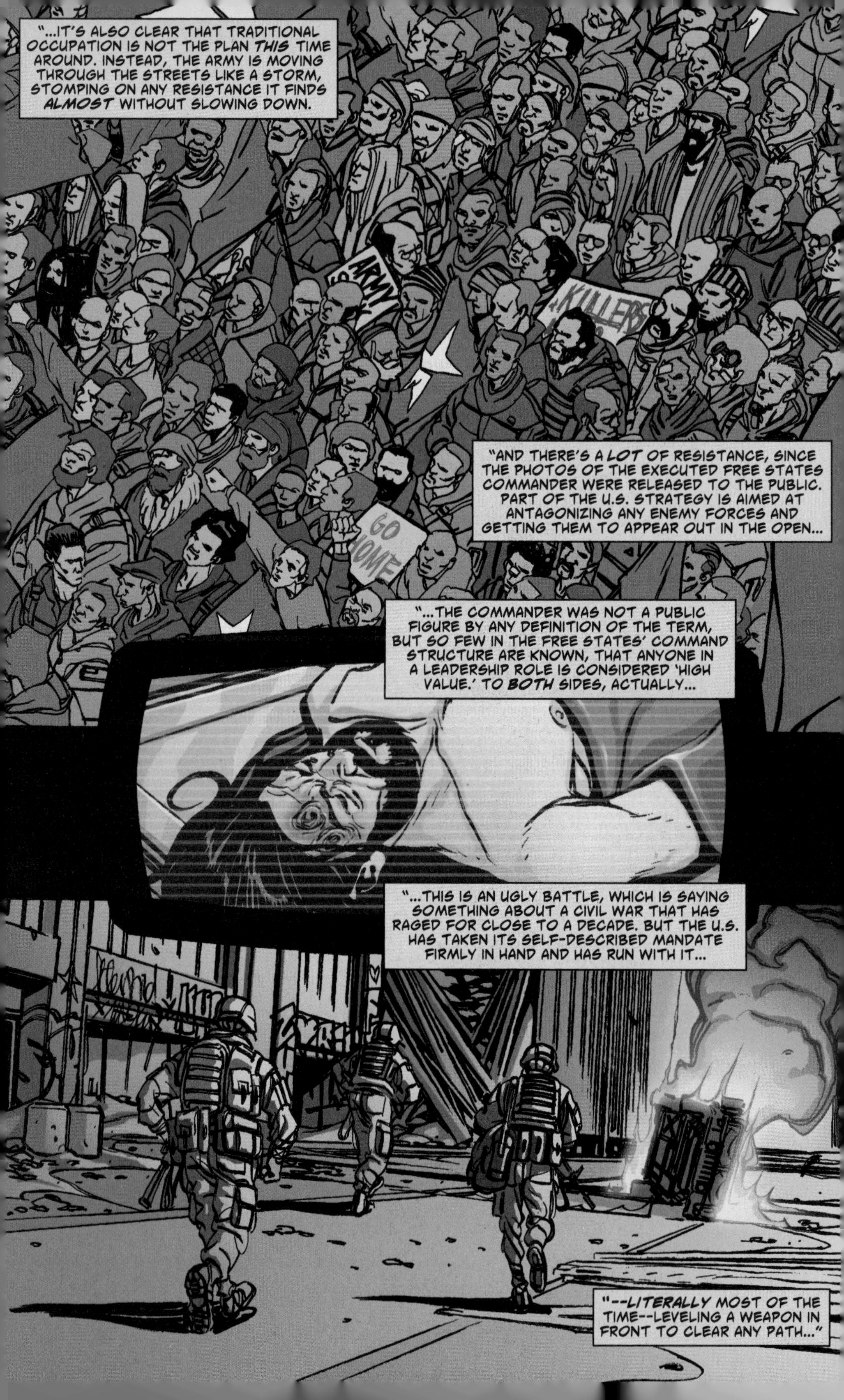
"...IT'S ALSO CLEAR THAT TRADITIONAL OCCUPATION IS NOT THE PLAN THIS TIME AROUND. INSTEAD, THE ARMY IS MOVING THROUGH THE STREETS LIKE A STORM, STOMPING ON ANY RESISTANCE IT FINDS ALMOST WITHOUT SLOWING DOWN.
ARMY
KILLERS
GO HOME
"AND THERE'S A LOT OF RESISTANCE, SINCE THE PHOTOS OF THE EXECUTED FREE STATES COMMANDER WERE RELEASED TO THE PUBLIC. PART OF THE U.S. STRATEGY IS AIMED AT ANTAGONIZING ANY ENEMY FORCES AND GETTING THEM TO APPEAR OUT IN THE OPEN...
"...THE COMMANDER WAS NOT A PUBLIC FIGURE BY ANY DEFINITION OF THE TERM, BUT SO FEW IN THE FREE STATES' COMMAND STRUCTURE ARE KNOWN, THAT ANYONE IN A LEADERSHIP ROLE IS CONSIDERED 'HIGH VALUE.' TO BOTH SIDES, ACTUALLY...
"...THIS IS AN UGLY BATTLE, WHICH IS SAYING SOMETHING ABOUT A CIVIL WAR THAT HAS RAGED FOR CLOSE TO A DECADE. BUT THE U.S. HAS TAKEN ITS SELF-DESCRIBED MANDATE FIRMLY IN HAND AND HAS RUN WITH IT...
"--LITERALLY MOST OF THE TIME--LEVELING A WEAPON IN FRONT TO CLEAR ANY PATH..."

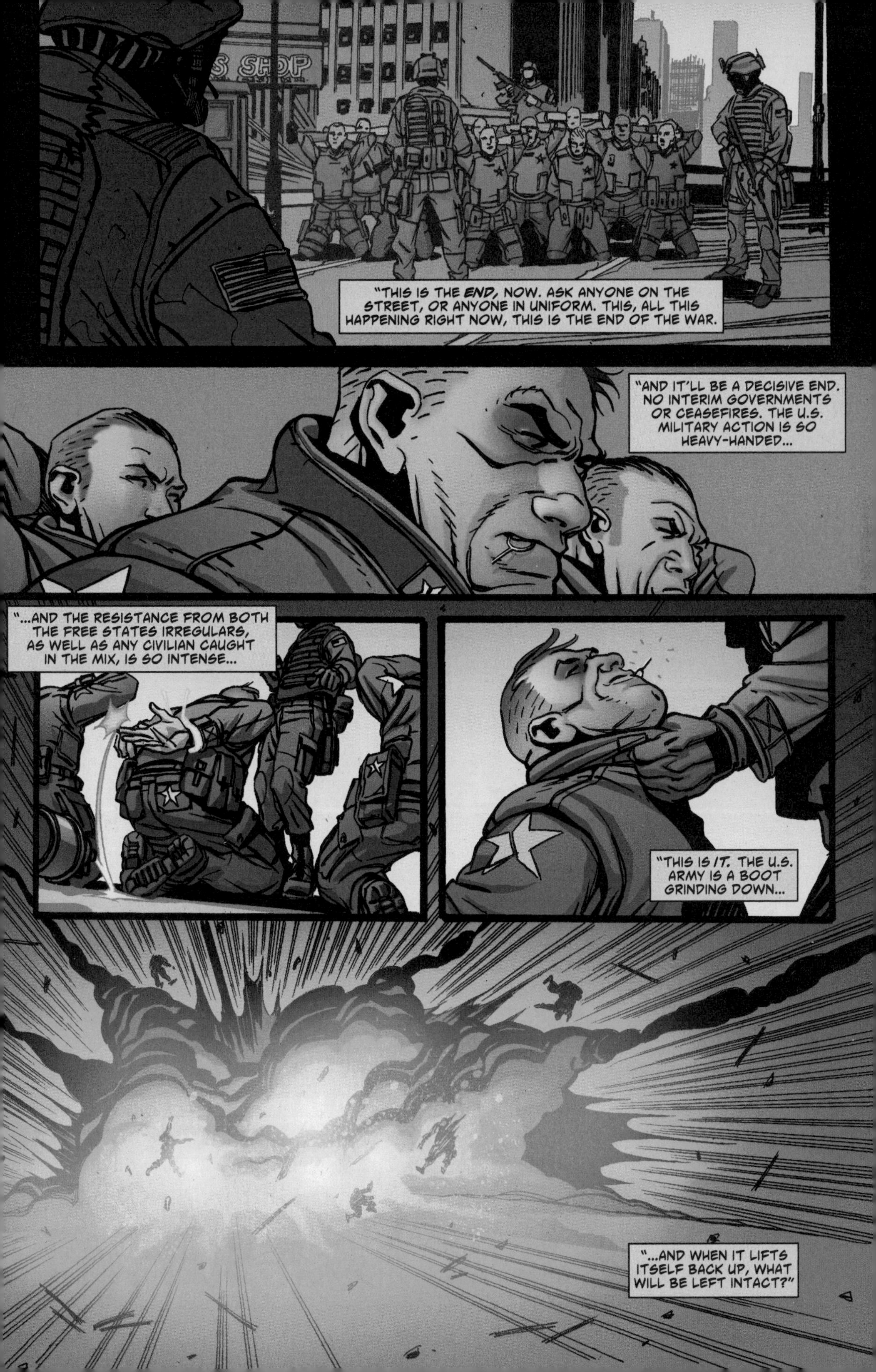

"THIS IS THE *END,* NOW. ASK ANYONE ON THE STREET, OR ANYONE IN UNIFORM. THIS, ALL THIS HAPPENING RIGHT NOW, THIS IS THE END OF THE WAR.
"AND IT'LL BE A DECISIVE END. NO INTERIM GOVERNMENTS OR CEASEFIRES. THE U.S. MILITARY ACTION IS SO HEAVY-HANDED...
"...AND THE RESISTANCE FROM BOTH THE FREE STATES IRREGULARS, AS WELL AS ANY CIVILIAN CAUGHT IN THE MIX, IS SO INTENSE...
"THIS IS *IT.* THE U.S. ARMY IS A BOOT GRINDING DOWN...
"...AND WHEN IT LIFTS ITSELF BACK UP, WHAT WILL BE LEFT INTACT?"

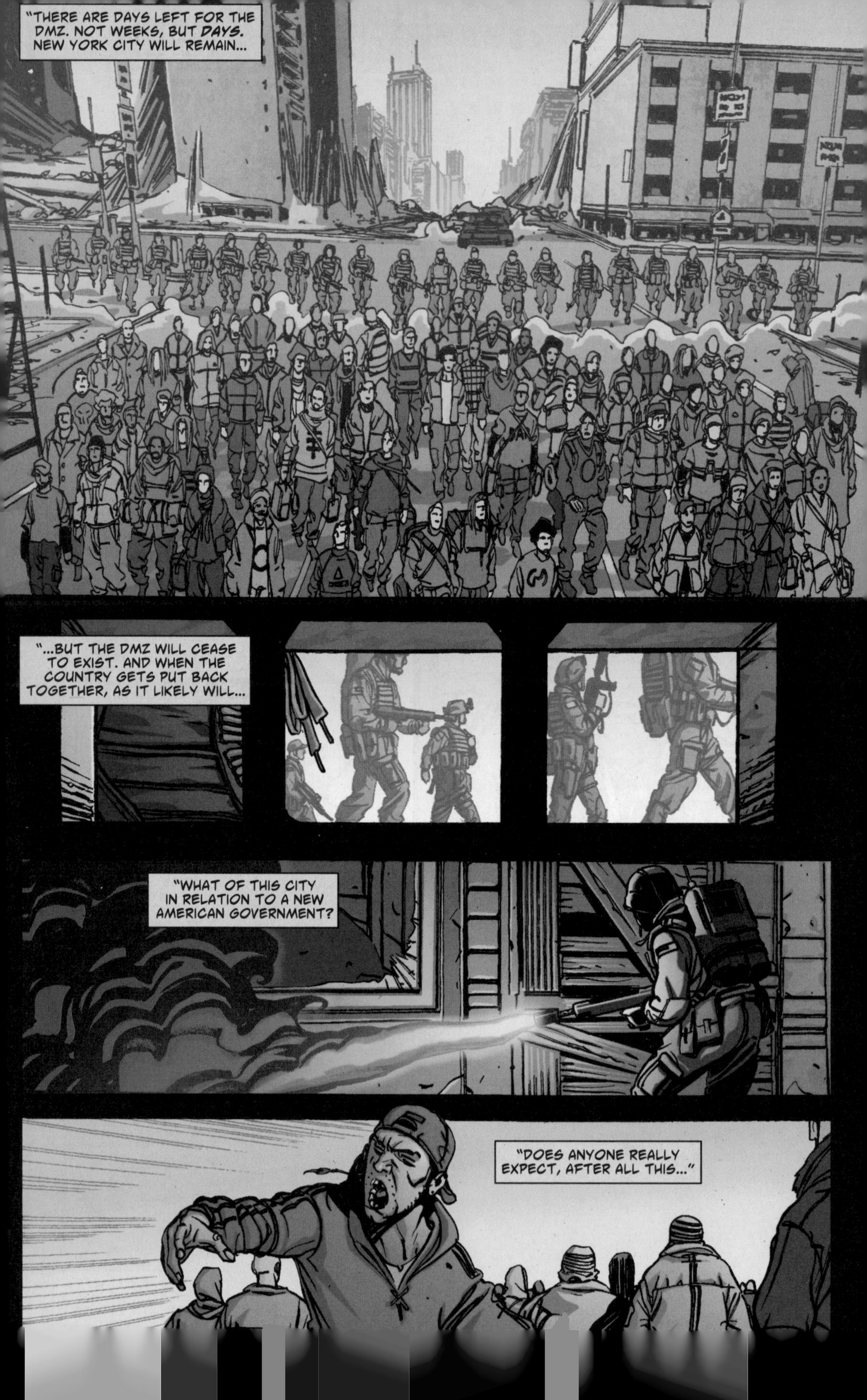
"THERE ARE DAYS LEFT FOR THE DMZ. NOT WEEKS, BUT DAYS. NEW YORK CITY WILL REMAIN...
"...BUT THE DMZ WILL CEASE TO EXIST. AND WHEN THE COUNTRY GETS PUT BACK TOGETHER, AS IT LIKELY WILL...
"WHAT OF THIS CITY IN RELATION TO A NEW AMERICAN GOVERNMENT?
"DOES ANYONE REALLY EXPECT, AFTER ALL THIS..."

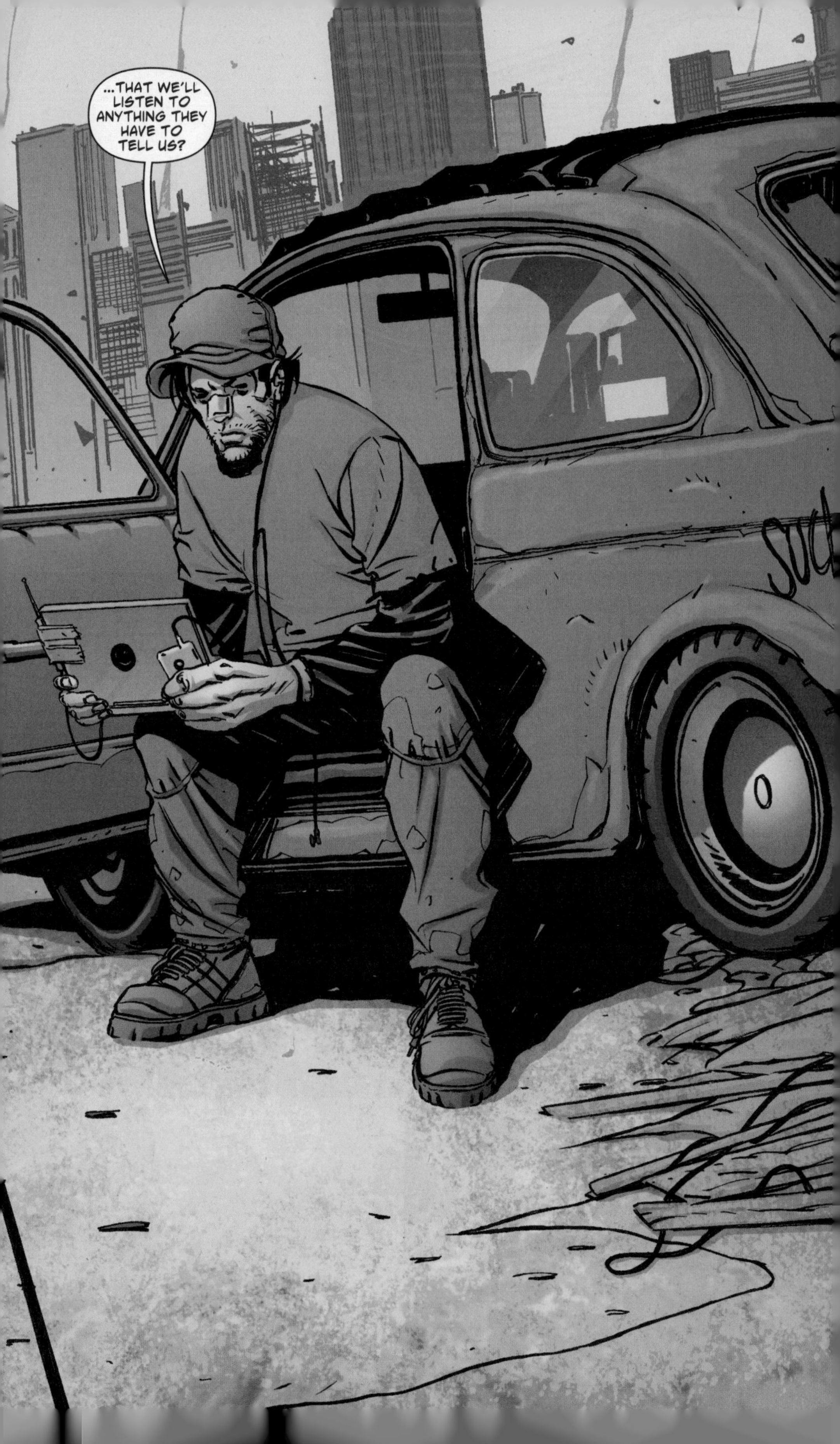
...THAT WE'LL LISTEN TO ANYTHING THEY HAVE TO TELL US?

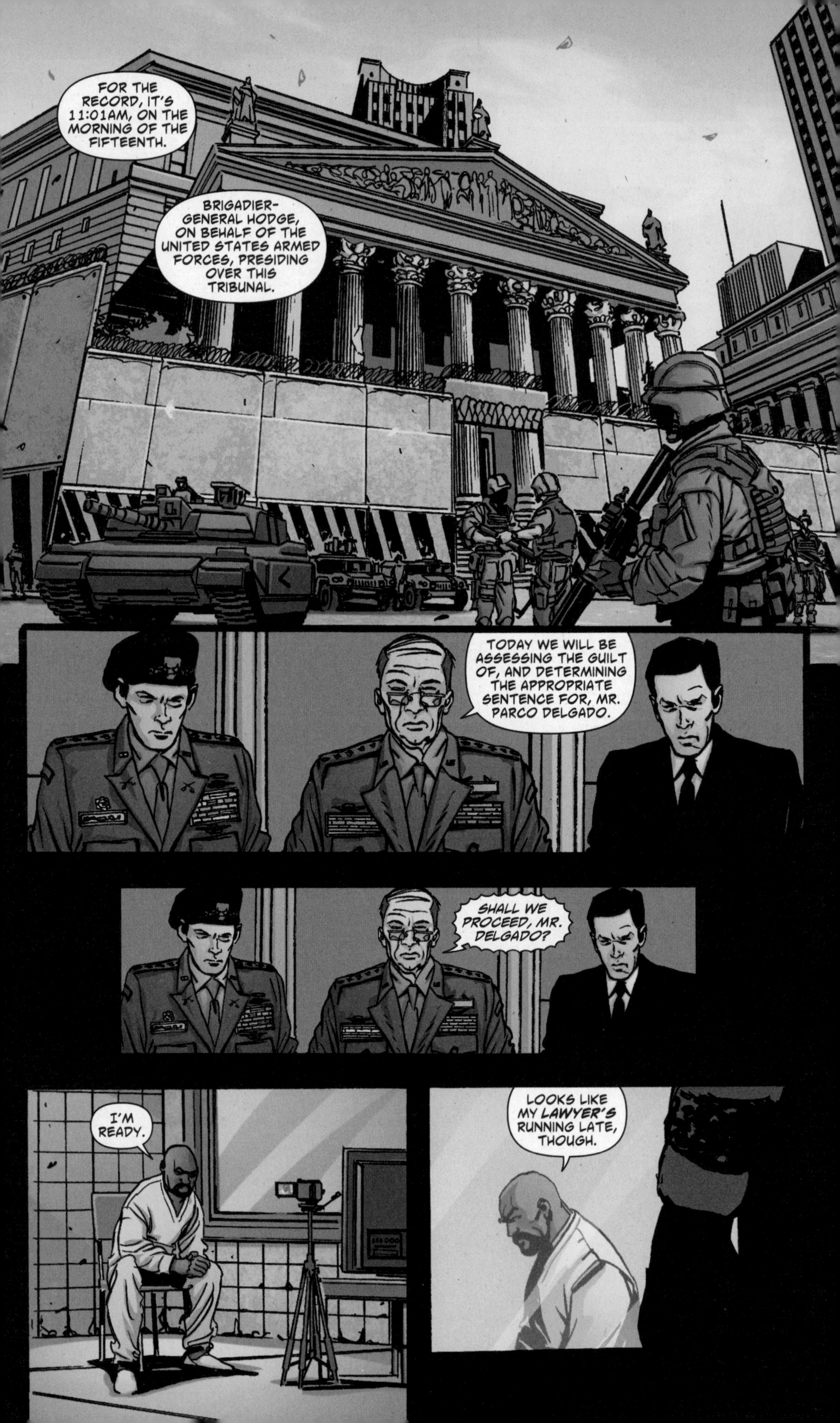
FOR THE RECORD, IT'S 11:01AM, ON THE MORNING OF THE FIFTEENTH.
BRIGADIER-GENERAL HODGE, ON BEHALF OF THE UNITED STATES ARMED FORCES, PRESIDING OVER THIS TRIBUNAL.
TODAY WE WILL BE ASSESSING THE GUILT OF, AND DETERMINING THE APPROPRIATE SENTENCE FOR, MR. PARCO DELGADO.
SHALL WE PROCEED, MR. DELGADO?
I'M READY.
LOOKS LIKE MY LAWYER'S RUNNING LATE, THOUGH.

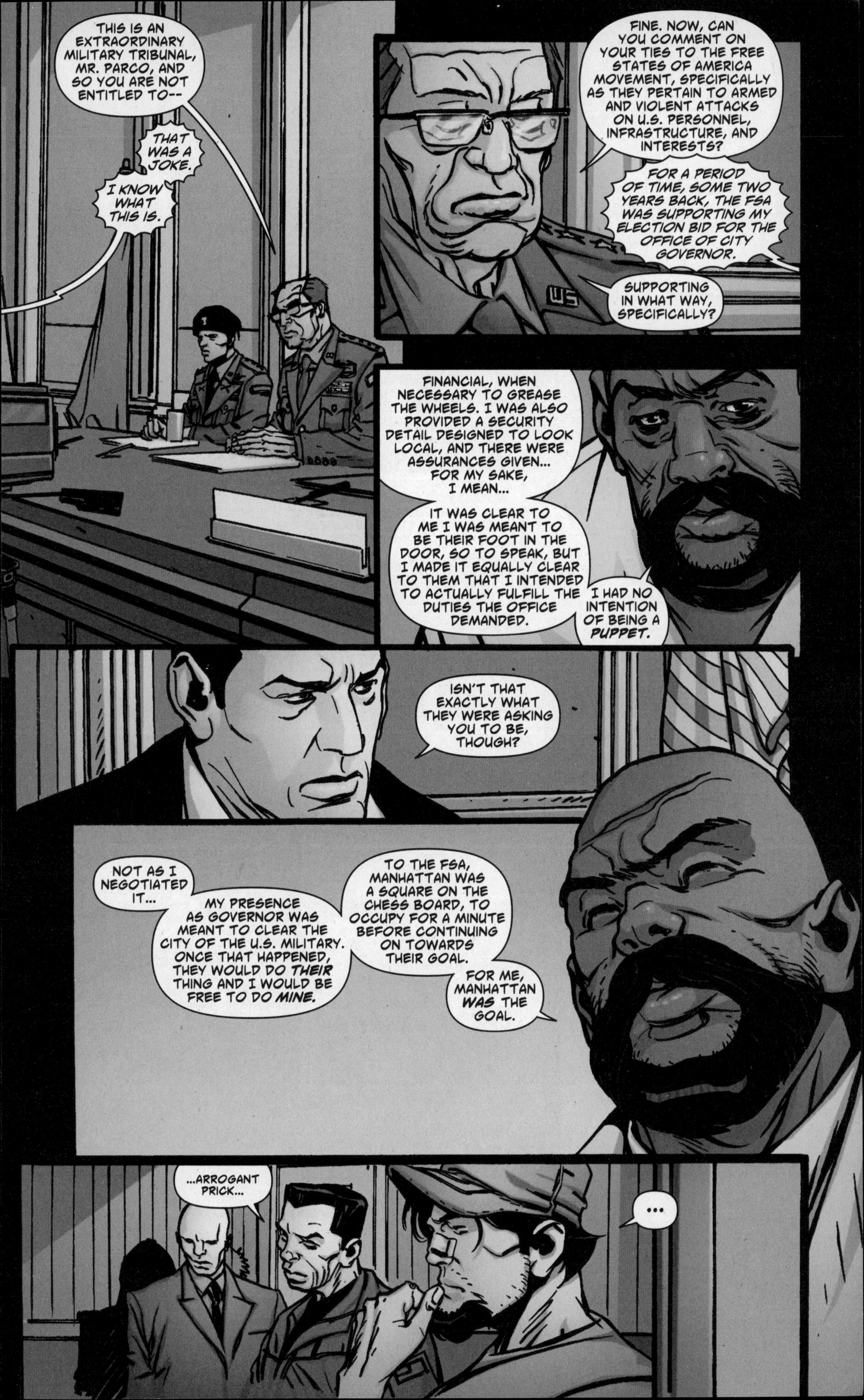
THIS IS AN EXTRAORDINARY MILITARY TRIBUNAL, MR. PARCO, AND SO YOU ARE NOT ENTITLED TO--
THAT WAS A JOKE.
I KNOW WHAT THIS IS.
FINE. NOW, CAN YOU COMMENT ON YOUR TIES TO THE FREE STATES OF AMERICA MOVEMENT, SPECIFICALLY AS THEY PERTAIN TO ARMED AND VIOLENT ATTACKS ON U.S. PERSONNEL, INFRASTRUCTURE, AND INTERESTS?
FOR A PERIOD OF TIME, SOME TWO YEARS BACK, THE FSA WAS SUPPORTING MY ELECTION BID FOR THE OFFICE OF CITY GOVERNOR.
SUPPORTING IN WHAT WAY, SPECIFICALLY?
FINANCIAL, WHEN NECESSARY TO GREASE THE WHEELS. I WAS ALSO PROVIDED A SECURITY DETAIL DESIGNED TO LOOK LOCAL, AND THERE WERE ASSURANCES GIVEN... FOR MY SAKE, I MEAN...
IT WAS CLEAR TO ME I WAS MEANT TO BE THEIR FOOT IN THE DOOR, SO TO SPEAK, BUT I MADE IT EQUALLY CLEAR TO THEM THAT I INTENDED TO ACTUALLY FULFILL THE DUTIES THE OFFICE DEMANDED.
I HAD NO INTENTION OF BEING A *PUPPET*.
ISN'T THAT EXACTLY WHAT THEY WERE ASKING YOU TO BE, THOUGH?
NOT AS I NEGOTIATED IT...
MY PRESENCE AS GOVERNOR WAS MEANT TO CLEAR THE CITY OF THE U.S. MILITARY. ONCE THAT HAPPENED, THEY WOULD DO *THEIR* THING AND I WOULD BE FREE TO DO *MINE*.
TO THE FSA, MANHATTAN WAS A SQUARE ON THE CHESS BOARD, TO OCCUPY FOR A MINUTE BEFORE CONTINUING ON TOWARDS THEIR GOAL.
FOR ME, MANHATTAN *WAS* THE GOAL.
...ARROGANT PRICK...
...

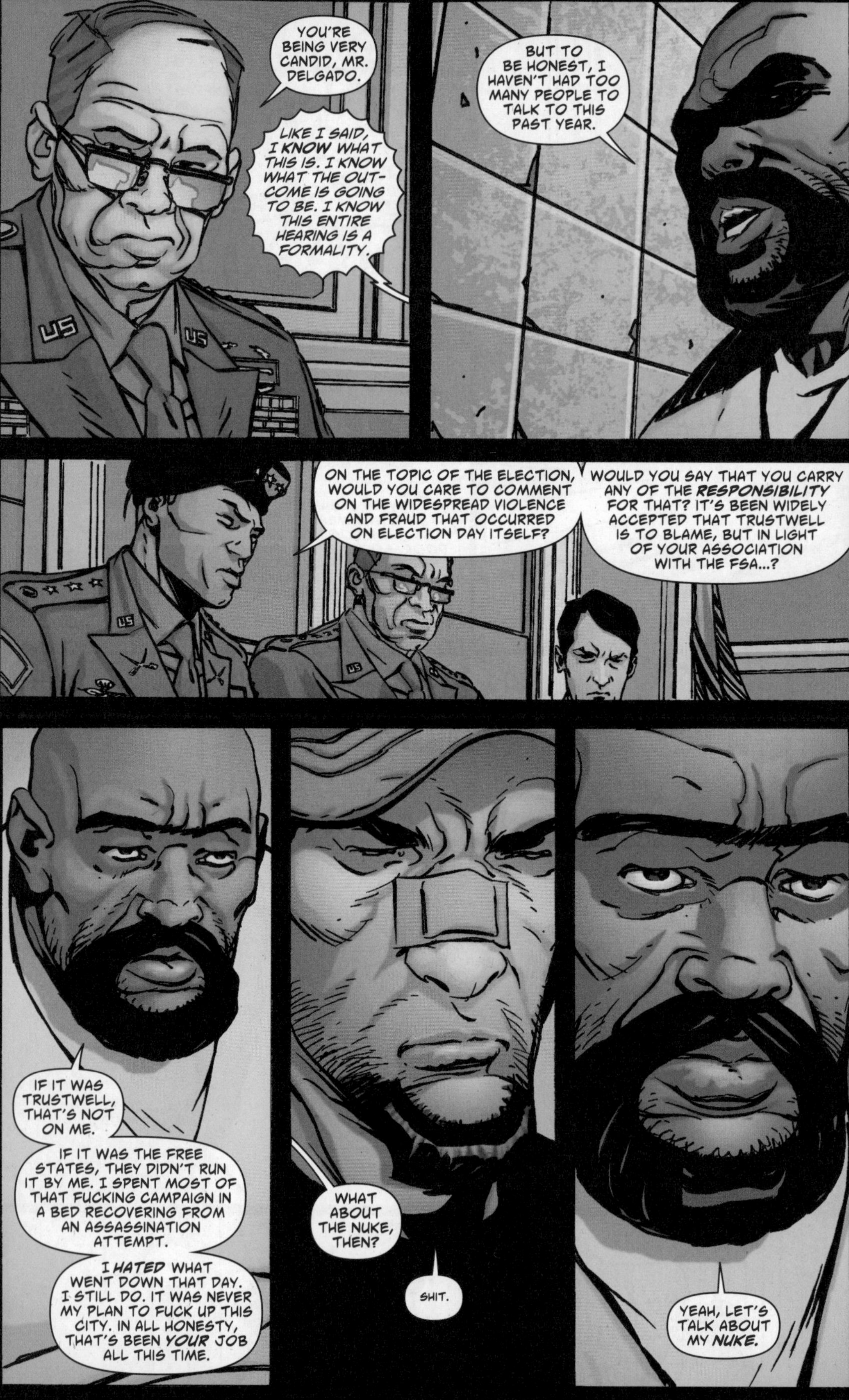
YOU'RE BEING VERY CANDID, MR. DELGADO.
LIKE I SAID, I KNOW WHAT THIS IS. I KNOW WHAT THE OUT-COME IS GOING TO BE. I KNOW THIS ENTIRE HEARING IS A FORMALITY.
BUT TO BE HONEST, I HAVEN'T HAD TOO MANY PEOPLE TO TALK TO THIS PAST YEAR.
ON THE TOPIC OF THE ELECTION, WOULD YOU CARE TO COMMENT ON THE WIDESPREAD VIOLENCE AND FRAUD THAT OCCURRED ON ELECTION DAY ITSELF?
WOULD YOU SAY THAT YOU CARRY ANY OF THE RESPONSIBILITY FOR THAT? IT'S BEEN WIDELY ACCEPTED THAT TRUSTWELL IS TO BLAME, BUT IN LIGHT OF YOUR ASSOCIATION WITH THE FSA...?
IF IT WAS TRUSTWELL, THAT'S NOT ON ME.
IF IT WAS THE FREE STATES, THEY DIDN'T RUN IT BY ME. I SPENT MOST OF THAT FUCKING CAMPAIGN IN A BED RECOVERING FROM AN ASSASSINATION ATTEMPT.
I HATED WHAT WENT DOWN THAT DAY. I STILL DO. IT WAS NEVER MY PLAN TO FUCK UP THIS CITY. IN ALL HONESTY, THAT'S BEEN YOUR JOB ALL THIS TIME.
WHAT ABOUT THE NUKE, THEN?
SHIT.
YEAH, LET'S TALK ABOUT MY NUKE.

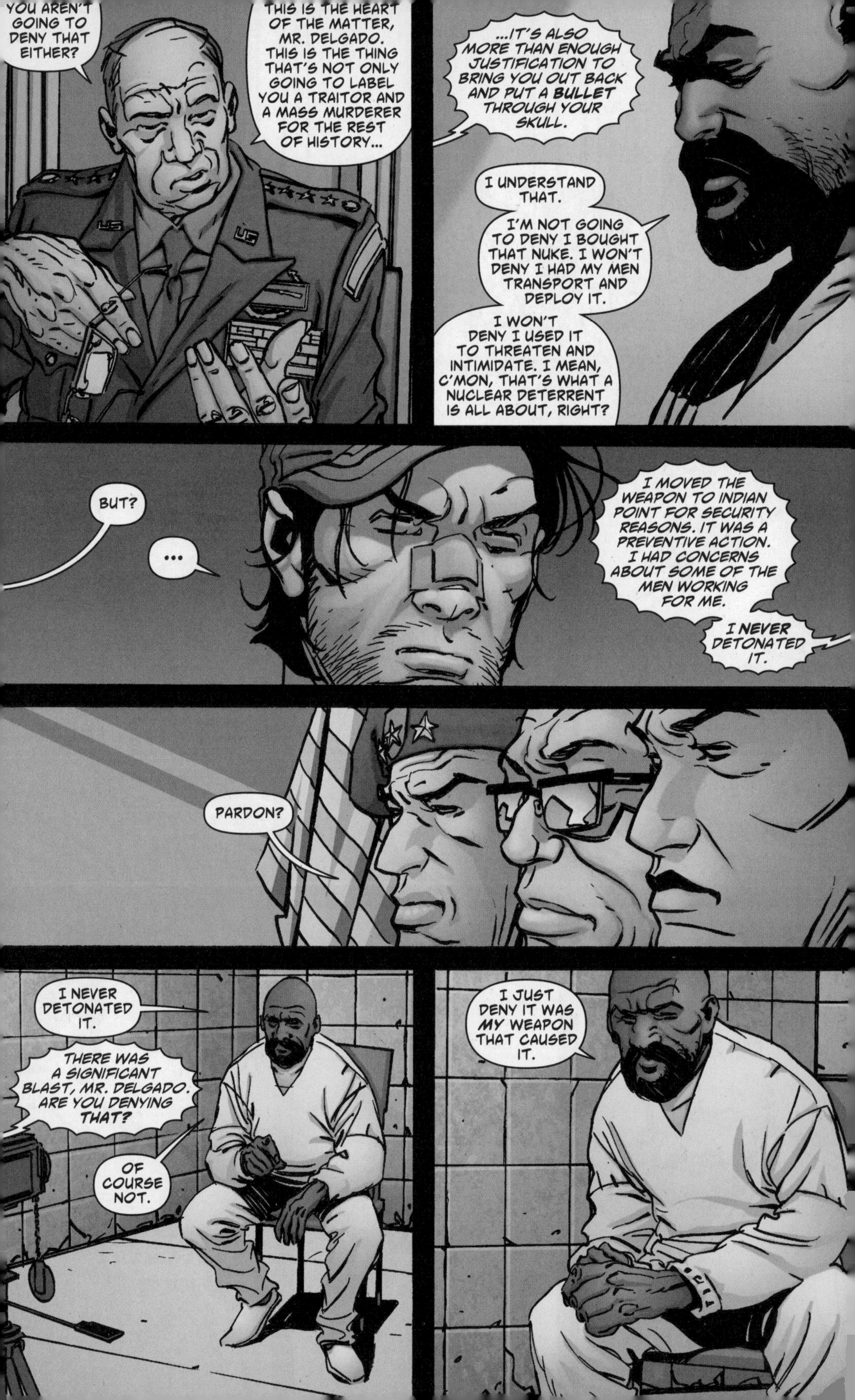
YOU AREN'T GOING TO DENY THAT EITHER?
THIS IS THE HEART OF THE MATTER, MR. DELGADO. THIS IS THE THING THAT'S NOT ONLY GOING TO LABEL YOU A TRAITOR AND A MASS MURDERER FOR THE REST OF HISTORY...
...IT'S ALSO MORE THAN ENOUGH JUSTIFICATION TO BRING YOU OUT BACK AND PUT A BULLET THROUGH YOUR SKULL.
I UNDERSTAND THAT.
I'M NOT GOING TO DENY I BOUGHT THAT NUKE. I WON'T DENY I HAD MY MEN TRANSPORT AND DEPLOY IT.
I WON'T DENY I USED IT TO THREATEN AND INTIMIDATE. I MEAN, C'MON, THAT'S WHAT A NUCLEAR DETERRENT IS ALL ABOUT, RIGHT?
BUT?
...
I MOVED THE WEAPON TO INDIAN POINT FOR SECURITY REASONS. IT WAS A PREVENTIVE ACTION. I HAD CONCERNS ABOUT SOME OF THE MEN WORKING FOR ME.
I NEVER DETONATED IT.
PARDON?
I NEVER DETONATED IT.
THERE WAS A SIGNIFICANT BLAST, MR. DELGADO. ARE YOU DENYING THAT?
OF COURSE NOT.
I JUST DENY IT WAS MY WEAPON THAT CAUSED IT.

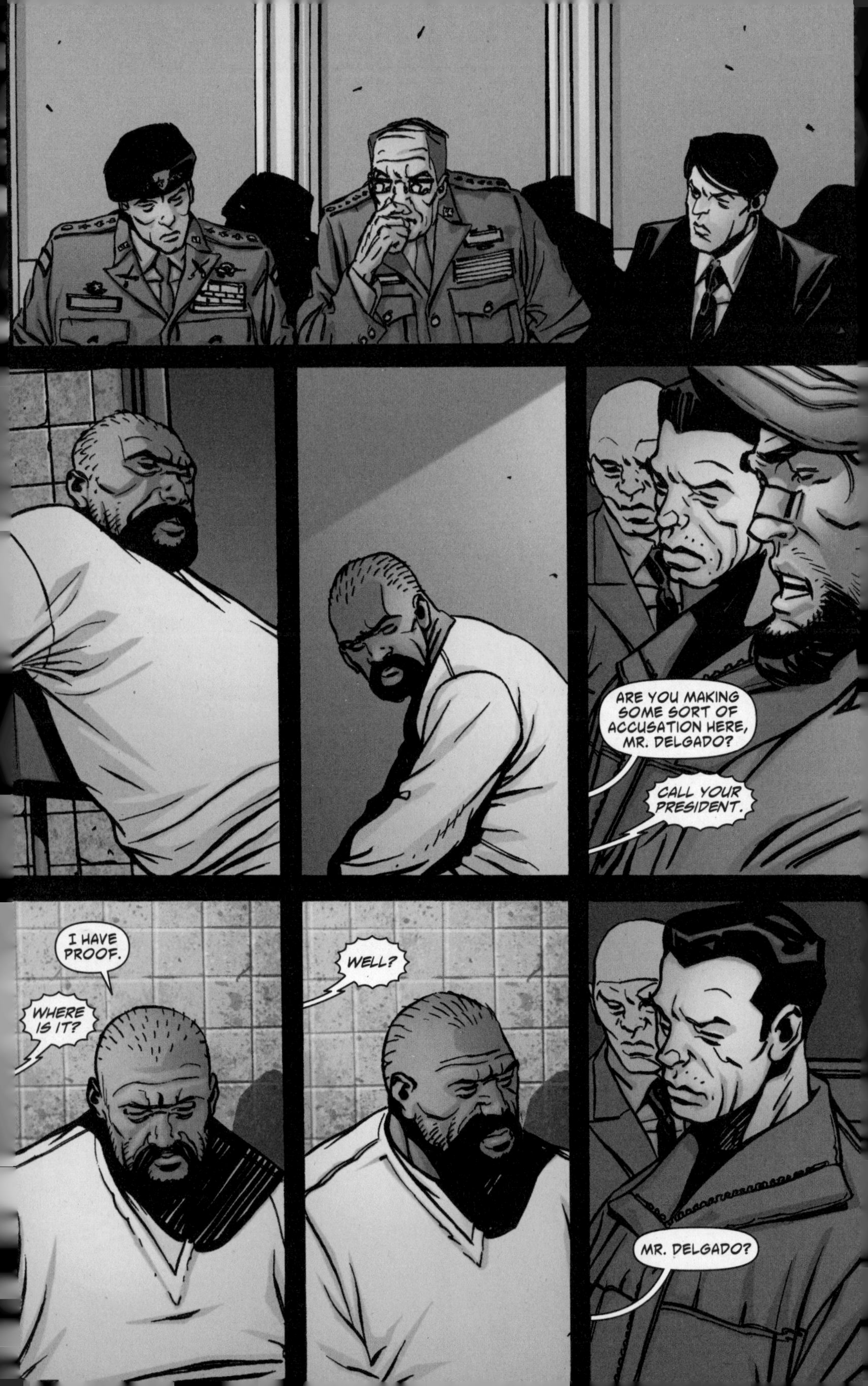
ARE YOU MAKING SOME SORT OF ACCUSATION HERE, MR. DELGADO?
CALL YOUR PRESIDENT.
I HAVE PROOF.
WHERE IS IT?
WELL?
MR. DELGADO?

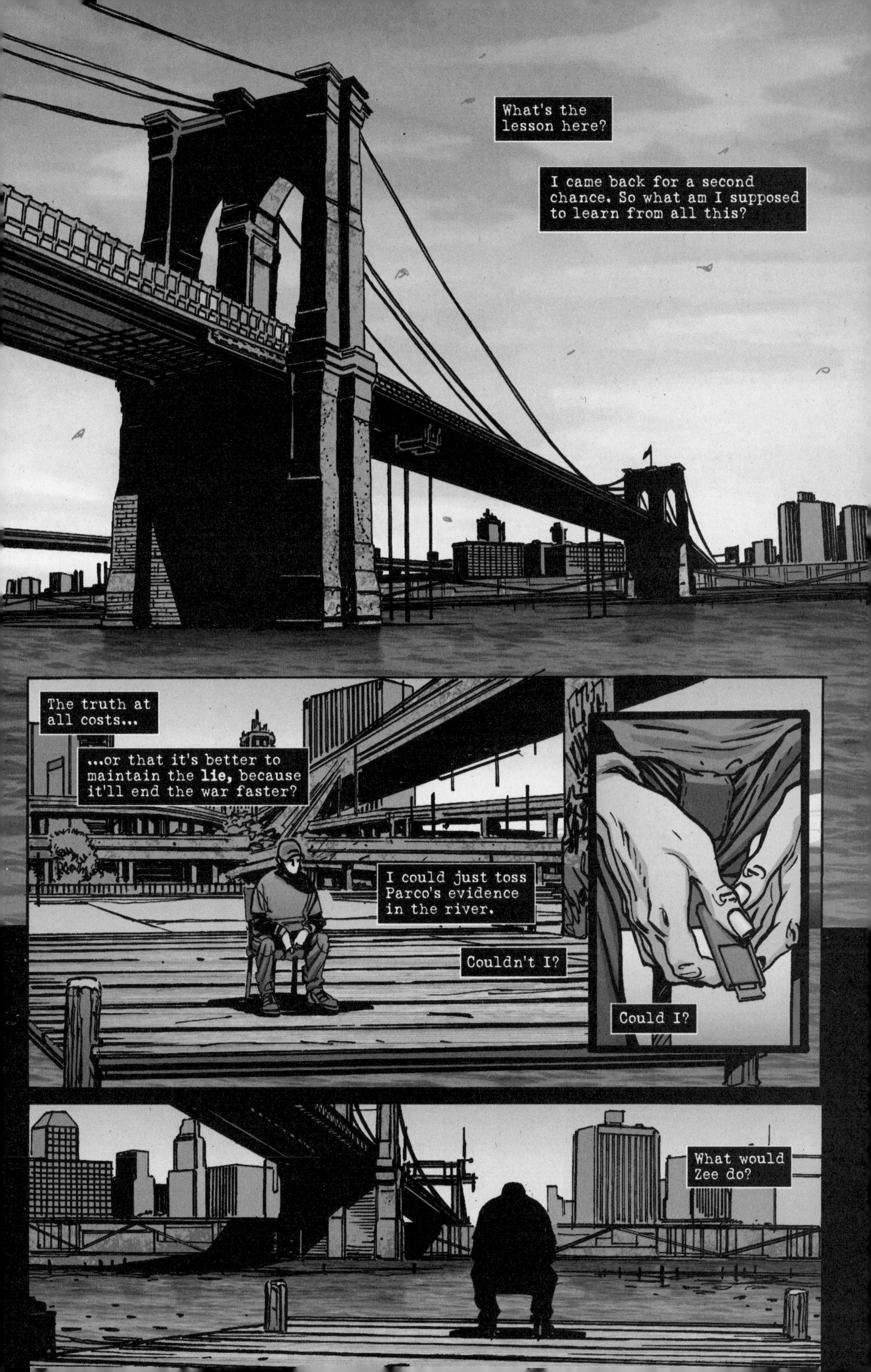
What's the lesson here?
I came back for a second chance. So what am I supposed to learn from all this?
The truth at all costs...
...or that it's better to maintain the **lie**, because it'll end the war faster?
I could just toss Parco's evidence in the river.
Couldn't I?
Could I?
What would Zee do?

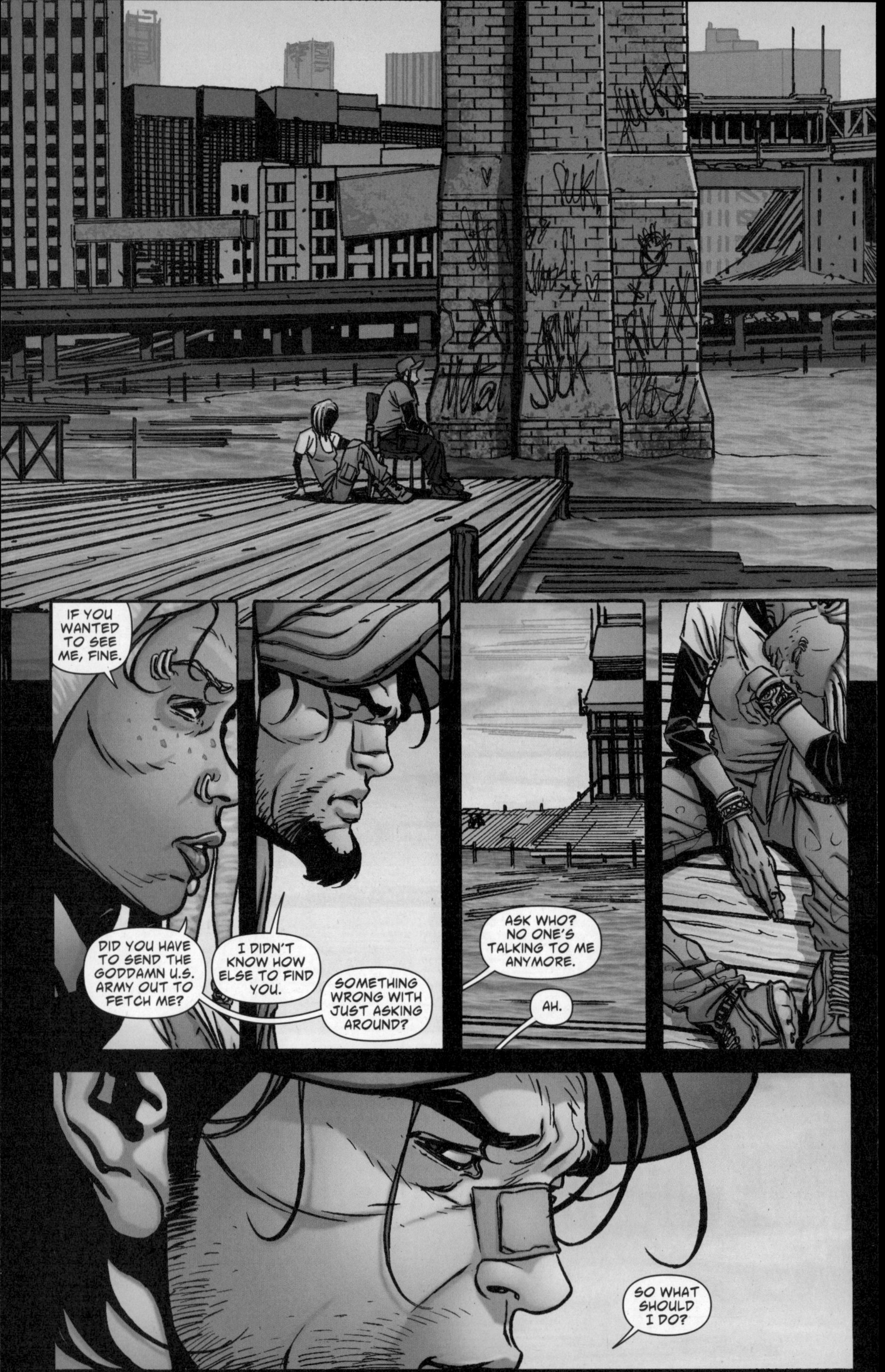
IF YOU WANTED TO SEE ME, FINE.
DID YOU HAVE TO SEND THE GODDAMN U.S. ARMY OUT TO FETCH ME?
I DIDN'T KNOW HOW ELSE TO FIND YOU.
SOMETHING WRONG WITH JUST ASKING AROUND?
ASK WHO? NO ONE'S TALKING TO ME ANYMORE.
AH.
SO WHAT SHOULD I DO?

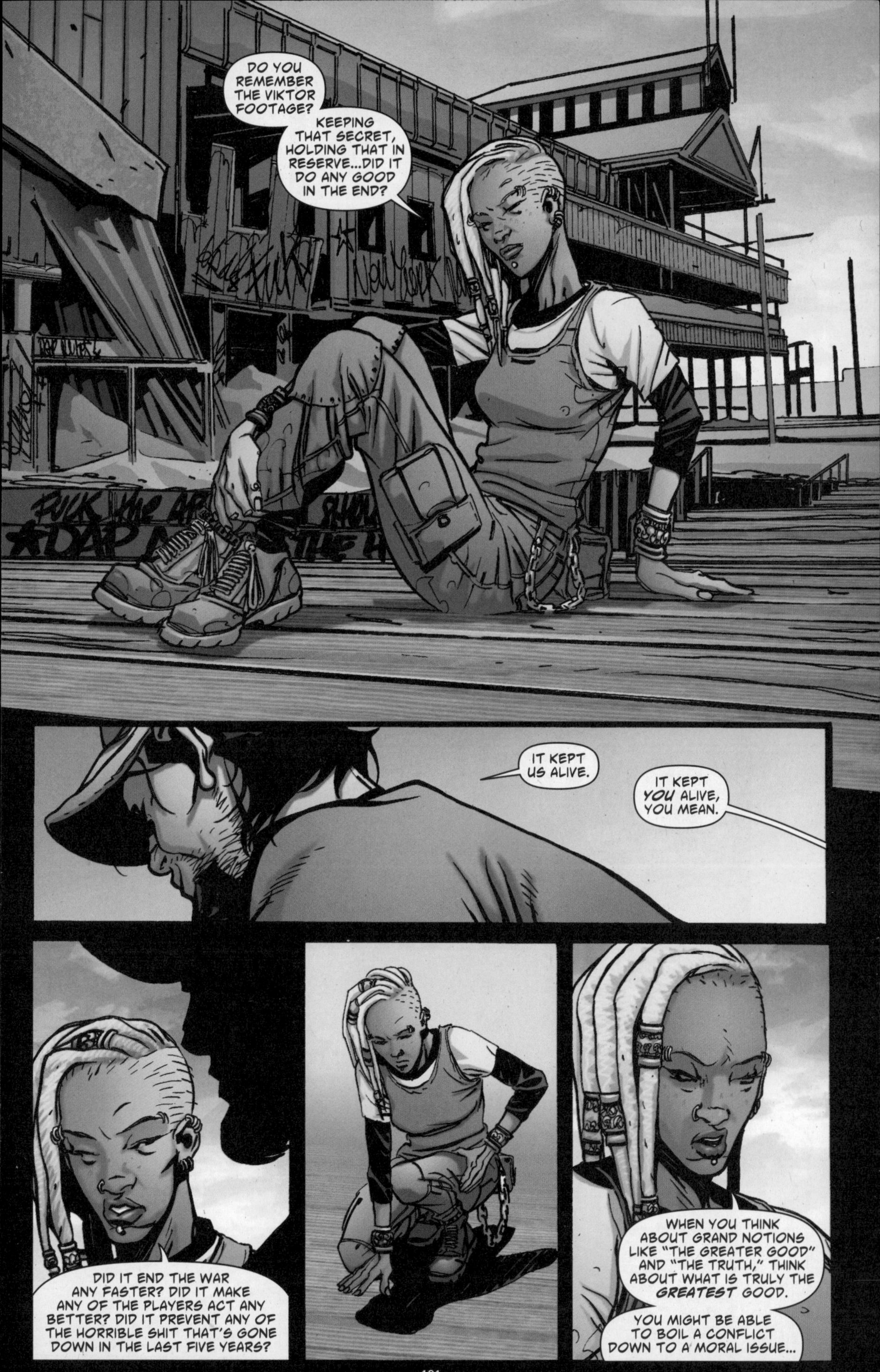

DO YOU REMEMBER THE VIKTOR FOOTAGE?
KEEPING THAT SECRET, HOLDING THAT IN RESERVE...DID IT DO ANY GOOD IN THE END?
IT KEPT US ALIVE.
IT KEPT *YOU* ALIVE, YOU MEAN.
DID IT END THE WAR ANY FASTER? DID IT MAKE ANY OF THE PLAYERS ACT ANY BETTER? DID IT PREVENT ANY OF THE HORRIBLE SHIT THAT'S GONE DOWN IN THE LAST FIVE YEARS?
WHEN YOU THINK ABOUT GRAND NOTIONS LIKE "THE GREATER GOOD" AND "THE TRUTH," THINK ABOUT WHAT IS TRULY THE *GREATEST* GOOD.
YOU MIGHT BE ABLE TO BOIL A CONFLICT DOWN TO A MORAL ISSUE...

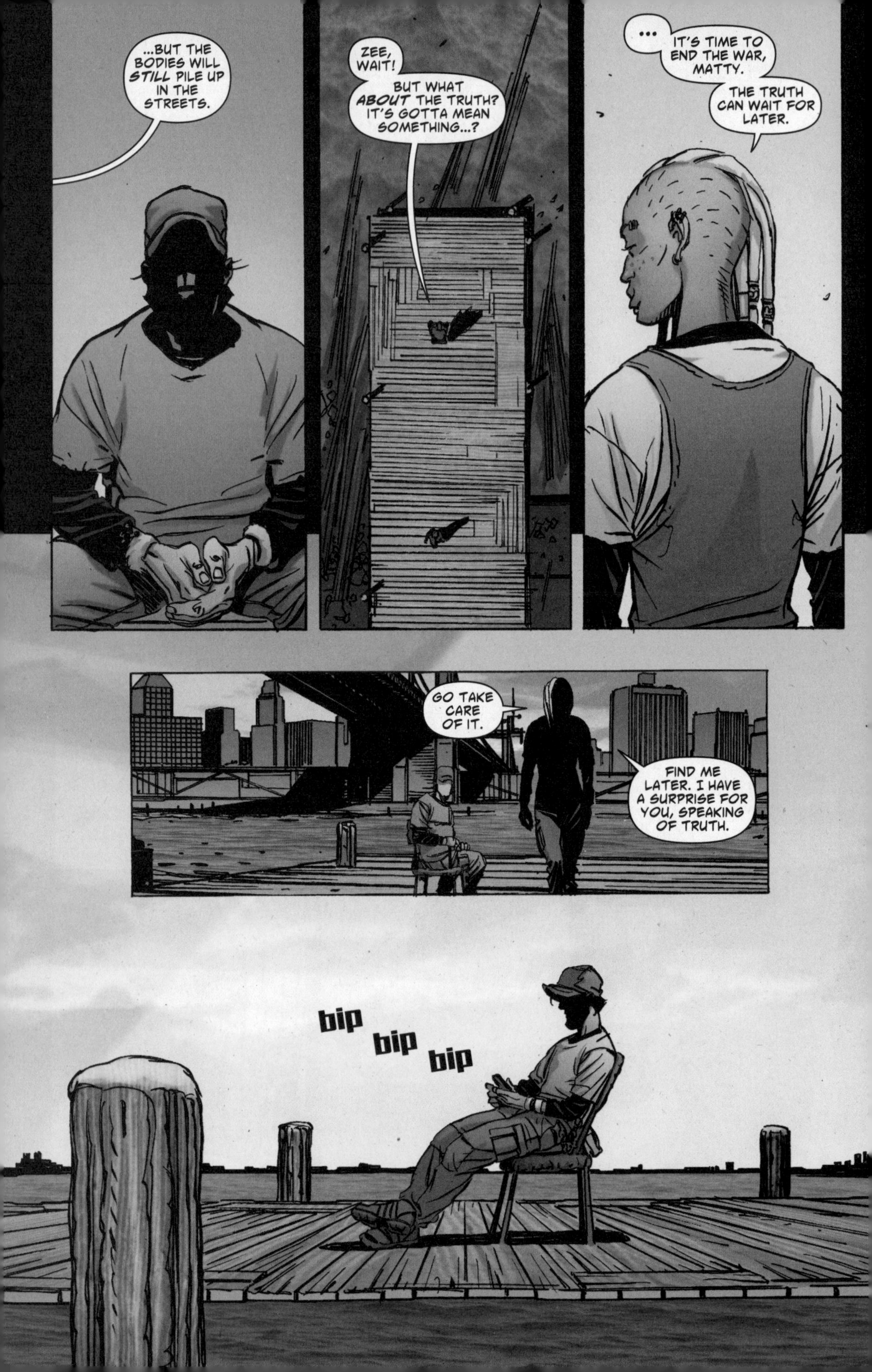
...BUT THE BODIES WILL STILL PILE UP IN THE STREETS.
ZEE, WAIT!
BUT WHAT ABOUT THE TRUTH? IT'S GOTTA MEAN SOMETHING...?
...
IT'S TIME TO END THE WAR, MATTY.
THE TRUTH CAN WAIT FOR LATER.
GO TAKE CARE OF IT.
FIND ME LATER. I HAVE A SURPRISE FOR YOU, SPEAKING OF TRUTH.
bip
bip
bip

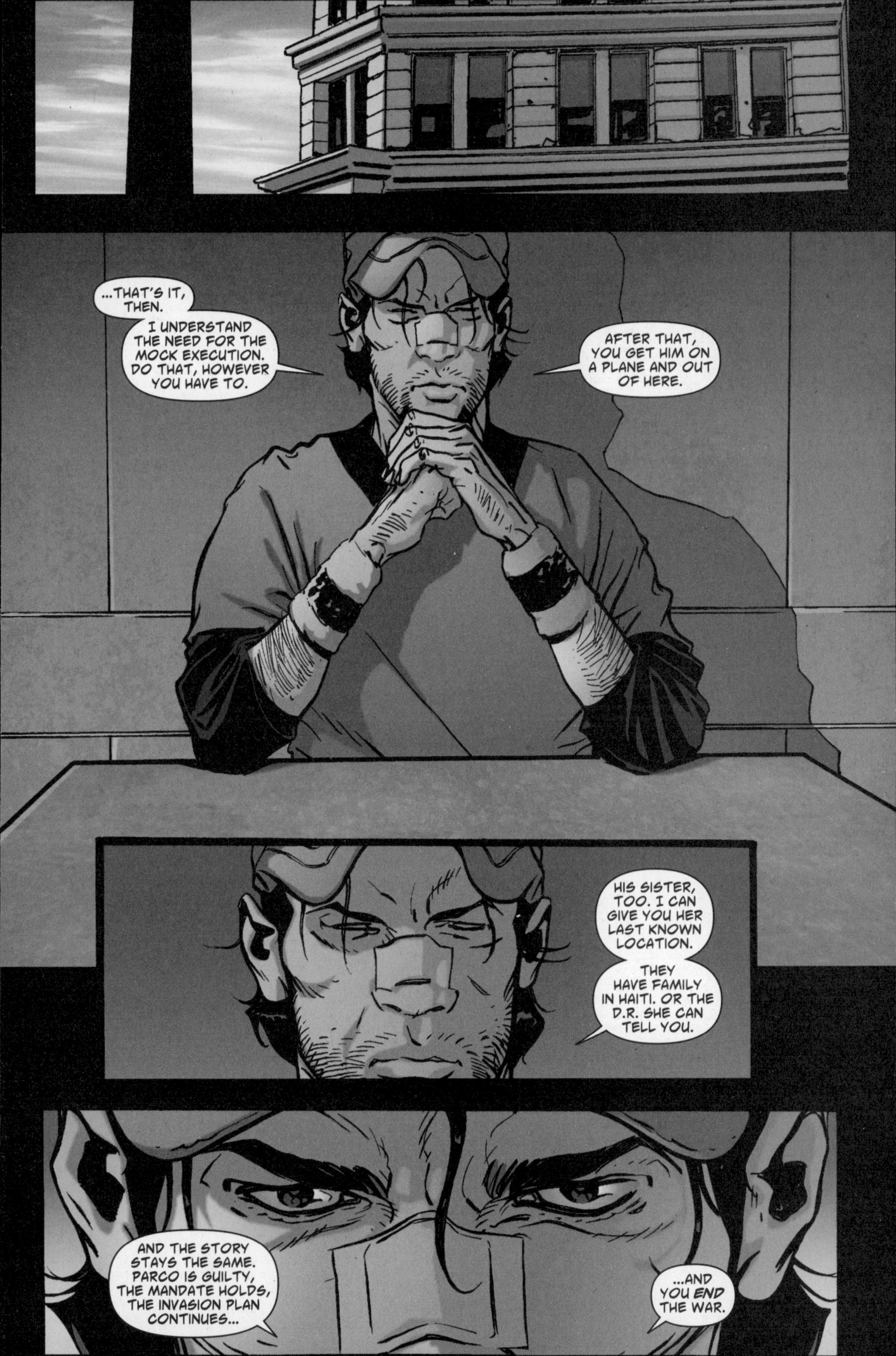
...THAT'S IT, THEN.
I UNDERSTAND THE NEED FOR THE MOCK EXECUTION. DO THAT, HOWEVER YOU HAVE TO.
AFTER THAT, YOU GET HIM ON A PLANE AND OUT OF HERE.
HIS SISTER, TOO. I CAN GIVE YOU HER LAST KNOWN LOCATION.
THEY HAVE FAMILY IN HAITI. OR THE D.R. SHE CAN TELL YOU.
AND THE STORY STAYS THE SAME. PARCO IS GUILTY, THE MANDATE HOLDS, THE INVASION PLAN CONTINUES...
...AND YOU END THE WAR.

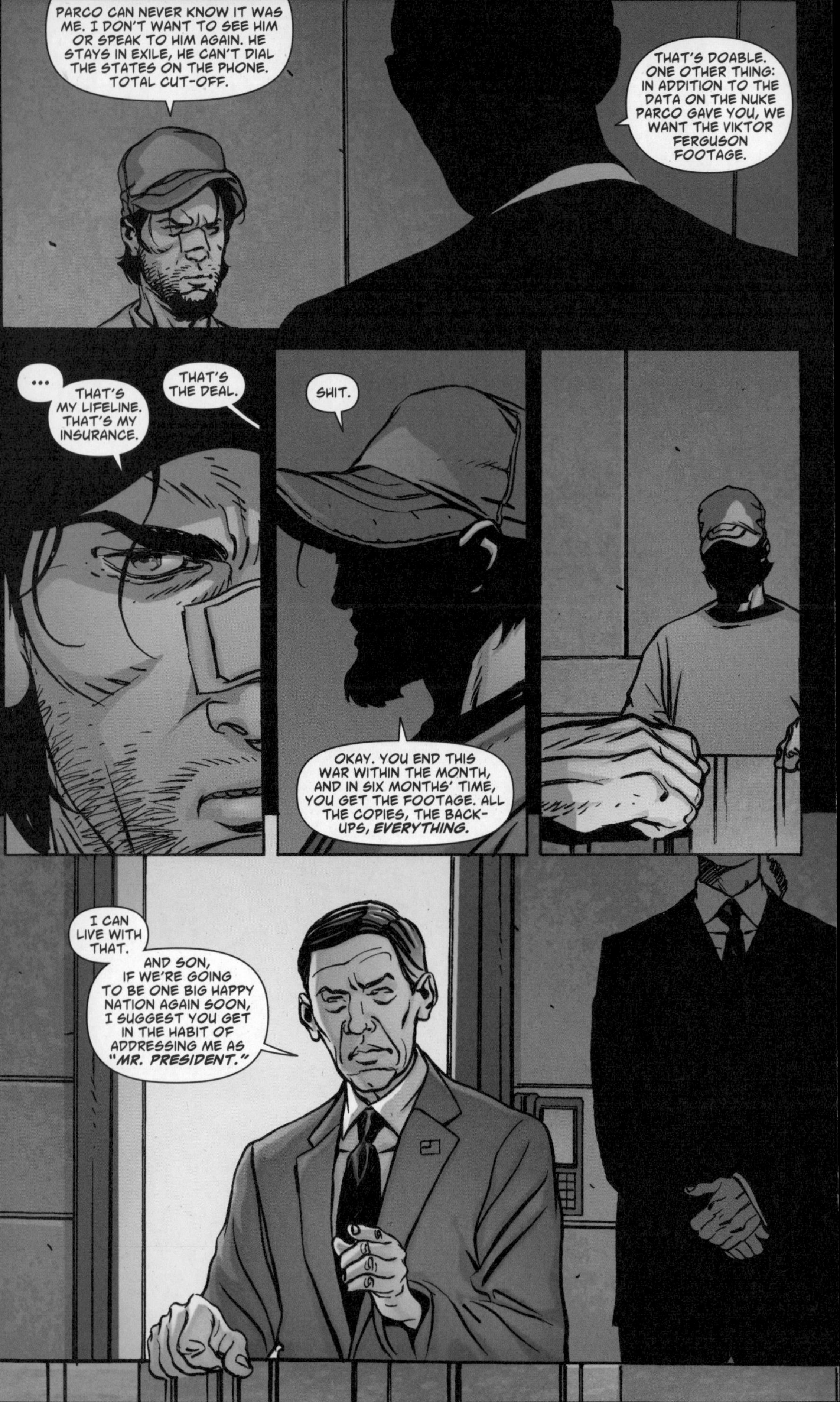
PARCO CAN NEVER KNOW IT WAS ME. I DON'T WANT TO SEE HIM OR SPEAK TO HIM AGAIN. HE STAYS IN EXILE, HE CAN'T DIAL THE STATES ON THE PHONE. TOTAL CUT-OFF.
THAT'S DOABLE. ONE OTHER THING: IN ADDITION TO THE DATA ON THE NUKE PARCO GAVE YOU, WE WANT THE VIKTOR FERGUSON FOOTAGE.
...
THAT'S MY LIFELINE. THAT'S MY INSURANCE.
THAT'S THE DEAL.
SHIT.
OKAY. YOU END THIS WAR WITHIN THE MONTH, AND IN SIX MONTHS' TIME, YOU GET THE FOOTAGE. ALL THE COPIES, THE BACK-UPS, *EVERYTHING.*
I CAN LIVE WITH THAT.
AND SON, IF WE'RE GOING TO BE ONE BIG HAPPY NATION AGAIN SOON, I SUGGEST YOU GET IN THE HABIT OF ADDRESSING ME AS "*MR. PRESIDENT.*"

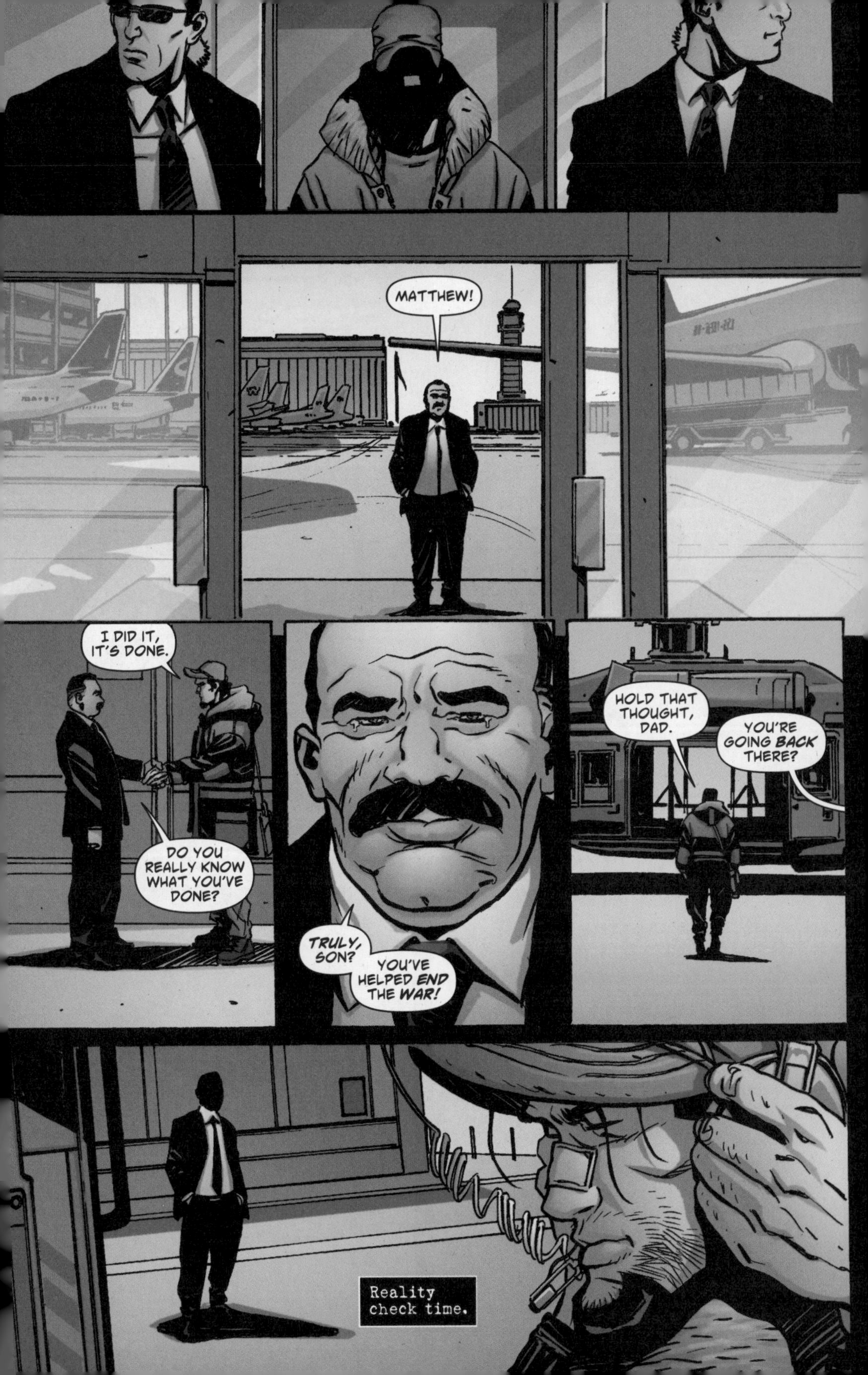
MATTHEW!
I DID IT, IT'S DONE.
DO YOU REALLY KNOW WHAT YOU'VE DONE?
TRULY, SON?
YOU'VE HELPED END THE WAR!
HOLD THAT THOUGHT, DAD.
YOU'RE GOING BACK THERE?
Reality check time.

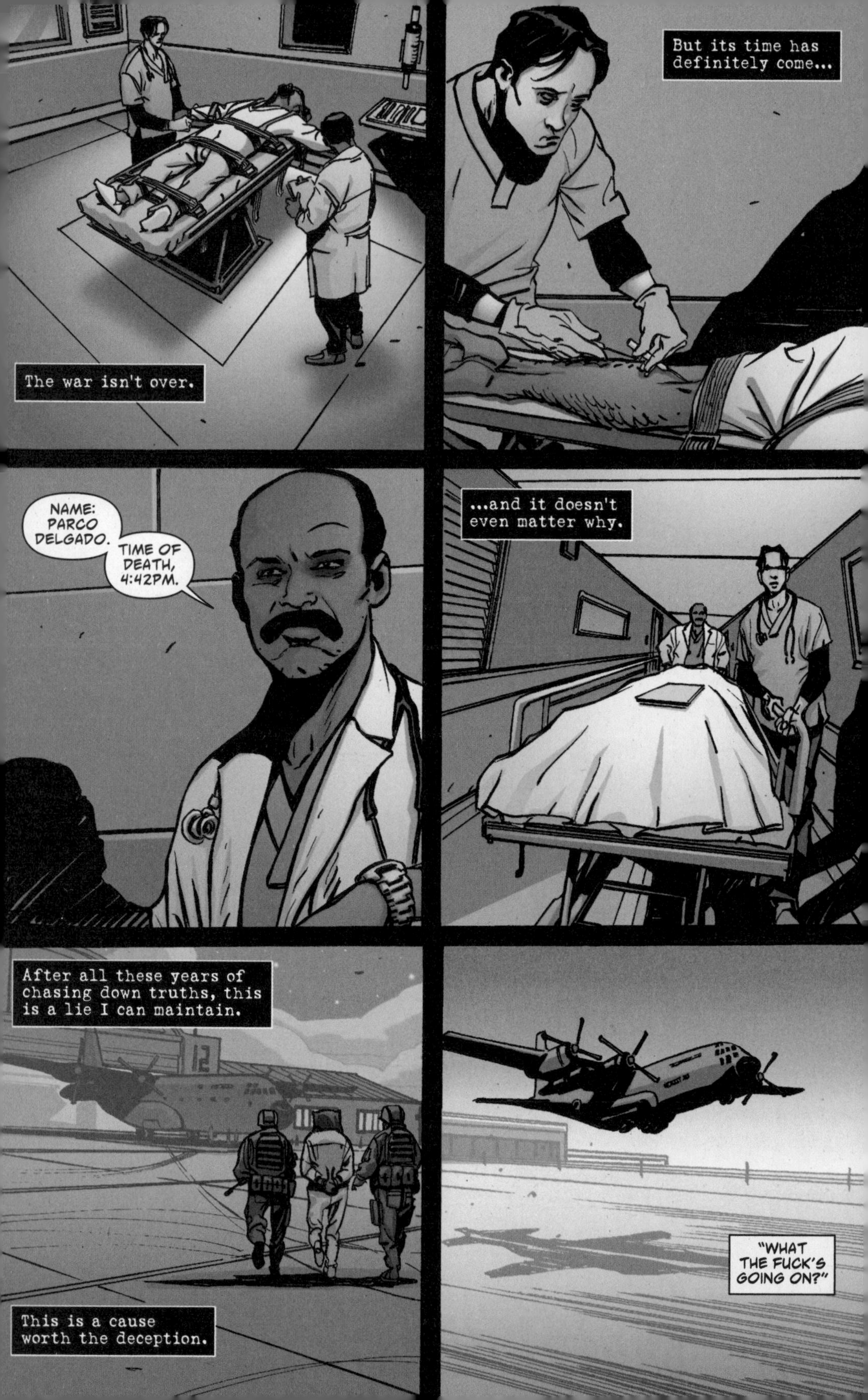
The war isn't over.
But its time has definitely come...
NAME: PARCO DELGADO.
TIME OF DEATH, 4:42PM.
...and it doesn't even matter why.
After all these years of chasing down truths, this is a lie I can maintain.
This is a cause worth the deception.
"WHAT THE FUCK'S GOING ON?"

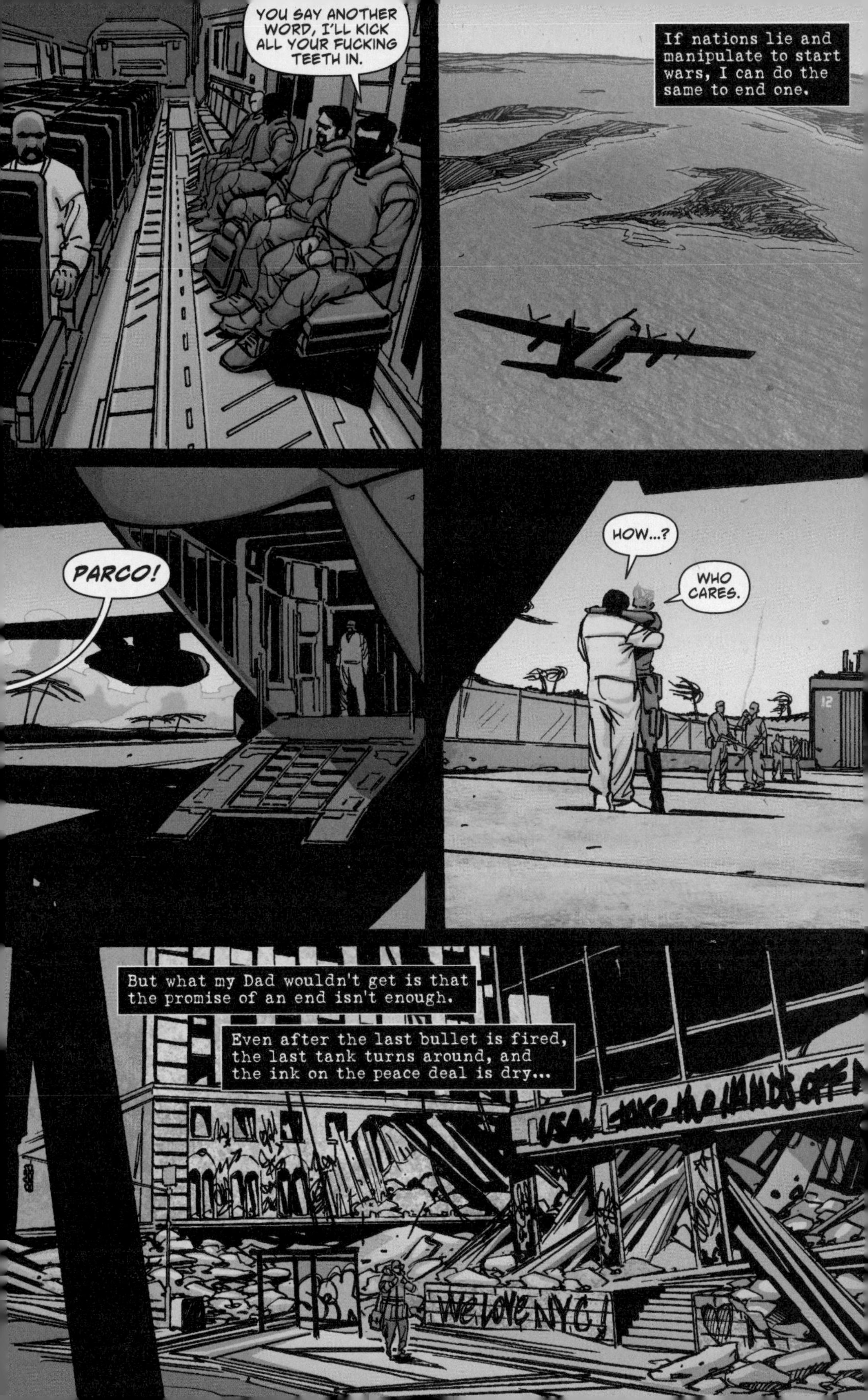

YOU SAY ANOTHER WORD, I'LL KICK ALL YOUR FUCKING TEETH IN.
If nations lie and manipulate to start wars, I can do the same to end one.
PARCO!
HOW...?
WHO CARES.
But what my Dad wouldn't get is that the promise of an end isn't enough.
Even after the last bullet is fired, the last tank turns around, and the ink on the peace deal is dry...
WE LOVE NYC!

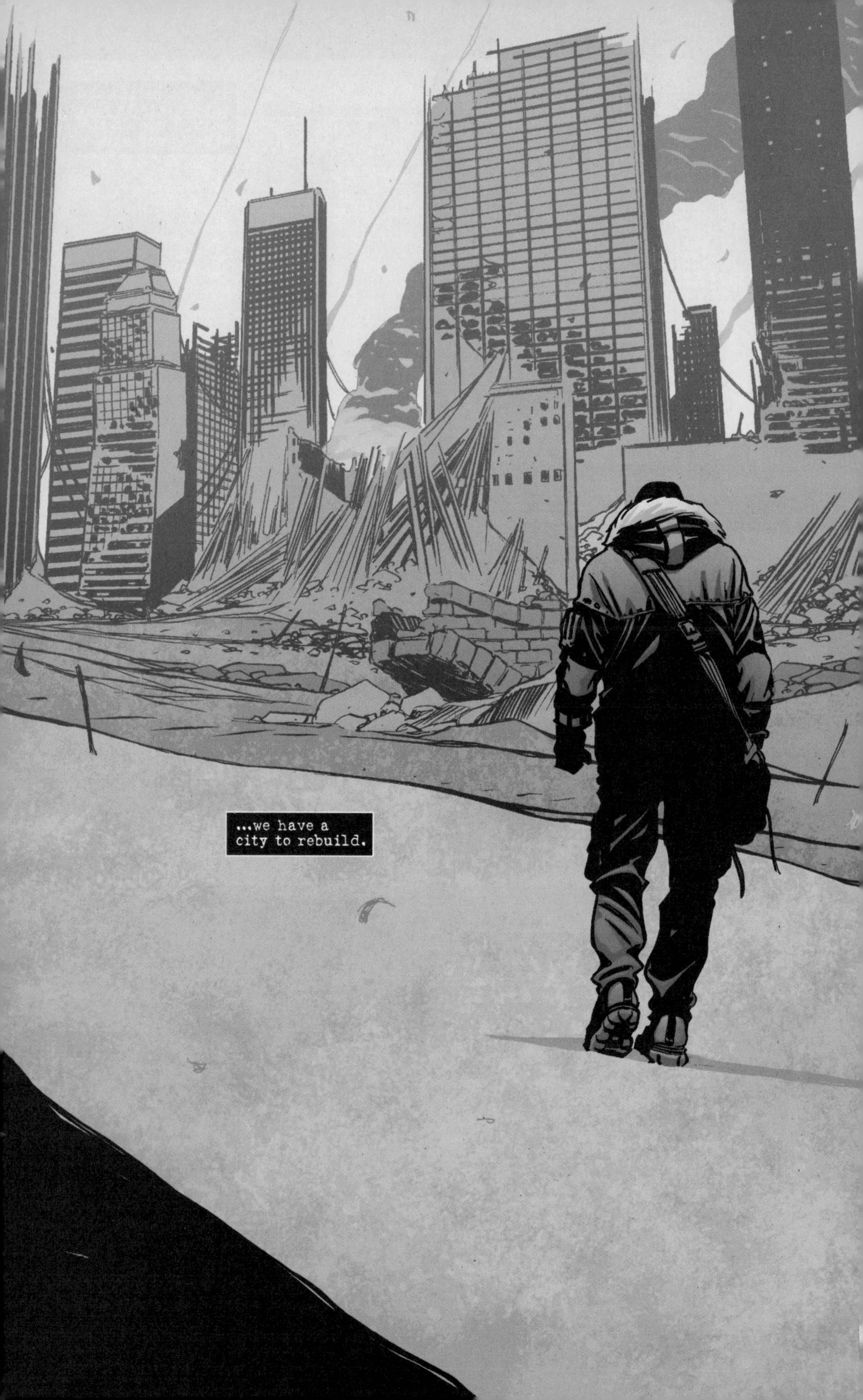
...we have a city to rebuild.

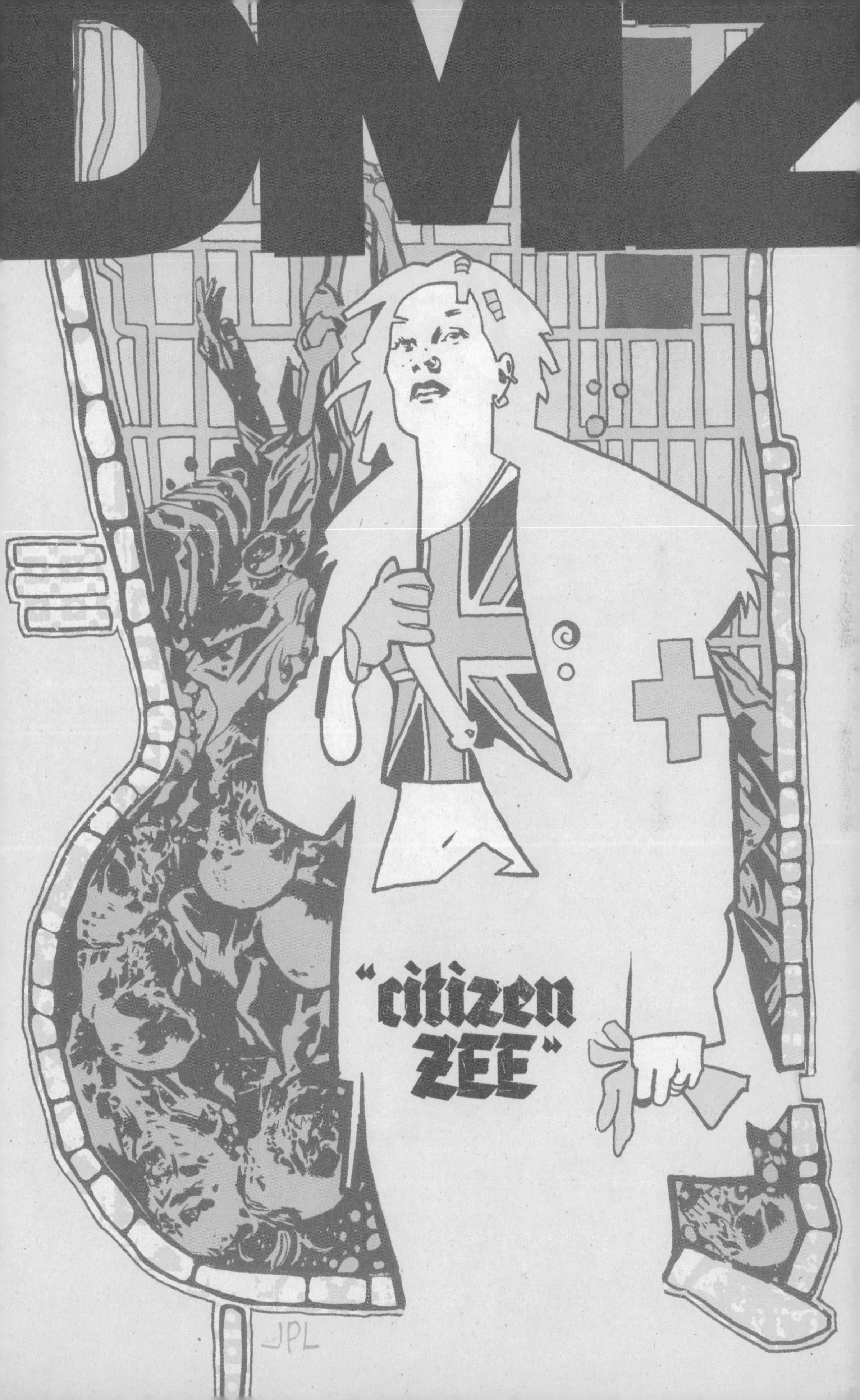
DMZ
"citizen ZEE"
JPL

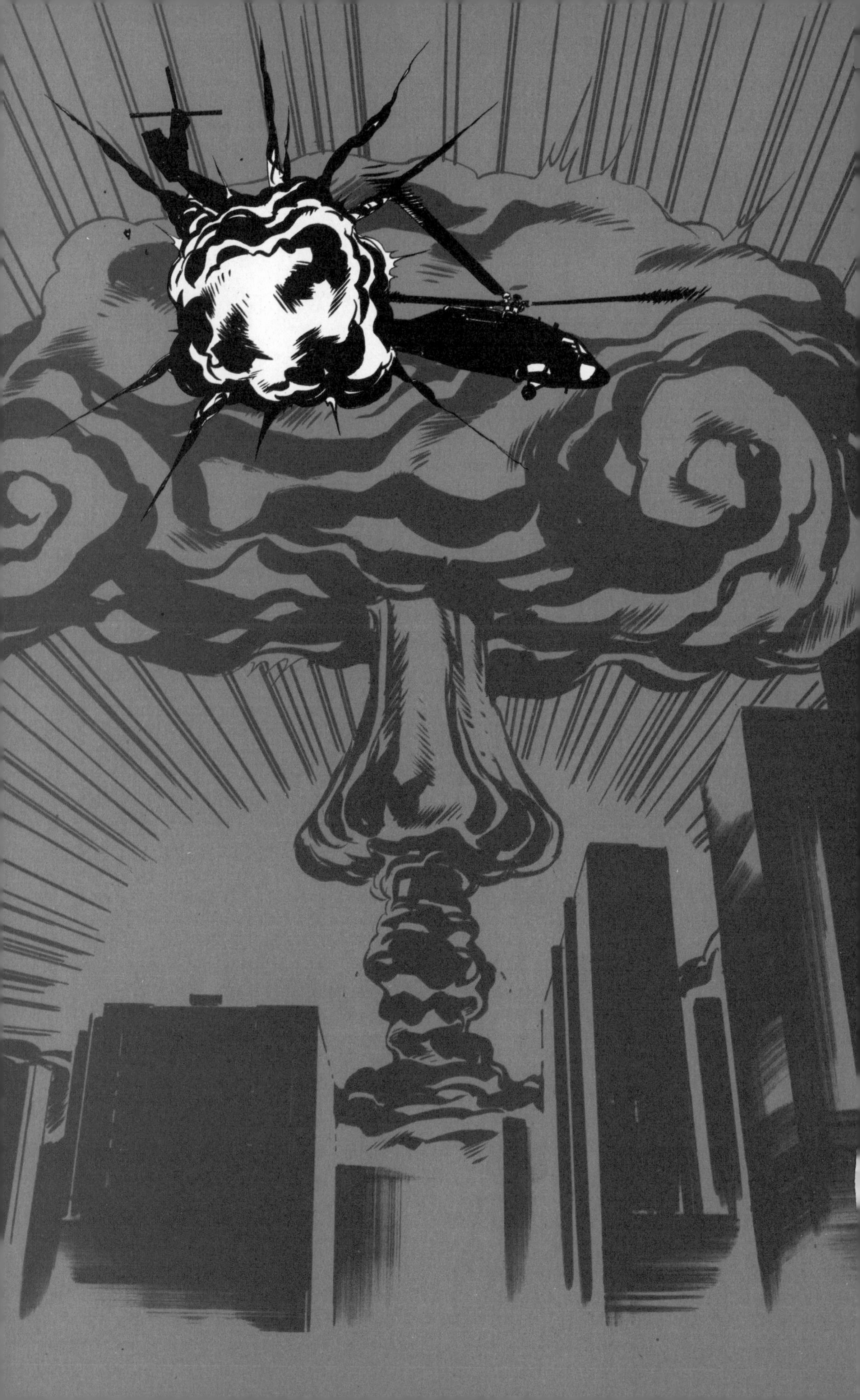

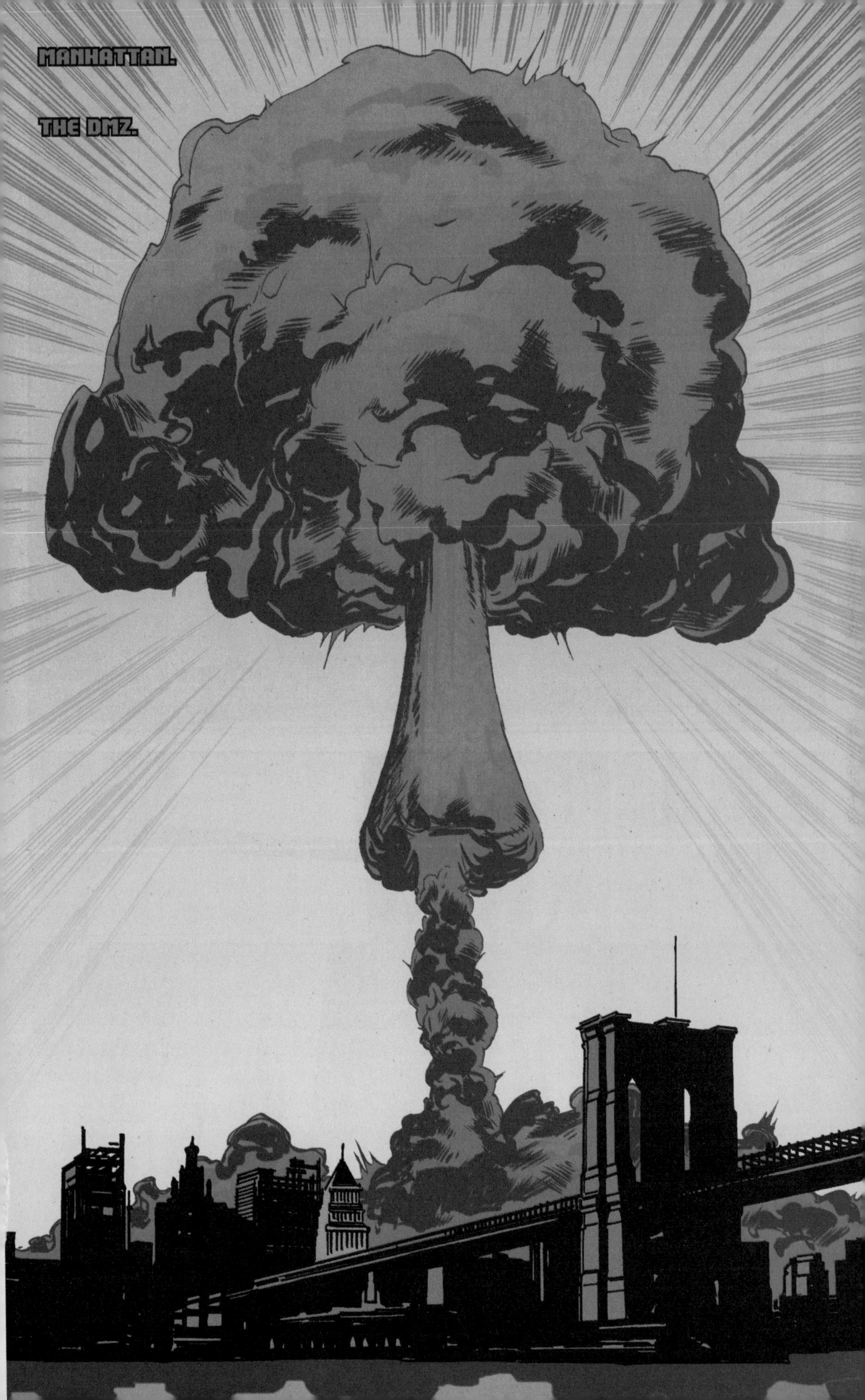
MANHATTAN.
THE DMZ.

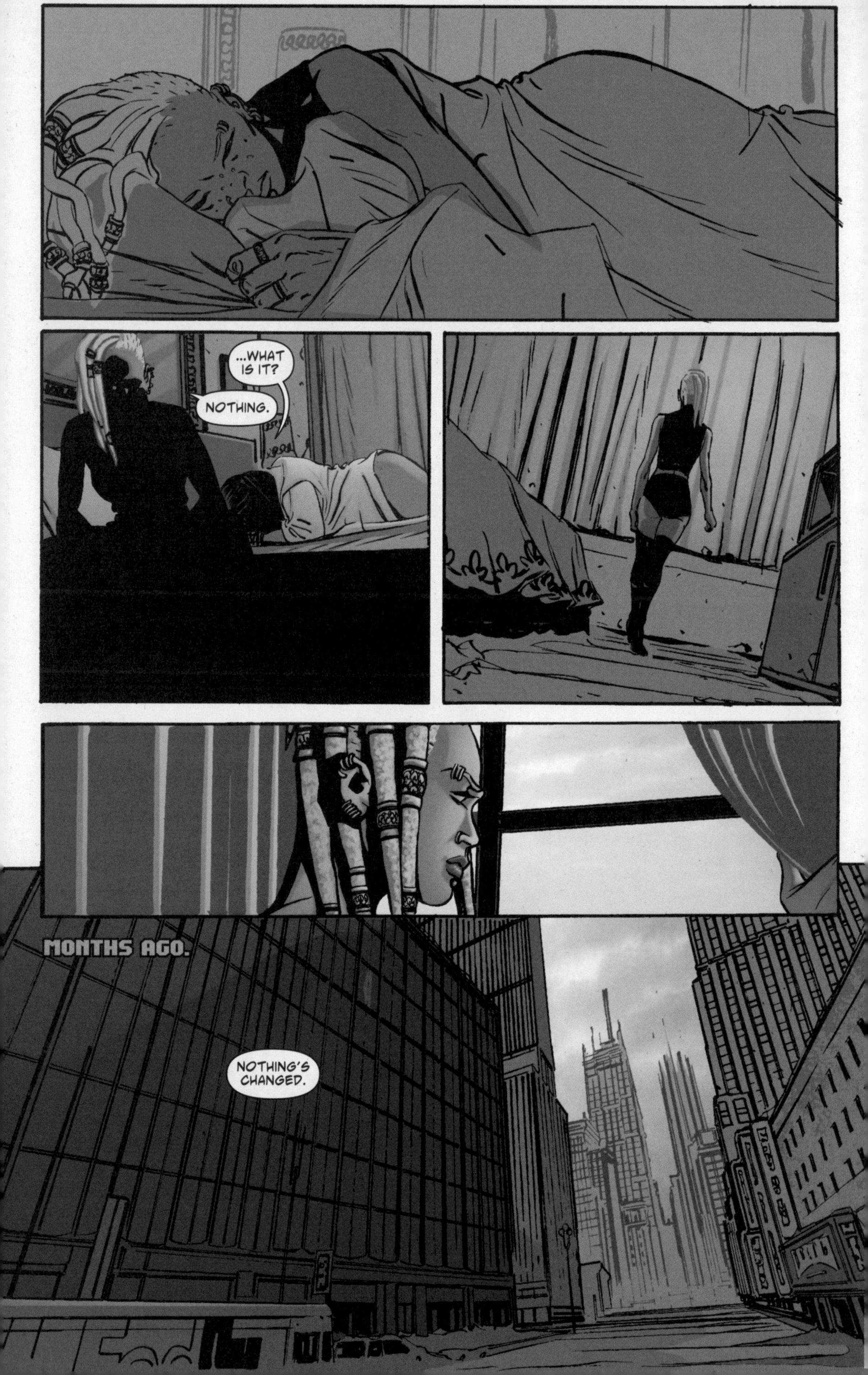
...WHAT IS IT?
NOTHING.
MONTHS AGO.
NOTHING'S CHANGED.

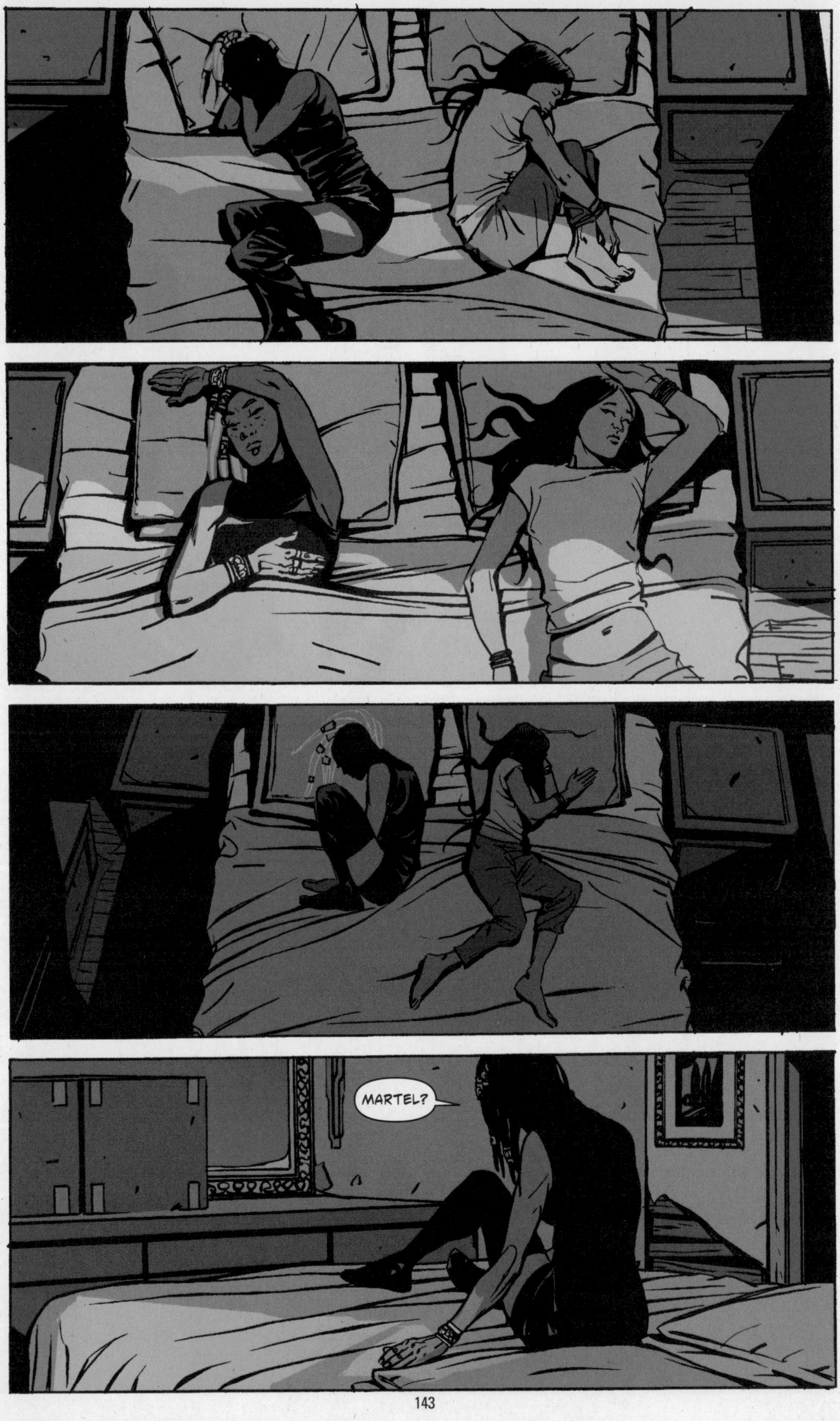
MARTEL?

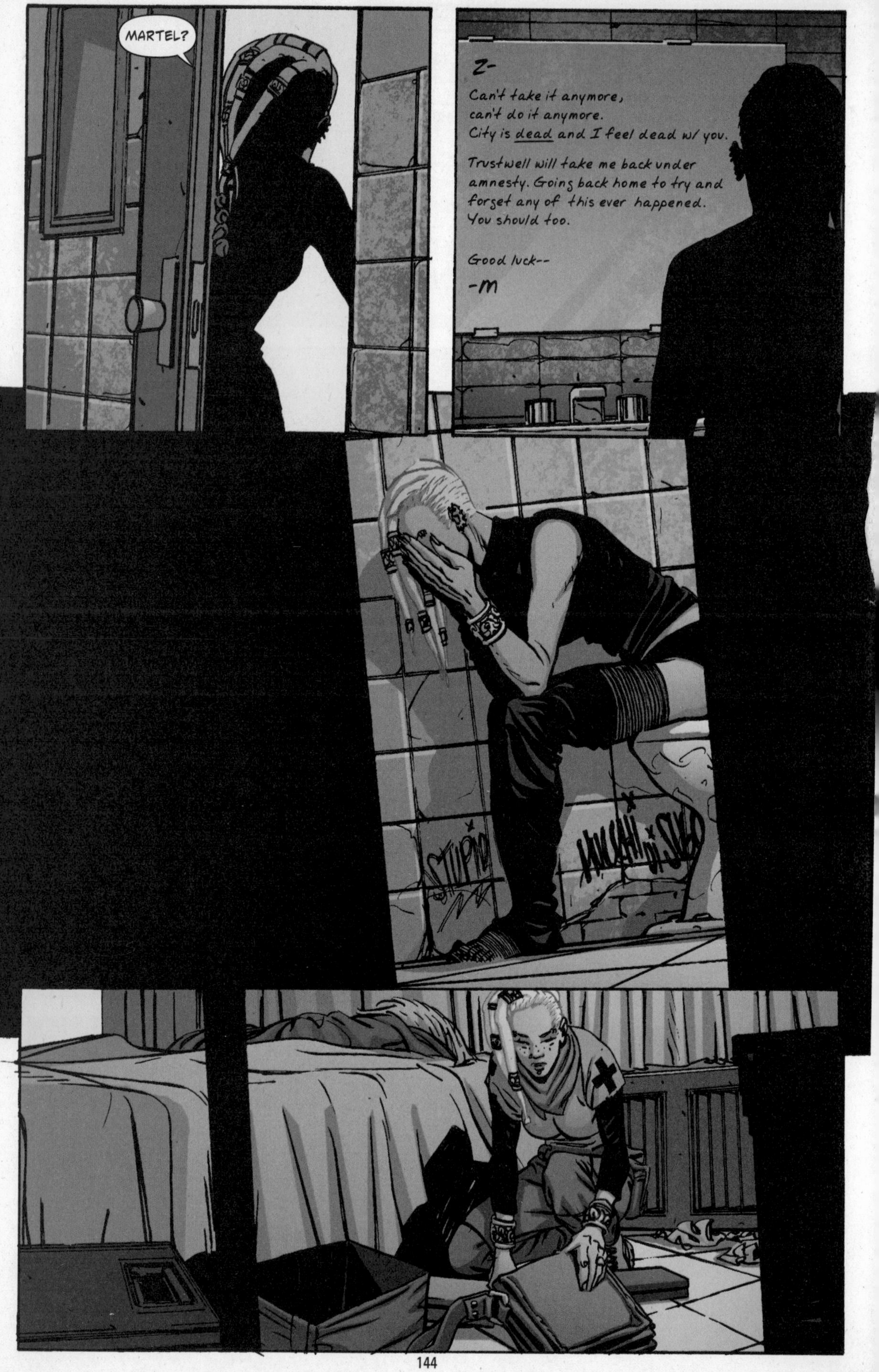
MARTEL?
Z-
Can't take it anymore,
can't do it anymore.
City is dead and I feel dead w/ you.
Trustwell will take me back under
amnesty. Going back home to try and
forget any of this ever happened.
You should too.
Good luck--
-M
STUPID

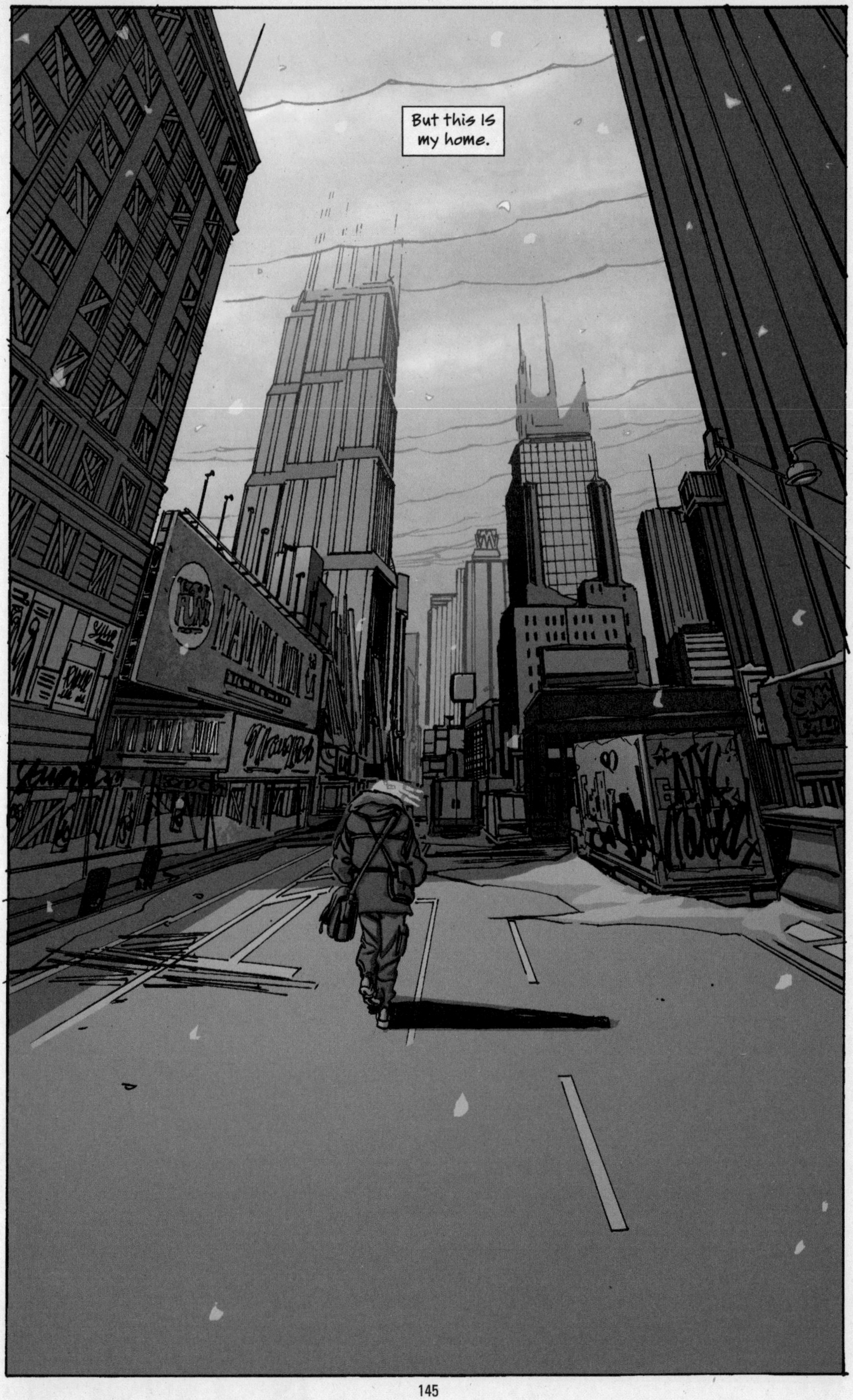
But this IS my home.

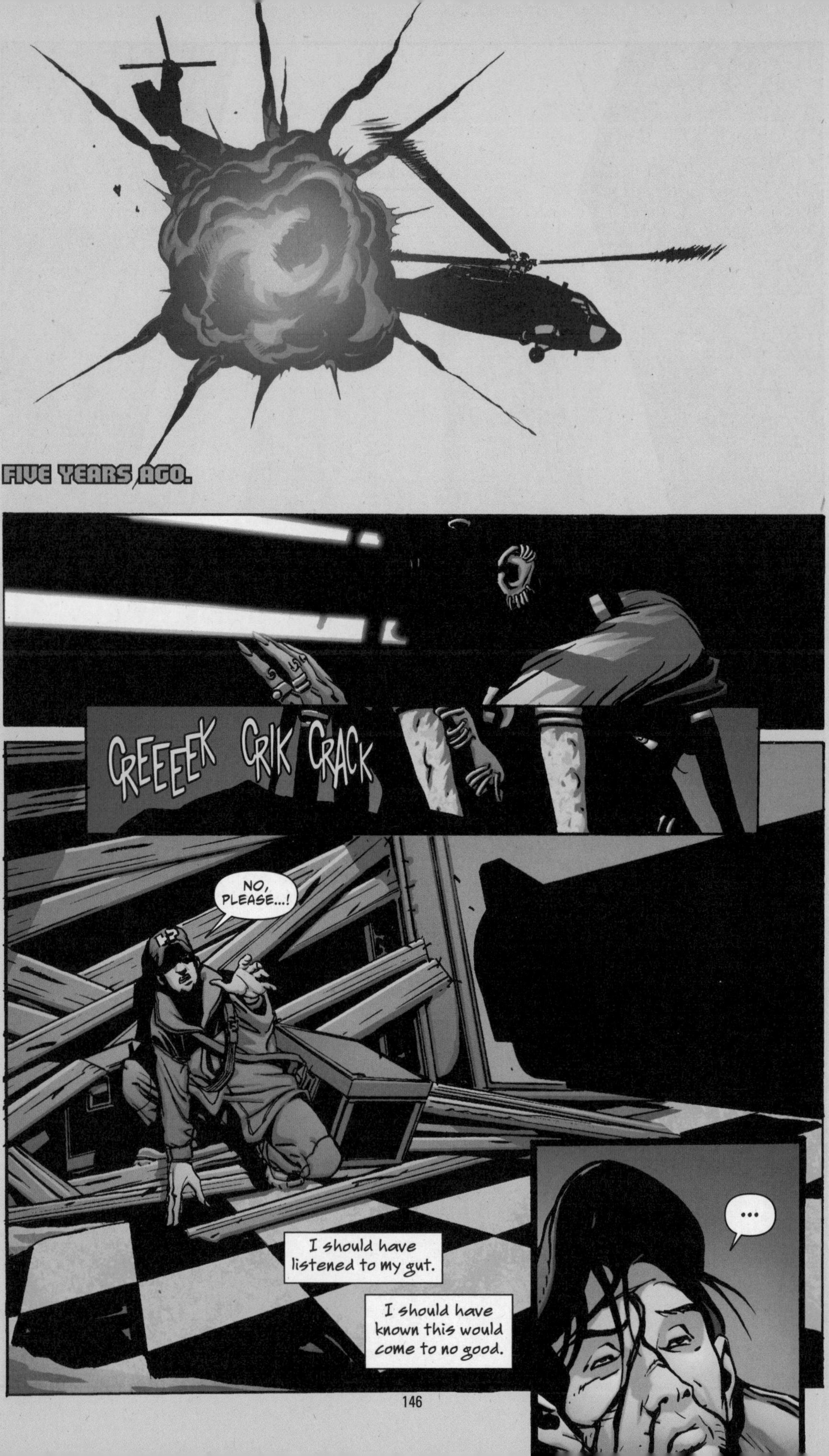
FIVE YEARS AGO.
CREEEEEK CRIK CRACK
NO, PLEASE...!
I should have listened to my gut.
I should have known this would come to no good.
...

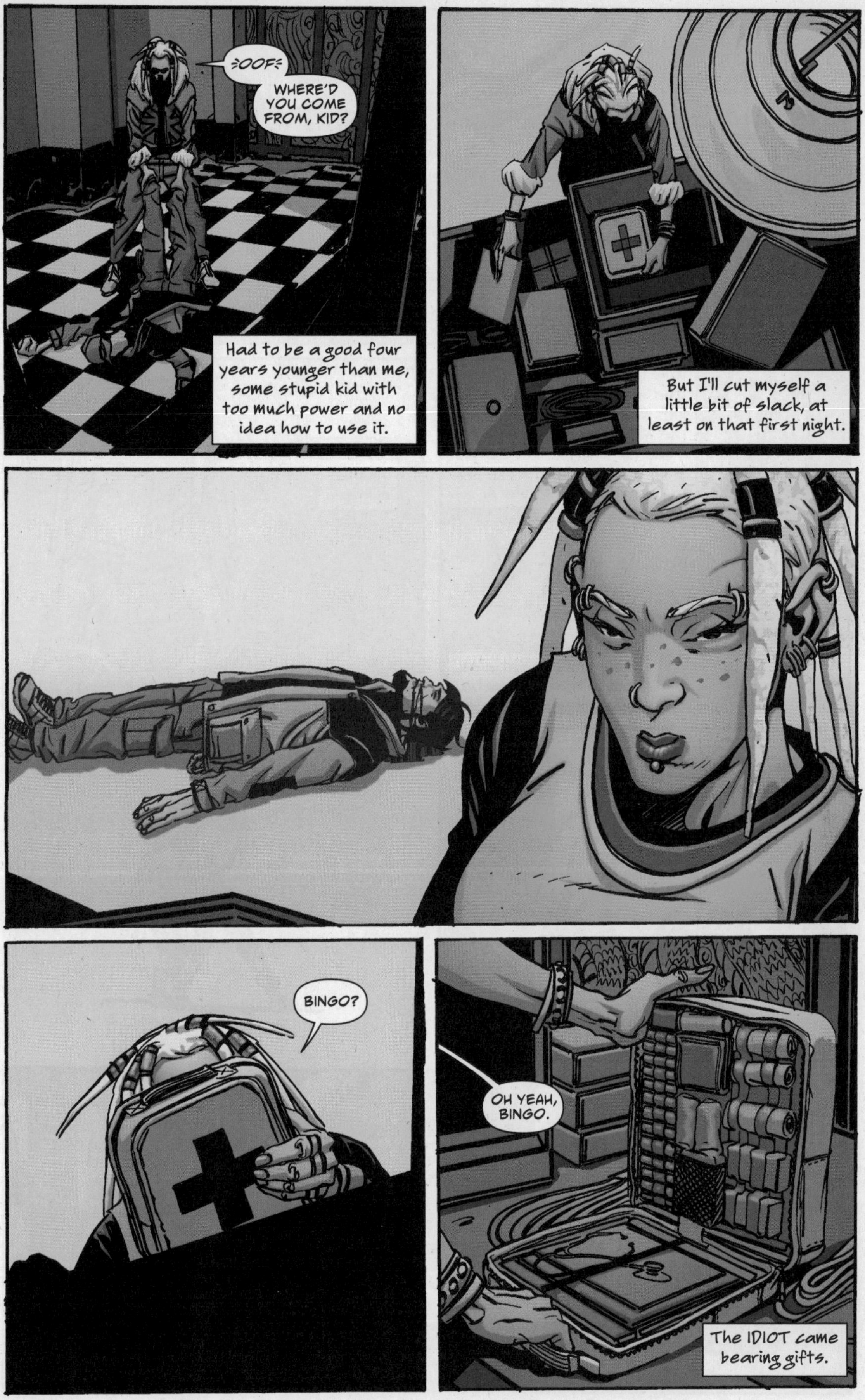

OOF
WHERE'D YOU COME FROM, KID?
Had to be a good four years younger than me, some stupid kid with too much power and no idea how to use it.
But I'll cut myself a little bit of slack, at least on that first night.
BINGO?
OH YEAH, BINGO.
The IDIOT came bearing gifts.

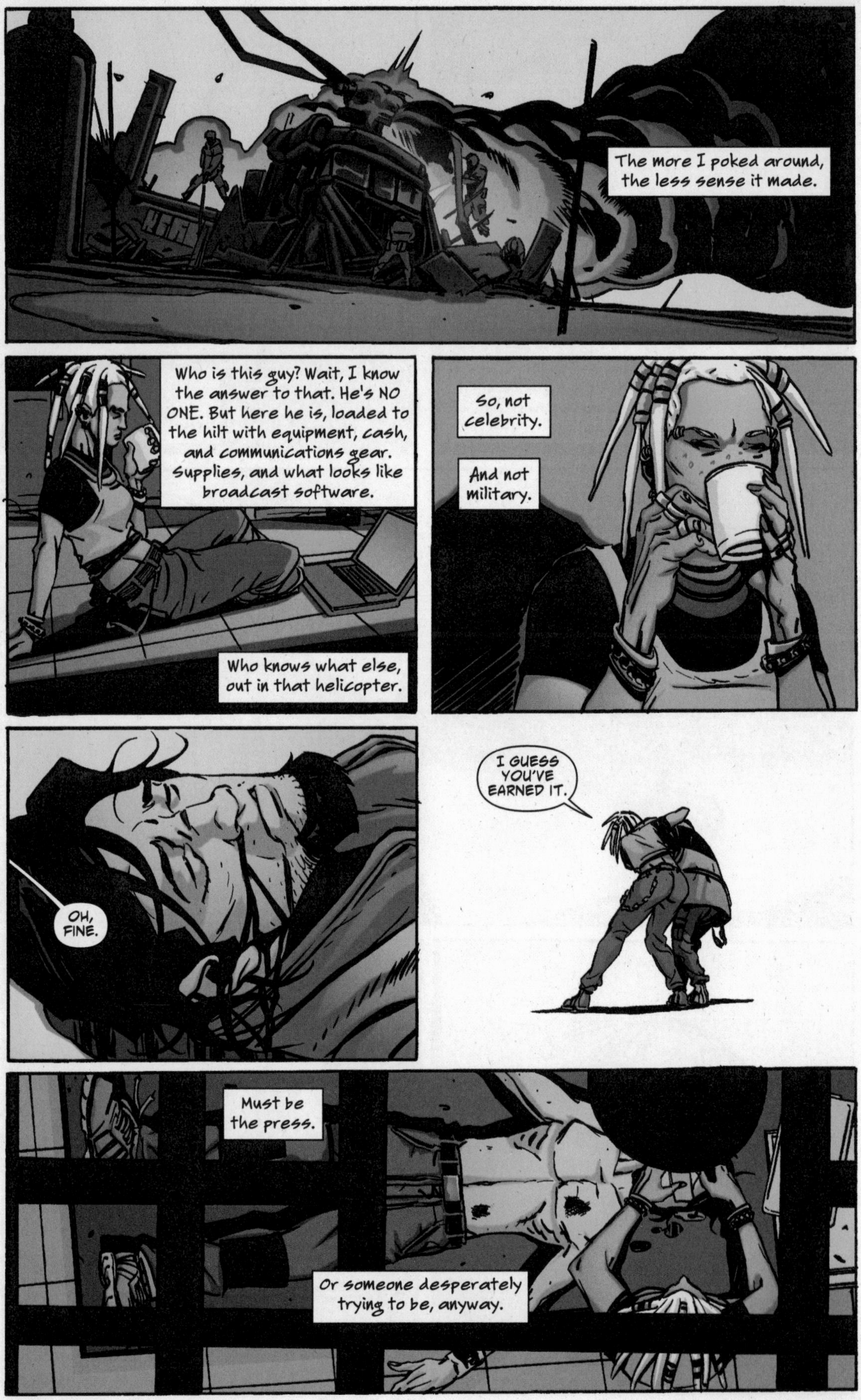

The more I poked around, the less sense it made.
Who is this guy? Wait, I know the answer to that. He's NO ONE. But here he is, loaded to the hilt with equipment, cash, and communications gear. Supplies, and what looks like broadcast software.
Who knows what else, out in that helicopter.
So, not celebrity.
And not military.
OH, FINE.
I GUESS YOU'VE EARNED IT.
Must be the press.
Or someone desperately trying to be, anyway.

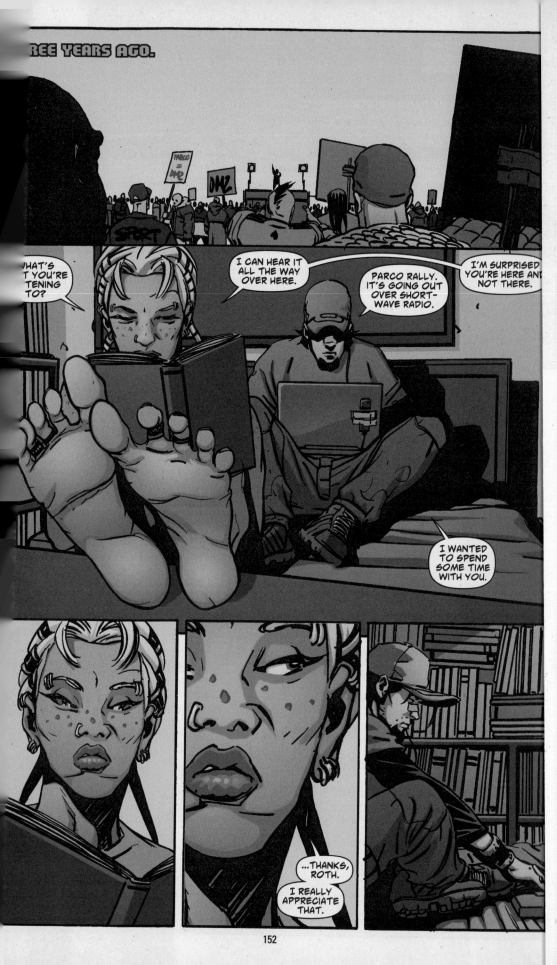

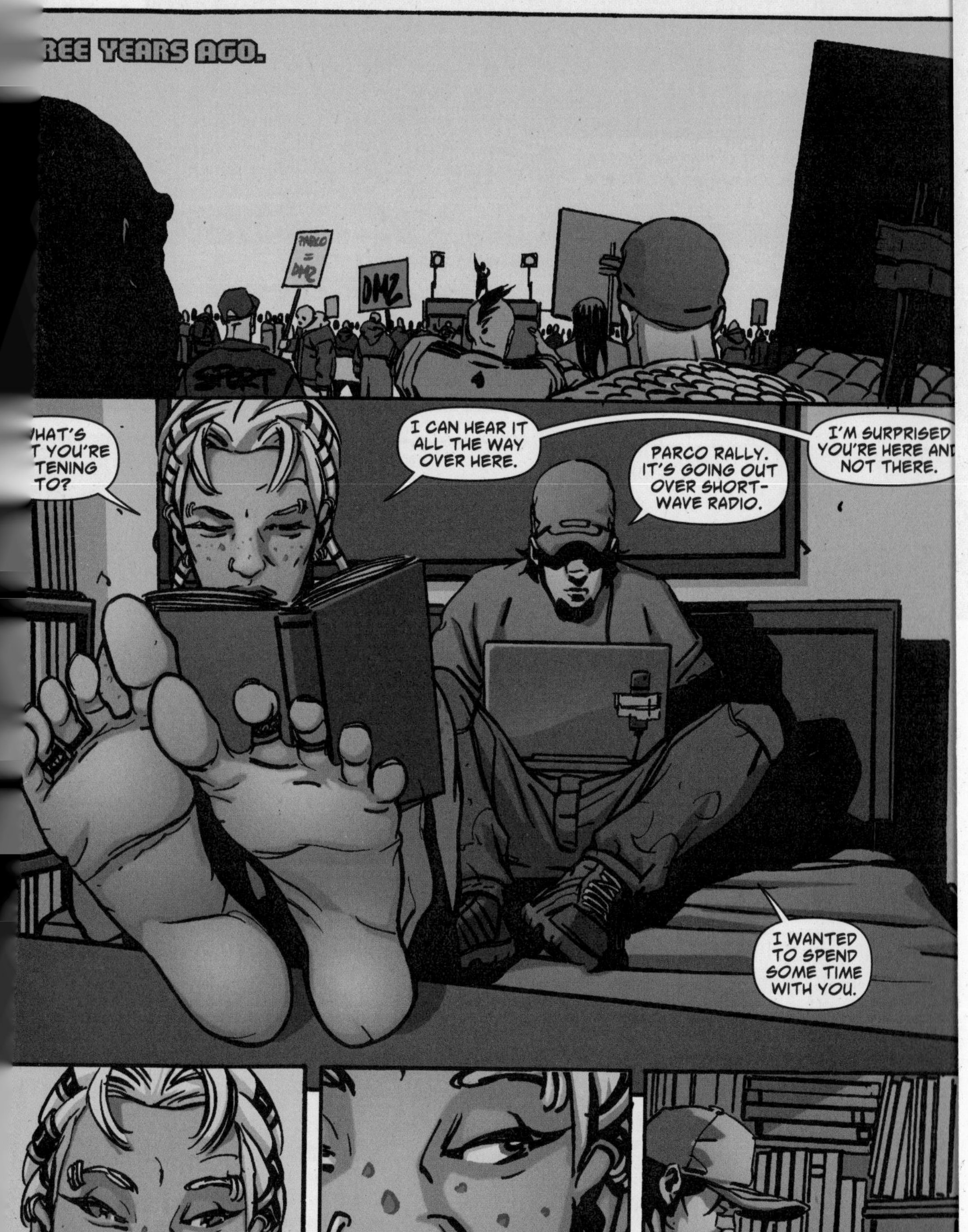
REE YEARS AGO.
HAT'S
T YOU'RE
TENING
TO?
I CAN HEAR IT ALL THE WAY OVER HERE.
PARCO RALLY. IT'S GOING OUT OVER SHORT-WAVE RADIO.
I'M SURPRISED YOU'RE HERE AND NOT THERE.
I WANTED TO SPEND SOME TIME WITH YOU.
...THANKS, ROTH.
I REALLY APPRECIATE THAT.

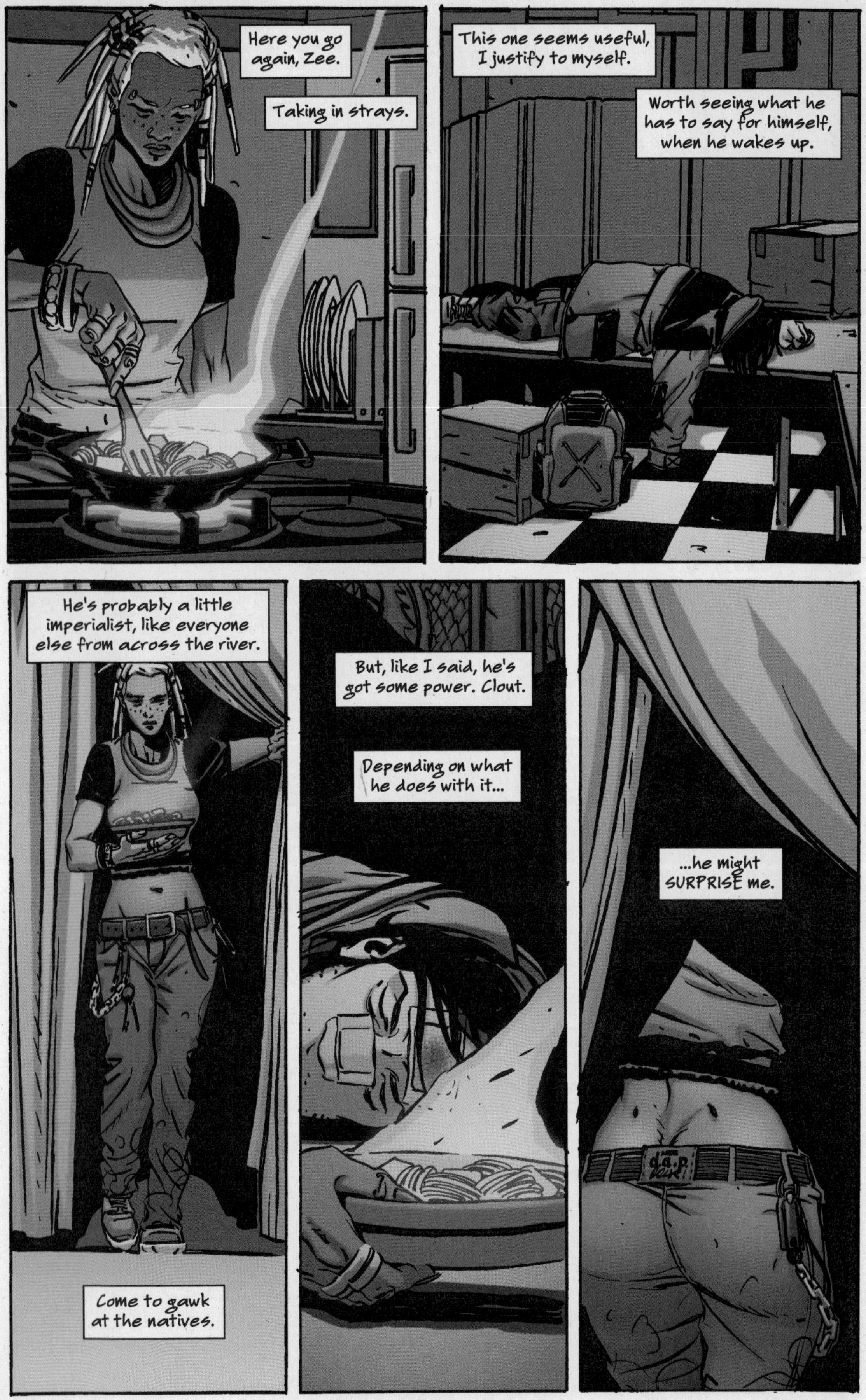
Here you go again, Zee.
Taking in strays.
This one seems useful, I justify to myself.
Worth seeing what he has to say for himself, when he wakes up.
He's probably a little imperialist, like everyone else from across the river.
Come to gawk at the natives.
But, like I said, he's got some power. Clout.
Depending on what he does with it...
...he might SURPRISE me.

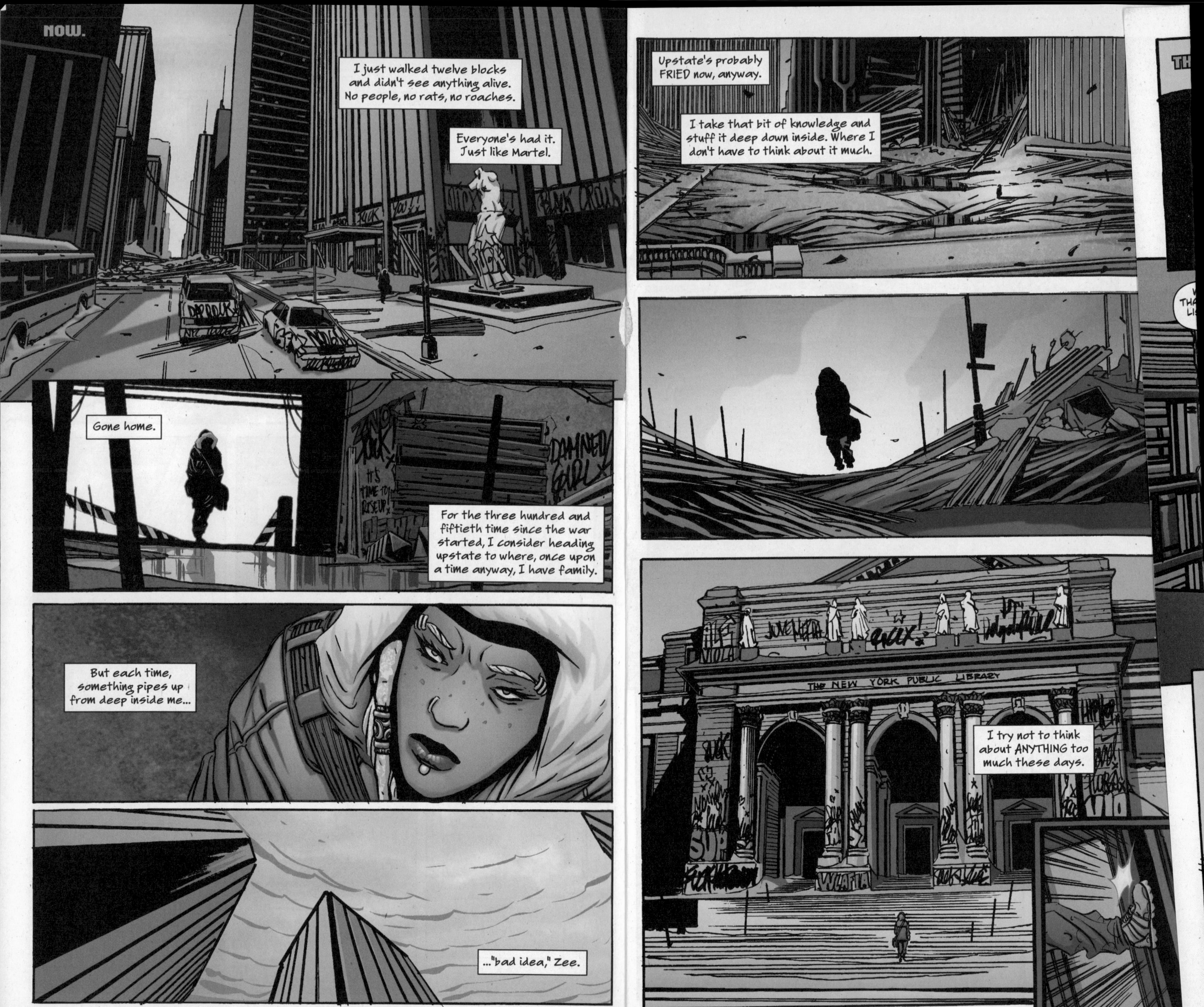
NOW.
I just walked twelve blocks and didn't see anything alive. No people, no rats, no roaches.
Everyone's had it. Just like Martel.
Gone home.
For the three hundred and fiftieth time since the war started, I consider heading upstate to where, once upon a time anyway, I have family.
But each time, something pipes up from deep inside me...
..."bad idea," Zee.
Upstate's probably FRIED now, anyway.
I take that bit of knowledge and stuff it deep down inside. Where I don't have to think about it much.
THE NEW YORK PUBLIC LIBRARY
I try not to think about ANYTHING too much these days.

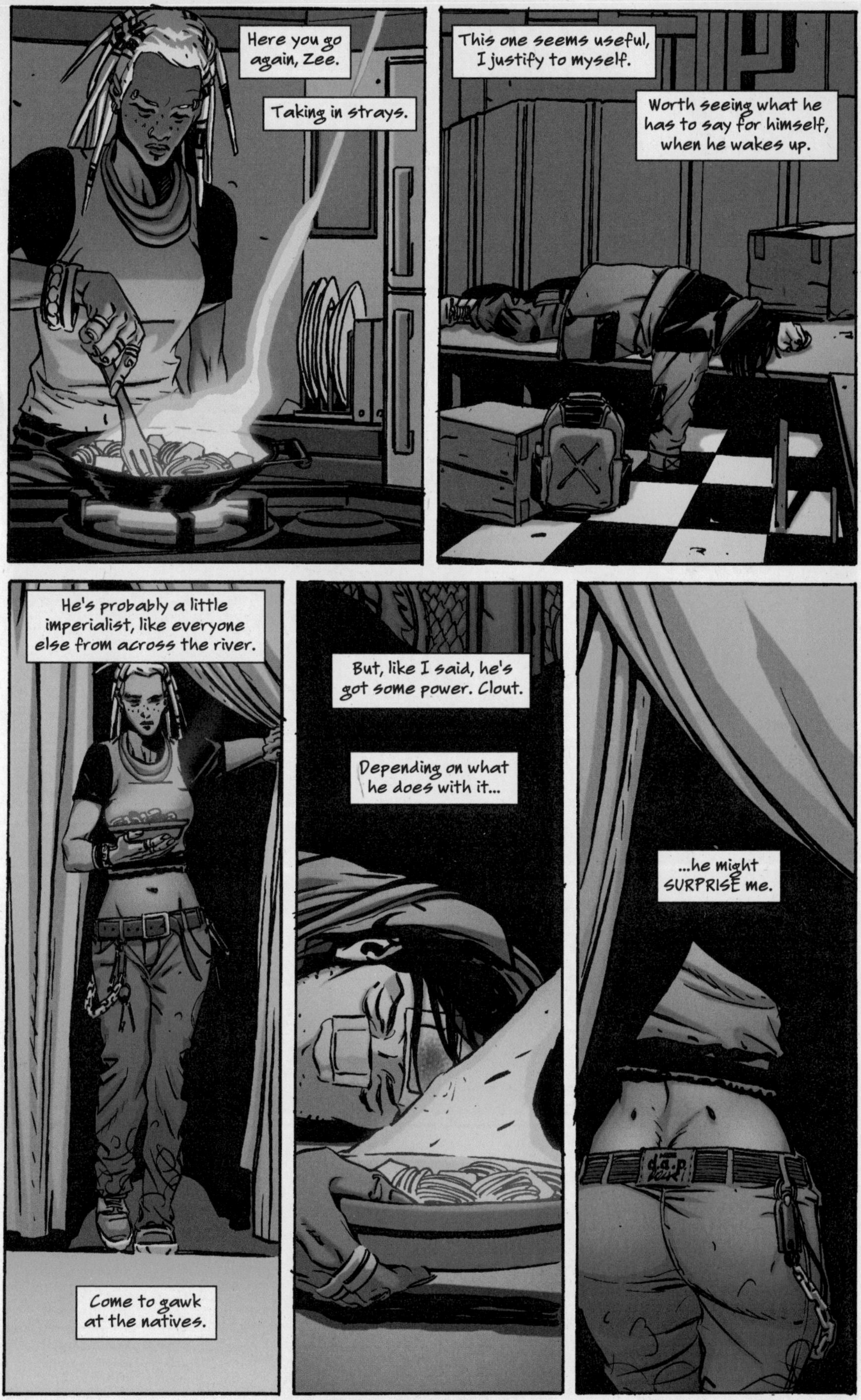
Here you go again, Zee.
Taking in strays.
This one seems useful, I justify to myself.
Worth seeing what he has to say for himself, when he wakes up.
He's probably a little imperialist, like everyone else from across the river.
Come to gawk at the natives.
But, like I said, he's got some power. Clout.
Depending on what he does with it...
...he might SURPRISE me.

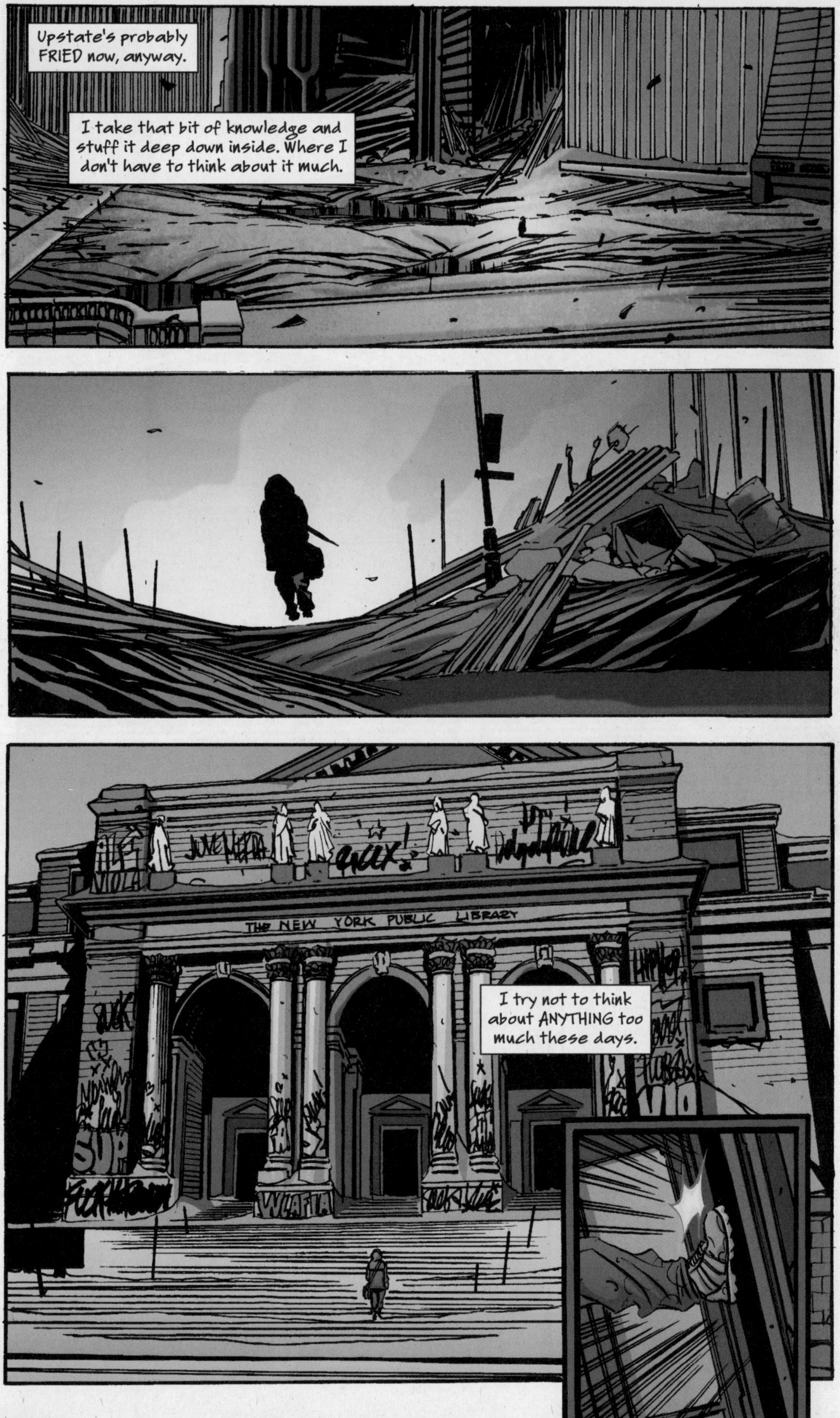
Upstate's probably FRIED now, anyway.
I take that bit of knowledge and stuff it deep down inside. Where I don't have to think about it much.
THE NEW YORK PUBLIC LIBRARY
I try not to think about ANYTHING too much these days.

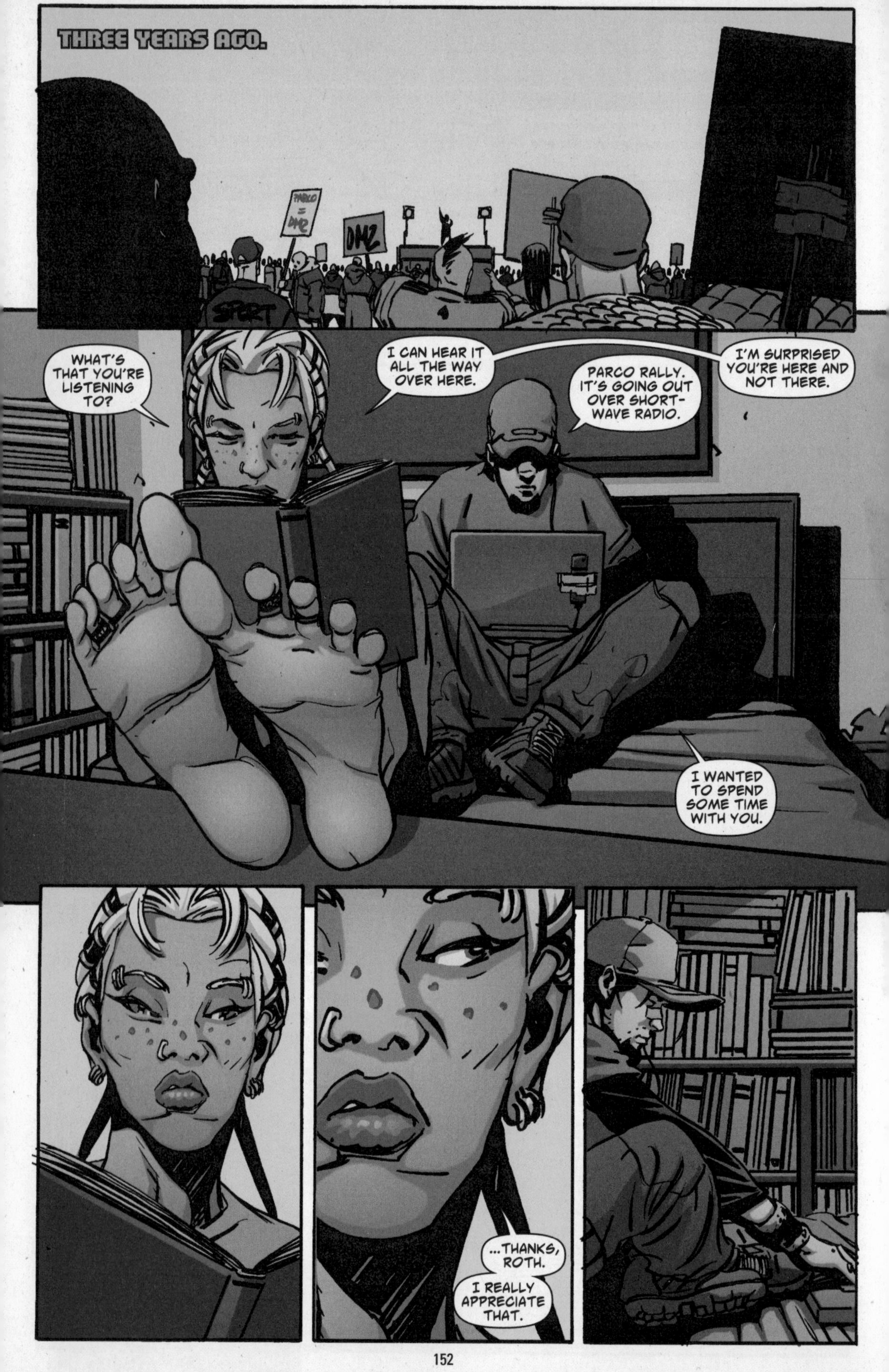
THREE YEARS AGO.
PARCO = DMZ
DMZ
SPORT
WHAT'S THAT YOU'RE LISTENING TO?
I CAN HEAR IT ALL THE WAY OVER HERE.
PARCO RALLY. IT'S GOING OUT OVER SHORT-WAVE RADIO.
I'M SURPRISED YOU'RE HERE AND NOT THERE.
I WANTED TO SPEND SOME TIME WITH YOU.
...THANKS, ROTH.
I REALLY APPRECIATE THAT.

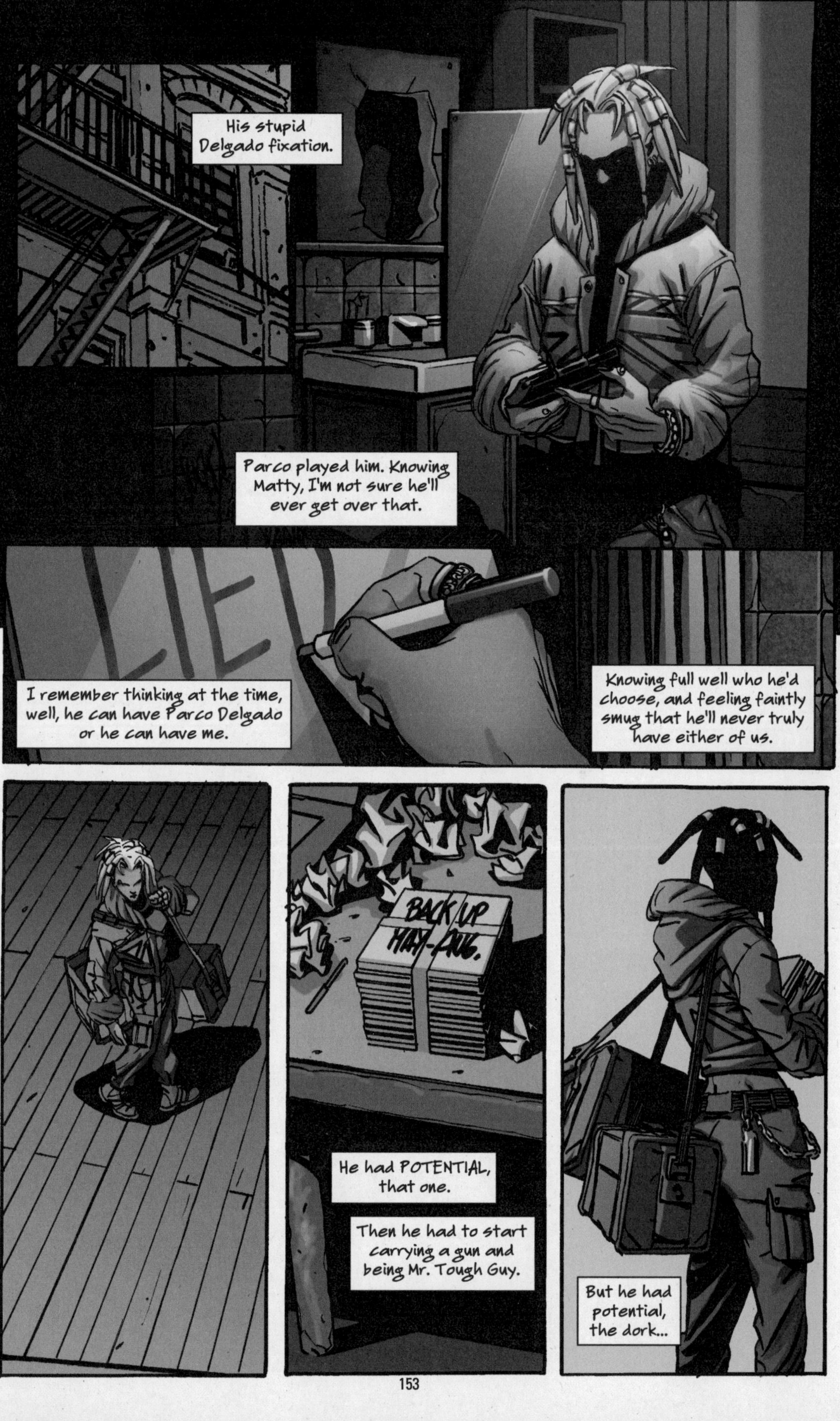
His stupid Delgado fixation.
Parco played him. Knowing Matty, I'm not sure he'll ever get over that.
I remember thinking at the time, well, he can have Parco Delgado or he can have me.
Knowing full well who he'd choose, and feeling faintly smug that he'll never truly have either of us.
BACK UP MAY-AUG.
He had POTENTIAL, that one.
Then he had to start carrying a gun and being Mr. Tough Guy.
But he had potential, the dork...

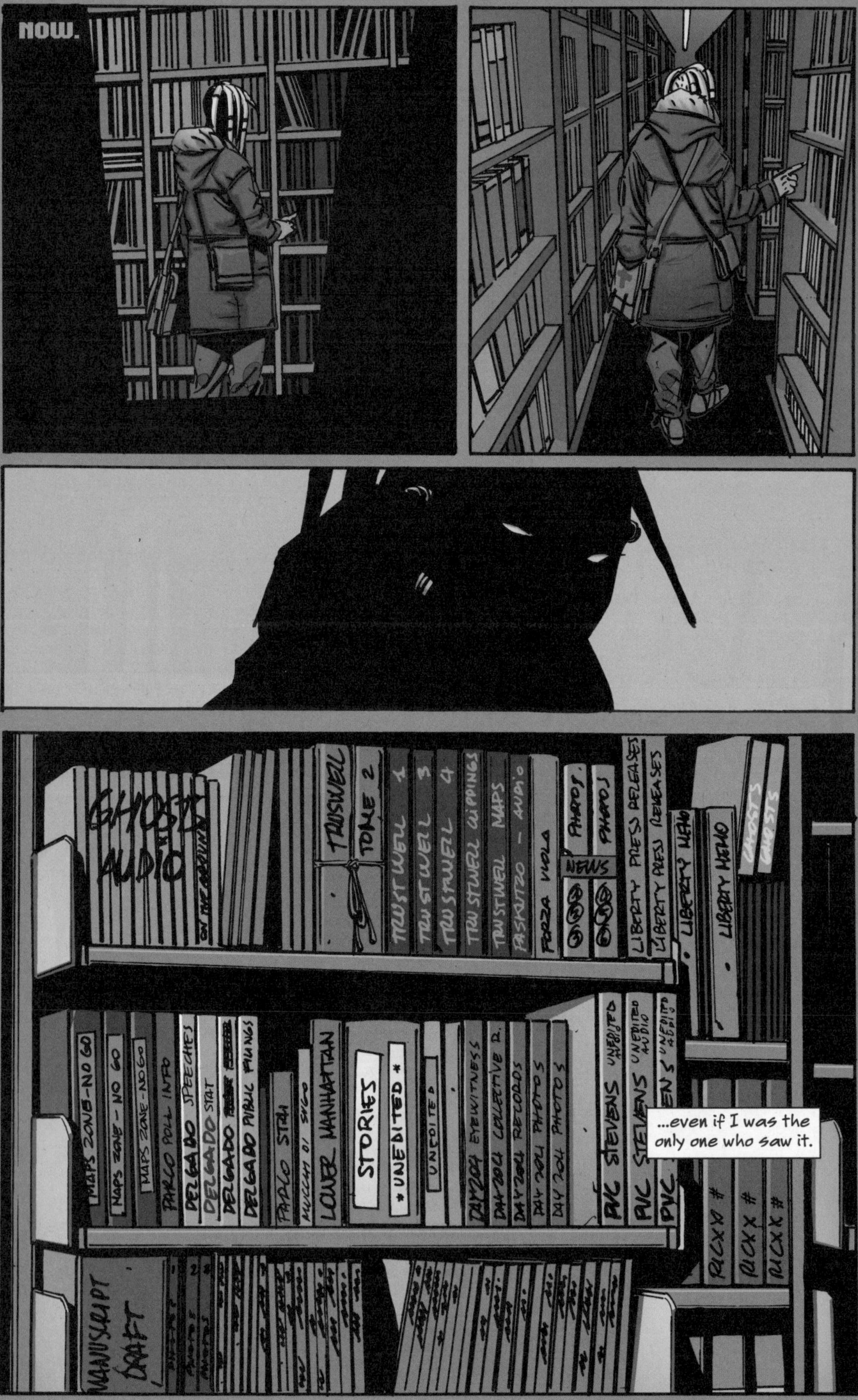
NOW.
...even if I was the only one who saw it.

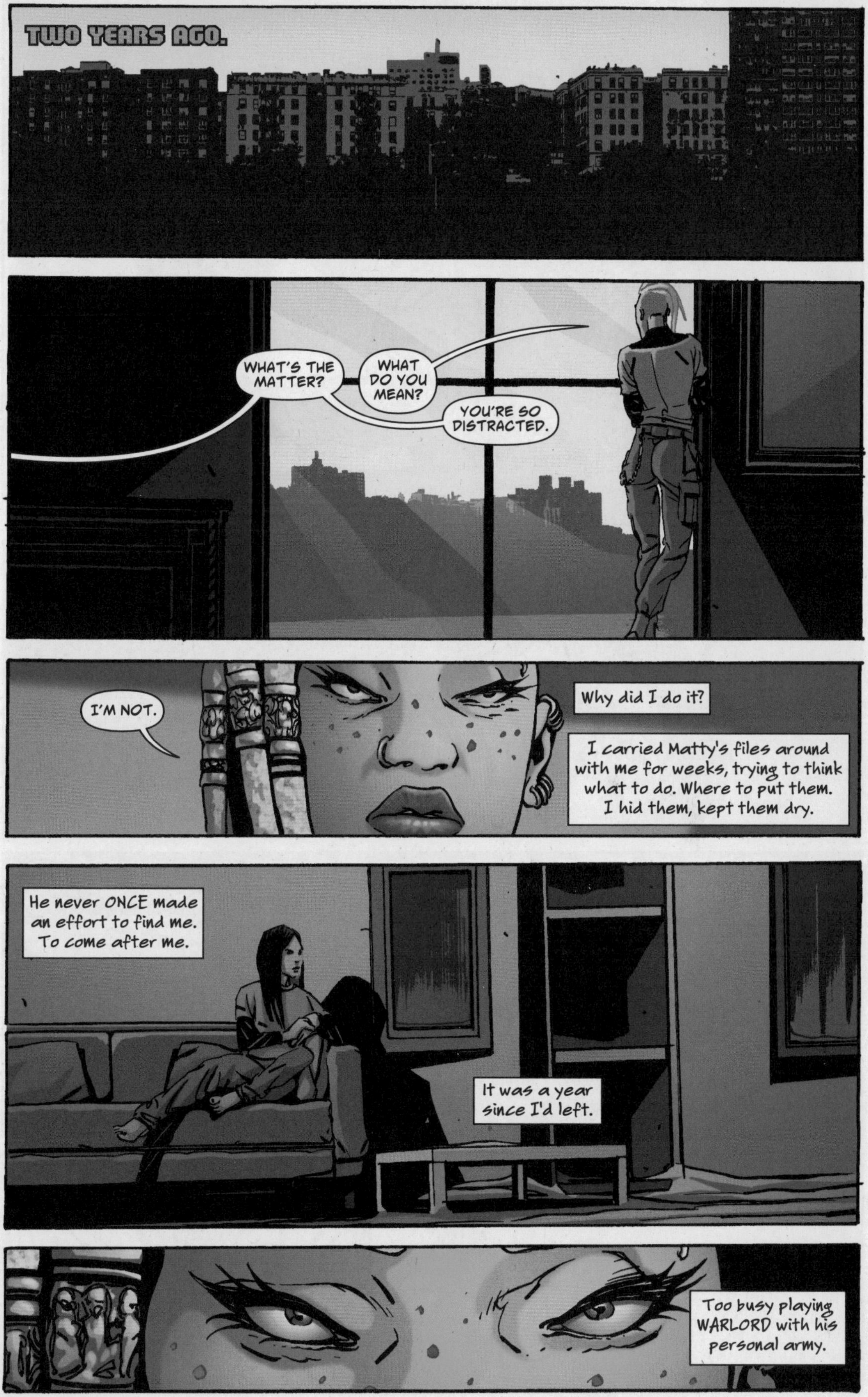
TWO YEARS AGO.
WHAT'S THE MATTER?
WHAT DO YOU MEAN?
YOU'RE SO DISTRACTED.
I'M NOT.
Why did I do it?
I carried Matty's files around with me for weeks, trying to think what to do. Where to put them. I hid them, kept them dry.
He never ONCE made an effort to find me. To come after me.
It was a year since I'd left.
Too busy playing WARLORD with his personal army.

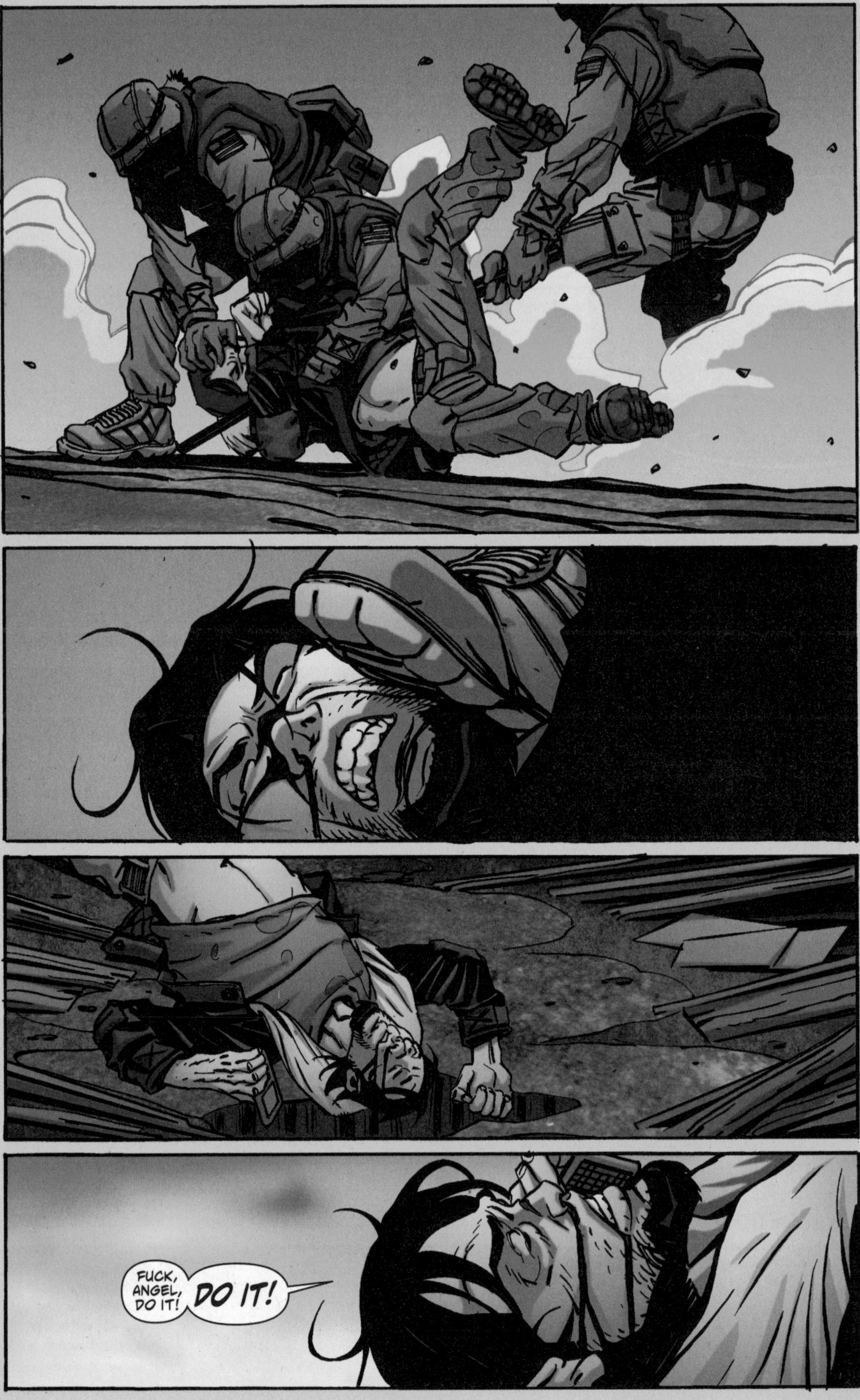
FUCK, ANGEL, DO IT!
DO IT!

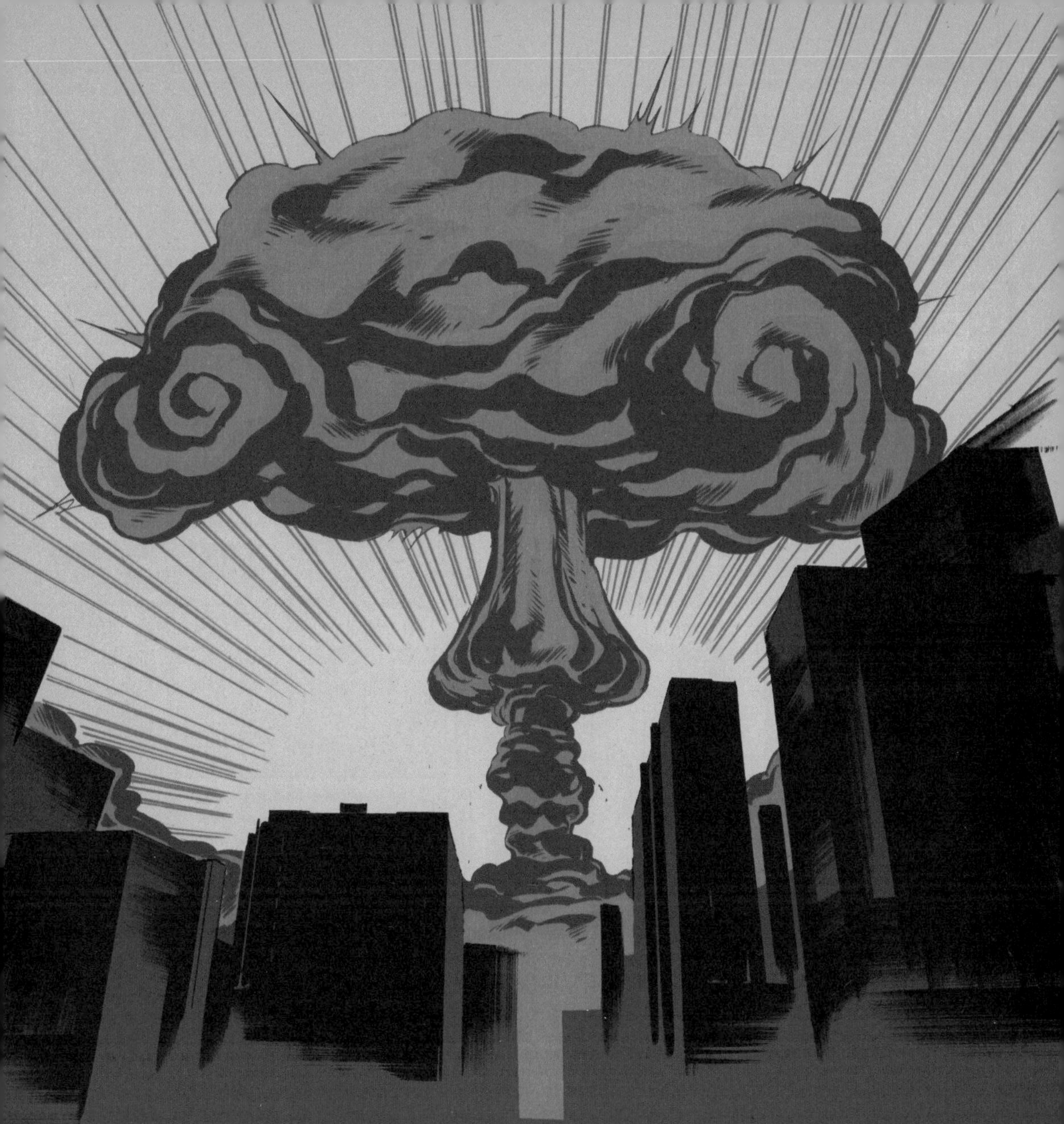

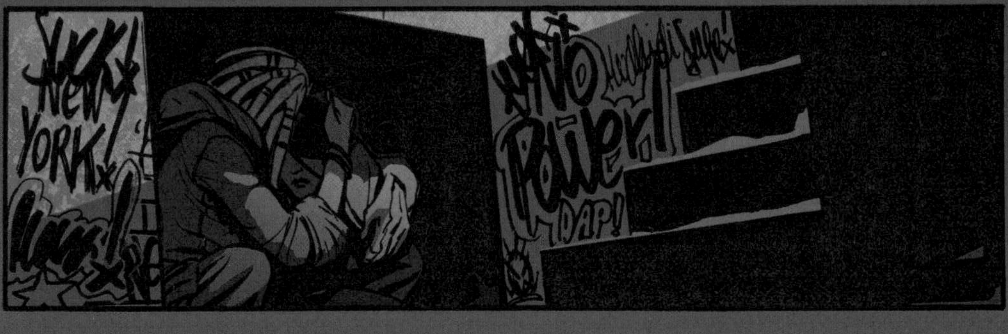
New YORK
NO Power!
DAP!

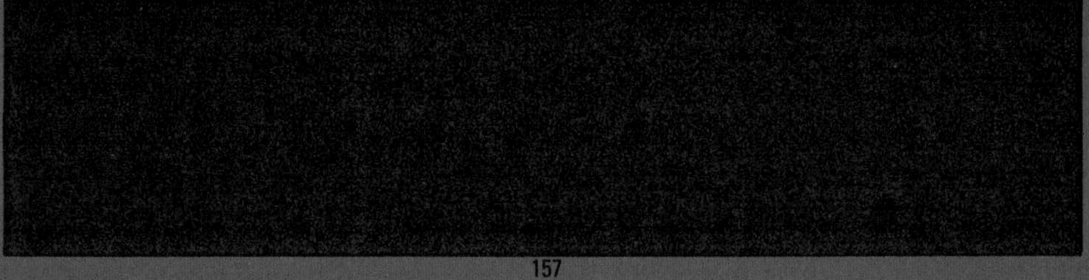

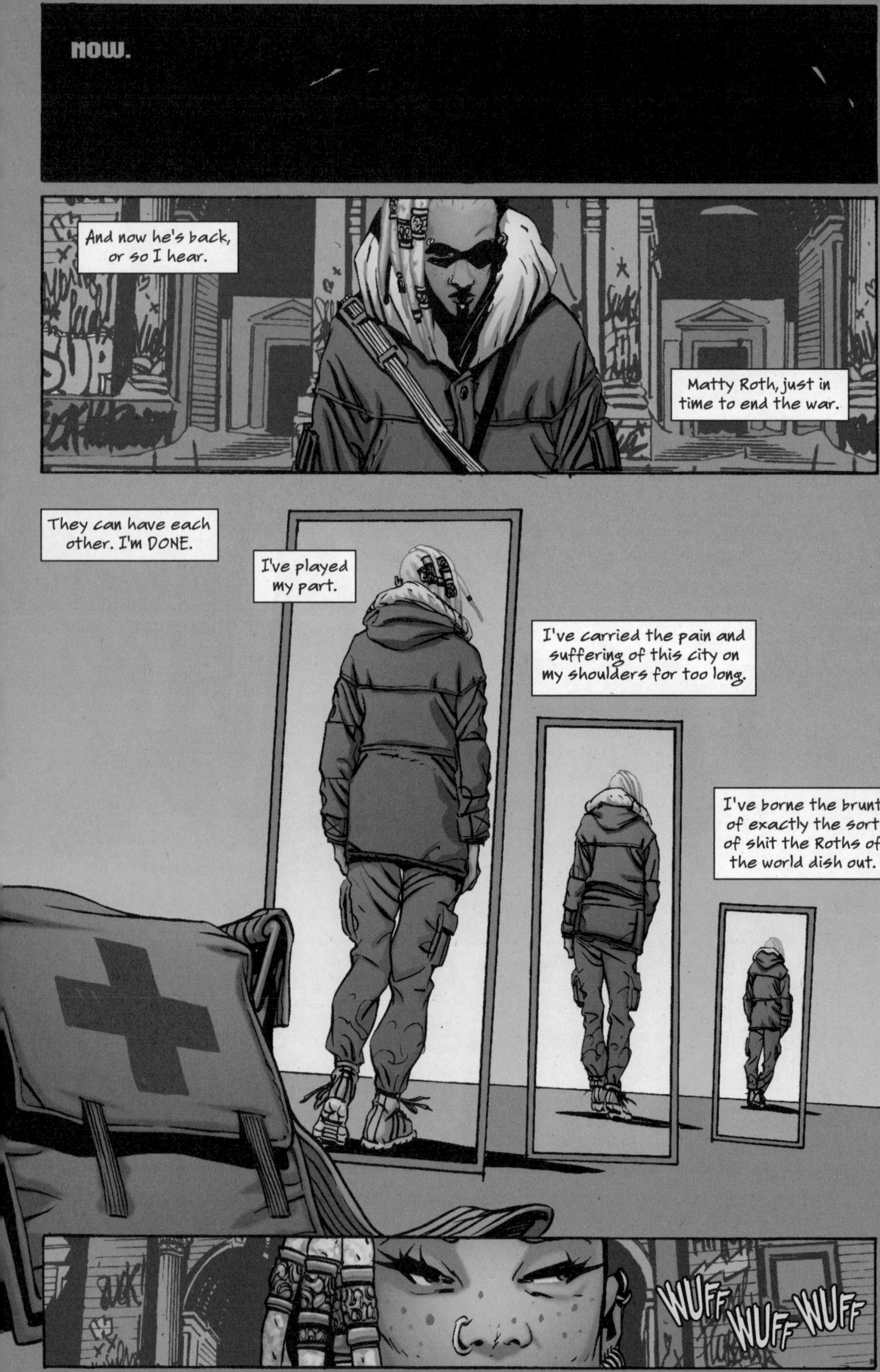
NOW.
And now he's back, or so I hear.
Matty Roth, just in time to end the war.
They can have each other. I'm DONE.
I've played my part.
I've carried the pain and suffering of this city on my shoulders for too long.
I've borne the brunt of exactly the sort of shit the Roths of the world dish out.
WUFF WUFF WUFF

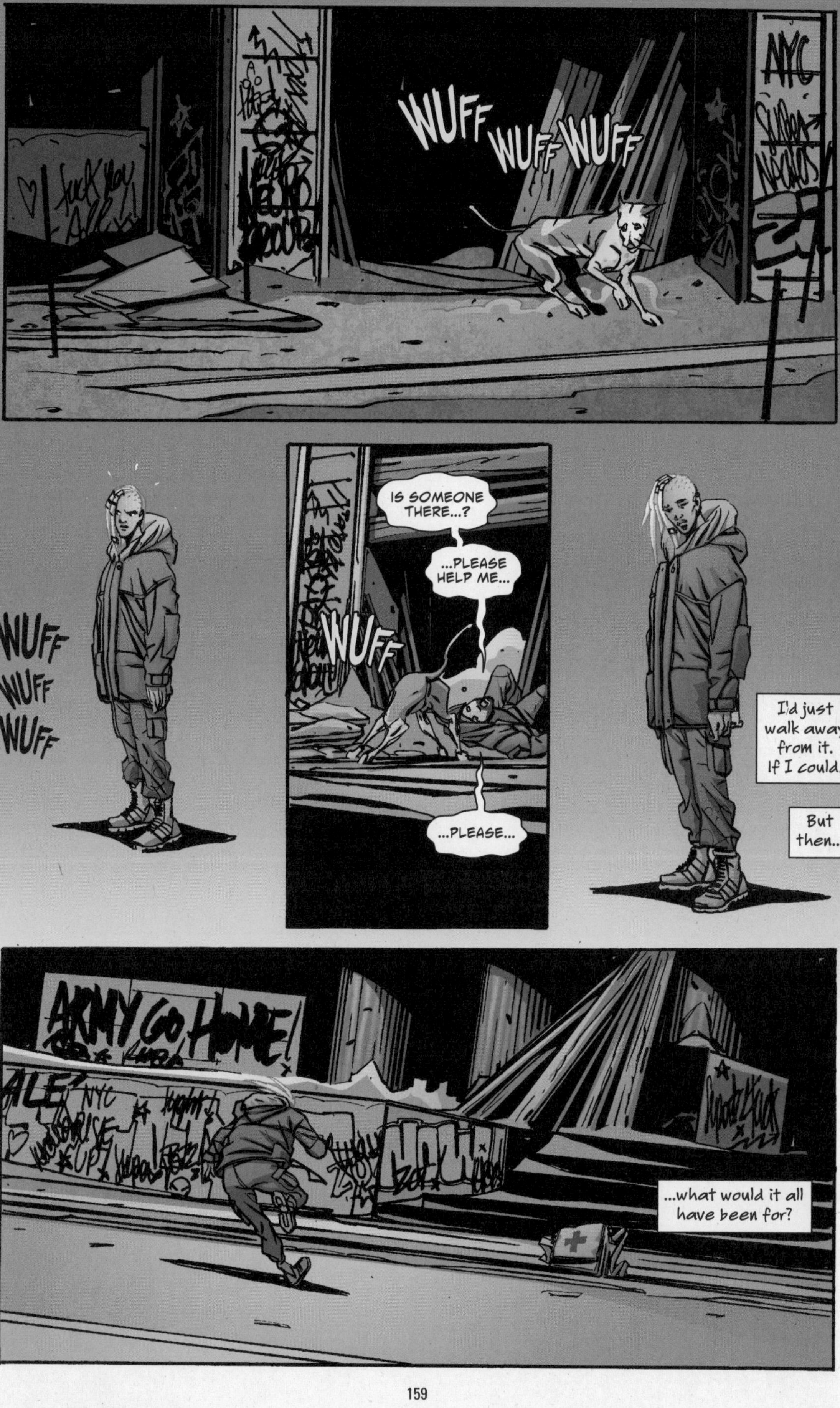
WUFF WUFF WUFF
IS SOMEONE THERE...?
...PLEASE HELP ME...
WUFF
...PLEASE...
WUFF
WUFF
WUFF
I'd just walk away from it. If I could.
But then...
ARMY GO HOME!
...what would it all have been for?

Long after the Parcos, the Martels, the Roths and the like have left me...

...I'll still be here.

Until the end of it all, and whatever comes after.